SAMUEL JOHNSON

SAMUEL JOHNSON

JOHN WAIN

THE VIKING PRESS / NEW YORK

ACKNOWLEDGMENTS

I am grateful to Dr Graham Nicholls, Curator of the Johnson Birthplace, Lichfield, Staffordshire, and to the Lichfield Corporation for their help in locating illustrations and for permission to reproduce plates 2, 3, 4, 6, 8, 10, 11, 12, 16, 17, 21, 23, 31, 34; to Dr Johnson's House, Gough Square, for 15, 22, 24, 25, 30; to the Trustees of the British Museum for 19, 27, 33; to the Hyde Collection, Somerville, New Jersey, for 7; to the National Portrait Gallery, London, for 9, 13, 18, 20; to the National Galleries of Scotland for 26, 35; to Courage Barclay Ltd for 28, 29; to the Tate Gallery, London, for 1, 14; to the Royal Academy of Arts, London, for 32; and to Haverford College, Pennsylvania, for 36. I also wish to thank Caroline Hobhouse of Macmillan, London, and Nanette Kritzalis of The Viking Press, New York, for their help with picture research.

J.W.

Published in 1975 by The Viking Press, Inc.
625 Madison Avenue, New York, N. Y. 10022

LIBRARY OF CONGRESS CATALOGING IN PUBLICATION DATA
Wain, John.
    Samuel Johnson.
    Bibliography: p.
    Includes index.
    1. Johnson, Samuel, 1709–1784—Biography.
PR3533.w33 1975   828'.6'09 [B]   74–6851
ISBN 0–670–61671–0

Second Printing, April 1975

Printed in U.S.A.

Acknowledgment is made to Macmillan Publishing Co., Inc., for permission to quote from "The Seven Sages" from Collected Poems of William Butler Yeats. Copyright 1933 by Macmillan Publishing Co., Inc., renewed 1961 by Bertha Georgie Yeats.

Ken's
1941–1974
in Staffordshire

Few can attain this man's knowledge, and few practise his virtues;
but all may suffer his calamity.

Rasselas

– He taught Laughing and Grief, they used to say.
– So he did, so he did.

Alice in Wonderland

Contents

Contents

Illustrations are between pages 196 *and* 197

Introduction

Samuel Johnson has not, I think, even yet come into his rightful reputation. Outside the English-speaking world he is virtually unknown, and within that world – or, at any rate, within England – certain stereotyped misconceptions about him still persist, not merely among the uneducated but among people who ought to know better and would enjoy knowing better.

This book, like all my work of the critical and expository kind, is addressed to the intelligent general reader. The specialist in Johnson studies has, in the last thirty years, been adequately catered for, even if I were capable of catering for him still further. Modern Johnsonian scholarship has advanced far into the work of editing and commentary. At last we are beginning to sort out what Johnson wrote and what he did not – always a difficulty in the case of a writer who wrote many fugitive and unsigned pieces and was also generous in giving his work away to others. And at last we are beginning to appreciate the complexities and niceties of Johnson's thinking about literature, about history, and about social and political issues.

I say 'we' because, after all, the work of the scholars is there for all of us to read. But in the nature of things the work of scholars is read primarily by other scholars. They talk to each other, and 'fit audience find though few'. Of course many of them are also teachers, and through their lectures and conversations a more accurate and enlightened attitude to Johnson might have spread to young people and thus slowly irradiated a generation. Might have. But it has manifestly not been happening. Young people for the most part still think of Johnson, when they think of him at all, as a stupid old reactionary. And not only young people. A highly intelligent and responsible journalist, whose life is spent in Fleet Street but very definitely on its respectable side, expressed surprise that I should be interested in Johnson. He hadn't thought of me as a reactionary kind of person: but Johnson, well, 'the arch-conservative . . .'.

Since he was speaking and not writing, I had no idea whether my friend intended the word 'conservative' to carry a large or a small c. But he evidently thought of Johnson, as so many people think of him, as an eighteenth-century ancestor of the typical modern Conservative. That is (to put the matter at its simplest) someone who in the eternal tug of war between labour and capital tends to find that his sympathies are with capital; who wants social change to be either gradual and cautious, or not to happen at all; who favours existing institutions rather than radical new solutions. This cap fits Johnson to some extent, but it obscures many of the finer and more humane points of his thinking: his opposition to colonialism and to every form of exploitation; his hatred of the slave trade; his pleas for a more merciful penal system; his insistence that the real test of any civilization lies in its treatment of the poor.

So there is still a job to be done, at the level of humble usefulness, in presenting a picture of Johnson as he actually was instead of as he is thought of. The average reader's picture of Johnson is still very much the one he gets from Boswell, or from one of the countless popularizers of Boswell. And Boswell was a sentimental–romantic Tory of a very different stripe. Being a Scot, he yearned over the Stuarts, though he showed no impulse to translate his yearning into direct politics; being the son of a laird and a bit of a snob, he deferred to titled people, where Johnson, for all his support of 'subordination', was just as likely to growl at them; being something of a Pasha where women were concerned, he thought it overstepping the limit when a lady suggested to him that perhaps the sexes would be equal in the next world ('Nay, Madam, this is to ask too much'); being untroubled by any notion of the basic rights of the human being, he thought the slave trade an excellent institution. Boswell naturally highlights those moods and opinions of Johnson's that match his own. What we lose in his portrait is the deeply humanitarian Johnson, the man who from first to last rooted his life among the poor and outcast.

Apart from that general wish to spread a just notion of Johnson among a less specialized circle of readers, I have, I suppose, one other motive for writing about him. Perhaps more than most, I am in a position to see his life from the inside. I was born in the same district as Johnson – some thirty miles away – and in much the same social *milieu*. I went to the same university, and since then have lived the same life of Grub Street, chance employment, and the unremitting struggle to write enduring books against the background of an unstable existence. The literary and social situation that Johnson knew in its early days, I know in its twilight; and perhaps even this will give my book, whatever its shortcomings, some documentary interest.

J. W.

1974

PART I

In the Midlands

CHAPTER I

'A Poor Diseased Infant'

Wednesday, 18 September 1709: the Market Square in Lichfield was quiet, for this was not a trading day. The occasional rattle of a cart, or the talk and laughter of a knot of citizens passing the time of day at a corner, would sound clear across the square, while at regular intervals the long swell of melody from the great cathedral bells came washing over the rooftops. All these sounds penetrated to the ears of Sarah Johnson, the bookseller's wife, as she lay in her bedroom in the handsome three-storied house that dominated the north-eastern end of the square. To Sarah, the day must have seemed a long one. At forty, she was giving birth to her first child, and the labour was prolonged and difficult. Her husband, Michael, had engaged the services of George Hector, the best man-midwife in the neighbourhood; beyond that there was nothing anyone could do but wait. Finally, at four o'clock in the afternoon, Hector was able to take up the strangely inert yet living body of the child and say encouragingly, 'Here is a brave boy!'

The news that mother and child were safe would spread quickly among the little circle of people with whom Michael and Sarah were intimate. They were, for the most part, middling people. The proud little city of Lichfield was the scene of a threefold life, being a country market town, a garrison, and a cathedral city with authority over a wide diocese. It would be too much to expect the fine officers and their ladies, or the grave dignitaries of the Close, to care much what happened to the bookseller's wife and her child. Michael and Sarah Johnson lived in one of the town's more dignified houses, but they were not grand people. Michael was a local man, born in the village of Cubley a few miles out in the country. (If you go to Cubley today you will see that the site of his birthplace is marked by a plaque on an unremarkable yellow and pebbledash house, for the people of these quiet lanes and fields do not easily let go the memory of a local worthy.) His wife, Sarah, was of slightly better stock, as the world reckoned such things; she was a Ford, of yeoman status or something a little more; there were connections, by marriage, with gentry and with the professions. Her father, Cornelius Ford, was a small-scale landowner and a man of some cultivation, neither of them attributes that Michael could point to on his side. Nevertheless Michael was well regarded by his fellow citizens in Lichfield, and in that very year of 1709 had been voted into the office of Sheriff. This dignity, and the birth of his first son, represented the peak of Michael Johnson's life, and he reacted with what for him, a man of habitual melancholy, was an unaccustomed euphoria. The next day he was due to perform the annual ceremony of riding round the boundaries of the city; this ritual, having outlasted its strictly legal and political justification, was beginning to decline in importance – after Michael Johnson only one more Sheriff made the Riding the occasion of public celebration. But this time Michael had a motive for combining personal with civic pride, and when they asked him whom he was going to invite to the Riding he replied grandly, 'All the town now.'

There spoke the happiness and relief of the new father. By ordinary standards, there was nothing much to rejoice about. The child was far from normally healthy. In place of the usual yells of the newborn, there was an ominous silence which the baby was at last persuaded to break with a few whimpers. Arrangements were made to have him christened that same evening, a natural and humane precaution in view of the torments promised by Christian theology for infants venturing into the presence of their Maker without a certificate of baptism. There was nothing to hold up the ceremony, for the man who had agreed to act as the child's godfather, Dr Samuel Swinfen, was under the Johnsons' roof as lodger; the choice of name may have been a compliment to him, though Sarah also had a brother Samuel. So, as promptly as possible, the baby's eternal welfare was signed for. It would have comforted George Hector and the Johnsons to be able, at that moment, to look into a crystal ball and learn that Samuel, the silent and sickly infant, would not in fact be departing this life for another seventy-five years.

Michael Johnson, twelve years his wife's senior and a man accustomed to taking charge of practical matters, gave instructions for the child's nursing. He was to go to a foster-mother to draw the nourishment in which Sarah was deficient. Michael's choice fell on Joan Marklew, the wife of a brickmaker in his employ. It was an unfortunate one. Joan Marklew's son, eighteen months older than Samuel Johnson, suffered from scrofula and, doubtless as a result, weak eyesight; in later life, his eyes were so defective that he could not earn a living. Sam, in his turn, also contracted scrofula – tuberculosis of the lymph glands – and also lost part of his eyesight.

His mother thought these diseases had been handed down from her own family, though why she thought so with the evidence of Joan Marklew's bad physical history before her it is impossible to say. It is likewise impossible to say why the Johnsons did not ask for, or at any rate did not get, the advice of their lodger, Dr Swinfen. A graduate of Pembroke College, Oxford, and a clever physician, Swinfen was a sufficiently close friend to stand as godfather to Sam; and he subsequently gave it as his opinion, to Sam himself, that the infection had come from Joan Marklew.

At all events, Sam stayed ten weeks at the Marklews'. Sarah visited him every day, which by present-day standards does not seem excessive, considering that only four hundred yards separated the two houses; but the eighteenth century had a very tough attitude to children, and Sarah knew, or thought she knew, that her neighbours would laugh behind her back if they saw that she was visiting her baby as amusingly often as once a day. So she varied her route, doubling and dodging, and once at Joan's house would purposely leave behind some small object, a glove or a fan, so that she could go back for it and catch Joan unawares if she was neglecting the baby in any way. (But she never was.) Finally, Sam was brought home, 'a poor diseased infant, almost blind'. The words are his own, in an autobiographical fragment he wrote down in his fifties. He must have been repeating what the older people told him.

Michael and Sarah did what they could for their poor diseased infant. In order to drain the infection out of his system, an incision was made in his left arm and kept open with thread or horsehair; he had to suffer this till he was six years old. They also made an effort to get the best possible attention for his afflicted eyes. Sarah Johnson had a first cousin named Mrs Harriots, a well-to-do widow who lived at Trysul, a large house near Wolverhampton. Here, in his second year, Samuel was taken so that he could be shown to Dr Atwood, a well-known oculist, who normally practised at Worcester but had, presumably, a branch at Wolverhampton. Whether he was able to do anything for the child's eyes is not known; all we know about this visit is that it was an unhappy one for the elder Johnsons. Michael, a man of decided spirit and independence, disliked what he took to be the patronizing airs of his wife's prosperous kinswoman, and took pleasure in irritating her in small ways, such as ordering his horses out of the stable on a Sunday, which she, with correct and conventional piety, regarded as a breach of the Sabbath.

In March 1712, when Sam was two-and-a-half years old, the couple decided on a more picturesque remedy. Scrofula was, of course, known as 'the King's evil', and the belief that it could be relieved by the touch of a royal hand was of respectable antiquity; Shakespeare, in *Macbeth*, represents it as being practised by the saintly Edward the Confessor. By the eighteenth century, this belief had naturally weakened a good deal, partly because of the Jacobite contention that the power did not descend to William, Mary or Anne. And in fact Queen Anne was the last British monarch to 'touch'. Not that the belief was merely a quaint survival among country people; in taking Sam to be touched Mr Johnson was acting on the advice of Sir John Floyer, an eminent physician of Lichfield.

Parents with a sick child will, notoriously, give anything a try; though Michael, who had made the journey to see Dr Atwood, was content this time to let Sarah go alone. She was nervous about the journey to London, shocked at the high expenses, afraid of being robbed and left without the means of getting back to the safety of home – a fear which she calmed to some extent by sewing two guineas into her petticoat. Thus equipped, they set off in the London stagecoach. The journey was horrible. Apart from anything else, the coaches of those days were not the sleek, well-sprung conveyances that developed in the heyday of stagecoaching, and particularly after the invention of the elliptical spring in 1804. The coach of 1712 was clumsy, heavy, unsprung; it had a window in each door, and sometimes an oval window on either side of the door, but these windows were small and did not open; they could hardly have admitted light and air sufficient for the six passengers who sat facing each other, three to a side. As the wooden frame jolted heavily along the rutted roads, the only shock absorber was the leather on which the coachwork was mounted. In fine weather, it might have been preferable – at first – to be one of the outside passengers who somehow wedged themselves into the large wicker basket at the rear, which they shared with the luggage and general cargo. Travelling in this way no doubt helped to foster the well-known ruggedness of the eighteenth-century English, but it was a poor means of conveyance for an ailing child. Sarah and Sam shared the coach with two female passengers; when little Sam was travel sick, one lady tried to comfort him, the other registered disgust. Once arrived after the two-and-a-half-day journey, they put up at a bookseller's – Nicholson of Little Britain, one of the best known in London and doubtless known to Michael Johnson through the trade. Years later, Samuel remembered playing with a bell on a string, and 'a cat with a white collar, and a dog, called Chops, that leaped over a stick'; or perhaps he only remembered hearing the grown-ups talk of these things; but he was sure he remembered 'a boy crying at the palace when I went to be touched', and 'a confused, but somehow a sort of solemn recollection of a lady in diamonds, and a long black hood' who was the Queen.

Like any other fond provincial mother, Sarah took the opportunity to buy her son a few treasures while they were in the metropolis. She got him a small silver cup and spoon, and instead of having them engraved with his initials only, caused them to be marked SAM. J. because her anxiously careful mind suggested to her that, since their initials were the same, they might be mistaken for her possessions and removed from him at her death. She also bought him a linen frock, known for ever afterwards as his 'London frock'. The ceremony once over, they went home, not by the coach as they had come but by the slower and less comfortable 'wagon': a concession to cheapness after the spending spree.

All things considered, the trip must have seemed to Sarah a successful one. It passed off without any of the major disasters she had feared, and if Sam was not actually cured of his scrofulous tendency, the fact that he lived to old age is sufficient indication that his constitution successfully resisted it: and if Sarah cared to attribute this to divine intervention through the medium of the Queen's hand why should she not? In any case, Sarah had other things to think of these days. She was pregnant again. Sam was shortly to have a brother, Nathaniel, his junior by three years. Always fearing the worst, Sarah had concealed her pregnancy lest the stagecoach company should make difficulties about carrying her or Nicholson about putting her up. Now, back home, she could prepare in peace for her second and last confinement.

What difference the birth of Nathaniel made to Sam we can only conjecture. Of course the birth of a second child always makes *some* difference to the first. In later life Samuel remembered the effort with which he had adjusted to the knowledge that he must now share his mother's affection with another boy; and also that at the time of his brother's christening Sarah had painstakingly taught him to spell and pronounce, syllable by syllable, the words 'little Natty'. Beyond that, we hear little of Nathaniel. Of all the people with whom life brought Samuel Johnson into close contact, Nathaniel was the one about whom he spoke least. Shadowy from birth, 'little Natty' vanishes into a deeper shadow some years before his early death. He sleeps now, with Michael and Sarah, under the floor of St Michael's Church in Lichfield.

When Sarah taught Sam to spell 'little Natty' she was, in addition to expressing her fondness for the newborn child and her wish to accustom Sam to his brother's presence, also mindful of the need to teach the boy his letters. She had already succeeded in setting him well on the road to reading and writing by the time he went, at the age of four or a little later, to the nearby 'dame school' kept by the widow Oliver. Before the days of ministries and diplomas and teachers' unions, the business of educating young children, at any rate those from families that could not afford to take in a governess or tutor, was handed over to a noble army of unqualified but more or less cultivated women. Whatever we might think of their methods today, these ladies succeeded in spreading the ability to read, write and reckon through a broad segment of the populace. Mrs Oliver, who was the widow of a shoemaker and who later went into business on her own account as a confectioner, must have been a very typical private or N.C.O. in this army. We know little enough about her, but what we know makes it certain that she was a kindly and patient soul. Sam, who lived less than a hundred and fifty yards from her school in Dam Street (it is still there), used to be seen there and back by a servant, lest he should meet with some accident owing to his near sight. Short as the distance was, there was always the possibility that he might be run over by a cart, or blunder into the hind legs of a horse, or be lost in the crowd on market day. Down the middle of the street was a 'kennel' or channel, exactly as in the Middle Ages, and this noisome obstacle on its own constituted a hazard. One day the servant did not appear, and Dame Oliver knew that Sam had inherited enough of his father's proud and stubborn temperament to refuse offers of a safe conduct from her. So, letting him start out by himself, she followed at a tactful distance to watch over him. When he reached the 'kennel', he got down on his hands and knees to be sure of seeing it clearly and estimating its width before stepping across it. Still Dame Oliver followed: until, happening to turn and see her, the child flew into a rage at this insult to his independence, rushed at her, and punched at her with all the strength of his little fists.

Between the efforts of Sarah Johnson and Mrs Oliver, Sam was now taking the first steps towards learning. And Sarah was equally concerned for his spiritual welfare. One day, in the same year that Nathaniel was born, Sam was lying in bed with her in the early morning, and she told him of two places on the other side of death: 'one a fine place filled with happiness, called Heaven; the other a *sad* place, called Hell'. Sarah was so eager for the boy to get these polarities well fixed in his memory that she made him get up, go and find their servant Thomas Jackson, and repeat the message to him.

In this, naturally, she thought of herself as doing no more than her Christian duty; in fact, when in later life her son reminded her of this first occasion on which she instructed him about the next world with its rewards and punishments, she was surprised to hear that she had left it so late. Certainly she was not the kind of mother to consider a carefree childhood more important than the inculcation of a sense of moral responsibility. There had never been much gaiety in her disposition, and what there was had been heavily shaded by life with Michael. The child Samuel lived with her admonitions continually in his ears, but because she lacked wide experience of life she seldom offered him the kind of moral teaching from which he could draw real, specific lessons: it was precept, precept, precept, with nothing concrete for his developing mind to seize on. 'My mother', he recalled years later, 'was always telling me that I did not *behave* myself properly; that I should endeavour to learn *behaviour*, and such cant: but when I replied that she ought to tell me what to do and what to avoid, her admonitions were commonly, for that time at least, at an end.'

The lack of real illumination, coupled with a constant wearying drizzle of admonition, was the more serious because the boy had very little balancing contact with his father. Michael Johnson was at no time a communicative man. He disliked talking business within the family circle; Sarah would not respect that wish, but on the other hand she had no real knowledge of trade and so was forever talking, in a grumbling or foreboding vein, of matters which she had only half grasped. As her son put it: 'Of business she had no distinct conception; and therefore her discourse was composed only of complaint, fear, and suspicion.' This can hardly have brightened the home, but in any case it is unlikely that the most cheerful spouse could have lifted Michael's spirits permanently. He suffered from constitutional melancholia; I suppose modern psychiatry would term him a 'depressive'; Boswell describes his affliction as

> that disease, the nature of which eludes the most minute enquiry, though the effects are well known to be a weariness of life, an unconcern about those things which agitate the greater part of mankind, and a general sensation of gloomy wretchedness.

Fortunately Michael had his own way of fighting off the black fits which, as Samuel was later to advise Boswell, are to be 'diverted by any means but drinking'. He would simply saddle his horse and ride away for orders. The countryside was dotted with fine houses whose libraries needed frequent replenishing; sometimes he took a calculated risk, as when in 1706 he bought the library of the Earl of Derby, nearly three thousand volumes in all. With this kind of thing to occupy him, Michael could get the sound of his wife's voice out of his ears and the healthy clatter of hoofs under his stirrups. If he had been stuck to a counting-house stool every day of his life, he might well have suffered that fate which his elder son never ceased to dread, and died insane, 'a driveller and a show'.

Samuel and Nathaniel, meanwhile, were thrown very much on Sarah's company, and it would have been hard for a sensitive child not to imbibe deeply of her anxiety and over-scrupulousness. One anecdote in particular stands out. When Sam was nine and Natty five or six, the two of them were sent to stay with some relatives at Birmingham. Part of the time they spent with their uncle, John Harrison, whose wife, now dead, had been Sarah Johnson's sister

Phoebe; and part with 'uncle Ford', who might have been either one of her two brothers, Samuel or Nathaniel. The sortie into the wider world does not seem to have brought the boys into uniformly edifying company; Samuel later described his uncle Harrison as 'a very mean and vulgar man, drunk every night, but drunk with little drink, very peevish, very proud, but luckily not rich'. However, the same autobiographical *Annals* go on to give, a few lines further down, an even more revealing passage:

> At my aunt Ford's I ate so much of a boiled leg of mutton, that she used to talk of it. My mother, who had lived in a narrow sphere, and was then affected by little things, told me that it would hardly ever be forgotten.

Here, for a moment, we catch an unforgettable glimpse of Sarah Johnson at work, moulding her son's character. Whether or not he was healthy, Sam was large and his physical appetites were correspondingly robust. Already, before his tenth year was out, these appetites had been associated with guilt and wrongdoing.

On another and very important level the boy had all this time been gaining self-confidence. From a very early age it had been recognized that, whatever plagues beset his body, there was no lack of vigour and suppleness in Sam's mind. His memory was astonishing, his precocity with words unusual. At a succession of schools, he rapidly assimilated everything the teachers put in front of him; from Dame Oliver's he went at six or thereabouts to a school kept by one Thomas Browne, about whom he recalled nothing in later life except that he 'published a spelling book, and dedicated it to the Universe'. This at least is proof of a manly self-esteem; Browne, like the widow Oliver's deceased husband, had been a shoemaker, and doubtless as proper men as ever trod in neat's leather had gone upon his work. At seven Sam moved on to Lichfield Grammar School, where for two years he was taught by the kindly under-master, Humphrey Hawkins. This crucial time was a happy one; 'I was', he wrote in his *Annals*, 'indulged and caressed by my master, and I think really excelled the rest.'

Sam shed tears when he had to leave the gentle Hawkins and enter the upper school to be taught by the Reverend Edward Holbrooke, whom he recalled as 'a peevish and ill-tempered man'. But, unpleasant as Holbrooke was, the head-master, Joseph Hunter, was worse, being not only severe but unfair. Early memories of injustice linger long, and smart; one's self-pity is reinforced by an objective pity for the child one used to be. Wounds like these, inflicted on the tender bark of a young tree, are the hardest to forgive. More than forty years later Johnson could still grow warm over the memory of Hunter's injustices, his failure to put himself in a boy's place. 'He would', he told Boswell, 'ask a boy a question, and if he did not answer it, he would beat him, without considering whether he had an opportunity of knowing how to answer it. For instance, he would call up a boy and ask him Latin for a candlestick, which the boy could not expect to be asked. Now, Sir, if a boy could answer every question, there would be no need of a master to teach him.'

Not that the mature Johnson disapproved of corporal punishment. Asked by his friend Langton how he came to have such an accurate knowledge of Latin, he replied simply, 'My master whipped me very well. Without that, Sir, I should have done nothing.' It is quite arguable that this is true; a subject like Latin, which requires endless attention to detail and continual effort of memory, was probably never learnt without coercion of some kind; certainly the disappearance of Latin and Greek from English schools has exactly kept pace with the obsolescence of the cane. Sam Johnson cannot have enjoyed being 'whipped very well' by the unpleasant Hunter, but he had the honesty to admit afterwards that it stimulated him in the long battle with accidence, grammar, and vocabulary on which the youth of all Western Europe for so many centuries exercised their intellectual sinews. And the big, ungainly lad with his short sight and pitted face had another motive besides avoiding too frequent contact with Hunter's cane. He could see that when he gave a solid demonstration of his mental powers people respected him. All his life it gave him a glow of pride to recall the early tributes. 'They never thought to raise me by comparing me to anyone,' he told Boswell. 'They never said, Johnson is as good a scholar as such a one; but, such a one is as good a scholar as Johnson.' In later life Johnson was constantly surrounded by a circle of admirers, drawn to him by his wisdom and the sheer strength of his character; but no circle ever gave quite such a remarkable demonstration of deference as the boys at Lichfield Grammar School. One of them was Edmund Hector, nephew of that George Hector who had assisted Sam into the world; and years later, when Boswell questioned him about Johnson's schooldays, the aged Hector recalled how a deputation of the boys used to call at Sam's house in the morning and carry him to school. 'One in the middle stooped, while he sat upon his back, and one on each side supported him; and thus he was borne triumphant.' Staffordshire schoolboys must have been more civilized in the eighteenth century than I remember them in the twentieth, when a boy who showed an aptitude for his studies had to keep the fact a dark secret or be taunted as a 'swot' and a quisling who had gone over to the side of the masters. But then Sam Johnson must have seemed very different from the skinny victimized swot whom schoolboys love to persecute. Already, with all his drawbacks, he was a giant among his peers, a natural dominator; in paying homage to him they felt themselves dignified rather than lowered; a fact which, as Boswell pawkily yet correctly remarks, 'does honour to human nature'.

Sam's mind was the great instrument by which he conquered the disadvantages of his physical and emotional constitution. It was, people already saw, an extraordinary mind, as colossal and in some ways as odd as its owner. To begin with, there was that prodigious memory. This, by itself, is not necessarily a proof of intelligence. Clinical psychiatry can show us examples of certain kinds of imbecile who can memorize a telephone directory. On the other hand, the hypothetical 'brilliant man with a bad memory', so faithfully trotted out by opponents of the examination system, clearly belongs to folklore. One never, in actual life, meets such a man. Every intelligent person has a more or less powerful memory, for the simple reason that the mind retains what it enjoys and is fed by.

Sam Johnson's memory seems to come somewhere between these points. All the faculties of his mind were powerful, but his memory seems to have been almost freakishly so. Soon after learning to read he had amazed his mother by repeating, after a couple of quick readings, a prayer she had set him to learn. Edmund Hector told Boswell of an even more remarkable example, from later in boyhood. He had recited to Johnson a passage of eighteen verses, presumably in Latin, and Johnson had at once repeated back to him the whole passage, making only one change – which, Hector generously added, was an improvement.

Sam's retentiveness was matched by his readiness of utterance, as it was to be all his life. It was his performance in this line that brought out the doting streak in the otherwise aloof Michael Johnson. Like any ageing father who realizes that he has produced a gifted child, Michael succumbed to the temptation to show off Sam's prowess to his scanty circle of friends; to the extent, indeed, that Sam learnt to run away and hide, sometimes up a tree, at the approach of a visitor. Michael even made up a quaint little set of verses, commemorating the accidental death of a duckling, and attributed them to Sam. No doubt these early experiences were at the root of Samuel Johnson's lifelong resistance to child prodigies. If any fond parent offered to have Missy or Master down to the drawing-room to perform, his head was bitten off in short order. One papa who wanted his two boys to repeat Gray's *Elegy* in turn, that the Doctor might judge who rendered it the better, was met with a counter-proposal: 'No, pray Sir, let the dears both speak it at once; more noise will by that means be made, and the noise will be sooner over.' This is one of those anecdotes about Johnson that 'everybody knows'; it is, in fact, not very typical; he could be short and brusque, but he was not often so rude. The unaccustomed snappishness points to the presence of a strong feeling, and it is only fair to Johnson to assume that such displays offended him not merely on his own account but on that of the victims. He relived, for a horrible moment, all those times when he had had to scramble up trees or skulk behind hedges, to avoid being shown off like a performing lapdog.

Michael's pleasure in his cleverness offended Sam because it was self-regarding and associated with parlour tricks; the other tributes he received, being unforced and disinterested, pleased him, as when he was 'caressed' by Hawkins or carried to school 'in triumph'.

Sam's mind was not only powerful and original: it had a highly idiosyncratic way of working. Long periods of sluggish idleness would be broken by flashes of a concentration almost terrifying in its singleness. He seems never to have been, as most of us are most of the time, more or less attentive, more or less alert. Either he was lost in daydreaming and vacuity, or he was focusing on what was in front of him with a fierce glare of attention. In this, undoubtedly, there was an element of the neurotic. During his fits of inertia, Sam literally *could not* concentrate. He would look up at the town clock, and though his eyesight was good enough to see the position of its hands he was unable to register what time it showed. He could not force the information into his mind.

Conversely, when he did find himself able to focus on what was in front of him, he became unconscious of everything else. Another of the things about Johnson that 'everybody knows' is that he never read a book all the way through; he leafed through it, snatching at the gist, 'tearing the heart' out of it. Readers without Johnson's incredible powers of concentration should be warned that this method will not serve them as it served him. To read a book steadily all the way through was probably impossible to him in any case. At a given moment he was concentrating either far more, or far less, than the rest of us normally do; so that to make his example a licence for careless reading and skipping would be a mistake.

In later life Samuel Johnson recognized the peculiar stop-and-start nature of his mental powers. In the autobiographical *Annals* from which we have been drawing so much of our information, he set down a recollection that illustrated how early this fierce, intermittent concentration had developed. It concerned the time when he and Natty had been sent to stay with their Birmingham relations. Uncle Harrison, the 'mean and vulgar' man who got drunk every night, had as housekeeper a sixteen-year-old niece named Sally Ford, a sweet-natured girl whom Sam remembered with fondness. One day Sam was sitting in the kitchen, writing away at a holiday exercise set by Hunter. 'I was writing at the kitchen windows, as I thought alone, and turning my head saw Sally dancing. I went on without any notice, and had finished almost without perceiving that any time had elapsed.'

If I were a classic painter of domestic interiors like Vermeer or Pieter de Hooch, I would paint that scene. In the quiet, sunny space by the kitchen windows Sam is at work. Sally enters: her sixteen-year-old heart suddenly seized by the joy of living, she forgets her chores and her curmudgeonly uncle, and begins dancing about the room. The boy turns, stares at her briefly, then goes back to his writing. His eyes have registered that she is there; his mind is hardly aware of her. Only when the work is finished, when his intellect relaxes its fierce grip, does he realize that while he was at work the world was going on, that Sally was dancing and time was passing. Already, in the strange, ungainly body, the mind had shown its ability to take command.

CHAPTER 2

Mentors

So boyhood passed into adolescence. New powers, new problems. The unusual intellectual power remained; he was not one of those bright children who, under the strain of puberty, suddenly become mediocre. On the other hand, the dangers and difficulties inherent in his temperament came into his consciousness in a way they could not have done in childhood.

His closest friend at this time was Edmund Hector, though he was also forming lifelong friendships with other schoolfellows – with John Taylor, with Robert James, even with poor Harry Jackson who came to nothing. Hector, his usual companion, soon found that he could do Sam no greater favour than to keep him company in idling about the fields on the outskirts of town. Unable to engage in the usual boyhood pastimes, Sam would stroll about the footpaths for hour after hour on days of leisure, and Hector, pacing beside him, noted that though he talked all the time, his talk had the quality of soliloquy; he liked to think aloud in the presence of an undemanding listener.

The fact is that, very early on, Samuel Johnson learnt to fear the hours of stagnant idleness forced on him by the pendulum swings of his mind. In these vacant hours undisciplined thoughts took over. He did not, at this age, suffer from the agonizing religious scruples that were to torment him in maturity; but already the periods of heaviness, when he was too sunk in his strange sloth to perform such simple acts of cognition as telling the time, must have been a source of perplexity and worry. All his life Johnson advised his friends, and that larger public whom he reached with his writings, to avoid mere vacant inactivity: busy yourself with *something*, as long as it is not something you know to be wrong; anything, except sin, is better than nothing. The advice crops up again and again: it is behind such odd observations as that smoking tobacco is justifiable because, without calling for any effort, it nevertheless 'preserves the mind from complete vacuity'; it is certainly behind the mature Johnsonian position that the ordinary sweat and toil of earning a living is good in itself because it keeps people occupied. Years later he remarked to Strahan the printer, 'There are few ways in which a man can be more innocently employed than in getting money.' Between this opinion and his lifelong detestation of money-grubbing and greed there is in fact no real inconsistency.

When he had no companion to saunter by his side, there was always the blessed haven of the bookshop. Michael Johnson may have been an unsatisfactory father, but he had made a priceless contribution to his son's life merely by his choice of a trade. No ordinary middle-class, middle-income family could possibly have afforded a private library of this extent and variety, and these were the days before the growth of free lending libraries. When his parents bickered, when Natty was a nuisance, or just when he felt an attack of low spirits coming on, Sam could always find an interesting book he had not read. What is more, both sides of his mind, the indolent and the fiercely energetic, could find satisfaction among his father's well-stocked shelves. In his idle fits he would sit for hours reading romances; not contemporary novels, like those of Richardson and Fielding, but those loftily non-credible tales of wonders and prodigies which seek only to enthral. In later life he was sardonic about these romances and drew a careful distinction between them and more serious literature; but in boyhood, and later, he indulged his half-ashamed taste for them. There was also much reading of a meatier nature. At school he had gone, like everyone else, through the rudimentary classical grind: learning rules, then parsing and construing, getting passages by heart – Latin, always Latin. Once the solid foundation of Latin was laid, there was an introduction to Greek; but the language of jurists and moralists, the language in which the affairs of a great Empire had once been conducted, leaving its mark in every country in Europe and in every area of life, was assumed to be much more important than the language of philosophers and poets. By the time the boys got to Greek they learnt faster, because they were older and understood how to set about studying a language; but they never took so tenacious a grip of Greek as of Latin, and in later life they forgot it more thoroughly. This is the basis of the mature Johnson's remark that Greek was like lace: every man got as much as he could of such expensive finery, but no one had very much. Lichfield Grammar School put him in possession of enough Latin, by the time he was sixteen, to read at sight the standard prose writers like Cato and Cicero, and the standard poets like Ovid, Virgil and Horace. Probably the syllabus did not stop at classical Latin but added a fair amount of reading in modern Latin writers such as Vives and Erasmus; so that it seemed natural to Johnson, all his life, to read the Latin works of a modern author as a normal and expected part of his output. In Greek, it is possible that they wrestled with a few passages of Pindar, Hesiod, Theocritus. (Johnson's later detestation of pastoral poetry, and his dismissal of the English 'Pindarique ode' with its tumid rhetoric, cannot be accounted for by saying that he did not know the Greek originals of these forms; Lichfield would have given him at any rate a nodding acquaintance with them.)

All a school education can do, in any case, is to put a man in the position to begin educating himself. The Latin drubbed into him by his teachers meant that Sam could devour the books in his father's shop indiscriminately. A good part of the stock of a respectable bookseller in the early eighteenth century would have been in Latin, and Sam had no need to pick over the books and sort out the English titles. He laid, at this time, the foundation of a learning that was as wide as Europe. No one directed his reading; he was fortunate, of course, in that the stock of the shop would contain far more weighty and serious books, and far less cheap trash, than that of a bookshop today. Chance association, chance discovery, led him to one important discovery after another. Somewhere in his boyish reading he came upon a reference to Petrarch as 'the restorer of poetry'. The phrase aroused his curiosity. What had happened to poetry that it needed restoring? And how did one restore it? Some time later he was groping round the shelves to see if Nathaniel had left any apples behind the books. (Apples always dry well on a wooden shelf.) He found a copy of Petrarch's *Works*. Down it came at once. The child was very clearly the father of the man. One of the mature Johnson's deepest interests was in the actual *process* whereby some great adventure of the human spirit had got into motion; its first faltering steps, its effortful stages of growth. Sitting in his father's shop reading Petrarch, trying to discover in what way Petrarch had 'restored' poetry, he was in fact plugging himself in to that great intellectual system of Renaissance Europe of which he was to be a late representative.

The English poets, of course, were also there. Sam would leaf through volume after volume of the more popular poets of his own day and the preceding century. There would be Herrick, Milton, Cowley, Dryden and, above all, Shakespeare. The foundation of his intimate, lifelong familiarity with Shakespeare's plays was laid in hours of boyhood reading by the kitchen fire. We know as a fact that he used to sit by the kitchen fire; the detail is vividly there in a tiny incident he recalled in later life. The kitchen, as so often in houses of that period, was a basement, connected with the street-door by a flight of stairs. Once, when Sam was reading *Hamlet*, the ghost scenes took such hold on his young mind that, suddenly noticing that he was alone in the room, he hurried up the stairs to the street-door 'that he might have people about him'.

Books of travels, descriptions of the manners and beliefs of faraway countries, also drew him strongly. (We even know the name of one such book that held his attention: Martin Martin's *Description of the Hebrides*.) He would have loved to travel himself, and explore the world; but the idea, for someone in his circumstances, was so unreal as to be not worth thinking about. So he tried to inform himself by books, even poring over atlases to make sure he got his countries right. In one atlas that happened to be his own property, he numbered the pages and made an index at the back. In this he showed not only his interest in geography but his appetite for particularity, for the concrete. When he read history, or biography, or anything else which studied the movements of men and ideas, he wanted to be clear about who came from where.

All this the bookshop gave him. By the age of sixteen, neighbours in Lichfield, and relatives scattered about the Midlands, began to take note of the fact that Sam Johnson had a great deal of knowledge in his head. Exactly what use he was going to make of it was less easy to say. In theory, the learned professions were all open to him; as the son of a grave and dignified tradesman, the respected holder of city offices, Sam fitted naturally enough into the class, or one of the classes, that habitually received liberal education. Though Michael's business went down, his standing in the community did not. From first to last his neighbours showed him respect. He was churchwarden of St Mary's in 1688, sheriff in 1709, magistrate in 1712, junior bailiff in 1718, senior bailiff in

1725. Nor was there any question of civil disability, such as often arose in those vexed years immediately following the accession to the throne of the House of Hanover. Like anyone who stood for election to public office, Michael Johnson had signed, not once but over and over again, pledges of allegiance to the Hanovers and renunciation of the Old Pretender. Boswell tells us that Johnson senior 'retained his attachment to the unfortunate house of Stuart, though he reconciled himself, by casuistical arguments of expediency and necessity, to take the oaths imposed by the prevailing power' – a passage which has led many readers to imagine fearful inner struggles, a final capitulation, a lasting sense of shame. But these things existed more in Boswell's vivid imagination than in the monochrome inner landscape of a solid Midland tradesman. Boswell, as a Scot, identified his national pride with 'the unfortunate house of Stuart'; he would be unlikely to take much account of the hard facts, that the Stuarts had been given a chance over two generations to govern England in a way that was to the liking of the English people, had made a mess of it, been replaced by a republic, been recalled after another generation and made a mess of it again. Michael Johnson, as a Tory, would obviously regret that it had been necessary to disturb the regular succession to the English crown, and he might have indulged in some nostalgic head-shaking over the departed Stuarts – especially in view of the utter charmlessness of the early Hanoverian kings! But that he had to bend the rules of his personal morality in order to conform to the existing order, to invent 'casuistical' arguments, is a bit of Boswellian nonsense on a par with his teasing suggestion that, if Johnson's mother had really wanted him cured of scrofula by the royal touch, 'she should have taken him to Rome', i.e., to be touched by the Old Pretender: who, again as a matter of hard fact, was not yet living in Rome in 1712.

Socially and legally, Michael Johnson was in a position to do all the right things for his gifted son. Financially, it was another story. He had been established in Lichfield since 1681, when he came from Cubley with his brother, Andrew. At first the two brothers were in business together, but before long Andrew moved to Birmingham and ran a bookshop there. He was, in fact, named on the title-page of the first book ever published in that city. But his nephew Samuel remembered him not as a tradesman with an honourable connection with literature but for accomplishments much more likely to win a small boy's respect: he spoke to Mrs Thrale of his 'uncle Andrew, my father's brother, who kept the ring at Smithfield (where they wrestled and boxed) for a whole year, and never was thrown or conquered'.

Michael Johnson was hard-working, enterprising, honest; but, whether surprisingly or not, these qualities never made him rich or even reasonably prosperous. Samuel Johnson's own terse description of his father's financial troubles, in retrospect, was: 'my father, having in the early part of his life contracted debts, never had trade sufficient to pay them, and maintain his family; he got something, but not enough'. No doubt Michael had originally set up his shop with the help of credit, and probably borrowed again in 1706 when he made his spectacular purchase from the Earl of Derby. For the rest of his life he was running hard to stay in the same place, and not always managing it. No one could have accused him of laziness or lack of enterprise. He maintained stalls on market-days at nearby towns such as Uttoxeter and Ashby de la Zouch, he sold stationery, maps and patent medicines at his shop as well as books. He even set up a parchment factory some quarter of a mile from home, in the field beside Stowe Pool, and tanned skins as well as made parchment. Before the seventeenth century was out, Michael Johnson was hard at work at three trades – bookselling, parchment making and tanning. Yet the profits never rose quite high enough. On his marriage to Sarah Ford he received some £440 from her family as dowry, but a counter-clause stipulated that he must deposit £100 in a trust fund, and somehow he could never get together this sum. The £100 remained unpaid year after year, and finally, when Sam was sixteen years old, one of Sarah's grand relatives came over to the Johnson household on a visit to sort matters out.

This was the Reverend Cornelius Ford, Sarah's nephew, the son of her brother Joseph, of Stourbridge in Worcestershire. At the time of his visit, in 1725, Cornelius Ford was thirty-one. Behind him he had a very successful academic career at Cambridge; he had been elected to a Fellowship at Peterhouse, and might easily have passed his life in lettered contemplation among the fens, had not livelier attractions drawn him away to London. He was a sociable, drinking, talking man; clever and well read, but liking most of all to bring his cleverness into play among a witty circle of friends. The Samuel Johnson who later came to the conclusion that 'a tavern chair' was 'the throne of human felicity' had been anticipated in this discovery by his older cousin. In later life Parson Ford appears to have cut a rather disreputable figure. Lord Chesterfield, that elegant but shadowy Svengali who hovered so consistently in the wings of Samuel Johnson's early life, making at last one brief and disastrous appearance onstage, presented Cornelius with a living in Rutland. He seems to have preferred, like so many eighteenth-century clergymen, to pocket the money and absent himself from the place for long periods, during which he was a familiar inhabitant of the fashionable *demi-monde*. In Hogarth's lively picture 'A Modern Midnight Conversation', a group of roisterers are sitting round, or attempting to sit round, the table in a tavern room. One drunk supports himself against a chair; another, leaning against the chimneypiece, seems to be getting ready to vomit; a third, in the foreground, crashes to the floor in a stupor. Seated composedly at the table, churchwarden pipe in his mouth, is a plump figure in clerical gown and bands, ladling punch from a generous bowl. This, according to tradition, is Cornelius Ford.

But we anticipate. Though Parson Ford was at no time of his life ideally suited to the cloth, the toss-pot side of his character was not always to the fore. At the time of his contact with Sam, Cornelius was in one of the quiet periods of his existence. Recently received into Holy Orders, recently married to an ageing lady whose ample dowry had fattened his lean purse, he was living soberly at Pedmore, near Stourbridge. Doubtless even the chore of going over to Lichfield to talk family business with Michael Johnson came as a welcome diversion; and there was, too, the interest of seeing for himself the bookish son who was beginning to be talked about in the family.

The contact proved immediately fruitful. The clever, polished young clergyman, who knew London wits and London haunts, who had read with scholars and drunk with poets, confronted the melancholy, raw-boned lad half his age, who had spent his life so far in poring among the bookshelves or mooning about the fields. Each recognized a power in the other. When Cornelius Ford concluded his business with Michael, and got into the saddle for Pedmore, he took Sam with him. Originally, the visit was to have lasted a few days. In the event, it lasted seven or eight months.

One is willing to believe that for Cornelius the long visit of his cousin was something more than a relief from tedium. He was a man of sufficient penetration and sensitiveness to recognize genius, even unformed genius, when he met it. Though the two drifted apart in later life, the long hours of their talk must have been valuable. To Cornelius, Sam's visit must have remained an important memory. To Sam, it was one of those experiences that change everything. For a whole blissful winter and spring, he was away from the narrow world of the family, his mother's over-anxious nagging, the sour drizzle of money worries; away from Hunter's unjust beatings and the aimless chatter of the boys at the Grammar School. His time was spent with a gifted and sympathetic man who directed his reading, putting at his disposal a library that did not rival the vast random collection of the bookshop but still contained much that he had not encountered before, and who discussed with him what he had been reading and offered good advice on how to assimilate knowledge. At the height of his fame and influence, Johnson could still remember how Cornelius Ford had taught him to set about a subject: to go for the essentials, 'grasp the leading præcognita of all things. . . grasp the trunk hard only, and you will shake all the branches'. The surviving fragment of advice showed that Ford did not only chat with his *protégé* but made a serious effort to train his mind. Sam took it all in. And the lighter, anecdotal side of Ford's conversation, the stray pieces of information about the literary life of London and the university towns in those opening years of the eighteenth century, was also packed away in Sam's capacious memory. The life of a man of letters, the possibility of getting closer to literature than the mere selling of books across a counter, began to come into focus in the boy's thoughts.

All this time Sam had been absent from school. Ford, realizing that some sort of countenance would have to be put on this absence, had given a more or less formal undertaking to oversee his education during that time. But when Sam at last returned home, in early June, he found that in Hunter's eyes such easygoing procedures were not good enough. Sam was deemed to have left the school, and when he sought readmission he found that the school had left him. Fortunately, Cornelius Ford accepted responsibility for the situation and did something about it. With the aid of his half-brother, Gregory Hickman, he managed to get Sam admitted to the King Edward VI School at Stourbridge. After only a few days at home, Sam packed and left once again.

He spent six months at this school, boarding in the headmaster's house; a fact which probably underlies his later remark that, whereas at Lichfield he learnt much from the school but little from the master, at Stourbridge he learnt much from the master and little from the school. Certainly the headmaster, John Wentworth, took enough notice of Sam to keep some of his routine exercises in translation, evidence that he saw what was in front of him better than Hunter seems to have done. For the rest, there was the welcome opportunity to keep up some contact with Ford at Pedmore, and to get to know other relatives dotted about the town, most of them substantial people who took him into their houses and treated him with consideration: the Hickmans, the Fords, the Moseleys, Mrs Harriotts of Trysull. One of the weapons with which Sarah Johnson so consistently belaboured her husband was the undeniable fact that her relations were of higher social standing than his. At Stourbridge, Sam was among these more prosperous siblings. By all accounts they treated him well. But it must have been very clear to him that he had to exert himself to deserve their esteem. They received him in the first place because of a common tie of kinship. Once there, he had to make himself welcome by the only quality he could bring to the bargain – his intelligence. Even his education at the Stourbridge school he owed to his prowess; according to a tradition reported by Boswell, the headmaster took Sam into the school gratis in exchange for help in teaching the younger boys. As so often throughout his life, he found himself among people who had more of the world's goods than he had; if they were to look up to him, it must be for his qualities of mind. The world owed no man a living, except of course those who were born to hereditary rank and privilege. Not far from Cornelius Ford's home at Pedmore stood Hagley Park, seat of the Lyttelton family. George, the future Lord Lyttelton, was just Sam's age; he was a pupil at Eton, but he would be at home during the holidays, and that Sam should have met him, under the auspices of Cornelius, is not at all impossible. More than half a century later, at the end of Samuel Johnson's life, it fell to his lot to have to write an account of George Lyttelton in his *Lives of the Poets*, and the portrait, which is far from an affectionate one, is unusual in that it gives a glimpse of its subject's physical appearance and bearing. Some of the major lives, dealing with important poets, do this, but it is rare among the minor ones. Here, suddenly, George Lyttelton looks out at us; he had, Johnson tells us, 'never the appearance of a strong or healthy man; he had a slender uncompacted frame, and a meagre face; he lasted however sixty years. . . .' Perhaps the gangling, thin-faced Lyttelton had been a little too casual or patronizing with the bookseller's son, and made a bad impression – though in the *Life* Johnson is careful to give credit where credit is genuinely due. To such as Lyttelton, in any case, the opinion of others could make little difference; rank and fortune and leisure were unalterably theirs. To Sam Johnson it was very clear that he must prove himself; and perhaps, among his friends and relations at Stourbridge, he had begun to do so.

The experience was obviously stretching and useful. In spite of his poverty, in spite of his ugliness – huge bones not yet adequately covered in flesh, wild staring eyes, scrofula-scarred face – he was growing up into the kind of man who might yet be outstanding in his generation. But for this some luck would be needed. And luck was coming Sam's way sparingly and in fits and starts. He was fortunate in having a cousin like Cornelius Ford; he was fortunate in leaving the brutal Hunter and finishing out his schooldays with the more equable Wentworth. On the other hand, Wentworth did not value him enough to keep him on at the school after the first six months. He returned home somewhat abruptly. Many years later Edmund Hector told Boswell that Sam had quarrelled with Wentworth over the exact phrasing of a Latin sentence. This, by itself, would hardly be enough to make his position at the school impossible, but the story rings true if one sees it as evidence that the two had been getting on one another's nerves and that real irritation flared up over a small matter – particularly a matter in which each was impugning the other's taste and scholarship. Whatever the reason, in the November of 1726 Sam was back at Lichfield. The Stourbridge experience had been a blind alley.

Now that Sam had acquainted himself with other places and other social circles, his native town emerged in clearer perspective. Certainly he would have judged it harshly. It is a law of nature that any adolescent regards his original setting of birthplace and family circle simply as a trap to be got out of. In later life, having explored to satiety the exciting landscape on the far side of the hills, he strikes a bargain with that early world, usually settling down to an attitude of mutual respect and tolerance, tinged on both sides with a certain amusement. This seems to have been Johnson's attitude to Lichfield when, in middle life, he again became a presence in its streets. At seventeen he would have been more conscious of its limitations to the extent that he was more hungry for change and experience. Even so, he could hardly have failed to register that Lichfield was a far more interesting place than some of the other towns in the vicinity in which it might have been his fate to be born. Compared with Uttoxeter or Stafford, it was metropolitan; compared with the booming industrial centre of Birmingham, which at that time was growing at the pace of a Klondyke, it was calm and meditative. 'We are a city of philosophers,' he remarked many years later; 'we work with our heads, and we make the boobies of Birmingham work for us with their hands.'

It was a lively, money-spinning, decent little place: not so little either, for a town of three thousand inhabitants made quite a figure when the entire population of England was less than six million. In some respects it must then have struck the eye very differently from today not only because of the inevitable depredations of the twentieth century but because of the boom Lichfield enjoyed between 1790 and 1840, when its position at the crossroads of so many important coaching routes brought it a wave of business. During those opulent years, the mediaeval buildings were pulled down and replaced by the plain but handsome Georgian brick structures which represent, today, the 'old' part of the town. So that the Johnson house in Breadmarket Street, a new house when Sam was born in it in 1709, is now one of the oldest.

In his time it would stand out even more as a newcomer, since it was one of the few Lichfield houses that had not needed to be extensively repaired and rebuilt. The Civil War of the 1640s had knocked the town about terribly. Some parts of England had been relatively undisturbed, but the Midlands had seen the full fury of the conflict, and when the guns fell silent the town was full of smashed walls and collapsed houses. The Cathedral, in particular, was almost completely ruined. Minster Pool, in those days, had two outlets which ran on either side of the Cathedral, forming a moat which, along with its size and strength, rendered the place defensible; and this patch of ground was savagely fought over, taken and retaken and taken again. All this was a long time ago by Sam's reckoning – before the birth of his elderly father – but the memories were still strong in the minds of Lichfield people, who pointed out to visitors the exact spot on which this or that Homeric action had been performed. The most famous of these was Dumb Dyott's almost incredible feat of marksmanship. It was at a time when the Cathedral was in Royalist hands, and the Parliamentary forces attacking it were under the command of Lord Brooke, a severe Puritan and implacable foe of episcopacy, who must have taken a particular pleasure in attacking a cathedral. Brooke had taken for his headquarters a house in Dam Street, now appropriately known as Brooke House, and on the morning of 2 March (the feast of St Chad!) he stepped out of the door to order the firing of a cannon he had set up in the street. Far up on the large spire of the Cathedral clung Dumb Dyott, a member of a well-known local family, a mute who had evidently compensated for his lack of speech by quickness of eye and hand. In spite of the distance, and the inaccuracy of seventeenth-century firearms, Dyott let fly at Brooke, and managed to get the bullet under the rim of his helmet so that Brooke, pierced through the brain, fell dead instantly. Such exploits make a man a hero in his native place. To this day Dumb Dyott is better remembered in Lichfield than the Dyotts who were active in eighteenth-century politics, or even than General William Dyott whose diary, printed in 1905, is an important source of Lichfield history.

Alterations and rebuildings notwithstanding, Lichfield was in one respect the same as it is now. The town is built across a shallow valley which runs right through it from west to east. In this valley occur several streams, and also marshy pools known locally as 'Moggs'. Streams and pools have changed their situation and shape often enough through the centuries, from natural causes and the interference of man, but together they have succeeded in making a broad stripe of land unsuitable for building, so that Lichfield then, as now, had grass and trees and water in its very centre. Both now and on his later visits as a mature man, Samuel Johnson was fond of strolling past the Moggs and round Stowe Pool, an extensive pond from which in those days two streams flowed out and presently united and ran into the River Trent. His father taught him to swim at the point where these streams twined into one and hid themselves under luxuriant overhanging boughs which in later years, to his pain, were cleared away.

Physically pleasant, enriched by associations with learning, piety and heroism, Lichfield was markedly more interesting than other Midland towns of similar size and wealth. Yet Samuel Johnson, stunned by the hammer strokes of disappointment, perplexed about his future, dissatisfied with his surroundings, might have anticipated Philip Larkin's words:

> Not a bad place to be;
> Yet it doesn't suit me.

Not that the place failed to do its best by him. The huge rawboned youth was not the most obviously attractive of companions at table or fireside. But among the respectable and well-to-do of Lichfield there was no lack of people who could see further than outward appearances. Such men as Theophilus Levet, the town clerk, John Marten, the apothecary (commemorated today by a plaque on his house in Sadler Street), Stephen Simpson, the lawyer, and Dr Swinfen made the boy welcome at their houses.

In later life Samuel Johnson was as remarkable for his knowledge of the law as for his depth in literature. If he became the first man of letters of his age rather than a great lawyer, that was – as he himself insisted – because he had lacked the funds, in youth, to study the law systematically. This remained, all his life, a sorrow to him. When a friend suggested that he might have been Lord Chancellor, he growled out, 'Why do you vex me by suggesting this, now that it is too late?' The twofold grasp of Johnson's mind, literary and juristic, is doubtless primarily a matter of the inherited structure of his brain. But something, also, must be due to early environment. Of the educated and liberal men whom he knew in youth, several were trained lawyers. Cornelius Ford's studies, it is true, had been almost exclusively literary. But in Levet and Simpson he would be meeting minds trained in the law. And now, in one of the decisive encounters of his life, he was to meet a man whose mind moved freely between literature, the law, administration and politics.

The new friend was Gilbert Walmesley, registrar of the ecclesiastical court of Lichfield. A bachelor of forty-seven, living in style in the bishop's palace – the stateliest building, after the Cathedral itself, in the entire Close – Walmesley was in a position to appreciate, and encourage, any new talent that showed its head in Lichfield. His table was well provided, and he was hospitable and civilized. He was ready to lend an ear to Sam Johnson and to the even younger David Garrick, son of the polite and courtly Captain Garrick who lived just round the corner from the Close, and was already showing signs of that histrionic talent that was to make him one of the most famous men in England.

So to the bishop's palace Sam went, often: to talk, to listen, to make new acquaintances and brush up old ones. It was here that he met again his older schoolfellow Robert James, now a young medical man just down from Oxford, who was destined to be another eighteenth-century celebrity, the author of a medical dictionary and the inventor of 'James's Powders', a nostrum which enjoyed the unwavering faith of the English people for a hundred years. It was here that he must surely have sat among the first audience to see David Garrick tread the boards; for the brilliant, restless child, already fired with stage fever, gathered the local talent about him and put on George Farquhar's *The*

Recruiting Officer, a classic stage comedy that had resulted from Farquhar's sojourn in Lichfield at the beginning of the century and set its action there.

But James and Garrick might be met elsewhere. It was the magnet of Walmesley's personality that drew Sam to the big house in the Close. Walmesley carried on the work that Cornelius Ford had begun: warming Sam's mind into life, extending his knowledge, making him show his paces like a young racehorse. Though too urbane to shout an opponent down, Walmesley was intellectually aggressive. He liked to direct an argument with all the skill of his legal mind. Since they disagreed about many things, Sam must often have found himself pointed into a corner. But he learnt quickly. It was at Walmesley's house that he began to develop that formidable skill in disputation that made it virtually impossible to get the better of him when he fairly 'talked for victory'.

Without doubt some of their arguments would be political. Walmesley was a Whig, no mere wearer of a party label but a very convinced and active supporter of the Whig cause. Sam Johnson was an equally convinced Tory. It is as well to get these two terms cleared up now, at the beginning of our story. Most of us have in our minds a vague notion of the Whigs as progressive, anti-clerical, jealous of the power of the monarchy; of the Tories as reactionary, anti-populist, suspicious of the power of commerce, supporters of the throne. This is not altogether incorrect; as Johnson put it in later years, in a statement he dictated to Boswell, 'The prejudice of the Tory is for establishment; the prejudice of the Whig is for innovation.' Back in the days of Charles II, the Whigs had angered the King by making a determined effort to bar the Catholic Duke of York from succession to the throne; they certainly had a tradition of keeping the monarchy in its place, and the Tories equally had a tradition of supporting it. We should not, however, deduce from this that their division was anything like the left–right division in present-day politics. Modern political systems are based, fundamentally, on the balance of power between labour and capital, which results in turn from the nature of industrial society. The England of Johnson's day was not yet industrial; the working class was not organized into a political force. On the occasions when the mob rioted over some political issue, it was more often on the Tory side; the Whigs represented wealth and power, the inherited wealth and power of the aristocracy as well as of the newer business magnates.

Above all, the Tories were the party of the losers. They had been defeated and outmanœuvred ever since 1688. Since so many of them had Jacobite sympathies, the first two Hanoverian kings regarded them with profound suspicion. All the important political offices in the eighteenth century were held by Whigs. From Walpole to Pelham to Rockingham to Charles James Fox, the powerful statesmen were Whigs. The Tories were too few and disorganized even to be an effective opposition, so that all the major political battles of the century were in fact between different factions of Whigs. When Sir Robert Walpole was hunted from office after a long period of unpopularity, it was not the Tories who got rid of him but a motley collection of rivals and discarded friends who patched up a semblance of unity by describing themselves as 'Patriots'.

Again, the centralized, disciplined party machine of modern times had not come into existence in the eighteenth century. We shall be on safer ground with the terms 'Whig' and 'Tory' if we think of them as attitudes, clusters of opinions and sentiments, rather than binding party labels. There were, indeed, politicians who described themselves as Tories; that is, they were politicians in as much as they stood for election and took their seats in Parliament. But once in Parliament the Tory member tended to give his main attention to the affairs of his own district. He was at Westminster to represent the interests of his neighbourhood, not to attain high office and disappear from the life of that neighbourhood altogether. His seat in Parliament was an adjunct, though an important one, to his usefulness and influence at home. Many Tories were indifferent to the power struggles that absorbed the career politicians; some of them, indeed, were hard to interest in matters of national policy at all. Like a certain type of politician in our day, they jumped to their feet only when something arose that concerned the folks back home.

Most people know that Samuel Johnson was a Tory, not because he very often described himself as one but because he so consistently used 'Whig' as a term of opprobrium. He evidently regarded a Whig as a person with a certain cast of mind, just as W. B. Yeats did when he wrote:

> . . .what is Whiggery?
> A levelling, rancorous, rational sort of mind
> That never looked out of the eye of a saint
> Or out of drunkard's eye.

To Johnson a Whig was someone who lacked the proper feelings of reverence for the past and respect for tradition. A Whig was dead to the noble imaginative associations of antiquity. The Whiggish impatience to sweep away the past came just as much from a lack of poetic feeling as from a desire to better the lives of men. Furthermore, to him most Whigs were shallow optimists who had not been forced into bruising contact with the realities of existence.

It tells us something about the stubborn intellectual courage of the young Sam Johnson that his contact with Walmesley did not turn him, even for the time being, into a Whig. Walmesley, with his knowledge of the world, his learning, his higher social position, his hospitable table, must have seemed to Sam exactly the kind of man he wanted to grow up to be. And if he had been a normally impressionable youth he would have taken over Walmesley's political opinions without a qualm. Most young people, even clever ones, do not think out political opinions for themselves; they take over the politics of others whom they admire and wish to resemble. That Sam resisted Walmesley's Whiggery can hardly have been due simply to the fact that he came from a Tory household. Michael Johnson's influence over him was never as strong as that, and his mother's example in a matter of this kind would be negligible. The boy's Tory cast of mind came from elsewhere, and Lichfield itself must have been largely responsible. Not in its political slant, for the parties were fairly evenly balanced there; some of the cathedral clergy would be High Tories, but the successive bishops, being political appointees, would in the nature of things be Whigs. No, the argument for tradition, the love and reverence Sam felt for the past, would come from the streets and squares of the old market town, and particularly from the three graceful spires of the Cathedral, their dark red sandstone rich against a changing Midland sky. The Cathedral was dedicated to St Chad, an ancient and half-legendary saint who had set a Christian example at a time when much of the region was ruled by the pagan Mercian King Offa. During the Civil War the Roundhead soldiers had stabled their horses in it, smashed its glass, disfigured its statues, in the name of a reforming and innovating movement that had also lopped off the head of an anointed king. Now it was restored and its serene beauty spoke to the young Johnson of a continuity of worship, a refuge against the misery of the world.

When, in his sixties, Johnson toured Scotland with Boswell, he registered shock and grief at the ruined state of the cathedrals. Since the reforming zeal of John Knox had been a prime agent in their destruction, Johnson spoke of Knox with a peculiar hatred. Boswell noted that, at St Andrew's, Johnson spent a long time pacing out the foundations of the almost vanished cathedral and that he kept his hat off during all the time he was standing on ground it had once hallowed. That Walmesley, who lived within the shadow of Lichfield Cathedral and was actually in its employ, should be a virulent Whig must have seemed particularly regrettable to his young friend. But they did not succeed in changing one another's views; and most of the time, we may be sure, they found other things to talk about.

The evenings he spent in civilized, literate talk at Walmesley's house were obviously a great solace and encouragement to Sam. But in another way they must have increased his discontent. The business in Market Street was not doing well. In spite of his energy, in spite of the diversification of his trade and the long miles he rode for orders, Michael Johnson was losing ground. It would have been only natural for the sorely tried man to imagine that with two sons growing up he might look forward to the day when they would take his business off his hands and, by working hard in co-operation, make it prosper at last. But Sam was obviously not cut out to be a tradesman; though he grudgingly went along with it, learning the elements of the business and becoming a tolerable hand at the practical skill of bookbinding, his resentment at the menial life of trade was always smouldering just below the surface. One day there was a nasty scene when he refused point blank to go to Uttoxeter Market, some ten miles away, and take charge of the stall which Michael regularly set up there. Michael was forced to capitulate: Sam just would not go, and other arrangements had to be made. As for Natty, he is, as always, a shadowy figure. Many years later, in one of the few surviving fragments that concern Nathaniel, his elder brother described him as 'a lively noisy man'. This is the kind of detail that enables us to reconstruct a life. If Nathaniel was 'noisy', the Johnson household in Sam's late teens must have resembled a beargarden. Today, when we make our decorous pilgrimages to the house in Breadmarket Street, climbing up the polished wooden stairs and peering into the small but beautifully proportioned rooms, it seems commodious enough. But when it had to house a book business with miles of shelves, the four Johnsons and their two or three servants, and all the clutter with which human beings surround themselves, there must have been times when it was bursting at the seams. All three of the Johnson males were large; when they squeezed past each other on the stairs, or in the narrow spaces between crowded bookshelves, they must have seemed like mastiffs in a terrier's kennel. And, since both Michael and Samuel were moody and melancholic, and Nathaniel was noisy, we can see one more reason why Sam was eager to get out of the house and visit Walmesley, or indeed anyone else who was willing to be visited. His old schoolfriend, Edmund Hector, lived in Sadler Street, and Sam was glad enough to keep up the connection; Hector was one of the earliest and most devoted friends he ever had, and besides there was his sixteen-year-old sister, Ann. Sam Johnson liked Ann Hector; he responded to her youthful beauty, and half a century later he still remembered how she had stirred his heart.

These diversions apart, it was a melancholy life. There was not much happiness at home, and whenever he looked towards the future Sam saw nothing but misery and frustration. His father's failure to amass even moderate wealth could have only one result on Sam's prospects: to abolish them. No learned profession would receive him, and he was fit for nothing else; only within a learned profession would his eccentricities be accepted. Tradesmen have to conform, and Sam showed no talent for conforming. As things were shaping for him, he would be lucky to avoid the workhouse.

Then came one of those reversals of fortune that one would never dare to put into a novel. (Though, since it was a stroke of luck afterwards ironically reversed, it would go well enough into a novel by Thomas Hardy.) Suddenly, enough money flowed into the Johnson household, or appeared to flow in, to buy Sam an Oxford education.

Two factors came together: one real, one illusory. The real one was a legacy of forty pounds which came to Sarah Johnson from her cousin, the widow Harriots. This was enough to get Sam over the threshold. The rest was provided for – in theory – by an offer from a young Shropshire squire, Andrew Corbet. Corbet had been one of the boarding pupils at Lichfield Grammar School, and as such had had plenty of opportunity to get to know Sam Johnson, with his incredible memory, his powers of intense spasmodic application, and his natural instinct to dominate the intellectual scene in which he found himself. ('They never said, Johnson is as good a scholar as such a one; but, such a one is as good a scholar as Johnson.') It occurred to Corbet, who was alone in the world and had plenty of money, that Sam would make an ideal companion during his Oxford years, and he came forward unbidden with an offer of financial help. He was already an undergraduate at Pembroke, the college most associated with Sam's immediate family and neighbourly circle. Dr Swinfen, his godfather, had been there; so had his uncle Henry Jesson; so had Richard Pyott, one of the trustees of Sarah's dowry and a reliable friend of the family.

So to Pembroke Sam was to go, following family tradition and under the financial umbrella of a boyhood friend and admirer. At last his wings were spreading. Walmesley must have nodded his approval; Robert James must have furnished details of what, in these days, an Oxford student was expected to be, and do, and wear. While Michael Johnson doggedly attended to his failing business, and Natty thumped and roared about the house, Sam was busy – with the whole-hearted help, we may be sure, of his mother – packing, sorting out clothes, buying whatever he lacked for his new life. The neighbourhood took due note: Dame Oliver, his first teacher, who had by this time given up education in favour of the confectionery business, came round with a present of gingerbread – her tribute to 'the best scholar she had ever had'.

At last it arrived, the great October day of the journey. From Lichfield to Oxford is no great distance – less than eighty miles even by the slightly longer route that would have been customary in the eighteenth century – but it was the longest journey Sam had yet taken, his first wider look at the English scene. Is it possible, one wonders, to wipe away everything that has happened since, and for a few moments to see England as it must have appeared to his eyes – the England of 1728?

Surface contrasts, of course, come easily to mind, and any biographer of an eighteenth-century figure could go on for pages about how they didn't have this which we have gained and did have that which we have lost. But it would be better to heed Cornelius Ford's advice to Johnson: 'Grasp the leading præcognita of all things – grasp the trunk hard only, and you will shake all the branches.' And the trunk, it seems to me, is the fact that England was a small country with a highly traditional way of life, under whose surface great changes were preparing.

European society in the earlier eighteenth century had a stability, a continuity of habit and tradition that in our change-ridden age is virtually unimaginable. For two or three thousand years – we can afford to be vague about the beginning, as we approach so nearly to the end – Western society had organized itself in a way that must have come to seem eternal. Everywhere, the bulk of the population worked on the land, and the agriculture to which they gave their working lives was predominantly a subsistence agriculture. Farms supplied their neighbourhoods. Apart from a few luxury items such as tea, coffee and ginger, most people even in the more comfortable middle class went through their lives without consuming or owning anything that had to be imported. As for the labouring class, they never saw, handled, ate or drank anything that came from more than a few miles off. Life was rooted and immobile to an extent that deeply affected everyone's outlook on it. To understand the eighteenth-century mind, as it shows itself in art, in politics, in conversation, in relationships, one has to start from that premise. When Johnson came to practise as a literary critic, for instance, he was able to build his work on the same foundation that had served Aristotle in the *Poetics*: 'Nothing can please many, and please long, but just representations of general nature.' The assumption is that human beings are basically the same everywhere and in all epochs, and that what appear to be differences between them are merely superficial accidents of time and place, which the poet loftily ignores. It follows that morality is invariable, since the same actions will be good or bad everywhere and by whomever performed; so that, again as Johnson was to write, the poet 'must disregard present laws and opinions, and rise to general and transcendental truths, which will always be the same'. The best artist is he who most nearly approaches universality, stripping away the incidental and the accidental, revealing the unchanging human form and the face which has always the same range of expressions. To reach back to this view, we have to unthink our modern notion of art and, for that matter, of truth itself, for our view is dominated by the notion of progress and advance; we think of sensibility and perception as a continual journey; our orthodoxy enforces reverence for the *avant garde*, brave and lonely voyagers who press on ahead of the rest of mankind into territory still untamed, and return to tell what they have seen and be met with misunderstanding and ridicule. The eighteenth-century view of art has no place for the *avant garde*; it seeks to 'please many', not just the enlightened few who have learnt to break away from fixed attitudes and prejudices, and it seeks to 'please long', not just till the next wave comes rolling in.

This changeless attitude arose naturally from the unvarying conditions of life, which had obtained so long that they had come to seem like laws of nature. In fact, of course, this old-European order of things was now in its last few years. The forces of change were at work under the crust of habit and expectation, and were beginning to send out seismic tremors which, as usual, were picked up first by imaginative people, so that literature and art entered the modern age before 1800, while most areas of life began to feel change only after the Napoleonic Wars. The scientific revolution had completed its first phase before Johnson was born and the apparent stability of life during his formative years was doomed; if, during most of his lifetime, the new knowledge appeared to have no very marked effect on daily life, that was because of the inevitable time lag between pure science and technological application.

New techniques, new means of communication and production, the revolution in transport brought about by the canal boat and shortly afterwards by the steam engine (a practical possibility within Johnson's lifetime) – all this made profound changes in the structure of English society. Once again, what Johnson saw in 1728 was a thin shell over a volcano. The country was finally emerging from its feudal past into its plutocratic future. In a feudal society, wealth and influence are reckoned in terms of ownership of land. In a plutocratic society, such as we have now, wealth and influence are reckoned in terms of money. The change was and still is heavily camouflaged by the fact that land is a valuable commodity, so that the owner of land is also rich in terms of money, which is why the aristocratic land-owning families have managed to stay near the top of the heap. Nevertheless, the jump from a feudal to a plutocratic society has been made. Land is no longer the means of producing wealth; even if oil or coal are found on one's land, the business of extracting and marketing them must be handed over to an industrial and commercial machinery of which the landowner, *per se*, knows nothing. Land is exchangeable for wealth, but that is not the same thing as being the means of its production. The change is important for an understanding of Johnson's mature attitudes. He showed impatience with what remained of the dead hand of feudalism. On the other hand he showed no great enthusiasm for the mere money scramble that has taken its place. If he is the man who resoundingly snubbed Lord Chesterfield, he is also the man who wrote to Boswell, 'I have the old feudal notions'.

But this is to get ahead of our story. At the moment we have young Sam Johnson riding eagerly with his back to Lichfield and his face towards Oxford – an Oxford unimaginably more beautiful and peaceful than she will ever be again. And on either hand of him, as he rides, even his short sight can take in the incomparably beautiful countryside, glowing with autumn. The hedge and field system, which transformed the English landscape, is just coming in; visually, the best period of English life is approaching its apogee.

Yes, perhaps that is what we should notice first, we twentieth-century people, if we could take our deafened ears and ugliness-affronted eyes back to the England of Johnson. It was a place in which ugliness was very rare; indeed, with the important exception of the ugliness that disease and disfigurement produce in human beings and animals, ugliness was unknown. This alone would make our England and Johnson's into two wholly different places. To us any object, from a city to a teaspoon, that is anything but hideous is immediately recognized as something special, probably the work of some world-famous artist. In his day there was probably no such thing as an ugly house, table, stool or chair in the whole kingdom. The reasons for this could only be adequately outlined in another book as long as this one, but obviously the main reason is known to all of us. It is that industrialism, by moving people away from the natural rhythms of hand and eye, and also from the materials which occur naturally in their region and to which they are attuned by habit and tradition, cannot help fostering ugliness at the same time as it fosters cheapness and convenience.

It was a beautiful England, then, through which Sam and Michael rode that autumn. To the eye, and to the ear. To the nose, it would compare more evenly with the England we have now. Obviously the air was much cleaner; still, in place of the stink of petrol and industrial smoke to which we are accustomed from birth, there would be the much more frequent smell of drains. The eighteenth century had not yet begun to tackle this important problem; the disposal of 'muck' was the responsibility of the individual citizen, and was surrounded by a thicket of complicated regulations as dense as that faced by the motorist in our time. Rules and penalties proliferated like weeds in a nightmare. It was practically impossible to get through one's lifetime without breaking some of them and indeed Michael had not done so. He is on record at least once as being 'fined 2d for a muck-heap in Bakers Lane'. It is interesting to recall that Shakespeare's father was fined in much the same way. Such details point up the similarity in social *milieu* that link Shakespeare and Johnson.

Clean water was the great shortage in Johnson's England as clean air is the great shortage in ours. In other respects the two societies can be placed quite closely side by side. In the eighteenth century there was a great deal of drunkenness, violence and whoring – almost as much as there is today – and because of the lack of an adequate police system these things were more openly in evidence; one was far more likely, for instance, to see a fight in the street. Again like us, they had rough spots in their society which all decent people wanted to see smoothed out but which somehow went on existing: the horrible treatment of lunatics resulted from the undeveloped state of that department of medicine; the equally gruesome treatment of debtors reflected the ethos of a commercial society during its frontier period. If trade was to be the foundation of the nation's greatness, then people who offended against trade must be destroyed; if they got into debt they were confined in a fever-ridden gaol until the debt was paid off, which was usually never, since the imprisoned debtor had no means of working. Forgers and coiners were, of course, simply executed out of hand.

So on could we go, contrasting and comparing, trying to decide which of the two Englands would be preferable to live in, safe in the knowledge that the issue can never be decided. To me personally, to think of the quality of life in the eighteenth century is inevitably, sooner or later, to think of Josiah Wedgwood's leg. Wedgwood, another Midlander who was to trade and commerce in many ways what Johnson was to literature, was troubled in his younger days by some kind of circulatory complaint in one leg. If he happened to knock it against anything, it swelled up and put him in bed for a few days; and, since he was constantly making journeys up and down England in the course of building up his business, he found the waste of time irritating and had the leg amputated.

Most of us, I fancy, would accept the fate of being a mediocrity in business rather than consent to have a leg amputated without anaesthetic. Wedgwood's decision symbolizes many features of eighteenth-century England – the toughness, the realism, the determination to be up and doing, whatever the price that had to be paid. In a thinly populated country such giant individualities stand out clearly. Wedgwood knew that if he did not succeed in the pottery industry, he could not simply subside into comfortable obscurity as the tenth vice-president in some large faceless corporation, with his name on the door and a carpet on the floor. He had to get out there and do what it was in him to do, or he would be nothing. In such a spirit, also, did Samuel Johnson live his life: that life which now, as the crisp leaves fell from the trees in the college gardens, entered a new dimension.

CHAPTER 3

'Ah, Sir, I was Mad and Violent'

The day on which a young man enters college is traditionally said to be that on which death seems furthest away: a statement which has never entirely convinced me, since I remember brooding intensely on death and mutability on the day I entered college, sitting in my room in terrifying solitude between arriving in the early afternoon and going in to dinner in the evening. What is undeniably true is that it is the day on which childhood, that incredibly long-drawn-out process, is finally over. As Sam Johnson rode towards Oxford his childhood came to an end; even though one of its chief irritants, his father, was by his side and going in the same direction.

His childhood had not, clearly, been a happy one. Sam had been bored by his mother's pious platitudes, furious at his ageing father's wish to show him off, probably jealous of his younger brother, and resentful of the harshness of his schoolmaster. He had dreaded the future because it had appeared to him as a life made up, like his father's, of chaffering and tying up parcels; but he had found nothing in the present, except the few delightful months at Pedmore and the golden evenings with Walmesley, that tempted him to linger. He felt, or wished to feel, deep affection for his mother, but his attitude towards her was at least partly condescending and even contemptuous. 'Poor people's children, dear lady,' he said years afterwards to his friend Hester Thrale, 'never respect them; I did not respect my own mother, though I loved her.'

With all this he gave no sign of wanting to replace the family system, or the school system, or the ordinary framework of middle-class life with anything different. Because his own early life in a family circle had been unhappy, he did not suggest that people should not have families or that children should be given numbers and brought up in State *crèches*. The fact that his parents were incompatible did not prevent him from marrying in his turn. Even the fact that he had been unjustly beaten at school did not lead him to maintain that schoolboys should not be beaten. And here, already, we see a pattern that was to persist. Johnson, as an individual, was highly independent and unbiddable. He did not fit smoothly into any system. Intellectually, on the other hand, he approved of systems. Free of any starry-eyed notion of the natural goodness of man, he insisted on the need to keep up the outward forms and conventions that act as some check on man's natural lawlessness. And he knew all about man's natural lawlessness because he felt its power in his own anarchic impulses.

In this we see something of Johnson's generous self-forgetfulness, his power to reach intellectual conclusions on impersonal grounds. Most people are entirely lacking in this quality. The average 'intellectual', especially, is the reverse of intellectual in his handling of theoretical questions. His deductive chain starts from self and ends at self. Because he has been ill at ease within the family, he wants to abolish the family. Because the power structure of his society does not automatically waft him to a position of unrestricted authority, he wants to abolish the power structure. The unspoken premise at the back of all his reasoning is that the world to be striven for is a world in which *he* will get what he wants.

Johnson's premise, on the contrary, is that the world must arrange itself in a way that suits the majority of its inhabitants and gives them a chance to live decent, peaceable and useful lives; and that he, and people like him, will then take their chance of happiness within that order. We see the difference if we compare Johnson's social attitudes with those of, say, Bertrand Russell.

At Oxford the pattern of Johnson's responses was to be demonstrated anew. In theory, Johnson liked Oxford. He approved of the idea of a great university, dating from the Middle Ages, renewing itself century after century, slowly evolving new forms and precedents, avoiding radical change. He liked the essentially democratic atmosphere of an association of men devoted to learning. (It approximated to his great and lifelong ideal: a closeknit society of free and equal men.) He enjoyed competition, and the atmosphere of any university is competitive. He even approved of the political and ecclesiastical tinge of Oxford thought; for Oxford, always ready to back a loser, was predominantly Tory, and the Master of his own college won his youthful allegiance as 'a fine Jacobite fellow'.

In theory, as usual, he saw the good points of the system. In practice, as usual, he showed little enough inclination to fit in smoothly with it. In the abstract, Oxford had no more loyal son than Samuel Johnson. In the concrete, he must have been as difficult a student as the university, in all her seven hundred years, has had to assimilate and absorb.

The Oxford experience began in a way that was trying enough, already, for Sam's limited patience. His father was at the old game of showing off his paces. Sam had been assigned to one of the Pembroke dons, William Jorden, for tuition. Michael, understandably but fussily, contrived to be introduced to Jorden on that first evening, and the three of them had a conversation in which Johnson *père* lost no opportunity of rubbing it into Jorden that he was tutor to a genius. Sam, also understandably, was largely silent, and the evening might have been a dreadful frost had not his interest in ideas got the better of his sullen embarrassment. The conversation happened to take a turn that interested him, and he struck in with an apt illustration drawn from, of all writers, Macrobius. An early fifth-century Roman grammarian and writer of miscellaneous observations on literature, history and mythology, Macrobius hardly came within the intellectual range of the ordinary undergraduate. But then Samuel Johnson had a special fondness for those gossipy, rambling, voluminous authors who meander through a rich field of knowledge and offer out-of-the-way information. He said in later life that Burton's *Anatomy of Melancholy*, a work of just this kind, was the only book that ever got him out of bed two hours earlier than he wanted to rise. Be that as it may, Jorden can hardly have failed to note that the strange-looking freshman was literate enough.

Jorden, like the widow Oliver, deserves a nod of recognition. He had to take a lot of back answers from Sam Johnson, and it is to his credit that he kept his temper and refrained from harsh disciplinary action which would have driven the youth still deeper into revolt. Their earliest brush came during Johnson's first week at college. Every morning the undergraduates were supposed to attend a session of formal instruction, conducted by Jorden, in the college Hall. Johnson showed up on the first morning, then stayed away the next four. What happened next is the subject of one of the most famous passages of Boswell's *Life*:

> 'On the sixth, Mr Jorden asked me why I had not attended. I answered, I had been sliding in Christ Church meadow. And this I said with as much nonchalance as I am now talking to you. I had no notion that I was wrong or irreverent to my tutor.' Boswell: 'That, Sir, was great fortitude of mind.' Johnson: 'No, Sir; stark insensibility.'

Jorden had his own way of dealing with stark insensibility on the part of his students. That same day he sent for Johnson to come to his rooms. Sam obeyed with – as he told Thomas Warton years afterwards – 'a beating heart'. But Jorden received him amiably; he had sent for him to drink a glass of wine, and to say that he was *not* angry at Sam's missing his lecture. Sam breathed again. 'Some more of the boys were then sent for, and we spent a very pleasant afternoon.' The story is valuable as showing that the Oxford method of pulling the rug out from under a revolting student has remained exactly the same through the centuries.

Good tutor that he was, Jorden saw that the way to help Johnson was to put him on his mettle. But how? In the ordinary way of routine tasks and assignments, it was very difficult to get him to take trouble. When they were all required to produce a set of Latin verses on the subject of November the Fifth, with its historical and political associations, Johnson was sunk in one of his fits of indolence and produced nothing. As a token gesture he dashed off a short set of verses called *Somnium*, describing in conventional enough terms a visitation from the Muse as he slept. Jorden knew that he was capable of something unusual and suggested that he might put into Latin Pope's *Messiah*, a celebrated poem by the most famous living poet. Johnson did the job so brilliantly that Pope himself, putting the two versions side by side, is said to have remarked that posterity would find it hard to say which was the original and which the translation. And Boswell tells us that this performance 'ever after kept him high in the estimation of his College, and, indeed, of all the University'. In the Oxford of 1728 it was already clear that one of the best of the new literary talents was Johnson of Pembroke.

In these early days, before the shoe of poverty began to pinch, we can imagine Johnson's life as happy enough. He was finding his place in a world that seemed his to conquer, confronting new challenges and acquitting himself to applause. Even the detail about 'sliding' (i.e. on the ice) on Christ Church meadow is a cheerful one, suggesting an ability to find companionship and simple-minded fun in the intervals of his sterner pursuits. (Incidentally, though early November very rarely sees ice in England, it is attested that the early winter of 1728 saw a cold snap, with travel made difficult by 'snow, frost and ice'.) And, although he was largely surrounded by men from much wealthier families, there was nothing in Johnson's position to make him feel subservient. The world of the Oxford undergraduate, like the world he would meet outside the college walls, was indeed frankly built on social and pecuniary distinctions. As today, there were scholars whose expenses were wholly or partly met by the college, and commoners who paid their own way; but in those days there were also gentlemen-commoners, who paid double fees and shared the 'commons' of the dons at High Table; and there were two ranks below that of scholar: battelers, who paid lower fees and did their own chores, and servitors, who, like many students in modern American universities, earned themselves an education by waiting at table and doing odd jobs. Johnson was a commoner. Evidently no one foresaw that he would have to count farthings at any time during his residence. Moreover, those who have examined the buttery books at Pembroke College, which show the charges for food and drink consumed above the bare minimum of the menu served in Hall, report that Johnson's charges were neither above nor below what might be expected in a commoner.

Johnson disapproved, in later life and doubtless at this time also, of the system which segregated into classes those who were gathered together for the common pursuit of knowledge. It was his considered opinion that the scholar's gown 'levels all distinctions of rank'. But he was honest enough not to make too much of his objection to this shortcoming. After all, the humblest servitor received the same education as the lordliest gentleman-commoner. Eighteenth-century Oxford servitors included many men who rose to high distinction: Dr Potter, Archbishop of Canterbury, for instance, or two men who became heads of houses in Oxford itself, Lancaster of Queen's and Royce of Oriel.

Socially, Johnson as a middling commoner must have felt quite secure; intellectually he was already marked out as a shining light. In these early days at least, his competitiveness, his exaggerated air of independence were not the result of any feeling that he was poorer than other people. They stemmed from the old causes: from the desire to overcome the handicap of his ugly appearance, to gain respect, to be secure against ridicule, to prove that he could win by the power of his mind the same prizes that others won by their charm or good looks or money.

His antinomian behaviour became a fixed pattern. Jorden, despite his adroit handling of Johnson in their first collision, had to endure further rudeness.

Johnson continued to cut his lectures; college discipline prescribed a small fine for non-attendance, and on one occasion when Johnson had to pay this fine he is reported to have told Jorden, 'Sir, you have sconced me twopence for non-attendance at a lecture not worth a penny.' Jorden's reply is not on record. In any case, he was soon to leave Pembroke College to take up a benefice in Johnson's native county of Staffordshire. His place as Johnson's tutor was taken by Adams, a young don who later became Master and was one of the firm friends of Johnson's maturity. Adams had the impression of Johnson as a merry fellow and a general favourite, but this seems to have been superficial. When Boswell reported to Johnson that this was how Adams remembered him, Johnson gravely dissented. 'Ah, Sir, I was mad and violent. It was bitterness which they mistook for frolic. I was miserably poor, and I thought to fight my way by my literature and my wit; so I disregarded all power and all authority.'

It was clear that when Johnson remembered himself as 'miserably poor' he was recalling chiefly the later months of his stay in Oxford. By the time consciousness of poverty came to reinforce his ingrained stubbornness and contentiousness, the mixture would be an explosive one indeed. But during the first six of his thirteen months, it was pure love of a contest, in which he might show his strength among his peers, that drove the big undergraduate with the wild eyes to spend so many hours lounging in the college gateway with a circle of idle friends, exchanging witticisms in the time-honoured fashion that never changes.

He could be rude and aggressive; the slightest touch of authority made him bristle; but for all that he loved the life of learning, and found the university a congenial place. Without seeming to study, and doubtless alternating, as usual, between the utmost intensity of concentration and the utmost slackness of non-concentration, he read a good deal: mainly Greek, on which he tightened his grip during these months, but also ethics and theology. Whatever his problems, Johnson never had to endure the agonising doubt and indecision that some young men go through while they try to decide what they really want to do and what part in life they are really fitted to play. Johnson wanted to be a man of learning and a writer. Once, when he was sitting in his room, the Master, Dr Panting, overheard him talking to himself. 'Well, I have a mind to see how they go on in other places of learning. I'll go and see the universities abroad. I'll go to France and Italy. I'll go to Padua. And I'll mind my business: for an Athenian blockhead is the worst of all blockheads.'

The fragment so happily preserved by Panting is interestingly characteristic. Two central Johnsonian positions are there. One is the internationalism. The Victorian caricature of Johnson as a kind of John Bull, and a London John Bull at that, ignores the essentially European nature of his sensibility and his excellent linguistic attainments. The boy who preferred Petrarch to apples had grown into the student who wanted to 'see the universities abroad'. Johnson already felt himself part of the great European system of literature and thought. The other remark is no less characteristic. An 'Athenian blockhead', one who has been liberally educated, is particularly offensive: crassness and impercipience are always more noticeable when they are accompanied by a lumber of scholarly knowledge. Cornelius Ford and Gilbert Walmesley, men who knew life as well as books and looked at both with the same eyes, remained his standard of what an 'Athenian' should be.

Johnson's irregular, stop-and-start manner of acquiring information has sometimes been attributed to his Bohemian way of life during the early hand-to-mouth years in London. But it is quite evident that it had started much earlier, and was already in evidence during his time at Oxford. Here, if anywhere, he had time to study methodically. And, with one part of his mind, he longed to do so. He drew up vast schemes of reading, and even made elaborate calculations of how much could be got through in a week, a month, or a year, allowing so much time for so many lines, trying to put it all on a time-and-motion basis. 'Thus,' says Boswell, 'I find in his handwriting the number of lines in each of two of Euripides's Tragedies, of the *Georgics* of Virgil, of the first six books of the *Aeneid*, of Horace's *Art of Poetry*, of three of the books of Ovid's *Metamorphoses*, of some parts of Theocritus, and of the tenth Satire of Juvenal,' with calculations of reading time. Those calculations became a familiar mental habit of Johnson's. He resorted to juggling with figures when he felt the grip of his mind slackening, and inertia or melancholy coming over him. It is easy to picture him, sitting alone in his room on the second floor of the gateway tower with his books piled on the table in front of him, knowing that he ought to get on with his reading, that this was a golden opportunity to acquire the knowledge that would make him a famous scholar, and, simply not able to rise to the necessary level of concentration, covering sheets of paper with calculations of the reading he was 'going to' get through.

Clearly, he was not an easy student to deal with. That his brilliance was recognized, that his rebelliousness in small matters did not obscure the fact that he was the right man in the right place, is something to the credit of the Oxford of that time. Eighteenth-century Oxford has, of course, a bad name. Certainly by comparison with the purposeful new university that emerged from the wave of Victorian reforms, it seems lethargic. Not much attempt was made to teach inspiringly, and still less to examine rigorously. There were, as ever, extenuating circumstances. The financial rewards of university teaching were much less than they are now. The dons were required to be celibate and in holy orders, which naturally meant that most college fellowships were held by young, or not-so-young, men who were waiting for the chance of a living. Since the colleges, then as now, disposed of a large number of benefices, Buggins's turn usually came along sooner or later. But a rich undergraduate, whose father lorded over half a dozen villages or had important political influence, could make the career of his tutor much more quickly if they happened to become friends. The temptation to spend one's time in drinking and social climbing must have been just as great as the temptation for present-day dons to spend their time running up to London to appear on television or acting as consultants to industry. I am aware of no convincing reason why twentieth-century Oxford should feel moral or intellectual superiority over eighteenth-century Oxford, though there is admittedly a difference in efficiency.

There are several famous denunciations of eighteenth-century Oxford by men who studied there. Of these the most celebrated is Gibbon's. Twenty-eight years Johnson's junior, Gibbon came up to Magdalen in 1752. To him it was a sad and shabby place. Intellectual stimulus there was none, and as for the personal character of the dons his famous phrases still blister. 'From the toil of reading, or thinking, or writing, they had absolved their conscience.' 'Their dull and deep potations excused the brisk intemperance of youth.'

Certainly the contrasting temperaments of these two great men come out in their respective attitudes to their university. Perhaps we might even call them the Whig and Tory temperaments. Gibbon, smooth and courtly, coming to Oxford from a background of leisure and spaciousness, despised what it had to offer, and in later life delivered himself of that scathing attack. Johnson, coming from a much more constricted *milieu*, aware already that opportunities for learning and original thought were painfully limited in the world, was prickly in his actual relationships at Oxford, yet loved the place, and testified to his love for the rest of his long life. Whenever the subject of universities in general, and Oxford in particular, came up, Johnson had something positive and encouraging to say about them. To Boswell in 1768 he praised Oxford for its 'progressive emulation':

> The students are anxious to appear well to their tutors; the tutors are anxious to have their students appear well in the university; and there are excellent rules of discipline in every college. That the rules are sometimes ill observed may be true; but is nothing against the system.

And about his own college he was openly sentimental. Several Pembroke men became recognized poets, though apart from Johnson's there is only one name, Shenstone's, that has survived; but this was enough to cause Johnson to remark, 'with a smile of sportive triumph', that the place was 'a nest of singing birds'. In 1782 the poet Hannah More happened to be in Oxford at the same time as Johnson, and remarked on the joy and pride that he took in showing her every part of Pembroke. 'After dinner Johnson begged to conduct me to see the College, he would let no one show it me but himself – "This was my room, this Shenstone's." ' Not so, we may be sure, did Gibbon show his friends round Magdalen.

Part of the explanation, certainly, lies in the different circumstances of the two men. But there is an emotional difference also. Gibbon, as a great historian, can hardly be said to have been indifferent to the past. But his was an intellectual passion:

> I insensibly plunged into the ocean of the Augustan history; and in the descending series I investigated, with my pen almost always in my hand, the original records, both Greek and Latin, from Dion Cassius to Ammianus Marcellinus, from the reign of Trajan to the last age of the Western Cæsars.

Johnson had no appetite for historical information as such. His attitude was emotional and æsthetic; in a word, poetic. The towers and spires of Oxford meant to him what the red sandstone of Lichfield had meant, only more so. That cluster of mediaeval and renaissance buildings, those streets where Duns Scotus and Erasmus and Friar Bacon and Davenant had walked, gave him so much that could never be taken away by a mediocre tutor or an irritating college regulation. To such a mind, especially in ardent youth, merely to be admitted to share the life of the university is to take part in an apostolic succession that goes on from generation to generation, in which the lustre of those names that have become famous shines over the dark yet living mass of all those who, without leaving any memory behind them, have thought and disputed and wrestled with problems in this square mile. As Johnson put it years later in strong, emphatic verse:

> When first the college rolls receive his name,
> The young enthusiast quits his ease for fame;
> Through all his veins the fever of renown
> Burns from the strong contagion of the gown;
> O'er Bodley's dome his future labours spread,
> And Bacon's mansion trembles o'er his head.

The great mediaeval scientific thinker Friar Bacon had his study in the gatehouse of Grandpont, now Folly Bridge, and the tradition was that the building would collapse when a man greater than Friar Bacon should pass under its shadow. This is why, in Johnson's poem (*The Vanity of Human Wishes*), the 'young enthusiast' feels it trembling over his head. Traditions and legends of this kind took a strong hold on Johnson's mind; the more rationalistic Gibbon would see them as, at best, interesting superstitions.

The pattern of Johnson's inner life, at any period of his existence, was complex enough, and the Oxford pattern is no exception. He loved the university, but irritably shrugged off the claims of authority; he wanted Jorden's approbation, but was unable to pay him the customary deference. As always, he eagerly drew in the breath of competition. Only one of his fellow undergraduates at Pembroke, Jack Meeke, approached him in brilliance as a scholar; and Johnson recalled years later that, at their classical lectures in the Hall, he sat as far as possible away from Meeke, so as not to hear him construe.

The detail is interesting because it reminds us that an eighteenth-century don was rather like a Victorian schoolmaster, who sat the boys down in rows and then, picking out this or that one, 'put him up to construe'. The modern tutorial system was just struggling into existence, but there seems to have been very little in the way of intercollegiate, university-wide teaching. Dons with the rank of professor were supposed to give lectures, but most of them contrived to be permanently on the point of doing so. Once he had entered a college an undergraduate received his instruction more or less tightly within its walls.

This fact underlies a characteristic small incident in Johnson's life. In March 1729 he was joined at Oxford by his old schoolfriend John Taylor. The reunion was a happy one. But, though he found comfort in Taylor's company and would obviously have liked to have him close by, Johnson vetoed Taylor's suggestion that he should enrol at Pembroke. The intellectual standard was not high enough; Taylor would do better at Christ Church, where there was a tutor named Bateman whose reputation stood high. So, at the last minute, Taylor went across the street to Christ Church. (The story suggests, among other things, that admission procedures were much more relaxed then than now.) Johnson had made a sacrifice, but he gained a little compensating benefit by going over every day to get Bateman's ideas while they were still fresh in Taylor's memory. That memory was rather sluggish, and what Johnson received must often have been sadly blurred. But he valued the companionship with someone whose roots were the same as his own. The challenging and stimulating Oxford environment laid him open to fits of homesickness and nostalgia for the protected atmosphere of childhood. Once, as he was turning the key of his rooms at Pembroke, he heard his mother say 'Sam'. Her voice fell on his ears with such distinctness that he remembered it ever afterwards and accepted the incident as – almost – evidence of extrasensory perception. Clearly, it was a momentary hallucination produced by the force of his longing for home and security.

In the ordinary way that longing would have diminished as he grew more accustomed to his surroundings and overcame his difficulties. As things stood, however, the difficulties increased. Corbet, his putative benefactor, seems never to have carried out any part of his undertaking. From October 1728 the battels and other charges listed against his name in the college books become irregular, and within three months they have ceased altogether. Obviously he either never saw Johnson at Oxford or, at most, barely overlapped with him before leaving for good. By the summer of 1729 Johnson's money had begun to run out. He did not return to Lichfield during the vacation, perhaps because it was cheaper to stay where he was; but when term started again in October it was evident that, unless a miracle occurred, he could not stay the course. No miracle occurred. Johnson's clothes became ragged. His toes poked through his shoes. A kindly fellow student placed a new pair of shoes by his door: Johnson threw them away angrily. His visits to Taylor ceased, for the well-to-do Christ Church men were beginning to notice his shabby appearance. Taylor, loyally, came to him instead, and continued his halting report of what Bateman had said on the classics, mathematics, ethics. Often he got it wrong. Once, unable to recall the solution Bateman had shown them to a problem in algebra, he went back to ask him to repeat it; Bateman kindly went over it again; Taylor hurried back to the waiting Johnson, but forgot the answer a second time as he crossed the street.

For Johnson life was proving difficult and discouraging. He had need to gather his strength about him. He began to think, and to feel, more deeply than he had done in boyhood. By the time he was twenty, two factors had entered his life that were never to leave it. One was his dreadful, disabling melancholic depression. The other was his vivid imaginative apprehension of Christianity.

Sarah Johnson, as we saw, had early instructed her son about Heaven and Hell. But we have his own word for it that, at about the age of nine, this religious teaching began to fade from his mind. The church he usually attended was undergoing some repairs, and the seating was inadequate; Sam was sent off to find a pew in any other church that took his fancy, but he was self-conscious about his short sight and disliked blundering into a church where he was not known and could not easily find his way. So he took to going into the fields and staying there till service time was over. As his adolescence went on he slipped still further from the teaching of his childhood: a sceptical, flippant tone crept into his talk. He was on the way to becoming a typical eighteenth-century rationalist. Then, at Oxford, a powerful lever was applied to his mind, forcing it on to different lines. He happened one day to take up William Law's famous book *A Serious Call to a Devout and Holy Life*: 'expecting', as he told Boswell, 'to find it a dull book (as such books generally are), and perhaps to laugh at it'. But Law's book proved impossible for Johnson to be flippant about. It has a bedrock seriousness, something Johnson always appreciated. Johnson later called it 'the finest piece of hortatory theology in any language', a judge-ment very much in line with his distrust of the purely speculative and preference for the concrete and practical. Law's concern is with the spiritual life of the individual. He writes an excellent prose, and he makes use of a technique resembling that of the eighteenth-century periodical essay: to embody and dramatize his thoughts, he invents characters who illustrate the various points of view, so that the book abounds in deft satirical portraits of worldly characters who are neglecting their own spiritual interests. There is also, on the positive side, a full-length portrait of a woman ('Miranda') who has found her peace in full acceptance and worship of Christ. That Johnson admired the book so much was doubtless because its method was entirely congenial to him, and indeed its influence can be seen in his own later work as a moral essayist.

Whether, on the other hand, it was a piece of good or ill fortune for Johnson that he became such a convinced Christian, is quite simply one of those un-answerable questions. We can no more imagine him without his religious faith than we can imagine him without his psychological burdens, his tragic fears and torments. To name the two factors together is to risk giving the impression that they are aspects of the same thing.

On due reflection, it is a risk I am content to take. Christianity, even more than most religions, is highly marriageable to the pre-existing character of the convert. When a man embraces Christianity, the pattern of his nature is not changed; it is merely ingrained more deeply and in stronger colours. When men of such different temperaments as, say, G. K. Chesterton and Graham Greene accept the Roman Catholic version of Christianity, it can hardly be said that their faith brings them together; it seems, if anything, to accentuate their temperamental differences. In Johnson's case, once he had made up his mind, at nineteen or twenty, that Christianity was true, the warring elements in his own mind proceeded at once to their action stations. Christianity provided fuel both for the constructive and the destructive forces in him. On the constructive side, it directed and energized his innate benevolence and generosity. The sheer number of people whom Johnson helped is astonishing, only less so than the unbelievable amount of trouble he would take on their behalf. His capacity for sympathy, provided the sufferer was really distressed and not acting a pantomime, was endless. Destructively, his Christianity helped to bring out, and to make more vehement, his tendency to irrational guilt and self-accusation. The child of ageing parents, constantly brought out to show his paces, he had lived out his infancy with a never-ending sense of being on trial. He had a deep need to give and receive love, but neither of his parents had any means of expressing affection; his mother's way of showing her love for him was to nag him as she nagged his father, and this had bred in him a sense of inadequacy, of a continual failure to come up to the required standard, so that with one deeply embedded part of his mind he felt that his existence was one long betrayal.

Given this pattern, it is understandable that the features of Christianity on which Johnson's mind laid its strongest hold were the minatory. He saw God not as a loving father but as a judge, who had the absolute right to consign him to an eternity of torment. Furthermore, being a Protestant, he had no prescribed set of rules for getting past this judge. Roman Catholicism provides the believer with a guaranteed rule of thumb for getting to Heaven. The Protestant has to plot his individual course. It was here that Johnson's sense of his own intellectual and spiritual power was a torture to him. For, if much had been given to him, correspondingly much would be asked. The parable of the steward who let his talent lie unused in a napkin was terrible to him. A standard of behaviour, of piety, of devotion, that would get most people clear of the gates of Hell might not be enough for Samuel Johnson. In childhood, he went to his mother for love and acceptance, and was met, all too often, with anxious reproaches; and by the time he came to accept God as his super-parent the pattern was fixed.

Small wonder that, during the last months of 1729, Johnson's energies failed and his spirits plummeted. That horrible depressive paralysis of the will, during which he could stare at the clock face without being able to tell the time, came over him again, reinforced now by anxiety and distress. If this seems a highly coloured description, it is no more highly coloured than Boswell's, referring to the same period:

> He felt himself overwhelmed with an horrible hypochondria, with perpetual irritation, fretfulness, and impatience; and with a dejection, gloom, and despair, which made existence misery.

Boswell goes further. He states positively that this condition was permanent and incurable:

> From this dismal malady he never afterwards was perfectly relieved; and all his labour, and all his enjoyments, were but temporary interruptions of its baleful influence.

Pinned down under an intolerable weight of depression, faced with insoluble problems, Johnson could think of only one step to take: to go home to Lichfield. There, he might possibly rake together some money; if he did not, there could be no thought of returning to Oxford, for he was already a full quarter behind with his fees. Term was over; he could go home without losing face; perhaps the calamity might still be avoided. He asked his friend Taylor to take care of his books while he was away. Then he closed the door of the room in the tower and went downstairs. It was to be a quarter of a century before he went up those stairs again.

Taylor rode with him as far as Banbury; the rest of the melancholy journey he took alone. Back home he found nothing to raise his spirits. Michael's business was still going down. Various biographers, beginning with Sir John Hawkins, have suggested that he was actually bankrupt, but this is not the case; he left property to his family when he died, which a bankrupt would not have been able to do. But that he was certainly going downhill is attested by the fact that two years later, in 1731, he received a grant from a Lichfield charity, the Conduit Lands Trust, and was described in its records as 'a decayed trades-man'.

Decayed Michael certainly was. Our last glimpse of him is a comic-pathetic one. The parchment business, that valiant effort at diversification, finally reached the low point at which it not only did not pay, but did not even bring in enough money to pay for its own upkeep, and the factory beside Stowe Pool became a semi-ruined building; the back wall fell down, leaving the structure open to the weather and to any tramp who wanted somewhere to sleep. In spite of this, as his son later told Mrs Thrale, Michael scrupulously locked the front door of the building whenever he came away. There is a touch of Laurel and Hardy in such solemn foolishness, but it is also a matter for tears. This is the kind of obsession that develops in us when we can take no more punishment from life.

In that black winter Sam Johnson sank under a tidal wave of depression and frustration. He made no move to bring home his books from Oxford, which would have been the last burning of boats in that direction; on the other hand, neither he nor anyone else could seriously imagine that he would ever go back. Where did his future lie? In the bookshop? But if it was failing already how would moody Sam and noisy Nathaniel be able to save it? Where then? In an independent career as scholar and man of letters? That meant working for the booksellers, and he had neither the energy nor the opportunity to go and scout for contacts among their suspicious fraternity. Schoolteaching? At semi-starvation level, possibly; no headmastership was possible without a degree, but perhaps some local school might be glad enough to employ an Oxford man – even one of only thirteen months' standing – as an assistant master or, as the barely veiled contempt of the age called it, an 'usher'.

An usher, then, Sam would be. But still many months went by before he could whip up the energy to go and look for a job. During 1730 he seems to have done little but hang about the neighbourhood, doing as little as possible in the shop, welcoming any opportunity to be taken out of himself by good company and good talk. Walmesley, once again, was a blessed source of comfort and inspiration. Sam was often round at the Palace. There he met a new luminary: Cornet Henry Hervey, whose regiment was just then quartered at

Lichfield. The fourth son of the Earl of Bristol, Hervey had charmed, drunk, gambled and seduced his way through twenty-nine glorious years. Like Sam, though for very different reasons, he was an Oxford dropout – from that same Christ Church whose lordly gates Sam's ragged kit had finally made it impossible for him to enter. He was married, recently, to an heiress of the Aston family, a relative of Molly Aston who would one day claim Sam's heart. And he was polite, affable, lettered – in the manner of his day and his class – up to a point. He wrote graceful verses, wore his clothes well, talked well and doubtless even knew when to listen. The part he played in Sam Johnson's life is easy to imagine. He was one of those graceful and charming people we sometimes meet at periods when we are very unhappy, and who have a strange mixed effect: partly, they make us feel more embedded than ever in our misery and inadequacy, since we can never float above it all as they seem to do; partly, they lift us up by taking kindly notice of us (if such people can find us worth talking to, all cannot be lost). Commonly we react to their casual kindness with what seems to others an excessive gratitude. So it was with Sam Johnson. When Harry Hervey's name came up, he was quick with his emphatic tribute. 'Hervey was a very vicious man. But he was good to me. If you call a dog Hervey, I shall love him.'

Into such frail receptacles, at this time, did the warmth and affection of Johnson's nature pour itself. It was a thin, sour season. Every avenue seemed bricked up. At last in the summer of 1731 news came that Stourbridge Grammar School, that same one where Sam had received part of his education, was in want of an usher. The present holder of the job had fallen out with Wentworth, just as Sam had done some years previously. He was going; but this time Wentworth was also going. On those terms it seemed a job that might suit the unemployed, degree-less former pupil. Besides, the thought of Stourbridge was always associated with the thought of Parson Ford, and those delightful conversations about literature and life that could now be renewed. This was a pinpoint of light at the end of the tunnel. Plans could, after all, be made. Life could go on.

Then Fate, as so often at this period of Johnson's life, dealt from the bottom of the deck. On 22 August Parson Ford died suddenly at the Hummums, an hotel of dubious reputation in Covent Garden, London. At one stroke Stourbridge was robbed of half its attractiveness. With a saddened heart the young man set out, nevertheless, to put in for the job and win what local family support he could. To be an usher was nobody's ideal. But it was a living.

CHAPTER 4

From Wolstan to Werburgh

Stourbridge did not want him. Perhaps Wentworth, consulted for his opinion just before leaving, had put in a bad report. More probably it was the fatal lack of a degree that influenced the governors. Back to Lichfield Johnson trudged. Even to be an usher, a job so menial that those who had done it usually concealed the fact in later life, was apparently above his reach.

For the rest of the summer and autumn he gloomed at home. It was a house of anxiety, then of illness and death. Michael Johnson died, and was buried on 7 December. The shop was, for the time being, carried on ostensibly by Nathaniel. For Samuel the bad times went on and on. We have little or no concrete information about what he did with himself, but it is not hard to imagine his irritable gloom and dejection. In the winter of 1729, he had formed the habit of taking long, solitary walks, hoping that by putting his body into motion he might still the demons that haunted him. At the very least, he could crash into bed and sleep the sleep of exhaustion after a day on the long muddy roads.

As a matter of record many poets, artists, and 'intellectuals' generally have been compulsive walkers. Dickens trod the streets of London for hundreds of miles, generally late at night, trying to 'still his beating mind'. Wordsworth's feats of perambulation were clearly motivated as much by the wish to deaden his emotional malaise as to be among his beloved lakes and mountains. The young Johnson fits well into this pattern. From Lichfield to Birmingham, reckoning from city centre to city centre, is a matter of some sixteen miles. Johnson would often walk there and back in a day. Probably what he saw in Birmingham did not interest him; his motive was the mileage. Still, even his dulled glance would take in the fact that it was, at this time, a bustling, burgeoning, rising place. One William Hutton, author of an enthusiastic *History of Birmingham*, related in his memoirs the impression the town made on him, only a few years after Johnson first saw it. 'I had been among dreamers, but now I saw men awake. Their very step along the street showed alacrity. Every man seemed to know what he was about.' The big, awkward young man who occasionally appeared in its streets, on the contrary, had scarcely any idea what he was about. Shabbily dressed, and wearing his own stiff brown hair instead of a wig – a direct defiance of the prevailing custom – he must have attracted curious glances from those Birmingham citizens whose attention was not entirely engrossed by the task of earning the next guinea. Sometimes, before turning about and making for home, it is reasonable to suppose that Johnson dropped in on one or other of his Birmingham friends. There was his faithful old schoolfellow Edmund Hector, who was now practising as a surgeon; there was the mercer Harry Porter, with his wife Elizabeth and daughter Lucy; there was Mr Warren, who in eighteenth-century fashion combined bookselling with book-publishing. There was even a quasi-familial link. His godfather, Dr Swinfen, was now in practice in Birmingham, and his daughter Elizabeth had married there. Her husband was a Huguenot refugee, Monsieur Desmoulins, who was a teacher at the Free Grammar School. We know that Johnson called on Dr Swinfen at any rate, because he consulted him about a possible cure for his depressions. Unfortunately Swinfen forfeited Johnson's confidence by a piece of tactlessness; Johnson had written out, in Latin, a complete account of his symptoms, and Swinfen was so impressed by the professionalism of this self-diagnosis that he showed it round among his friends. Johnson, who considered his confidence betrayed, never went near him again. But his relations with Elizabeth Swinfen Desmoulins, and the other members of their set, were unchanged. These people formed the nucleus of a 'circle' for Johnson at Birmingham. But he was, in this bad year of 1731, too sunk in misery and frustration to make new friends or even to be much aware of anything that went on outside the depths of his own mind.

So matters stood for long, weary months. Then in the summer of 1732 the offer of a job came up: usher at the school in Market Bosworth, Leicestershire. On 16 July Johnson took himself thither – *ex pede*, as he noted in his diary, on foot.

He never took a more unlucky walk. The period at Market Bosworth was a hell of insult, drudgery and humiliation. The school was under the patronage of Sir Wolstan Dixie, the local squire, who lived close by in his large, handsome residence, Bosworth Hall. On paper, the job of usher was supposed to carry a salary of twenty pounds a year and a free house. When Johnson got there, he found that Dixie had forgotten about the house and arranged for him to board at Bosworth Hall, where he had to perform the loosely defined duties of domestic chaplain. If Johnson opened his mouth to protest, he closed it again. A man without a degree could not talk terms with any prospective employer.

Sir Wolstan Dixie is remembered only because of his brief contact with Johnson. Nevertheless, as a social type he is not without interest. He was the typical hard-drinking, hard-riding, red-necked country squire of the earlier eighteenth century, ruling the local roost as much by strength and aggressiveness as by social position. If a neighbour trespassed on his land, Dixie did not send for the constable; he took off his jacket and thrashed the man with his own big fists. One of these punch-ups makes the basis for the best-known anecdote about Dixie. When, as a matter of routine for a baronet, he was presented to King George II, the German-born monarch caught at the name 'Bosworth' and, eager to show that he was not totally ignorant of English history, remarked that he had heard of a great battle there. His Teutonic Majesty had in mind the events of 1485; but Dixie, his memory going back to one of his own fist fights, replied proudly, 'Yes, Sire, but I thrashed him.'

It seems incredible to us that such a tyrannosaurus should exercise power and patronage in an English Midland county rather than on some surf-beaten Atlantic island. The root of the explanation lies in the nature of eighteenth-century agriculture. The revolution in farming methods associated with the names of Jethro Tull and Viscount 'Turnip' Townshend did not accomplish its work overnight. It would in due course transform subsistence farming into farming for surpluses which made a profit. But in the earlier part of the century many country districts lived as they had always lived; the land provided for local needs, there was nothing left over to sell elsewhere and in consequence no incentive to look beyond one's own neighbourhood. As William Hutton wrote of the inhabitants of this same district of Market Bosworth: 'Surrounded with impassable roads, no intercourse with man to humanize the mind, no commerce to smooth their rugged natures, they continue the boors of nature.' That was in 1770. What the district was like forty years earlier we can only conjecture. If a squire like Dixie chose to treat his tenants in much the same way as a nineteenth-century Texas rancher treated his Mexican hands, there was the same lack of interference or supervision from outside.

Exactly how Dixie treated Johnson we do not know in detail. Boswell merely records that Johnson called it 'intolerable harshness'. He adds that Johnson never willingly looked back on this period of his life. In later years, when staying with John Taylor at Ashbourne, he tended in his walks to avoid that side of town on which lay the road to Market Bosworth; such was the 'horror' (Boswell's word again) with which the memory of the place inspired him. If one were writing an historical novel about Johnson instead of a biographical study, this would be a fine opportunity for some chiaroscuro. As things are, we must leave the episode behind the veil drawn by Johnson's own hand. Within a year he had made his escape. He wrote to Taylor, laconically: 'Mr Corbet has, I suppose, given you an account of my leaving Sir Wolstan Dixie. It was really *e carcere exire* [getting out of prison].'

The 'Corbet' mentioned there was, incidentally, the younger brother of that same Andrew Corbet who had been going to underwrite Johnson's Oxford career. John Corbet was sometimes in the district because Dixie's sister had married Andrew. Pleasant though the young man was as a companion, eagerly as Johnson sought him out as a civilized youth among all these boors, his presence must have brought back rueful memories of the unfulfilled Oxford life, of his books lying there under the care of John Taylor (who had by now gone down – what had happened to the books?), and of Andrew Corbet's thoughtless pseudo-generosity. Yet, characteristically, Johnson is not on record with one single bitter remark about Corbet and his defection. He made a point of never blaming others for his misfortunes – not even those who were at least partly responsible for them.

Checkmated again, back home in a worse state of mind than ever, Johnson was rescued by the kind offices of a friend. (No wonder he continued all his life to set such a high value on friendship.) Edmund Hector, hearing that Johnson was inactive and doubtless deducing his low state of mind, invited him to be his guest at Birmingham. Once again, as on the visit to Pedmore, Johnson set out with no definite ideas about the duration of his stay; once again it lengthened out into many months. Birmingham had more to offer than Lichfield; on the other hand, to go there was not a terrifying break with his lifelines as it would have been to go to London. Birmingham was a big town, wide open to a man of talent not only in trade but also, to some extent, in the liberal arts; yet it was an extension of his own neighbourhood, where he felt secure.

Edmund Hector boarded at the house of Mr Warren the bookseller, and it was there that Johnson joined him. Warren was an enterprising man, whom Boswell describes as 'the first established bookseller in Birmingham', and he soon realized that his roof was sheltering a man of letters, young but already accomplished. Warren ran a newspaper called *The Birmingham Journal*, and at his invitation Johnson wrote some of the essays on general subjects which, in accordance with the custom of the time, padded out the editorial section. At least, the tradition that he did so is reliable enough to be reported by the cautious Boswell, and has never been discredited, though it cannot be authoritatively confirmed because all copies save one of *The Birmingham Journal* have perished. But it has the ring of truth and, if so, it is a help in building up our picture of Johnson's days in Birmingham. His later reputation was to be raised first on the platform of the periodical essay, at which he was such a skilled hand and which attracted the attention of discerning readers. If Warren gave him his first chance to practise this art, the more credit to Warren.

After some six months as Hector's guest, Johnson moved out and took a room on his own, doubtless feeling that, since he could earn the occasional coin, it was unfair to freeload on Hector indefinitely. The two continued to see much of each other, though Johnson in his solitude became moody, indolent and somewhat difficult. A quarter of a century later, renewing his friendship with Hector by letter, he confessed, 'From that kind of melancholy indisposition which I had when we lived together at Birmingham, I have never been free, but have always had it operating against my health and my life with more or less violence.' The old melancholia, the loss of mental grip, the dejected *accidie*, were on him again, never wholly to cease. And now he felt more isolated than ever. He had done the sensible thing by going to a doctor with his troubles, and the doctor had betrayed him to the idle curiosity of bystanders. That was how Johnson interpreted the episode of Dr Swinfen and the Latin document, and he was surely justified. But the experience inhibited him from seeking help again. Living in a rented room in Birmingham, unwilling to go back to the decaying Lichfield shop, unemployable as a schoolmaster except by such bosthoons as Dixie, at the age of twenty-five he felt his life crumbling away.

Then Hector had a good idea. The talk at Warren's house had often turned on books, and Johnson had mentioned that during his days at Pembroke he had enjoyed reading a Portuguese travel book, Father Jerome Lobo's *Voyage to Abyssinia*. There was no English translation; Johnson knew it in a French version by Joachim Le Grand. Hector now reminded Johnson of this book. A somewhat shortened translation of Le Grand's version might make a saleable commodity for Warren. A travel book set in some exotic corner of the earth could always find readers, and besides there was a certain political mileage to be got out of the book's Portuguese origin. The Whigs had firmly sewn up an alliance with Portugal; Tories like Johnson were unenthusiastic about it; the worthy Jesuit missionary had some unpleasant facts to report about the behaviour of the Portuguese in their colonial territories. In so far as the book had any political tendency, it would be against the Whig establishment; which, from Johnson's point of view, would give it an extra spice.

The work was begun. Warren employed a printer named Osborn, and in short order Osborn began printing off the material supplied by Johnson. But the old influences were at work. After an initial flurry of activity, Johnson once more sank under indolence and frustration. While Osborn chafed, he sat staring at the wall. Fortunately, in this crisis, Hector showed the resourcefulness that made him a natural Birmingham citizen. He told Johnson that Osborn and his family were in want; that the unfortunate man could undertake no other work until he had finished the present assignment; that procrastination would plunge him into ruin and hunger. Johnson agreed that Osborn must be helped. Indifferent to his own fate, he could not resist the story of someone else's troubles. Even this, however, was not sufficient to get his pen into the inkwell. Again Hector had the answer. He sat beside Johnson's bed; Johnson, his vast body lying inert among the pillows, mustered the energy to hold the book up in front of him and translate extempore while Hector wrote. The story is wonderfully characteristic of both young men. Especially when we add to it the fact that Hector, after getting the original idea, had scoured Birmingham for a copy of Le Grand's translation, failed to find one, and ultimately borrowed the book from Pembroke College Library. (It gives us a small but heartening glimpse of the intellectual atmosphere in that much-maligned Oxford of the 1720s to know that Pembroke College Library contained a travel book, written in a foreign language and published only three or four years earlier.) Hector then made a fair copy of his scribbled-down version, to make Osborn's task easier, and rounded off the performance by reading the proofs. Not a bad record for a young surgeon with his practice to build up.

The *Voyage to Abyssinia* was published in 1735, with a title-page that claimed 'London' as the place of publication, though it originated from Birmingham; 'a device', says Boswell severely, 'too common with provincial publishers'. What it really points to is not so much dishonesty on Warren's part as the growing stranglehold of London on the rest of the country, fostered by better communications. Warren belonged to the same provincial culture as Michael Johnson; and, like him, fought a losing battle. He went bankrupt in 1743; as late as 1755, Johnson, in a letter to Edmund Hector, is still asking for 'news of poor Warren'. He felt a soft spot for the man. The five guineas Warren paid him for the Lobo translation was not very much – Boswell mentions the sum with disapprobation – but, considering that Johnson was unknown in the world of letters and that he did most of the work without getting off his back, it compares favourably with what a young literary journeyman can earn today, for a shilling in the 1730s bought what a pound buys now.

The translation of Lobo was never a matter of much pride to Johnson. He saw it for what it was – a dashed-off job. The preface, to be sure, contains a good ironic passage, three paragraphs long, which Boswell picked out for quotation and which has found a place in most subsequent selections from Johnson's work – the earliest passage to do so. Those paragraphs are good debunking stuff. The rest is routine. But it served its threefold purpose, which was to keep Johnson busy at a bad time, to earn an honest penny, and to oblige Warren. It also had the desirable side effect of bringing Johnson his first critical attention. The *Literary Magazine or Select British Library* devoted a long article of fifteen pages to an examination of the book, with copious quotations.

Early in 1734 Johnson wandered back to Lichfield. For the next year or two he was back and forth between the two places, unable to settle for long in either. His tension and misery continued. Clearly, they were not entirely due to objective causes. There was an element of disease. He knew the trouble that dogged him to be of pathological origin, and feared it all the more for that reason. If it was a disease, then his best-willed efforts might be insufficient to prevent its progressing until he finally went mad. Dr Swinfen, indeed, had given him a clear warning that this might come. On receiving that celebrated Latin auto-diagnosis which subsequently caused the trouble between them, Swinfen had written back, physician-like, in the third person: '. . . from the symptoms therein described, he could think nothing better of his disorder, than it had a tendency to insanity; and without great care might possibly terminate in the deprivation of his rational faculties'. But what kind of 'great care' is useful in such a case?

Now and throughout his life, Johnson fought his mental anguish with two chosen weapons: work, including activity of every kind, and sociability. These two do not, of course, go naturally together, in fact they cancel one another out; which helps to explain why in later life, after the award of his pension, Johnson did so little of the kind of work that meant shutting himself up in a room alone. At this early stage, however, a diet of unrestricted sociability would have meant starvation. Before leaving Market Bosworth, he had received his share of the money bequeathed by Michael Johnson; most of this, understandably, went to provide for Sarah, and the amount that reached Sam was nineteen pounds – enough for a frugal man to live on for about three months. If there was to be any more, it would not come until his mother's death; 'which', he piously wrote in his journal, 'I pray be late'. There was nothing for it but to work, at something, anything. He was still, in theory, looking round for a schoolmastering job. In the meantime, he decided on an appeal to the literary public by way of a familiar eighteenth-century method, that of publishing by subscription. The hopeful author collected the guineas of intending purchasers and, when enough had come in, the book was printed. Accordingly, Johnson began to whip up support, mainly in his own neighbourhood, for an edition of the poems of the Renaissance Latin writer Politian. He was always fond of neo-Latin poetry and presumably intended to aid Politian's fame as well as his own finances. Once again, as in the case of Lobo, he had no copy of his own and was obliged to borrow the one in Pembroke College Library. Since he had gone down owing a quarter's fees, he could hardly write and ask for the book, and this problem might have capsized the enterprise had it not come to Johnson's ears that a clergyman named Boyse, whose parish was in Smethwick near Birmingham, was an old Pembroke man and was on the point of going there for a visit. Johnson asked him to borrow the book, and in the surviving register of the library we read that it was duly taken out on 15 June, borrowed by the Rev. Mr Boyse 'for the use of Mr Johnson'. The librarian who oversaw the transaction was that same Jack Meeke whose proficiency at the daily 'classical lecture' had aroused Johnson's jealousy and caused him to sit on the other side of the hall.

So the works of Politian duly found their way to Lichfield. As so often happens with books that are borrowed by one person 'for the use of' another, it seemed to be nobody's job to return it. The volume was duly found among Johnson's books at his death, but its subsequent fate is unknown and Pembroke are still waiting for it to be returned.

After all this, Johnson's edition never got off the ground. Hopefully he issued proposals which announced that subscriptions would be received by 'the Editor' or by 'N. Johnson, bookseller, of Lichfield' – a concrete piece of evidence that Natty had taken charge of the shop. But not enough subscriptions rolled in, and the idea faded from sight.

It seemed that nothing was going to work. Whichever way Johnson looked, he saw only a solid log jam of difficulty and frustration. But now, suddenly, his life was once again pulled into a new shape. In September 1734 Harry Porter the mercer died. As we have already noted, Harry and his wife, Elizabeth, were members of Johnson's circle of acquaintances in Birmingham. Porter seems to have been a decent man, an industrious though not particularly successful merchant, coming from a solid middle-class background – his father had been a governor of King Edward's School, Birmingham – and doubtless a pleasant and welcoming host to the young prodigy from Lichfield. Exactly what Porter thought of Johnson we do not know. Mrs Porter's first reaction to him, however, is on record. After her first conversation with the strange, gaunt youth, she said to her daughter, Lucy, 'This is the most sensible man that I ever saw in my life.' The vivacious blond lady in her mid-forties, accustomed to the respectful attentions of men, penetrated clearly enough beyond the veil of the young man's ugly appearance. She 'saw Othello's visage in his mind'. Substantial good feelings existed between the two of them before Harry Porter's unexpected death at forty-three.

Elizabeth Porter had been two or three years older than her husband. Now, at his death, she was in early middle age and by no means ready to finish with life. She looked with favour on Sam Johnson and Johnson got the message. Doubtless it was he who first brought up the subject of marriage, but he would hardly have done so if she had not smoothed the way. Those conversations, in the late months of 1734, are among the dialogues of the dead that one most longs to be able to go back and hear. But time has rolled on and we shall never know just what Sam said to Elizabeth and what she replied. One thing is certain: he soon dropped her full name and began calling her 'Tetty', one of the then common abbreviations of Elizabeth and a sound well adapted to the expression of fondness and the softer feelings.

On Tetty's family, the effect of the suggestion that she should marry the penniless and uncouth Johnson was appalling. Her late husband's brother, a man who had done well in business, tried to bribe her with a large annuity to see no more of her suitor. Her elder son, a young naval officer, renounced her and never saw her again. Her younger son, destined to spend most of his business life in Italy, took years over his grudging acceptance of the situation. Only the daughter, Lucy, who lived at home, went along with the new arrangements and, outliving her mother by thirty-four years, became one of the permanent fixtures of Johnson's life.

So the marriage was agreed to. Sarah Johnson raised no objections, probably realizing that it would make no difference if she did. Boswell calls it 'a very imprudent scheme, both on account of their disparity of years, and her want of fortune'. But what, one wonders, would have been a prudent marriage for Johnson in 1734? Doubtless he ought, as every writer ought, to marry a seventeen-year-old girl with a docile disposition and a million pounds in the bank. But he seems to have neglected his opportunities for getting to know such a girl and winning her affections. His sexual desires were strong and he had held them down long enough. Everyone who knew him well in those years had testified that his life contained no casual amours and no whoring. His religious scruples were already too fierce for any such liberties; the dread of hellfire was strong enough to torture him even within the framework of a life whose weak spots were of omission rather than commission. He injured no one, was a threat to no one's livelihood, broke no promises, yet frequently sweated in fear of eternal punishment. How he would have suffered if his feet had strayed into the wrong bedroom can only be imagined. Certainly it never happened. All the more reason why he should be delighted with the partiality, the open attraction, shown by a handsome widow. What is more, Boswell's misgiving about her 'want of fortune' is very much the point of view of one who was heir to broad acres. Tetty had at any rate seven or eight hundred pounds which would be available as capital for her hopeful young husband. Harry Porter had died insolvent, but this money was her own, tied up where it could not be touched by his creditors.

In planning to marry Tetty, then, Johnson was being realistic and sensible. He needed a wife, and his frightening appearance would have put off any girl of his own age. He well understood this himself; years later he told Henry Thrale that until he was past thirty he never tried to make a good impression on anyone, 'considering the matter as hopeless'. He expected everyone he met to be disgusted or terrified by his looks and his nervous mannerisms, his convulsive starts and twitches. For such a young man, the approbation of an experienced and still attractive woman can be a lifesaver.

We have on record many unflattering descriptions of Tetty Johnson. But most of them date from her later years. David Garrick spitefully called her 'a little painted poppet, full of affectation and rural airs of elegance'. But this is the verdict of a man of the theatre, surrounded by actresses who know how to deploy their beauty and poise to the best advantage. Such men have very high standards. In any case, the crack about 'rural airs' comes awkwardly from one whose background was so similar to Mrs Johnson's. Even Garrick bore into later life the simple tastes and economical habits of Lichfield; when he was living with the actress Peg Woffington, he used to complain that she made the tea too strong and sent up the household bills.

It is probable that on the day of her marriage to Johnson, when she was two months short of forty-six and he two months short of twenty-six, Tetty still retained some of her earlier prettiness. In terms of physical attractiveness, a woman of forty-six may have very little ahead of her. Johnson, however, was willing to settle not for what his wife had ahead of her but for what she had at that time. It was a love match, on both sides.

They got married on 8 July 1735. The ceremony took place at Derby. It was the quietest of quiet weddings; the couple set off alone, on horseback – from Lichfield, presumably, though Johnson's famous account of the journey, to Boswell, does not specify. Their ride to church, a distance of some eighteen miles, was like a scene from *The Taming of the Shrew*. Tetty was acting up. She refused to keep pace with Sam; now riding ahead, accusing him of dawdling, now falling behind and saying he made too much haste. After a little of this Sam decided to begin as he meant to go on. He pressed forward at his own pace, knowing that the road lay between hedges and that she could not miss it. Soon, deaf to her petulant cries, he was out of sight. With the lesson well driven home, he reined in his horse and waited; she appeared, with tear-wet cheeks; they rode on together.

The wedding took place in the church that has been variously known as St Warboro's, St Warbridge's, St Warbere's, St Warburge's, St Walburg's and St Werburgh's. The latter is the name that has stuck. As at Lichfield, Johnson could feel himself within the aura of an ancient and native saint, for St Werburgha was the daughter of King Wulfhere, who died at Trentham in 699. The God in whom Johnson believed was worshipped on this spot before the Danes arrived to establish the township that we know as Derby. And the life of St Werburgh's goes on; in a number of ways it provides an emblem of the complicated life of the Church of England. It stands in what is still a busy part of Derby, in the commercial district, at the meeting-point of five main thoroughfares. It is also built on treacherous ground. Two streams flow under it. Throughout its long history the church has been plagued by flooding, and for this reason has been completely rebuilt a number of times.

In the nineteenth century, when funds must have been plentiful, it was enormously enlarged. The church in which Sam and Tetty Johnson took their vows became a chapel within a larger church. In the twentieth century further changes have come. The huge barn-like building, now too large for the needs of the neighbourhood, had to find ways of employing its space. In recent years a youth centre has been set up, actually within the walls of the church, where the

adolescents of Derby maintain their links with the Church of England by drinking tea, coffee and cokes, playing billiards and table tennis and hearing pop
music. A few steps away is the chapel. Once over its threshold you are in the
eighteenth century. All is elegance, dignity, repose: cool white pillars and dark
wood. Above the altar the Ten Commandments are inscribed in beautiful
eighteenth-century lettering; surmounting them, the arms of Queen Anne.
Outside, the traffic rumbles on the five main roads; beneath, the streams gather
for the next flood. Yes, St Werburgh's is worth a visit. So much humanity is
concentrated there, so many vibrations have gone into its walls, and into the
walls that were there before them, and the walls before that. It is the kind of
place where, as somebody or other has put it,

> the past flows with the present
> in the deep pool of Now.

And there it happened. What happened? They were married: whatever that
means in respect of any man and any woman. Elizabeth Porter was a widow,
and we may feel, as we trace out her story, that a widow is what she remained.
But on that July morning Sam Johnson became a husband.

CHAPTER 5

Time of Decision

'At Edial, near Lichfield in Staffordshire, young gentlemen are boarded and taught the Latin and Greek languages by Samuel Johnson.' The idea, it seems, had been Gilbert Walmesley's. Always brimming over with goodwill towards his *protégé*, Walmesley had noticed that Edial Hall, a large brick-built house with a walled garden some two or three miles out of Lichfield, was standing empty and was of the right size and impressiveness to make a private academy. Hence the quietly confident, modestly terse advertisement which appeared twice (June and July 1736) in *The Gentleman's Magazine*, that successful London miscellany which, a few short years later, was to depend so heavily on the pen of Samuel Johnson.

So it was to be schoolmastering again. True, Johnson had tried the work several times, always with disastrous results, but what else was there? In any case, his previous experiments had mostly ended in mutual hostility between Johnson and whoever was employing him; if he could be master of his own school, there would be no employer and all might be well. These, indeed, were the only terms on which he was likely to get started at all. In the short interval between his marriage and the setting up at Edial, he had made another attempt to land an usher's job, this time at Solihull in Warwickshire. But again he was turned down. The trustees of the school had heard of Johnson; they knew he was a good scholar and a gifted man, but they knew also that he had uncontrollable nervous tics and they concluded, rightly, that this would lead to disrespect on the part of the pupils and finally to insurmountable problems of discipline. For Johnson it was to be his own school, or nothing.

So, using Tetty's money, the couple leased and fitted up the large, rather depressing house. From the beginning, a smell of failure seems to have hung about the enterprise. The 'young gentlemen' of Staffordshire stayed away from the school in large numbers. According to Boswell, there were only three pupils, whom he names: David Garrick and his brother Peter, and a boy called Offley, who died young. That the Garrick brothers should have attended the unpromising establishment is a touching evidence of neighbourhood solidarity on the part of their father, Captain Garrick, and doubtless also of the devoted work of Gilbert Walmesley behind the scenes; there may also have been a touch of desperation in it, since David, in the fashion of most boys who will grow up to be star entertainers, had no relish for sitting still on a classroom bench and was shunted from school to school until he was blessedly old enough to leave. Apart from these three, there may well have been others: Sir John Hawkins, a steady and reliable biographer who had the advantage over Boswell that he had known Johnson much earlier in life, when these memories would be fresh, puts the probable number as high as eight. But even at that optimistic estimate the school was obviously not doing well. A successful academy cannot be built on eight boys, and the Johnsons must have known that it could not last.

Johnson was a conscientious schoolmaster. Hopelessly unfitted for the work by his stop-and-start temperament and by the physical peculiarities so fatally easy to mimic, he nevertheless invested some hard thinking in the planning of a curriculum. He drew up an elaborate scheme, which happens to have survived because he sent a copy of it to his cousin Samuel Ford, a clergyman in Herefordshire. Printed by Boswell in the appropriate part of his narrative, it shows that the classical studies of the young gentlemen were, in theory at least, carefully regulated. The school did not fail through lack of diligence and forethought; it just failed.

Meanwhile, life had its compensations. Whatever may have happened to the Johnson marriage in its later years, it was at Edial a real sexual and emotional relationship, which gave the young man a much needed outlet for his energies. There were also, as there should always be in one's twenties, bright dreams of the future. Johnson was at work on a tragedy, to be called *Irene*. He had come across the story in Knolles's *General History of the Turks*, a book he had borrowed from David Garrick's elder brother, Peter, perhaps with a view to digging a good plot out of it. The source is not without significance, for the East (or rather both the Easts, 'Near' and 'Far') laid a spell on Johnson's imagination all his life. When he adventured a work of imagination, rather than of criticism and commentary, it was generally in the framework of an exotic setting somewhere to the east of Europe. Evidently he found stimulation and release in these Oriental tales. Since there was, in eighteenth-century Europe, little or no accurate knowledge of the eastern part of the world, the poet was liberated from a too hampering concern with probability, chronology and documentary reference; and in the heightened atmosphere, the lyrical or lurid colouring, of the tales reaching him from those far-off lands he could find a welcome corrective to the placid fields and grey skies of his normal surroundings. But, as Johnson combed through Knolles, he was looking for more than just a suitable story. His imagination needed solid meat as well as sherbet. A story might take his fancy as being colourful and dramatic, but it would not hold up as a Johnsonian platform unless it had also a moral. In the story of *Irene*, the beautiful Greek slave who was the favourite of Sultan Mahomet II, Johnson found a political martyrdom and also a demonstration that 'absolute power corrupts absolutely'. The Sultan's armies have overrun Greece, a country whose sinews have been slackened by vice and self-indulgence until it has become an easy prey. Some of the other Greek prisoners, though not Irene herself, enter into a plot with a sinister caliph who intends to murder the Sultan; the plot is discovered and, though Irene has had no part in it, she is executed with the rest so that Mahomet can prove to his followers that he has not gone soft under the influence of his love for a Christian.

Johnson clearly found a great deal in this story. Among other things, it fell into line with his political thinking. He distrusted despotism as much as mob rule; his ideal was always a system of checks and balances. Thus, in the rough draft on which the finished work is based, we find that the Caliph, Mahomet's would-be assassin, has been driven to make a deal with the enemies of his country 'that he might have a retreat in his Necessity'; he dare not trust the Sultan, and

> . . . here he launches into the misery of absolute governments, where if a man serves his country counterfeit plots and false suspicions, then breaks out into the praises of that country (after having blamed the Eastern tyranny) which he has heard of in the north where king and people own one common law, one common interest, mutual duties and feel one happiness and one misfortune

This, in itself, is a handsome anachronism, since the England of that day was engulfed in the Wars of the Roses, but in planning this lofty work Johnson was in no mood to stoop to petty considerations of the calendar. In celebrating the rumoured virtues of British democracy he has Cali Bassa say, in the finished version,

> If there be any land, as fame reports,
> Where common laws restrain the prince and subject,
> A happy land, where circulating power
> Flows through each member of the embodied state

– a reference to the circulation of the blood, which at that time was still undiscovered. Later, in the more sober pages of *The Rambler* (No. 140), he was to laugh at himself for this high conflation of historical periods; but this was Johnson in his Shakespearean vein, perfectly willing if necessary to give a sea coast to Bohemia.

The hopeful poet, dreaming his strange dream in which the rich profusion of the East was to group itself according to a Christian and Anglo-Saxon sense of moral responsibility and divine providence, was also the happy bridegroom. It was this side of his life, indeed, that provided the only material for future reminiscence. Everything else about Edial was forgotten, but the love-making of the pair was preserved as if in amber by the extravagant comic art of Garrick.

'The young rogues', says Boswell, 'used to listen at the door of his bed-chamber, and peep through the keyhole, that they might turn into ridicule his tumultuous and awkward fondness for Mrs Johnson.' 'Tumultuous and awkward' is good; it gives an exact impression of what Johnson must have been like as a lover. Such scenes, whether actually glimpsed through the keyhole or merely constructed by imagination from the sounds audible in the corridor, made an irresistible opportunity for David Garrick. As a youth he convulsed his schoolfellows with his imitation of Tetty lying in bed urging her husband not to keep her waiting, and Johnson stumbling about the bed hastily undressing and exclaiming, 'I'm coming, Tetsie, I'm coming, my Tetsie.' Or he would represent

Johnson as sitting by the bedside absorbed in creative labour on *Irene*, deaf to Tetty's reproaches and importunities, finally rising and short-sightedly stuffing the bedsheet into his breeches in mistake for his shirt. Garrick made a party piece of the Johnsons' marital relations for the rest of his life; it was his most successful burlesque act; he would be surrounded by friends with tears of laughter running down their faces, begging him to stop before they burst. These wild scenes of merriment, at London supper parties in the sixties and seventies, proved to be the only legacy of the months at Edial. The time was, indeed, approaching when Johnson had to make one more attempt to build success on a foundation of failure. The school was, inevitably, going down. It had been opened early in 1736, and after struggling along for just over a year it closed its doors finally. February, never the most cheerful month in the country-side, found Johnson facing the fact that the school would not keep them. His thoughts, naturally, turned to the only other possible means of livelihood. In the Birmingham days he had scratched a few guineas out of working for Warren, the optimistic publisher who suppressed 'Birmingham' on the title-page of his book and boldly substituted 'London'. The capital city was where books and periodicals came from, and where, on the whole, people expected them to come from. To London, then, Johnson's thoughts turned. And he resolved, in this bleak winter period as all his earlier hopes crumbled, that his assault had to be a serious one. He must go to London in person. He had tried, once before, to interest Edward Cave, owner and editor of *The Gentleman's Magazine*, without taking the gamble of leaving his Staffordshire roots and throwing himself into Cave's world. A couple of years earlier he had sounded Cave out with a cautious letter in which he offered, on behalf of a shadowy third person, to raise the stan-dard of the magazine's literary section. The unnamed author would supply not only 'poems . . . never printed before' (most young writers have a few of these in stock), but also 'short literary dissertations in Latin or English, critical re-marks on authors ancient or modern, forgotten poems that deserve revival', etc., etc. Still boxing with his guard well up, Johnson had signed the letter 'S. Smith', with a request that Cave should address his answer to the Castle Inn, Birmingham. The pseudonym could have several explanations. Either Johnson was hoping to arouse Cave's curiosity by using what inevitably seemed to be a false name (was the real writer someone too important to own his identity? A person of quality, even?), or perhaps he had already tried Cave before, in a letter now lost which had carried his true name. Whatever is the reason, 'S. Smith' offered the services of his *alter ego* in vain. Though Cave wrote on the letter 'Answered 2 Dec', there is no knowing what kind of hope his answer held out; all that we know is that nothing came of it. Not surprisingly. Cave was a downy bird, a self-made man of business who formed his estimate of people by looking into their faces as much as by reading what they had written, and he was falling for no long-range offers from Birmingham inns. Besides, the letter had come at a bad moment. Cave, always seeking ways to improve business, had recently advertised a prize of fifty pounds for the best poem on 'Life, Death, Judgement, Heaven and Hell'. (The eighteenth century's idea of a bestseller was more dignified and serious than the twentieth's.) As a frugal tradesman, coming from a background of poverty, Cave had imagined that fifty pounds would set all the most famous pens in the kingdom scribbling in a fever of competition. In fact, the bait proved too small to attract first-rate material. On top of that, when Cave invited well-known men of letters, some of them at the universities, to act as judges of the entries, he had the humiliation of being refused.

In the letter from 'S. Smith', Johnson had complimented Cave on the 'generosity' of the fifty-pound offer; and indeed, though apparently not high enough to get results, it was not at all bad payment for that miserable epoch in the fortunes of authors. The price of literary wares rose steadily throughout the eighteenth century, and in its second half there are records of very respectable payments: Fielding got £700 for *Tom Jones* and £1000 for its much inferior successor, *Amelia*; Gay's *Poems* earned £1000, while Hawkesworth's book on the South Sea expeditions made no less than £6000. But in the 1730s generous pay was simply not to be looked for, and Cave with his fifty-pound trophy had to be reckoned a good employer. To Cave, then, Johnson would go. The school was closed down; the few pupils who were left seem to have had no difficulty in making other arrangements. Lawrence Offley was going up to Cambridge; he was a well-connected young man, related to the Aston family with whom Johnson was to have quite a lot to do in one way and another, and no doubt he had only been marking time at Edial Hall. The Garrick brothers were also assigned to new schools. It was at this time Captain Garrick's intention that David should follow the law, and it was to this end the tireless Walmesley had arranged that he should continue his education at the Free School at Rochester in Kent.

So the Edial venture was over, the pupils departed, and the big house must have been dark and silent in those cold, wet months. If ever there was a time for resolute action and sweeping changes, it was now. Johnson was young; he had behind him the whip of failure, in front of him the dream-landscape of success. His tragedy, *Irene*, was well along; three out of the five acts were written. Always solicitous of Walmesley's good opinion, Johnson showed him the play as far as it had gone. Walmesley objected to the way the plot was developing. Irene had been plunged so deeply into black misfortune, he complained, that there was nothing left to inflict on her before the final curtain. Johnson, out-pointed so many times in their conversations, at last saw the chance of a knock-down retort. 'Sir,' he said, 'I have enough in reserve for my purpose; for, in the last act, I intend to put my heroine into the ecclesiastical court at Lichfield, which will fill up the utmost measure of human calamity.' Walmesley's reply is not on record. Probably he had none to make. The ecclesiastical court, which it was supposed to be his job to regulate, had irritated local people so much by its high-handed ways that they had petitioned Parliament for its reform. From the fact that he continued to be a friend of Johnson's after this riposte, we know Walmesley to have been a generous man.

Yes, this was the moment. Tetty would stay behind until he was settled, and since she had the company of her daughter Lucy she would be able to stand the separation. His mother in Lichfield had her companion, Catherine Chambers. Such business as came into the failing shop she could cope with. It ought, of course, to have been Nathaniel's business now. But another blow had fallen on the household in Breadmarket Street. Nathaniel, it seemed, was in trouble. At about the same time as Sam had taken the Edial house, Nathaniel had moved the short distance to Burton-on-Trent to take charge of a branch of the bookshop. There, some false move or other plunged him into disgrace. The details are lost, but it appears from a letter which Nathaniel wrote to his mother that he had committed what he called 'crimes' and that these were the result of a period of frustration and disappointment. Nathaniel had been interested in acquiring a shop at Stourbridge, that town in which the Johnsons had respectable and prosperous connections. This scheme had been baulked, probably because Sarah declined to give him certain help which was within her power.

'It is true,' Nathaniel wrote to his mother, 'I did make a positive bargain for a shop at Stourbridge in which I believe I might have lived happily and had I gone when I first desired it none of these crimes had been committed which have given both you and me so much trouble. I don't know that you ever denied me part of the working tools but you never told me you would give or lend them me. As to my brother's assisting me, I had but little reason to expect it when he would scarce ever use me with common civility and to whose advice was owing that unwillingness you showed to my going to Stourbridge.'

From this letter we can get a glimpse of what the situation must have been. Natty, seeing that Sam had found substantial support and encouragement among the Fords, the Moseleys, the Actons, the Hickmans, all those solid Stourbridge families, had wanted his own squeeze at the orange. He had formed the scheme of setting up there in trade, and somehow or other Sam had blocked it. Natty, who had not inherited the brains of the family and who was content with the lowly status of a tradesman, would have cramped his elder brother's style. He would have been a living reminder, daily walking the streets of Stourbridge, that the Lichfield Johnsons were seedy, unsuccessful shopkeepers and that the fact of Sam's being an Oxford man of letters was an accident, a sport in the family history.

These were unworthy motives. Perhaps this is the only time in his long life that Samuel Johnson gave way to an impulse that had in it a trace of meanness. And, if we care to be forgiving about it, we can do so without much straining. He was very young, very poor, very threatened. Chances were limited, and the scales weighted heavily against him. He was desperate to find some way up from frustration and failure, and the Stourbridge circle must have seemed his only firm foothold for a leap. If Nathaniel had set up in Stourbridge, we now see, it would not have made any difference in the end; London, not Worcestershire, was to be the essential springboard. But in the 1730s Sam could hardly have foreseen this. He needed every chance he could get, and Nathaniel's presence seemed to threaten one of the best he had.

Yes, we can make allowances. But for Nathaniel it was the end of the road. He wandered to Frome in Somerset, with the vague idea of emigrating to

North America. 'I know not', he told his mother in the same letter, 'nor do I much care, in what way of life I shall hereafter live, but this I know that it shall be an honest one and that it can't be more unpleasant than some part of my life past. I believe I shall go to Georgia in about a fortnight. . . .'

But there was to be no future life, in Georgia or at home. Nathaniel came home from Frome a fatally sick man; he must have died on 3 or 4 March because on 5 March he was buried at St Michael's Church.

The exact date of his death is of interest because we know the date of his brother's departure for London. It was 2 March. This makes it certain that Nathaniel was still alive, for Sam would never have set out on the very day he died. Why was the death so sudden, that its coming was not foreseen even one day before? Was it suicide? If so, the matter was hushed up very thoroughly, or he could never have been buried in consecrated ground. Was it the sudden worsening of an illness that did not appear to be fatal? This could be; dying people often seem to be recovering and then suddenly go off while one's back is turned.

Whatever the reason, Natty died while Sam was on the road to London. The letter he wrote to his mother, the only residue of his twenty-four years on earth, lies now in the birthplace in Lichfield: still at the same house where it was delivered, and where Sarah Johnson opened it and – we have to believe – cried over it.

Sam, for his part, kept his feelings on the matter to himself. He made no reference to them, then or at any other time; or at any rate none that has survived. If it matters to us, and surely it must, we are thrown back on conjecture. The house at Lichfield seems to have become, for the next twenty-odd years, a focus of guilt and deep-seated fear. It was associated for Johnson with his early shortcomings: the parents he had not loved enough, the brother he had injured. As we shall see, he went back there for a brief visit in the early months of 1740, a couple of years after leaving for London. On that visit he saw his mother for the last time, and for the next twenty-two years he kept well clear of Lichfield and his birthplace. In later years, when Lucy Porter was living in the house, Johnson did not often sleep under that roof on his visits, preferring to put up at the Three Crowns, a couple of doors away; was this solely to avoid inconveniencing Lucy, that pernickety old maid, or did something inside him shrink from lying down to rest in that house where he had been betrayed and had betrayed others?

In any case, London claimed him. The battle was joined, and if he had tears to shed about Nathaniel, if in later life there would be phantoms of guilt to exorcize and appease, that time was not yet. His wife, Walmesley, Taylor, Hector, all the friends who had believed in him, were waiting for him to show his powers.

The journey to the capital was amusing enough, since it was made in company with David Garrick, who had to pass through London on his way to Rochester. In later life both men took a certain pride in humorous exaggeration of their humble entry into the new life. Johnson once said to Garrick at an evening gathering that he himself had arrived in London with twopence-ha'penny in his pocket – 'and thou, Davy, with three-halfpence in thine'. Garrick, for his part, used to tell people that they had journeyed by the method known as 'ride and tie', which allowed two men to use one horse. In such sportive mood did they look back, from the heights of eminence, on a journey that was not, fortunately, as romantically rugged as they painted it. Johnson had a few pounds from the wreck of Tetty's dowry, enough to live on while he took stock of the London situation; Garrick may have been short of spending money, but he was still a carefree schoolboy going from one kindly shelter to another. Even so, if they were not the sturdy vagabonds they amused themselves by depicting, neither of them had any margin for failure. For both of them, but more especially for Johnson, London held out a clear choice. Swim, or sink. And the penalties for sinking, in eighteenth-century London, were too frightening to contemplate. As the city came into sight, Johnson must have been acutely aware that in the next few years, while his strength lasted, he had either to conquer this place or go the way of Nathaniel.

PART II

Grub Street

CHAPTER 6

At St John's Gate

Once arrived in London, Johnson, characteristically, did nothing for weeks on end. The immediate objective he had set himself was to finish *Irene* and see if he could get it staged or at least printed. But the uncompleted play languished among his luggage that spring as he sat in coffee houses or wandered about the streets.

It was enough, for the moment, to be taking in the absorbing spectacle of London itself, a big new place to get used to, the city that was to be his principal home from now until the end of his life. After two centuries of levelling-down and levelling-up, we can hardly imagine the extent to which eighteenth-century London was a city of extremes. The beauty of the buildings, the fine clothes and gilded carriages, the haughty elegance of the *beau monde* made a permanent bizarre contrast to the filth running in the streets, the beggars and syphilitics and idiots, the nightly stabbings and beatings-up, the hundreds of whores and foot-pads and pickpockets, the impulsive violence of the mob. After the quiet streets and squares of Lichfield, even after the busy rush of Birmingham, these juxta-posed worlds were enough to throw the young newcomer off balance. On the other hand, London was not as claustrophobic as it is now. Megalopolis had not yet arrived; the big city was an invention of the nineteenth century and in fact a consequence of the steam engine, since before steam there was no means of hauling the colossal daily loads of food and materials needed to supply the London of Dickens or the Paris of Baudelaire. Johnson's London was served by wagon or boat, which meant that by modern standards it was tiny. Its half-million inhabitants were crammed into a few miles. Open country began at Hyde Park, and farmers drove their herds through the streets.

Johnson took lodgings with a Mr Norris, staymaker, in a quiet cul-de-sac off the Strand. Norris had Staffordshire connections, so that a little of the old life projected reassuringly into the new. At the very beginning, Johnson was still in the company of David Garrick, who had suddenly to cope with drastic changes in his situation: his father had died, back in Lichfield, at just about the same time as Nathaniel Johnson. Hurried new plans were made, and the notion of going to school in Rochester was abandoned. Garrick had a legacy waiting for him when he became of age, but that was a couple of years in the future, and for the moment he was short of cash for necessities. So he and Johnson, lending each other moral support, went to a bookseller named Wilcox in the Strand, with whom Garrick had some slight acquaintance, and asked for the modest loan of five pounds. Wilcox advanced them the money (it was punctually repaid), though he could not resist a little joke while doing so. Hearing that Johnson proposed to earn a living from literature, he glanced meaningfully at his strong and burly frame and suggested that he might find it easier to get work as a porter.

Johnson took this in good part. He was beginning to find his feet in London, and he felt, for the time being, in a confident mood. He accepted the necessity of living on as little money as possible – enjoyed it, even, as an interesting challenge to his ingenuity and practical sense. Years afterwards he was pleased to give the attentive Boswell a detailed account of how he managed it. Near his lodgings there was a little neighbourhood tavern called the Pine Apple; Johnson fell in with the regulars who always had their midday dinner there, and remembered them as 'very good company'. 'Several of them had travelled', an important recommendation in the eyes of this young man who wanted so much to know about the varieties of men and customs. Another thing he remembered about them was that they 'expected to meet every day, but did not know one another's names' – exactly like the *habitués* of every pub and restaurant in the world, and the sort of small, vivid detail that shows there was a novelist somewhere inside Johnson.

The Pine Apple provided him every day with food and conversation, and cheaply too. 'It used to cost the rest a shilling, for they drank wine; but I had a cut of meat for sixpence, and bread for a penny, and gave the waiter a penny; so that I was quite well served, nay, better than the rest, for they gave the waiter nothing.' Johnson was learning fast. His mind went back to an Irish painter he had known, back in his Birmingham days; this character, whose name has not come down to us, had expounded to Johnson the system of economy he had followed during some years in London, where, he declared, a careful man could live for thirty pounds a year 'without being contemptible'. The rather pathetic series of shifts which this Hibernian limner found necessary to live on such a sum – doing without supper, frequenting a coffee house for an expenditure of threepence a day and conducting one's business there, and paying social calls only on 'clean-shirt days' – evidently struck Johnson as the height of practical commonsense, and he would not hear the man ridiculed. To live on a pittance and keep one's self-respect is better than letting go and sliding into vagabondage, and Johnson respected it as a discipline. At the same time, he was also capable of seeing good in a very different life style. His aristocratic friend of Lichfield days, Harry Hervey, was in London, ostensibly serving as a Captain in Lord Robert Montagu's regiment, but actually living it up, as usual, in a fine house in St James's Square. Johnson and Garrick found a welcome there, good food, good talk, handsome company. Doubtless there was plenty of good drink too, but this meant nothing to Johnson at this time. He was going through a period of rigid abstinence from alcohol. This was natural in one who had to watch his money, but there may have been another explanation also. Johnson seems to have given up drinking at the time of his marriage; it is natural, again, for a man to turn over a new leaf on getting married, but there is also the possibility that

Tetty, who certainly drank too much in her later years, was already too fond of a glass and that her husband was trying to set her a good example.

In this fashion the first few London weeks slipped away. By July the novelty was wearing off, and it was time for another of Johnson's pendulum swings from idleness to high-pressure work. He moved from town to the quiet of Greenwich; there, in lodgings in Church Street, he set about finishing *Irene*. The work went slowly; all along this play gave him trouble; it was and it remains the only exception to the rule that Johnson's writings were produced at white heat and with inconceivable rapidity. The stiff, ponderous lines came slowly from his pen, the dramatic structure was hewn out with hard labour. He was working against the grain of his natural inclination. There must have been moods of depression and discouragement as he doggedly worked to put together something that looked like a classical tragedy, and probably it was one of these that determined him to find another string for his bow. In July he took up again his original intention of getting in touch with Cave. Abandoning the cardboard mask of 'S. Smith', he wrote from Greenwich to Cave's office in St John's Gate, Clerkenwell. This time, instead of a large general undertaking to turn his hand to anything literary, he came up with a specific proposal: a translation of Father Paul Sarpi's *History of the Council of Trent*. This book already existed in a seventeenth-century English translation, but it had been recently put into French and provided with scholarly notes by one Le Courayer, and Johnson proposed to work from this rather than from Sarpi's original Italian.

Since Cave did in fact commission this work, we must assume that Johnson's letter elicited a reply and that it was favourable. Probably this month of July saw a meeting between the shrewd bookseller and his prospective contributor. So that when Johnson returned to Edial that summer to report to Tetty and convince her that he was ready to make a life for her in London one of the most important things he had to tell her would be his impressions of Edward Cave.

Cave could hardly have been called an attractive man, though Johnson discerned admirable qualities in him from first to last, and after his death wrote a biographical sketch which showed him in a good light. Cave's nature looks plainly enough out of the two surviving portraits of him. In one, he is the successful man of business, dressed in full fig to have his picture painted, with his large round face surmounted by a full, neatly combed wig, and one hand tucked into his finely brocaded waistcoat in such a way as to show off the lace at the wrist. The face is smooth, bland, confident; the painter is working hard to show the self-made man as he wished to see himself. The other picture shows Cave in working gear, with a tradesmanly round cap on his head, an open-necked shirt, and a loose coat unbuttoned all the way down. The eyes are watchful and slightly shifty, the face as moon-like as in the set-piece portrait but much more lined. One hand holds what looks like an invoice; the other is held out towards the onlooker as if Cave were saying 'Hand it over' – whatever 'it' might chance to be, the money of a debtor or the copy of a contributor.

Cave was a man who had risen from poverty, first by a brainwave and then by steady attention to the job of seeing that his brainwave paid off. He was no more than an ordinary jobbing printer when in 1731 he had the idea of starting *The Gentleman's Magazine*, which pioneered monthly journalism of that miscellaneous kind and consistently overshadowed the opposition. When Johnson came to write his *Dictionary*, he remembered Cave; the word 'magazine' is defined first in its primary sense, and then in the sense given to it by Cave:

1. A storehouse, commonly an arsenal or armoury, or repository of provisions.
2. Of late this word has signified a miscellaneous pamphlet, from a periodical miscellany named *The Gentleman's Magazine*, by *Edward Cave*.

Cave found a place in his magazine (or 'storehouse') for anything that might interest a gentleman or contribute to the comfort of his household – medical, culinary, legal, political; the improving, the uplifting, the entertaining. His pages were filled by a team of hacks whose busy pens hardly ceased moving over the paper. Cave saw to it that they worked as many hours as were needed to fill the magazine and bring it out punctually, and that they were paid frugally and, if necessary, in driblets. 'He would', Johnson later recalled, 'contract for lines by the hundred, and expect the long hundred.' He cultivated a cold, slow manner; working with literary men, he refused to be jolted by their temperaments, stampeded by their enthusiasms, or melted by their hard-luck stories. When a newcomer was shown into his office, Cave would remain seated behind his desk, and as often as not say nothing for the first few minutes, forcing the visitor to do the talking – an excellent method of making people blurt out all sorts of things they had previously determined to keep to themselves. When he did decide to speak, Cave's usual way of beginning the conversation was to put into the visitor's hand some item from the next number of the magazine, and ask his opinion of it. He also had the valuable art of appearing not to be listening when in fact he was taking everything in and storing it in his memory.

The insecurity of Johnson's state at this time is well illustrated in the letters he wrote to Cave, which come as near to being anxiously deferential as his sturdy nature would permit. The first letter from Birmingham had been independent, even rather haughty; it began with a cool assumption that Cave knew how low was the standard of the poetry he published in the magazine:

Sir
As you appear no less sensible than your readers of the defects of your poetical article, you will not be displeased, if in order to the improvement of it, I communicate to you the sentiments of a person who will undertake on reasonable terms sometimes to fill a column.

But this high-handed approach had got no results. The letters written from London are much more cap-in-hand. The opening one, in which Johnson is trying to interest Cave in his translation of Sarpi, begins with a compliment anxiously framed to put Cave in a good mood and keep him reading.

Sir
Having observed in your papers very uncommon offers of encouragement

to men of letters, I have chosen, being a stranger in London, to communicate to you the following design, which, I hope, if you join in it, will be of advantage to both of us.

When Cave answered, Johnson again applied the flattering varnish as fast as his brush could fly.

Sir
When I took the liberty of writing to you a few days ago, I did not expect a repetition of the same pleasure so soon; for a pleasure I shall always think it to converse in any measure with an agreeable and candid man. . . .

All this is very forgivable. Cave, after all, was a decent tradesman; by treating him with politeness, even with deference, Johnson was not having to swallow his scruples as men do who find it expedient to flatter the powerful and wicked. Furthermore, he was desperately eager to get his foot in the door. He had left behind such security as the Midlands afforded, which was little enough, and had not yet established himself in London. If Cave turned him away the only thing waiting for him was the pavement. Even when he was safely on the strength of the magazine, one of Cave's regulars and a trusted coadjutor, Johnson was still very careful to treat Cave with politeness and to remember their relationship as employer and employed. Once, when Cave had evidently sent a note indicating some kind of dissatisfaction, Johnson quickly made clear his readiness to set matters right:

Sir
I did not care to detain your servant while I wrote an answer to your letter, in which you seem to insinuate that I had promised more than I am ready to perform. If I have raised your expectations by anything that may have escaped my memory I am sorry, and if you remind me of it shall thank you for the favour.

Yet, however much he had to pick his way, Johnson quite clearly did not suffer actual insolence from Cave. The relationship was not one that left behind any flavour of resentment. If Cave was a careful tradesman who put business first and the graces of life second, Johnson had experience of a long line of men who had had to do the same, beginning with his own father. When he got back to Edial in that summer of 1737, and poured out to Tetty his report of how he had fared in London, the account of Cave would be a cheerful one. He would also be able to give her an impressive description of the physical surroundings from which the celebrated magazine came forth. St John's Gate was the gatehouse of an ancient monastic foundation; its two square towers, astride a broad archway, would have reminded Johnson pleasantly of his rooms in the tower of Pembroke College. Impressed by the solid reputation of *The Gentleman's Magazine*, and pleased by the dignified building, Johnson on his first visit 'beheld it', as he told Boswell, 'with reverence'.

At all events, his account of London was encouraging enough to induce Tetty to cut adrift from the Midlands and follow him. The house at Edial was closed up, Lucy Porter moved into Lichfield to live with Sarah Johnson and help with the dwindling trade of the bookshop, and before Christmas Johnson and his wife were established in London, and at a good address too: in Castle Street, near Cavendish Square.

It was a time for action. Before finally deciding to go to work regularly for Cave, there was the matter of *Irene* to be settled one way or the other. Johnson sought out David Garrick's brother, Peter, and read the whole five acts aloud to him, sitting in a tavern. Peter had no great theatrical career ahead of him – he was, in fact, destined for the wine trade – but he had some useful connections in management and he had always been encouraging about Johnson's play. He did his best to get it put on at the Drury Lane Theatre but without success. The then manager, a man called Fleetwood, was a show-business shark of the worst type, who had patience for nothing except pantomimes, and helped along the success of his productions by infiltrating the audience with ruffians paid to assault anyone who hissed the show. He refused even to read *Irene*, and the project went to sleep for another ten years and more. For the disappointed dramatist it had to be St John's Gate or nothing.

So it was that Johnson joined the team of industrious journalists who were in and out of Cave's office. There was Tom Birch, historian and biographer, member of the Society for the Encouragement of Learning, a man whose head was stuffed with information about everything, mostly within a framework of anecdote. His talk was inexhaustibly interesting, but, as often happens, he was unable to write as well as he talked. Johnson's way of describing this disability of Birch's was to say, 'Tom is a lively rogue; he remembers a great deal, and can tell many pleasant stories; but a pen is to Tom a torpedo, the touch of it benumbs his hand and his brain.' But, always willing to praise a man for what he genuinely did well, he remembered Birch all his life for that amazing fund of anecdote. As an old man, riding along with Boswell in the Hebrides, he would not allow Birch to be put down by comparison with Bishop Percy, a man of great and miscellaneous learning. Boswell said that Percy's flow of stories went on like one of the streams that ran by the roadside. Johnson retorted, 'If Percy is like one of the brooks here, Birch was like the river Thames.' Then there was William Guthrie, a decent and hardworking Scot, whose special interest was in political writing and who had an impressive grasp of the history of Parliament. As a Jacobite he had felt unable to accept any official post under the Hanoverian Government, and had left his native country to come and earn a living by his pen in London. Johnson found much to respect in Guthrie. Another contributor was Moses Browne, a self-educated and prolific poet, whom Cave evidently thought of as a star contributor and to whom he introduced Johnson one evening as a special treat; Johnson thought highly enough of Browne to encourage him, some years later, to undertake an edition of Walton's *The Compleat Angler*. There was Elizabeth Carter, a learned young woman who was later, like Johnson himself, to soar above the confines of monthly journalism, but who at this time was glad enough to send in regular contributions of rather feeble verses. Johnson, who met her through Cave, admired her greatly and made a lifelong friend of her. She had been schooled in the Greek and Latin classics by her father, but the other necessary skills had not been forgotten, and Johnson once remarked approvingly, 'A man is in general better pleased when he has a good dinner upon his table, than when his wife talks Greek. My old friend, Mrs Carter, could make a pudding as well as translate Epictetus.'

Besides all these people and more, there was one who came to the office in St John's Gate who was to engage more closely with Johnson's life than any of them. This was Richard Savage, poet and dramatist, man about town, Jacobite politician, author of *The Bastard*. Savage was, or claimed to be, the illegitimate son of the Countess of Macclesfield by her lover, Earl Rivers. Now aged forty-two, he was nearing the end of his years in London. In 1739 his friends, tired of digging into their pockets for money which the poet instantly spent on carousal, organized his departure for the soothing quiet and convenient distance of Swansea. But if Johnson was one of the last friends Savage made in London he was also one of the closest. It was Johnson from whom Savage parted, in the summer of 1739, 'with tears in his eyes'. But to his bizarre story we must return later.

Once accepted by Cave, Johnson began immediately to pull on his oar. Cave had been scurrilously attacked by rival publishers enraged at his success, and Johnson's first contribution to the magazine, in March 1738, was a Latin poem, *Ad Urbanum*, which was in fact a counter-attack on these enemies. Cave's own occasional contributions to the magazine were over the signature 'Sylvanus Urban', and Johnson's poem praises Urban for his industry, the usefulness of his work, and the steadiness of his indifference to his rivals' malignancy. Doubtless the poem was a sincere enough expression of Johnson's feelings – his wish to identify with the magazine and to reply to attacks on the editor, his respect for what Cave had managed to accomplish, and his almost pathetic gratitude at the prospect of regular employment. But this is not to say that it called out any of his real strength. He obviously saw it as an exercise, a task to be performed, rather like the kind of thing he had written for Jorden at the university. Probably it was the result of one of his sporadic bursts of energy. Meanwhile, the poet in him was also busy with a more sustained work, conceived and executed at a deeper level. He was writing a poem about (what else?) London.

Striking while the iron was hot, Johnson approached Cave immediately after the acceptance of *Ad Urbanum*, and told him of the new and more ambitious work. But with a curious rush of caution to the head he returned to something like the old deviousness that had marked 'S. Smith'. He told Cave that he was acting on behalf of another hard-up writer. Perhaps the idea was that he could drive a more unblushing bargain if he could claim to be representing someone else. Or he may have thought that the anti-government sentiments expressed in the poem would be offensive to Cave, whom it was terribly important not to alienate at this stage. Whatever the motive, a complicated mating dance ensued, at the end of which Johnson sold the poem to Cave for ten pounds and Cave brought it out with the name of another publisher, Dodsley, on the title-page. The author remained anonymous.

London is an interesting poem in itself. It established Johnson's reputation as a poet within the Augustan mode and one can see why. But in the biography of a writer one tends to view his works as episodes in his life, and from this point of view also *London* is of especial interest. It is, on the face of it, an exercise in the then highly fashionable mode of writing known as 'Imitation'. Since eighteenth-century English literary taste was saturated in the classics (Greek up to a point, Latin more thoroughly), it was at all times possible to attract attention with a well-turned version into English of some familiar Latin poem. 'Imitation' went one stage beyond this. It provided a framework of translation, always taking off from some poem which the reader would know in the original, but it substituted contemporary English references for Roman. It brought the original up to date, while continually implying that *plus ça change, plus c'est la même chose*. Responding to an 'Imitation' is always a matter of reading it on two levels at once, which in turn means having one foot in ancient Rome and one in modern London. Only a culture with definite points of reference in the past can produce such a genre.

Johnson's starting-point is Juvenal's *Third Satire*. This is a ferocious attack on Rome – its corruption, its vice, its physical unpleasantness. Juvenal is a highly scurrilous writer who likes abuse for its own sake. Johnson is not. He raises the tone a good deal, cutting out the scabrous detail, preferring lofty rebuke to pelting abuse. But, that apart, he sets about London as heartily as Juvenal had set about Rome. He speaks of it as a doomed city. Corruption, spreading from the top, has gone down to the very foundations. Only in country retirement can the traditional virtues be found.

On this side, the poem is of course hostile to London. And we have no need to question its sincerity. Lonely, insecure, aghast at much of what he saw, Johnson would obviously experience moods of revulsion from the city. These moods would flow strongly enough into his measured couplets and dense, emphatic language – as well as fitting in amicably with Juvenal's diatribe. But on another level the poem welcomes London. In tone, in strategy, in the nature of its art, it is metropolitan. It signals an acceptance of the values of eighteenth-century civilization at their most urbane and sophisticated. It reminds us that Juvenal himself had no intention of living anywhere but in the Rome he thrashed so hard.

In this dual nature the poem is true to its author. Johnson always saw London as a heartless city, where those who fell were trampled without mercy. At the same time he always accepted it at the level of intellect and art. He once remarked to Boswell that there was more 'learning and science' within ten miles of where they were sitting than could be found in all the rest of the country – including, no doubt, Oxford and Cambridge. In view of the vast amount of scholarly and literary work that went on in country parsonages, the remark is (quantitatively) dubious. But in London as an intellectual and artistic centre Johnson never ceased to believe; and his poem *London*, satiric though it is on one level, is at another level a gesture of support for London 'culture' and a calculated attempt to interest a London audience.

This meant, among other things, that it was almost bound to be strongly political. At that time the struggles of rival factions engrossed everyone's attention, or at any rate every Londoner's. The long opposition to Sir Robert Walpole was gathering to a head; England was about to plunge into the 'War of Jenkins's Ear', against Spain, whose disappointing progress would in fact be one of the causes that toppled Walpole. Johnson was at this time seeing a good deal of Richard Savage, a man of violently unbalanced views on most things, and they encouraged one another in a heated opposition to the Walpole administration. That he himself regarded *London* as a bold political satire is shown by his offering to alter any passage that Cave felt particularly uneasy about. Cave does not seem to have taken him up on this; perhaps the poem was not so vitriolic as its author thought it. Extreme, however, it certainly was.

Johnson was at this time going through that stage, experienced by most spirited young men, of violent dissatisfaction with the prevailing authority. When we are young, and before we have had to try exercising authority ourselves, we find it blissfully easy to see the weak points of any system of government and to magnify them into blunders and crimes. Johnson himself, in later life, wrote with high tolerant irony of 'that indistinct and headstrong ardour for liberty which a man of genius always catches when he enters the world, and always suffers to cool as he passes forward'. He himself always found it easier, in any case, to identify with the opposition rather than the established power, and at this time of his life he was hotly rebellious rather than judicially sceptical as he became later. He swallowed whole the accusations of corruption and perfidy which were so freely made against the government of the day and in particular against its leader, Sir Robert Walpole.

Walpole had, indeed, a resoundingly bad press. A number of gifted writers disliked him – always a misfortune for a public man – and with them a crowd of venal, poisonous scribblers. Much of the hostility was overdone. Walpole may not have been a likeable man; he belonged to that type, the technician of power with a cool head and a cool heart, which makes very few close friends; but he was not a disaster for the country, as his opponents claimed. He was just about the first prime minister in the modern sense, and he held his position for some twenty years, longer than any of his successors have done, during which time he managed to keep England out of wars and embroilments generally, while the prosperity and comfort of life steadily rose. Probably Walpole had so many enemies just because his Whig administration was solidly powerful. The Tories were so outclassed that they scarcely bothered to attend the sessions of Parliament, and this monolithic pressure inevitably had a fissiparous effect on the Whig party: factions and splinter groups appeared, the most notable taking the name of 'Patriots', and joined with the grumbling remnants of the Tory party to keep up a constant harassment of Walpole.

It is clear that, in his present unsettled state, the widespread strident abuse of Walpole and the government fell like music on Johnson's ears. He was in a mood for scolding and haranguing; partly because life had not so far treated him kindly and partly because, like many another young man newly arrived on the scene, he was spoiling for a fight and ready to join in any pitched battles that happened to be going on. *London* had contained measured denunciation, in general terms, of the corruption of manners and morals, the decline of martial vigour and the old-fashioned hardy virtues, which Johnson chose to lay at the door of the Walpole administration. But he was soon to descend into the arena, to lay aside lofty art and pick up the weapons of direct controversy. In 1739, the year after *London*, he published two anonymous pamphets: *Marmor Norfolciense* and *A Compleat Vindication of the Licensers of the State*. Both were attacks on the administration, and both were in a vein of savage irony.

Marmor Norfolciense, 'the Norfolk Marble', adopts a simple scheme. In Walpole's home county, a mediaeval inscription has been discovered on a long-buried block of marble. After the usual circumstantial details of the finding of the marble and its laborious deciphering, Johnson gives a 'translation' into eighteenth-century satirical couplets. It turns out to be the expected jeremiad, in the form of a prophecy of the state that England will be in when the stone is uncovered. One couplet in particular was political dynamite:

> Then o'er the world shall discord stretch her wings,
> Kings change their laws, and kingdoms change their kings.

The reference to kingdoms changing their kings was calculated to flick the Hanoverian dynasty on the raw. Many Englishmen still felt that they had no sufficient title to the throne, that they had been arbitrarily brought in from Germany and could be just as arbitrarily sent back there. Michael Johnson, as we saw, had regretted the dispossession of the Stuarts and though, like a sensible tradesman, he went along with the new settlement that brought stability to the country without noticeably curtailing its freedom, he did so with no relish. His son's feelings, round about this time, were more edgy. It was to be another twenty years before Samuel Johnson could feel himself fully reconciled to the House of Hanover. But to challenge it directly, even to cast as much doubt on its stability as is cast by that couplet, was distinctly imprudent in 1739.

Like most controversial writing, *Marmor Norfolciense* appealed strongly to those who found their own opinions mirrored in it. Alexander Pope, who as a Catholic born in the very year 1688 would have no tenderness for the political arrangements of his lifetime, found it 'very humorous'; several opposition papers mentioned it favourably. Today it is unreadable, though slightly less so than Johnson's next controversial musket-ball, *A Compleat Vindication*. This is a tongue-in-cheek statement of support for the action of the Lord Chamberlain in banning a play by Henry Brooke, *Gustavus Vasa*, which had offended by its libertarian sentiments and faintly revolutionary tinge. The pamphlet mockingly purports to come from a spokesman of the government, who utters the usual reactionary opinions with an air of impatient disbelief in the good faith of people who talk about freedom of speech or inalienable human rights.

Cave published neither of these efforts. As a cautious man, he did not care to stir up a wasps' nest, and in any case he had his own problems with the law. Since July 1732 he had been making a feature of reporting the debates in

Parliament. The idea had originally come from one of his rivals, *The London Magazine*, but Cave had quickly seen its possibilities and taken it up. In those early days, the debates had been roughly reassembled from notes taken in the public gallery, and simplified by giving to two or three principal speakers a variety of arguments put forward by lesser-known members. A perfunctory veiling of identities went as far as printing W——le for Walpole, P-lh-m for Pelham, etc., but it was clear that no one expected to be prosecuted. The House of Commons had gone on record with a resolution to the effect that it was a breach of privilege to make known any of its proceedings, but there was a general belief that this prohibition obtained only during the actual session. When Parliament was in recess, journalists believed, the debates of the past few months could safely be published.

All this changed on 13 April 1738, when the House of Commons unanimously adopted a resolution that it was 'a notorious breach of the privilege of this House' to make public any of its debates, 'as well during the recess as the sitting of Parliament'. This would appear to have put Cave into a quandary. But the ingenious *London Magazine* quickly came up with a solution, and once more Cave followed suit. The *London*'s method was to describe the debates of a political club of young noblemen and gentlemen, who hoped one day to enter public life and were preparing themselves by debating questions of the day. Headed 'Proceedings of the Political Club', the series managed to make public the main outline of what was going on in Parliament.

Cave, with the ready assistance of his staff, promptly went one better. Drawing on the vogue of Swift's *Gulliver's Travels*, which had been published in 1726, he began in June 1738 a series which boldly transferred the Mother of Parliaments to Lilliput. There, the little men debated matters of the day in two chambers, Hurgoes (Lords) and Clinabs (Commons). At the end of 1739 the magazine published a key to all the fictitious names.

Exactly how much of this was suggested by Johnson we cannot now establish. But it seems reasonable to suppose that he, one of the liveliest and most creative people at St John's Gate, would have played a leading part in setting up this zestful exercise, partly in mockery and partly in the assertion of democratic rights. The series led off with an amusing narrative of how the grandson of the original Captain Gulliver undertook his own voyage to Lilliput and the state of affairs he found there. And this, at least, reads very like something written by the early Johnson.

At first the actual writing-up of the debates had been assigned to Guthrie. But right from the moment of that reorganization of 1738 the probability is that Johnson helped him, and finding nuggets of Johnson in the Debates for 1738–40 has become a fascinating parlour game for scholars. In 1741 controversy ceases because in that year Johnson took over the sole authorship and continued it till March 1744.

These Parliamentary Debates are an important part of Johnson's work. On the score of length alone, and even allowing for the uncertainty as to how much he actually wrote, they amount to well over half a million words. To compose so much, and so fast, was necessarily to put on journalistic muscle. According to Sir John Hawkins, the only one of his biographers who actually knew him at this time, it was Johnson's practice to shut himself in a room at St John's Gate, alone except for the printer's devil who ran between him and the waiting compositor, and write his material 'faster than most persons could have transcribed that quantity'. But at no time of Johnson's life, either now or later, did rapid composition mean thin or ill-considered work. It was simply a product of his incredible power of concentration. The Debates are, in fact, very highly finished.

Johnson was, of course, composing the speeches rather than reporting them. His own account of the matter, as recorded in Murphy's *Life*, was that

> I never had been in the gallery of the House of Commons but once. Cave had interest with the doorkeepers. He, and the persons employed under him, gained him admittance; they brought away the subject of discussion, the names of the speakers, the side they took, and the order in which they rose, together with notes of arguments advanced in the course of the debate. The whole was afterwards communicated to me, and I composed the speeches in the form which they now have in the Parliamentary Debates.

'Afterwards' is right. There was no question of rushing the Debates to an impatient public. Cave's policy was never to publish during the session of Parliament in which the debate had taken place, so that months would go by in which Johnson had the material before him. In one celebrated case, the Commons debate on a motion of lack of confidence in Walpole, his account did not appear until two years after the event. Clearly, the rapidity of execution was forced on him not by a reporter's tight schedule but by the historian's need to think his material into a coherent shape before beginning to write. For this he needed all the time he could get; and when we add his constitutional inability to begin work at anything until the last possible minute we have sufficient reason why the Debates were composed rapidly; but they had been thought out carefully and closely.

On the same occasion when Johnson described to Murphy and others his method of working on the Debates, he added in jocular self-mockery, 'I took care that the Whig dogs should not have the best of it.' Here again we have one of those Johnsonian *mots* that 'everybody knows'. Ask the average person – I mean, of course, the average literate person who has heard of Johnson at all – what he knows about the 'Debates in the Senate of Lilliput', and after wrinkling his brow for a few moments he will recall something about not letting the Whig dogs have the best of it. The story has done its share in building up the popular notion of Johnson as an entrenched, reactionary bigot. In fact, his impartiality is remarkable. On the evidence of *London*, and of the hot-headed rhetoric in *Marmor Norfolciense* and *A Compleat Vindication*, one might have expected the Debates to keep up the 'Patriot' line of implacable hostility to Walpole and the stacking of the cards against him. On the contrary. When Johnson comes to report (for instance) the debate in the Commons in which Walpole's opponents finally felt strong enough to confront him and heave him out (13 February 1741), he employs the full power of his pen to give Walpole a speech in his own defence which is dignified, reticent, and extremely effective. Archdeacon Coxe, in his *Memoirs of the Life and Administration of Sir Robert Walpole*, a careful and semi-official work in three volumes (1798), reports the same speech quite differently, making Walpole defend himself at length, with a mass of detail, and in a tone of querulous resentment. Johnson gives him a speech worthy of a character in some great stately drama of political life. Rising at last, after speaker upon speaker has accused him of corruption and personal enrichment, Walpole begins with a brief nod of thanks to the few who have defended him:

> The gentlemen who have already spoken in my favour have indeed freed me from the necessity of wearying the House with a long defence, since their knowledge and abilities are so great that I can hope to add nothing to their arguments, and their zeal and friendship so ardent, that I shall speak with less warmth in my own cause.

As for the rich gifts he has allegedly obtained from the Crown:

> All that has been given me is a little house at a small distance from this city, worth about seven hundred pounds, which I obtained that I might enjoy the quiet of retirement without remitting my attendance on my office.

Walpole then glances down at the star of the Order of the Garter; it is normally given only to persons of royal blood or the higher ranks of the nobility and, indeed, after Walpole the next commoner to wear this star was Sir Winston Churchill. He goes on – that is, Johnson makes him go on:

> The little ornament upon my shoulder I had indeed forgot, but this surely cannot be mentioned as a proof of avarice; nor, though it may be looked on with envy and indignation in another place [i.e. the House of Lords], can it be supposed to raise any resentment in this House, where many must be pleased to see these honours which their ancestors have worn restored again to the Commons.

Walpole-Johnson ends with a calm pride:

> I shall wait the decision of the House without any other solicitude than for the honour of their counsels.

It is a brilliant performance, intensely dramatic and intensely flattering to the man Johnson had so vehemently abused a few years earlier. Why the change? Why the decision to let this leader of the 'Whig dogs' have such a fair crack of the whip?

Part of the answer lies in the very nature of the work. For everyone except the most brainwashed hack, it is an enlightening experience to be immersed in the actual process of political decision. The young enthusiast soon learns that doctrinal purity, the rigid adherence to a 'line', the inflexible refusal to dilute one's ideological brew are not always and everywhere the virtues he took them to be. The spokesmen for his own side lose their wings and harp, those on the opposite benches their horns and tail. Of course an impatient man will come away from the experience still impatient. Charles Dickens was a Parliamentary reporter in his youth, and it seems to have left him with a contempt for the confusion and leisureliness of democratic assemblies. But while Dickens was a gallery reporter, using shorthand to put down everybody's wafflings, Johnson was processing a sheaf of notes into an exchange of oratory worthy of Thucydides. The task was one that continually drove his mind back on to political principle. How shall a society govern itself? What is the degree of liberty that best produces happiness? What are a man's rights and what are his duties? These questions were steadily before him. If he emerged from the experience a 'conservative', suspicious of utopian and libertarian views of the human condition, he remained also a strong democrat and an egalitarian. In 1739 he wrote in one of his *Gentleman's Magazine* pieces ('To Mr Urban') that 'the happiness of twenty thousand is of twenty thousand times more value than the happiness of one' – a Johnsonian anticipation of Jeremy Bentham's 'greatest happiness of the greatest number'. The years of immersion in political thought did not shake that position.

Johnson's formal education, at Oxford, was cut short after thirteen months. But in the three years of writing the Debates he found a better education than money could have bought. It was a training for pragmatic wisdom. The depth and solidity of his later judgements about politics and society can be traced to these long sessions at St John's Gate, with his head down to the facts: who precisely had said what precisely, and what happened as a result.

But it must now be confessed that in order to deal with the period of the Debates as a whole, and not split the discussion of so important a matter into splinters, we have run slightly ahead of our narrative. Johnson commenced sole author of the Debates in 1741. By that time he was already a different Johnson from the young firebrand of 1738 with his 'indistinct and headstrong ardour for liberty'. Two sobering experiences had intervened, both of them in 1739. One was the departure of Savage from London that summer, an event at which we have already glanced briefly. The other is the extended visit to the Midlands which Johnson began in the autumn of 1739 and continued until the spring of 1740.

This visit is important in a number of respects. To begin with, it disposes finally of the popular stereotype of Johnson as the delighted Londoner, the ancestor of all those provincials who consider their arrival in the metropolis as the beginning of 'real' life, and the years that went before as a waste of breath. Even though Johnson had begun to swim above the tide of London, even though he had found employment, made friends, published work that had attracted notice, he was still ready to give it all up in favour of schoolmastering in the country. The immediate object of his visit was that he had heard of a vacancy – the headmastership of the Grammar School at Appleby, Leicestershire. When he failed to get the job he still did not return, but lingered on month after month, while Tetty waited and wondered in London. Part of this may have been the familiar Johnsonian inertia, the unwillingness to heave himself out of any chair into which he happened to have sunk. But most of it, beyond doubt, was that he liked the Midlands and enjoyed the company he found there. Small wonder. These were gifted and amiable people; less frenetic than Savage, less tradesmanly than Cave, more tolerant of his fads and fancies than his wife. There must have been times, during that autumn and winter, when he thought that he had at last found the circle of friends he had been looking for since boyhood.

First, however, came the rebuff. The trustees of the Appleby Grammar School did not require his services. Probably they would not have taken him in any case, since by this time his unsuccessful record as a pedagogue would be common knowledge in the Midlands, but there was also a formal bar: the post called for a man with the degree of M.A. An effort was made to get over this hurdle; Pope, who had no knowledge of Johnson except that he had read with approval *London* and *Marmor Norfolciense*, wrote on his own initiative to Lord Gower to enlist his aid as a prominent Midland landowner who might be expected to take an interest in a gifted man from his district. Gower did his best; from his seat at Trentham he wrote to a friend in Dublin, asking if he, the friend, could approach Dean Swift and see if a Dublin M.A. could be fixed for Johnson. (Why Pope, who was a personal friend of Swift's, did not write to him with this request is not clear.) Gower wrote of Johnson to his Dublin acquaintance:

> They say he is not afraid of the strictest examination, though he is of so long a journey, and will venture it, if the Dean thinks it necessary, choosing rather to die upon the road, than be starved to death translating for booksellers, which has been his only subsistence for some time past.

That unexpectedly vivid image, *rather to die upon the road, than be starved to death translating for booksellers*, stands out conspicuously in His Lordship's dignified but undistinguished prose style. It sounds like a phrase that has come to his ears from Johnson's own talk. If so, it is a strong indication of Johnson's preference for a settled position in country society as against the up-and-down life of a London man of letters.

In any event, nothing happened. No response came from Swift, and the headmastership went, predictably, to someone else. By the end of 1739 the matter was settled and there was no reason why Johnson should not have gone back to London and Tetty. But he stayed on, comfortably installed as a guest in the house of John Taylor, the same faithful friend who had hastened across the street from Christ Church to Pembroke with reports of Bateman's lectures. Taylor was at that time in the process of making up his mind to switch professions, from the law to the church, and was in fact ordained the following summer and presented with his first benefice by – of all people – Johnson's old enemy Sir Wolstan Dixie. He had a large and comfortable house at Ashbourne, and while he did not get on at all well with his wife their domestic jangling, if any, did not disturb Johnson's repose. Besides, Taylor introduced him to the cluster of families who made up the gentry of the neighbourhood: the Meynells, the Fitzherberts, the Boothbys and the Astons.

All of these families had their own particular attractions for Johnson. At the Meynells' house at Bradley, there was the amusing if sometimes terrifying figure of Littleton Meynell, the head of the family, an English country squire straight out of folklore, with his horses and hounds (to this day one of the most famous of Midland hunts is called 'the Meynell'), his irascibility, his religious scepticism, and his remark quoted by Johnson years afterwards: 'For anything I see, foreigners are fools.' There was his wife, a model of sweetness and piety; and their eldest daughter Mary, whom Johnson, at no time a male chauvinist, later described as the most intelligent human being he had ever met. Mary Meynell married a pleasant, unassuming man called Fitzherbert, who lived nearby at Tissington; and, probably at their house, Johnson made the acquaintance of Sir Brook Boothby and his sister Hill, grandchildren of Sir William Boothby who, back in the 1680s, had been an enthusiastic customer of Michael Johnson's. He greatly admired Hill Boothby; in 1756 he told John Taylor that this spinster, one year his elder, was the only woman with whom he ever corresponded regularly – and very affectionate letters they were, addressing her as 'Dearest Madam', 'My Dearest Dear', 'My Sweet Angel'. In these early days their friendship had not ripened to quite this extent; but Johnson was always susceptible, and it is clear that this attractive and witty woman, not yet thirty, could make his heart beat agreeably fast.

Less than two years after Johnson's visit, the clergyman-novelist Richard Graves was appointed to a living at Tissington, and the life he found there was to provide him with a chapter or two in his amusing and good-humoured novel *The Spiritual Quixote*. Several local characters appear in thin disguise, and among them Hill Boothby, whom Graves jestingly canonizes as 'Miss Sainthill'. She is shown as deeply pious and robustly combative. When 'Colonel Rappee', a cowardly ruffian whose chief military exploit has been to run away faster than anyone else at the Battle of Prestonpans, teasingly insults her, choosing as targets both her religious principles and her appearance, she quickly chops him down:

> As soon as prayers were ended, Colonel Rappee again made his appearance; but was rallied by Miss Sainthill (a very sensible maiden lady, a friend and companion of Lady Forester's), on 'his fondness for private meditation, and the care he took to avoid all appearance of hypocrisy'. Rappee said 'he knew no reason why a man could not say his prayers as well in private as in public, in a walk upon the terrace as well as in a closet; that religion was a mere personal affair, and the like.' He hinted, however, 'that he might have as much true devotion, as those who were always canting about religion, and pretended to set up for Reformers.'
>
> Miss Sainthill replied, 'that, to be sure, people might say their prayers in any place, or in any posture, and even in a warm bed; but she could not but think there was a natural decency of behaviour due to the Supreme Being, as well as to our fellow creatures; and she was afraid' (she said) 'those who

deferred their prayers till they lay down upon their pillows (as she fancied the Colonel did) very frequently fell asleep without saying them at all.'

'Well', says the Colonel, 'there is one part of my devotions which I shall never forget; and that is, thanksgiving. I have always thanked God for three things.' 'Pray let me hear those curious particulars', says Miss Sainthill, 'I suppose the first is that you are not an old maid.' 'No,' says Rappee, 'the first is that I was not born in Russia.' 'What! because you are afraid of the cold I suppose?' says Miss Sainthill. 'No', says the Colonel, 'because I am afraid of the knout, and do not like arbitrary governments.' 'Well, and what is the second particular?' 'Why, that I was not bred a cheesemonger.' 'What! because you do not love the smell of cheese?' says Miss Sainthill; but, 'For a like reason, you should not have been bred a soldier', continued she. 'Why so?' (says the Colonel). 'Why, because you do not love the smell of gunpowder.'

Rappee bowed, and smiled; but said 'he was most thankful for the third particular.' 'And, pray, what may that be?' says Miss Sainthill. 'Why, that I have not a very *long nose*', cries the Colonel. Miss Sainthill courtesied, and took a long pinch of snuff, being conscious how liberal Nature had been to *her* in that respect, and being willing to give Rappee a short triumph by inviting a laugh in his favour at her own expense; of which he was not a little conceited. Miss Sainthill, however, retorted, and said, 'A long nose would certainly be very inconvenient to the Colonel in the day of battle, especially if he should ever face the Highlanders again; as it would be more exposed to the stroke of a broad-sword.'

Reading such a passage one is struck by how much freedom these eighteenth-century ladies enjoyed. England had not yet entered the long Victorian penumbra during which eligible misses were supposed to simper over a fan and faint at the least hint of anything that outraged their delicacy, while older women were expected to withdraw into a gaggle and talk about children and servants. In memoirs and novels of Johnson's time, there is a wonderfully bracing directness in the social relationships between men and women. And one sees it as clearly in this cultivated provincial circle as in the world of Mrs Montagu or Charlotte Lennox or Sarah Siddons.

If Johnson admired Mary Meynell, if he something more than admired Hill Boothby, he was knocked completely over by 'Molly' Aston. Sir Thomas Aston, Bart, had one son and eight daughters; one of the daughters, Catharine, was married to Henry Hervey, the polished rake for whose courtesies Johnson had shown such gratitude, and he had seen her fairly regularly in the previous winter when paying calls at their London house. Another daughter, Magdalen, had become the young wife of the middle-aged Gilbert Walmesley, and was installed in the Palace at Lichfield, that scene of so many of Johnson's happiest hours; doubtless he would be often there again now, renewing his friendship with Walmesley and perhaps envying his solid matrimonial comfort. Mary Aston, generally known as Molly, was not yet married, though in the end she bestowed herself on a sea captain. Johnson long outlived Molly Aston but he never forgot her; 'Molly,' he said to Hester Thrale, 'was a beauty and a scholar, and a wit and a Whig . . . she was the loveliest creature I ever saw!!!' Her one surviving portrait shows a face handsome rather than beautiful, shining auburn hair, a long smooth neck, and eyes in which one reads intelligence and challenge. If she had lived two centuries later and known Yeats rather than Johnson, there would probably have been immortal poems about her, for she was the type Yeats generally chose to hymn: 'Pallas Athene in that straight back and arrogant head.'

These people – well-to-do without having money to throw away, well bred without being too grand to know a bookseller's son, well read and cultivated without being a nest of squabbling intellectuals – made up the kind of educated provincial *milieu* in which Johnson had his deepest roots. He himself belonged to the shabbier underside of this society, because of his father's lack of success in trade. Yet the mere fact that Michael Johnson *was* a bookseller, however he may have failed to grow rich by it, is evidence of a book-buying, cultivated society in the Midlands at that time. And now his brilliant elder son had the freedom of that society. But too late. He was without a degree, and could get no post that would keep him in the district; he was married, and could not hope for an alliance with any of the attractive and respectable young ladies who now enjoyed his company and listened to his talk.

A weaker and less generous man might have been driven down into bitterness. In fact, Johnson accepted the situation and seems to have found this interlude calming and steadying. He kept up his friendship with Taylor, even though it was to be years before they could once again see each other regularly; and he found a warm place in his heart for the whole of that circle of families. And here we can begin to see why his political writing, once he found himself back at St John's Gate, was so much less virulent and partisan. He had always met with kindness and encouragement from comfortable Whigs like Gilbert Walmesley and the families of the Stourbridge district. Molly Aston was a Whig who, as he said, 'talked all in praise of liberty'. Taylor was a Whig. The Meynells, indeed, were Tories, which may have been one reason for Johnson's amused tolerance for earthy old Littleton Meynell, but most of these gentle, gracious, well-intentioned people were Whigs or Whiggishly inclined. Johnson was not tempted to emulate them; from his point of view, they were people whom life had handled with kid gloves, never putting their fine sentiments to the test of rough experience. But they cured him, finally, of his political acerbity, and though for the rest of his life he always used 'Whig' as a term of abuse he did so with a glitter of humour ('I see, Sir, you are a vile Whig,' etc., etc.). The remark about not letting 'the Whig dogs have the best of it' is typical of the rough jesting vein in which Johnson habitually spoke of his political opponents. Anyone who has met with real political rancour, the cold-eyed, tight-lipped unforgiving venom that politics so often breeds in modern people, can see the difference at once.

Happiness is a great sweetener of opinions, and during these months Johnson knew happiness. In later life, asked by Henry Thrale to name the happiest period of his past life, he replied that 'it was that year in which he spent one whole evening with Molly Aston. That indeed (said he) was not happiness, it was rapture; but the thoughts of it sweetened the whole year.' Thrale's widow, writing down this reminiscence, adds primly the evening was 'not past *tête à tête*, but in a select company, of which the present Lord Killmorey was one'. But, whether alone or not, Molly Aston's presence could throw Johnson into 'rapture'. Never again could he automatically declaim against Whigs.

The early months of 1740 were bitterly cold. But Johnson passed them comfortably enough with his mother at Lichfield. The house by the market place had settled down into a long twilight. Sarah Johnson was ostensibly running the business, but there was not much business to run. For company and support she had Tetty's daughter, Lucy, and her own faithful maid-companion, Kitty Chambers. The three of them took turns at answering the shop bell. According to Anna Seward, a Lichfield blue-stocking of a younger generation, Miss Porter was not above 'thanking a poor person who purchased from her a penny battledore'. One is glad to hear of it. As a daughter of her mother's, Lucy would have too much realism and good sense to engage in trade while keeping up the airs of a person who was too good for trade. But the detail about the penny battledore is also interesting. Odds and ends of this kind, one suspects, were more often passed over the counter these days than handsome calfbound volumes.

If the three ladies wondered what kept Sam for so long away from his wife, their speculations are not on record. Of Johnson's mother, in particular, there is virtually no remaining impression from this time. Probably, with one son more or less launched and the other in his untimely grave, she was quietly slipping out of life. Her last recorded utterance is a question she put to Samuel on his previous visit, when he came back to fetch Tetty away to London. Recalling her own one and only sight of the big city, when she took him to be touched by Queen Anne, she remembered how people jostled for the drier and cleaner strip of footpath that was nearest the wall and therefore furthest from the mud and sewage of the 'kennel'; and she asked Sam which category he belonged to – those who took the wall, or those who gave it. The detail came back to Johnson's mind many years later, when he himself was of a like age, and he mentioned it to Boswell as evidence of the progress of civilization. 'Now it is fixed that every man keeps to the right; or, if one is taking the wall, another yields it, and it is never a dispute.' His mother's memories came from a London that was disappearing even when he first went there: the turbulent, overgrown country town that Dryden had known, still full of people who could remember the Civil War, and the Plague, and the Fire, and the Dutch warships sailing up the Thames.

How long Johnson might have idled on in Lichfield and Ashbourne we cannot tell. Tetty, meanwhile, was still in Castle Street, Cavendish Square, wondering gloomily when she would see him again. Finally, in January, events took a hand. She fell over somehow and injured a tendon in her leg. Beyond doubt the accident really happened; but it is also likely that Tetty welcomed the occasion to write her husband a letter which would at last sting him into action.

> Dearest Tetty [Johnson hastily wrote]
> After hearing that you are in so much danger, as I apprehend from a hurt on a tendon, I shall be very uneasy till I know that you are recovered, and beg that you will omit nothing that can contribute to it. You have already suffered more than I can bear to reflect on, and I hope more than either of us shall suffer again.

Clearly he was feeling guilty at leaving her alone for so long; and his next thought is to reassure her that once he is back with her he will stay back.

> One part at least I have often flattered myself we shall avoid for the future, our troubles will surely never separate us more.

The letter goes on to speak of money. She is to get a good surgeon – more than one, if she likes. There is money available; he will send her twenty pounds on Monday.

In this we know that he was confident. He had, that very day, raised eighty pounds by mortgaging the Lichfield house to his old acquaintance Theophilus Levet. Johnson and his mother both signed the document, she as owner of the property, he as 'son and heir'. With the money firmly promised, he proceeded to reassure Tetty on more personal matters.

> Of the time which I have spent from thee, and of my dear Lucy and other affairs, my heart will be at ease on Monday to give thee a particular account. Be assured, my dear girl, that I have seen nobody in these rambles upon which I have been forced, that has not contributed to confirm my esteem and affection for thee, though that esteem and affection only contributed to increase my unhappiness when I reflected that the most amiable woman in the world was exposed by my means to miseries which I could not relieve.
> I am my charming love Yours
> SAM: JOHNSON

It is impossible to miss the defensive note here. He is conscious of having neglected her for too long, even though he has been 'forced' on 'these rambles'. (What rambles? Was it not just a matter of going to Appleby and, when the job did not materialize, straight back?) However, all will be well in the future. And he has other news too. Someone has written from London to say that *Irene* might be put on after all. 'Mr Fleetwood promises to give a promise in writing that it shall be the first next season, if it cannot be introduced now.' Ah, those promises that people promise to make when they get round to it! Production of *Irene* was still nine years in the future.

From Johnson's undertaking to give his wife 'a particular account' of what he had been doing all this time, it is clear that he had been neglecting to write adequate letters to her. Perhaps, even, that he had not written at all. And if word got back to her that he had been enjoying the company of Molly Aston Tetty would have uneasy thoughts for company by her solitary fireside in Castle Street. For of Molly she was unfeignedly jealous, as we know from the famous story that Johnson told to Mrs Thrale.

> She was jealous to be sure (said he), and teased me sometimes when I would let her; and one day, as a fortune-telling gipsy passed us when we were walking out in company with two or three friends in the country, she made the wench look at my hand, but soon repented her curiosity; for (says the gipsy) your heart is divided, Sir, between a Betty and a Molly: Betty loves you best, but you take most delight in Molly's company: when I turned about to laugh, I saw my wife was crying. Pretty charmer! She had no reason!

Exactly when this country walk took place we cannot be sure. Johnson may have already known and admired Miss Aston before he and Tetty moved to London. Or the gipsy may have met them in a lane outside London itself, at some time after the 'blissful' evening he never forgot. But when Johnson fondly said of his wife that she had 'no reason' to weep over his feelings for Molly he was talking like every husband who is convinced that things would be all right if his wife would only be reasonable. While Johnson's morality was far too strict to allow of his deserting his wife, it is also true that Tetty was insecure and that she had reason to be. Even before this long separation, she had recently lived through a bad period. The details cannot now be reconstructed, but it is clear that for long stretches in 1738 and 1739 the Johnsons were not living together. Sir John Hawkins thought that they were apart at the time of Johnson's friendship with Savage. What probably happened was that Tetty found the smoke and stench of London unpleasant, and Sam found lodgings for her at Hampstead, then well out in the country, where she had for company Mrs Desmoulins, the daughter of Johnson's godfather, Dr Swinfen. In pure air and with someone to talk to, she might have been happy enough. But she must have wondered what her husband was doing. And we know what, for a good deal of the time, he was doing. He was living in a pattern of Bohemianism so extreme that it bordered on vagrancy, treading the streets of night-town with thieves and prostitutes. And beside him, inseparable as a shadow, pouring out wild opinions and wilder stories, went that strangest of strange characters, poet, conversationalist, sponger and freeloader *par excellence*, 'the Bastard', Richard Savage.

CHAPTER 7

'The Friend of Goodness'

Life was hard in those winters of 1738 and 1739; not only for Johnson but for all the underpaid, overburdened creatures whose fate it was to scratch out a living with their pens. The conditions of authorship have always been difficult, but during the second quarter of the eighteenth century they were monstrously so. The class that had come to power in England after the Revolution of 1688 had at first been willing to treat the literary man with respect and channel some of their wealth his way; the generation of Addison and Rowe, Swift and Gay and Prior had on the whole been treated well by the rich and aristocratic. But as the century went on it became clear that writers were not, after all, much use to the governing power; there were plenty of professional politicians who for suitable reward would fight one's battles more effectively. Large sums could still be made, it is true, by newspaper writing of an openly partisan nature; Walpole had on his payroll a number of propagandists who did quite well out of him, and when his dealings were investigated by a Secret Committee they reported that in a single decade, from 1731 to 1741, he had paid out £50,077 18s to the writers and printers of newspapers. But, except for the fact that he writes words down on paper, the 'scribbler for a party', as Johnson put it, hardly qualifies as a writer at all. And the position of the real writer – the poet, novelist, biographer, critic, translator, essayist – was at its most precarious during these years. The age of munificent patronage, of well-paid government posts going automatically to men of literary reputation, had faded almost over the horizon; the new daylight, that of the direct relationship of author and public, was as yet no more than a dapple in the sky. As communications improved, as printing became cheaper and faster, as the growth of trade fostered a more comfortable and literate middle class, there came into being that triangle of author, publisher and reader which gave a shape to literary endeavour from the middle of the eighteenth century to the middle of the twentieth, when it collapsed again into a chaos of subsidiary rights and complicated side deals. Johnson lived to see the era of the triangle. Not that he was ever entirely a man of the new order. He believed passionately in the more free and fluid relationship of writer to reader, but he never lived in that world as totally as Scott or Dickens was to do. Most of his writing was commissioned in one way or another; he was always working for some employer or group of employers who had suggested the job and agreed a payment for it. This put him a step or two away from patronage but still not quite in the position of the writer who launches his books out on the choppy sea of public favour, not knowing whether they will be wrecked or bring home a cargo. And there was also his pension, which we will come to in due time. What concerns us at the moment is that though Johnson lived until well within the era of a direct, trading relationship between the writer and the public his early years were spent in the unsheltered epoch when neither the patron nor the ordinary book-buying reader was doing anything to help the writer. A dramatist, once estab-lished, could wring an uncertain income out of 'the players'; for other writers the only hope of avoiding starvation was to stand well with 'the booksellers', a race of men who combined the functions of printing, publishing, bookselling and the dissemination of news. One and all they drove a hard bargain. We have Johnson's own testimony that Cave would buy lines by the hundred 'and expect the long hundred', but he was a model of generosity by comparison with some of his *confrères*: a man named Gardner, for instance, who signed up two authors, Rolt and Christopher Smart, to produce a monthly miscellany. This was to cost sixpence and they were to have a third of the profits between them. It sounds good until one gets to the small print: neither man was to write any-thing else during the period of the contract, and it was to last ninety-nine years. Small wonder that the lurid miseries of this period provided Macaulay with the material for one of the liveliest pages in his *Essays*.

All that is squalid and miserable might now be summed up in the word Poet. . . . Even the poorest pitied him; and they well might pity him. For if their condition was equally abject, their aspirings were not equally high, nor their sense of insult equally acute. To lodge in a garret up four pairs of stairs, to dine in a cellar among footmen out of a place, to translate ten hours a day for the wages of a ditcher, to be hunted by bailiffs from one haunt of beggary and pestilence to another, from Grub Street to St George's Fields, and from St George's Fields to the alleys behind St Martin's church, to sleep on a bulk in June, and amidst the ashes of a glasshouse in December, to die in an hospital and to be buried in a parish vault, was the fate of more than one writer who, if he had lived thirty years earlier, would have been admitted to the sittings of the Kitcat or the Scriblerus Club, would have sat in Parliament, and would have been entrusted with embassies to the High Allies; who, if he had lived in our time, would have found encouragement scarcely less munificent in Albemarle Street or in Paternoster Row.

Or, as Oliver Goldsmith put it more succinctly and from bitter personal experience, in his *Enquiry into the Present State of Polite Learning*:

The poet's poverty is a standing topic of contempt. His writing for bread is an unpardonable offence. Perhaps of all mankind an author in these times is used most hardly. We keep him poor, and yet revile his poverty. Like angry parents who correct their children till they cry, and then correct them for crying, we reproach him for living by his wit, and yet allow him no other means to live.

'Grub Street' has long enjoyed the status of a semi-proverbial expression; what Tin Pan Alley is to music, Grub Street is to literature. But it was, in Johnson's time, a real street in the Moorfields district, and not yet ashamed of its name – there was, for instance, a *Grub Street Journal*. The street was inhabited by printers and booksellers, who found it convenient to concentrate in one neighbourhood; and in the cramped, ill-furnished upper floors of their premises were to be found the shivering and peevish figures who provided the pabulum for their growing industry; ragged, hungry and thirsty; resentful of the wretched hand their society had dealt them, yet, like literary people of every epoch, unable to make common cause and ready at any time to bite and tear one another while their real enemies stood smiling by. These are the men whose names are mentioned in the *Dunciad* and its long, melancholy train of notes, their talents wasted in mean employment and puny quarrels, their gifts turned sour, their condition a disgrace to the society that tolerated it.

Johnson never actually lived in Grub Street but he shared its life, and some of the most picturesquely wretched of its inhabitants were his associates and friends. In the security of his later years, among people who had no first-hand notion of what he was talking about, Johnson would occasionally mention an episode that came back to his mind. Characteristically, he never mentioned his own privations; the story always concerned someone else. The poet Samuel Boyse, for instance, who was often driven to pawn his clothes to get something to eat; the trouble was that when the clothes were duly accepted, and the pawn ticket and a few shillings were in his hand, Boyse would send out for delicacies like truffles and mushrooms to sweeten his bare existence. On one such occasion Johnson put himself to a great deal of trouble to help Boyse get his clothes back; 'the sum', Johnson later recalled, 'was collected by sixpences, at a time when to me sixpence was a serious consideration'. The clothes came out of pawn; two days later they went in again, and Boyse was sitting up in bed covered with a blanket, in which he had punched two holes for his arms so that he could write. Scamp as he was, Boyse was a gifted man who deserved a better fate. He could write verse almost as fast as prose, he had an ear for music and some talent for drawing; he turned his hand to translating from the Dutch and the French, and modernized some tales of Chaucer, for which he was paid threepence a line; he was the complete literary journeyman, and his reward was to die a pauper and lie in an unmarked grave. Even the circumstances of his death, in 1749, were in doubt; one report said that he had been run over by a coach when lying drunk in the street, another that he had been found dead of starvation, pen in hand, in his bed.

Such a life does not encourage prudence and careful budgeting. Boyse was not the only Grub Street inhabitant who reached for such luxuries as came within his grasp, and to hell with tomorrow. Johnson's steadiness, his sturdy root of Staffordshire commonsense, protected him from sliding into incurable habits of improvidence and self-indulgence. But it is noteworthy that these were always among the faults he found easiest to forgive. He never looked down on unfortunate people who snatched at immediate pleasure to make their lives tolerable. Nothing, for instance, irritated him more than to be told that it was a mistake to give money to beggars because they only spend it on drink. He always took the attitude that if you push a man down into the gutter, you must expect him to relish the pleasures of the gutter rather than have no pleasures at all. Everyone who knows anything about Johnson remembers his famous rebuke to someone who talked in this strain, as recorded by Mrs Thrale: 'Life is a pill which none of us can bear to swallow without gilding; yet for the poor we delight in stripping it still barer, and are not ashamed to show even visible displeasure if ever the bitter taste is taken from their mouths.' It was a lesson he had learnt from the poor, during the time when he was one of them.

Feckless, disreputable, these men and women commonly were; and Johnson, the abstainer from drink, the married man with high standards of sexual morality, did not let their ways become his ways. Yet he never despised or blamed them. And to the biggest tearaway of all, the most unteachable, irre-deemable Bohemian drifter, he opened his heart in love, admiration and pity. Richard Savage was, arguably, the most hopeless case among all Johnson's acquaintances at this time. A rakehell, a sponger who had long ago decided that it was the privilege of lesser men to empty their pockets for his support, a self-pitying martyr whose grievances, real or imagined, had left him with a sense of injury and resentment that never slept for an instant, Savage was at first sight a strange companion for the strong, honest, realistic Johnson. Was he really, as he claimed, the natural son of the Countess of Macclesfield? It hardly matters: what is important is that he believed himself to be. If his claim was false, it still went far deeper than a mere cynical imposture. If Savage had dreamed it up, he had long since forgotten having done so, for he had woven the story into the fabric of his being. Every thought that came into his head, every emotion that shook his frail form, was directly related to his sense of being the rightful heir to wealth and rank, cruelly cheated and dispossessed.

Johnson, too, believed it. Pacing the streets at Savage's side, he listened with tingling sympathy as his friend poured out the tragic story: how his mother had put him out to the care of a poor woman, with instructions that he was never to learn of his parentage; how she had further seen to it that he was apprenticed to a shoemaker; how, on the death of his foster mother, he went through her few belongings and found letters which told him the true situation; how he appealed to his mother's natural feelings, with no result; how she banished him from her presence, repulsed him from her door, gave orders that he was never to come near her. Other episodes of complicated misfortune followed. Savage was befriended by one person after another, as the story of his sufferings aroused pity and the increasing evidences of his literary gift awakened admiration; he was supported in turn by Sir Richard Steele, by the actor Wilks, by the actress Mrs Oldfield, by his mother's kinsman Lord Tyrconnel, finally by Queen Caroline herself, who granted him a pension: in each case the misfortune that pursued him everywhere managed to intervene between him and his benefactors. He fell out with one friend and well-wisher after another and was banished from their generosity. Even the pension from

Queen Caroline came to an end at her death, while a firm promise from Walpole that he should have the next profitable sinecure that fell vacant was never honoured and was probably not sincerely meant in the first place.

Savage was, in fact, typical of all those brilliant and charming *ratés* who never lack friends and never fail to wear them out by incessant demands and outrageous behaviour. At the time Johnson knew him, he had run through most of those who were in a position to give him substantial help, but still he could count on a long-suffering circle at whose tables he could feed himself up, while a supply of drinks was never further away than the nearest tavern, for he was a fascinating talker and could hold any stranger in conversation as the bottle emptied. Johnson, with no more money in his pocket than Savage, did not come into either of these categories; what he provided was companionship and an attentive ear for Savage's flow of anecdote. At forty-one, Savage was not very much older than Johnson, but he had been about town much longer, had mixed on terms of equality with the great and the famous, and generally had looked on the spectacle of life from vantage points not yet attained by the Lichfield bookseller's son. In particular, he had known well some of the most famous writers of the literary generation that was just passing its zenith – Pope, James Thomson, Steele. In their hours of talk, Johnson soaked up many details which in years to come would enrich his talk and his writing.

Their poverty was also a bond. Shared misfortune is a great forcing house of friendship, and before they had known each other very long Johnson and Savage had been hungry and cold together. For lack of money to go for a drink, they would walk the windy streets late at night, and on at least one occasion they had nowhere to sleep and were forced to keep moving till dawn round and round St James's Square. Stimulated by one another's company, buoyed up by their high-hearted friendship, they kept warm also by the heat of political ardour. Savage was a violent Opposition man, inveighing against Walpole and all his works; and Johnson remembered in later life how, that night, the two vagabond writers had vowed to 'stand by their country'.

Johnson loved and admired Savage, and for a complex of reasons. On a superficial level, the older man was universally allowed to have charming, courtly manners; and Johnson, whose physical handicaps had put a smooth, graceful bearing for ever out of his reach, valued it all the more in others. Savage fascinated him in something like the same way as Harry Hervey had done. He also respected him as the veteran of many desperate hand-to-hand struggles with life. In a way their relationship must have been like that of Othello and Desdemona:

> She loved me for the dangers I had passed,
> And I loved her that she did pity them.

There were also deeper emotional reasons. Savage had, by his own account, been cruelly rejected by an unnatural mother. Now Johnson, as we have seen, had strong and ambivalent feelings towards his own mother. On the one hand, he naturally wished to love her. His ardent, generous nature always longed to love and be loved. But the fact remained that he had, as a child, turned to his mother with this longing and found himself bouncing off the wire mesh of her narrow, fussy anxiety.

This resentment of Sarah for her failure to give him love and emotional security was buttoned down tightly out of sight and watched over by an unsleeping censor. All the more eagerly did he listen to Savage's tirades against the mother who had similarly, and far more spectacularly, failed him. Chords which his own fingers were forbidden to touch became vibrant at the eloquent recital of Savage's wrongs.

How deep did Savage's influence go? Very deep, I think. His presence touched the hidden springs of Johnson's deep feelings, and may, here and there, have caused some strange streams to gush from the rock. He was, for some crucial months, closer to Johnson than anyone else was. Certainly closer than Tetty. She was asleep in her bed at Hampstead; or perhaps not sleeping, but reading romances and pouring herself stiff drinks, which is how old Robert Levet remembered her in later years. In any case, Johnson found the journey back and forth too long for a busy man to take every day, and Savage a more stimulating companion than his tired and increasingly querulous wife.

If the Johnsons needed a rest from each other at frequent intervals, the fact is not one to be wondered at. The physical and emotional release of marriage to a buxom, forthcoming woman of forty-six was undoubtedly there in the early days, but it did not last. Tetty seems to have been at a peak of vitality round about the time of her remarriage, and to have declined steeply from then on. It would be reasonable to conjecture that she found her husband's sexual needs more than she could comfortably cope with. But in fact there is no need for conjecture. Elizabeth Desmoulins, née Swinfen, used, as we saw, to pay extended visits to the Hampstead *ménage* during these years. On the nights when Johnson was able to get out to Hampstead, it was Elizabeth who waited up for his arrival. Tetty always went to bed early; she spent, in fact, a greater and greater share of her time in bed. Johnson, by contrast, always hated to go to bed. So Elizabeth, younger than himself by seven years and younger than Tetty by twenty-seven, would sit with him. And when Johnson did finally retire, he would call her into his room to sit on the bed and talk. Sometimes they did more than talk; he would take her hand, caress her, even put his arms round her as she lay with her head on the pillow. Beyond that, things never went. Mrs Desmoulins (but for whose frank confiding in Boswell we should know nothing about these nocturnal incidents) was a well-conducted young woman. As for Johnson, he was far from being the ordinary married man looking round for a few extra helpings of sex. He was in dire emotional and physical need, disappointed by his wife as he had been disappointed by his mother. Even the thought that a younger woman could care for him and feel close to him was desperately important. These bedroom conversations as Tetty slumbered in the next room, the occasional kiss and hug, were things he could snatch at to save his life.

But this brings us back, by another route, to the question of Johnson's relationship with Savage: a man he loved and in many ways admired deeply, and who was certainly not troubled with any scruples about sexual promiscuity. Sharing Savage's way of life, Johnson would be brought into contact with many a Doll Tearsheet. He would beat off temptation so long as it was a matter of corrupting a virtuous young woman like Elizabeth Desmoulins. But it might have been harder to resist when confronted with a whore to whom one sexual encounter more or less could hardly make any difference.

Here, of course, we enter conjecture. The sexual life of someone who lived two hundred years ago is never possible to reconstruct exactly unless, like Boswell, he happened to be under a psychological compulsion to write it all down. Those who want to believe that Johnson was never physically unfaithful to Tetty are perfectly free to do so. Those who picture him as being led, now and then, to share the adventures of Savage are equally free to do so. Nor is there any specific evidence, one way or another, in Johnson's frequent expression, in his prayers and diaries, of a sense of guilt and sin. These expressions tend to occur often when he is thinking of Tetty; at the recurring anniversary of her death, for instance; and he several times mentions his 'resolutions on Tetty's coffin'. But any man as deeply pious as Johnson would naturally feel that a crisis in his life, such as the death of a wife with whom he had lived for over sixteen years, brought him face to face with the whole nature of his relationship with God, his sins and expiations. There is no need to read into the guilt and self-accusation any reference to one specific offence. Anyone who lives with another person will be guilty of shortcomings, denials, failures of love and understanding; and when the relationship is ended these things remain like the thorns in a bunch of roses.

Johnson's feelings of guilt, in so far as they concerned his wife, do not add up to a concrete indication of sexual laxity. He certainly quarrelled and bickered with her, neglected her comfort, failed to make a good living for her, left her alone for long periods. But the guilt he felt when he thought of her in later life is probably not related to these but to the deep emotional and psychological gulf that opened between them. It seems to me likely, and more than likely, that Johnson within a few years came to regret his marriage to Tetty. He married her at a time when he considered himself so repulsive that he was grateful to any woman who would come near him. Quite soon afterwards he would begin to discover that this was not so. The fascination of his talk, the tidal pull of his powerful mind, the appeal of his honesty and goodness, drew towards him sweet, sensitive, lively women. Meanwhile Tetty's charms rapidly faded. If this was so, Johnson must have been guilty of the one and only basic offence against a wife – wishing in his heart that he had not married her. In a mind like his, both generous and scrupulous, both strong and self-distrusting, this would be enough to produce the emotional disturbance that always accompanied his meditations on Tetty after her death. The mere fact that he knew he ought to love her, while also knowing that he did not, would put her in the same category as his mother: another woman whose image was connected with deep emotional whirlpools.

I bring in all this here, rather than at some other point in the story, because Boswell, towards the end of his great book where he is writing about Johnson's death, explicitly links Johnson's guilt feelings and fear of death with the possibility of some episodes of sensual indulgence: 'his conduct, after he came to London, and had associated with Savage and others, was not so strictly virtuous, in one respect, as when he was a younger man. It was well known, that his amorous inclinations were uncommonly strong and impetuous . . . in his combats with them, he was sometimes overcome,' etc., etc. Boswell's motive here is perfectly clear. He is defending Johnson against the charge of over-scrupulousness. Other writers had represented Johnson as the kind of neurotic who transfers his guilt feelings to trivial matters. Boswell is offended, on his hero's behalf, at the suggestion that 'the sins, of which a deep sense was upon his mind, were merely such venial little trifles as pouring milk into his tea on Good Friday'. No, no, Johnson must have done something really wrong, as the world understands wrongness. And Boswell (with the concurrence of the sedate and careful Sir John Hawkins) sited these misdemeanours in the months of Johnson's association with Savage 'and others', though it is not clear what others he had in mind.

We shall never know for certain. It is a matter of assembling the shreds of evidence and probability, and shuffling them into a shape. Tormented by his unassuaged sexual appetites, surrounded on all sides by a metropolitan society which, though it had fortunately never heard of the *word* 'permissiveness', had the *thing* in unlimited supply, Johnson was on his own admission fascinated by whores. Boswell again: 'He owned to many of his friends that he used to take women of the town to taverns, and hear them relate their history.' If he played with fire, it may have happened sooner or later that he burnt his fingers. Who could blame him? And we may well feel, with Boswell, that it was the friendship with Savage that gave the decisive last push.

As far as direct contact went, that friendship was to last no more than two years. In the summer of 1739 Savage's remaining friends got together and undertook to find him fifty pounds a year for life, on condition that he left London and betook himself to some quiet place where he could not be tempted to extravagance. The idea caught his fancy; the country life, about which he knew nothing, suddenly appeared to him as an idyllic dream; and in any case it would not be for long. Once he was comfortably installed in a cottage with roses round the door, brilliant plays, poems and essays would flow from his pen, and he would return in triumph to London. Rich and successful, he would of course have no need of the fifty pounds from his friends, who would, with admiring smiles, release him from his obligation to live at a distance. Johnson detected in all this the usual note of fantasy, and tried to persuade Savage, if he meant to work hard at writing, to stay in London and get on with it there. But the soap-bubble iridescence of Savage's dreams lured him forward into the new life and, though he shed tears at parting from Johnson, he had long ago formed a decidedly jaundiced view of most of the other people he knew in London; especially the subscribers to his remittance fund, who showed an annoying tendency to take decisions over his head. Why – he told Johnson, trembling with rage – they had not even trusted him with the money to get himself a new suit of clothes. Having decided that he should be kitted out, they had sent a tailor of their own choosing to measure the poet's limbs rather than put the money in his hand.

At last, in July 1739, Savage shook off the dust of the metropolis, like 'Thales' in Johnson's *London*. Also like Thales, he was bound for Wales ('Give to St David one true Briton more,' as Johnson put it) – a coincidence which has tempted some to identify the real with the fictitious setting out, though I cannot see that *London* would have been any different if Johnson had never met Savage. Heading for Swansea, Savage got as far as Bristol; no ship being immediately available to carry him across the water, he fell into his old habits; made new acquaintances, captivated them, was invited to their houses, wore out both his hosts and his welcome, proceeded to Wales, did the same thing, floated an unsuccessful scheme for publishing his poems by subscription, returned to Bristol, was arrested for debt, treated with unusual kindness by his gaoler, aroused the resentment of the principal citizens by satirizing them in a poem, quarrelled at long range with his benefactors in London, and died in prison of a sudden illness which sounds like a physical expression of sheer despair.

Savage departed this life on the night of 31 July 1743. At once Johnson conceived the idea of writing a Life of his friend. Cave was more than willing to publish the work, and published in *The Gentleman's Magazine* an announcement, written by Johnson, warning off possible competitors:

> It may reasonably be imagined that others may have the same design, but as it is not credible that they can obtain the same materials, it must be expected they will supply from invention the want of intelligence, and that under the title of the Life of Savage they will publish only a novel filled with romantic adventures and imaginary amours.

The warning was successful; no one else appeared in the lists, and Johnson worked, that summer, with the usual relentless application he showed when he could bring himself to work at all. By the autumn he was writing to Cave with a hurried request for more material. 'Towards Mr Savage's life what more have you got? I would willingly have his trial, etc., and know whether his defence be at Bristol.' Johnson is referring to the *cause célèbre* of 1727, when Savage stood trial for murder; he conducted his own highly eloquent defence, and Johnson, evidently not knowing if any transcript of this had survived, was wondering if it lay among Savage's remaining papers at Bristol. Cave scraped up what he could, and Johnson worked on, taking part of his information (as he acknowledged) from a short account of Savage's life published in 1727, in the wake of the trial, and part from his personal knowledge of the man. In spite of having many other jobs on hand, Johnson managed to complete the *Life of Savage* by mid-December. It was published by Cave, disguising himself for some reason behind the imprint of a publisher named Roberts, early in the following year. Johnson was paid fifteen guineas.

The *Life of Savage* is Johnson's first major work. The omnicompetent Cave may have seen it merely as an opportunity to cash in for the last time on the already well-exploited story of Savage's misfortunes. But for Johnson it was an all-important emotional outlet. The contact with Savage had stirred him deeply. He had loved the man, partly because he had fallen under the spell of Savage's famous charm but also simply because Savage had been genuinely fond of him, and his nature was such that he thirsted deeply for affection and was unfailingly grateful to anyone who reached out to him. Whether he felt special pity for Savage because he believed his story, or believed his story because he felt special pity for him, hardly matters now. What is important is that the sufferings of his friend roused in him feelings which found their vehicle in the *Life*. Savage was an imaginative man, a poet, a wonderful talker, and a man who, lacking an elaborate formal education and lacking opportunities for leisured study, had made himself creditably well read and well informed. Johnson was all these things. Savage was poor, insecure, sometimes even destitute. So was Johnson. Savage was, or claimed to be, cruelly wronged by an unnatural mother. Johnson had his own deeply hidden and unconfessed doubts about his mother's love. The special plangency of the *Life of Savage* arises from Johnson's profound identification with its subject. His stoicism, his sturdy rejection of emotional self-indulgence, sealed his lips against the uttering of any complaint against the hardness of his own fate. But he could be all the more convincingly eloquent about the fate of Savage:

> On a bulk, in a cellar, or in a glasshouse among thieves and beggars, was to be found the author of *The Wanderer*, the man of exalted sentiments, extensive views and curious observations; the man whose remarks on life might have assisted the statesman, whose ideas of virtue might have enlightened the moralist, whose eloquence might have influenced senates, and whose delicacy might have polished courts.

In such passages we see not only the depth of Johnson's involvement but also his thrust towards generalization. He is not saying only that it was a pity that Savage should be in such a plight; nor even that it was a still greater pity that Sam Johnson should share that plight with him. Both these particular statements are made, but beyond them there is another and a general one. Any society that allows this kind of thing to happen to gifted men, men of vision and creativity, is pouring away a priceless resource. It is as near as Johnson's pride will let him come to uttering a lament over the sad life of a writer in the 1720s. And of a gifted poor person generally. An anonymous well-wisher, noticing that Savage was out at elbow, once left a new suit of clothes for him at a tavern. Savage was told of this gift, but something in the manner of the telling offended him, or in the nature of the gift itself, and he refused to enter the tavern until the clothes had been removed. Johnson could find an emotional release in telling this story; it was a way of alluding, as it were in code, to his own proudly angry rejection of the new pair of shoes left for him outside his door at Pembroke.

There are other reasons for the dark emotional strength of the *Life of Savage*.
Savage was a deeply erring man. Many people tried to help him and were first
discouraged and finally turned away by his outrageous behaviour. Johnson
brings this out in the beautifully contrived structure of his story. Up to about
half-way point, he concentrates on the misfortunes that rained on Savage from
outside. After that he shifts the emphasis to the damage that Savage did to
himself, and shows that it was just as extensive. The wrongs done to him by
others aroused pity and brought him friends; his impossible temperament drove
them away again.

> To supply him with money was a hopeless attempt; for no sooner did he
> see himself master of a sum sufficient to set him free from care for a day,
> than he became profuse and luxurious. When once he had entered a tavern,
> or engaged in a scheme of pleasure, he never retired till want of money
> obliged him to some new expedient. If he was entertained in a family,
> nothing was any longer to be regarded there but amusements and jollity;
> wherever Savage entered, he immediately expected that order and business
> should fly before him, that all should thenceforward be left to hazard, and
> that no dull principle of domestic management should be opposed to his
> inclination, or intrude upon his gaiety.

In other words, Savage had to bear through life the cross of a constitutional
inability to do what was expected of him. And Johnson had more than enough
reason for suspecting the same kind of trouble in himself. He was a depressive,
subject to paralysing fits of *accidie* accompanied by dire anxiety; he had failed to
honour his father, been uncharitable to his brother, never reached a satisfactory
relationship with his mother, been 'mad and violent' at the university, clashed
with several people who had tried to employ him, and now he had married a
wife and was not making a conspicuous success of that either. What was wrong
with him? And, whatever it was, did he not stand in as much need of tolerance
and forgiveness as Savage ever did?

We may go further, admittedly only in speculation. If it were indeed true
that Johnson had been tempted to share some of Savage's sexual indulgences,
and had yielded to that temptation, he may well have thought of himself and
Savage as fellow sinners, standing together before the judgement seat of men
and of God. And this would give a deeper note of urgency to his repeated plea
that Savage's failings should be looked at with a merciful eye. Not that Johnson
whitewashed Savage. In cataloguing his faults, he left nothing out. For instance:

> It was always dangerous to trust him, because he considered himself as
> discharged by the first quarrel from all ties of honour or gratitude; and
> would betray those secrets which, in the warmth of confidence, had been
> imparted to him.

And:

> He appeared to think himself born to be supported by others, and dispensed
> from all necessity of providing for himself; he therefore never prosecuted

any scheme of advantage, nor endeavoured even to secure the profits which his writings might have afforded him.

On the other hand, he is equally firm in defence. This takes three forms. He represents Savage as the victim of persecution, with the right of all such victims to be treated sympathetically. And also as a man of exceptional gifts and powers, who if properly treated would have been valuable to society. Looking at some of the things Johnson has to say under this second heading, it is hard to believe he did not realize that he was talking as much about himself as about Savage:

> His mind was in an uncommon degree vigorous and active. His judgement was accurate, his apprehension quick, and his memory so tenacious that he was frequently observed to know what he had learned from others in a short time, better than those by whom he was informed; and could frequently recollect incidents, with all their combination of circumstances, which few would have regarded at the present time, but which the quickness of his apprehension impressed upon him. He had the peculiar felicity that his attention never deserted him; he was present to every object, and regardful of the most trifling occurrences.

Thirdly, Johnson is at pains to represent Savage as a man who, however backsliding in his life, never sought to corrupt others into following his example. His work, Johnson insists, is blameless and teaches a sound morality. To a modern literary taste, it may well seem a pity that Savage did not write directly out of his experience of profligacy and degradation; but perhaps we overdo our preoccupation with these subjects. To Johnson, if a man could not lead a virtuous life, at least he could do his best to *write* from a virtuous standpoint. Savage, he admits, was not a good man; but he was 'the friend of goodness'. And now that he is dead, Johnson submits, his writings ought to plead for him. He was an author, 'and he now ceases to influence mankind in any other character'. Without doubt Johnson would have made the same claim for himself. He had fallen short in life, but he had kept up high ideals in his work, which was likely to reach more people, and for a longer time, than his personal example would do. So he took the opportunity, in this very work, to make a clear statement of his positive values. Disliking as he did the cant of self-indulgent misanthropy, the facile contempt for mankind that is so useful a means of dramatizing one's commonplace discontents, he pointed out that Savage, who had known real suffering and injustice, did not in fact take a low view of human nature:

> The knowledge of life was indeed his chief attainment; and it is not without some satisfaction that I can produce the suffrage of Savage in favour of human nature, of which he never appeared to entertain such odious ideas as some, who perhaps had neither his judgement nor experience, had published, either in ostentation of their sagacity, vindication of their crimes, or gratification of their malice.

The story does, of course, contain one full-scale example of human wickedness: the Countess of Macclesfield. Johnson's denunciations of 'the enormity of this woman's conduct' are justly famous:

> This mother is still alive, and may perhaps even yet, though her malice was so often defeated, enjoy the pleasure of reflecting that the life, which she often endeavoured to destroy, was at least shortened by her maternal offices; that though she could not transport her son to the plantations, bury him in the shop of the mechanic, or hasten the hand of the public executioner, she has yet had the satisfaction of embittering all his hours, and forcing him into exigencies that hurried on his death.

It must have taken some courage to let fly in this vein against a rich and powerful opponent; even if the Countess could get no redress at law (and I am by no means certain that she couldn't), there must have been risks involved. Dryden, not many years before, had been beaten up in a narrow Covent Garden street by ruffians in the pay of a nobleman who had felt the lash of his satire. And Dryden, at the time of this occurrence, was a famous poet with an assured position among the classics, who might have expected some degree of public support and protection. Johnson was, relatively, a nobody. If the Countess had cared to, she could have made a lot of trouble for him. But nothing could stem the tide of his scornful denunciation. This was the woman who had injured his friend, and who thus came to personify those forces of hostility, of denial of love, of treachery and inhumanity, that threatened all sensitive and vulnerable beings. Where some writers – Swift, say – might have made the Countess's behaviour the text for a biting sermon on the shortcomings of human nature, and others – Sterne comes to mind – might have seen in it an interesting psychological curiosity to be analysed, Johnson chose to treat it as melodrama. He makes no attempt to probe the Countess's psychology; he accepts that she was a monster of (almost) unbelievable wickedness, and this enables him to show Savage as a victim who can, in many respects, typify all victims; as he writes, heaping up example after example of Savage's undeserved misfortunes, he can allow himself to be

> Moved by fancies that are curled
> About these images, and cling;
> The notion of some infinitely gentle
> Infinitely suffering thing.

At other times, for this short work is wonderfully varied and many-faceted, he can speak of Savage with grave reprobation, inviting the reader to profit by seeing his mistakes and follies; and in another mood again he can smile at some of his friend's wrong-headed fancies, as he does when describing the rosy state of mind in which Savage left London for the country. As Johnson writes with affectionate humour, Savage

> could not bear to debar himself from the happiness which was to be found in the calm of a cottage, or lose the opportunity of listening, without

intermission, to the melody of the nightingale, which he believed was to be heard from every bramble, and which he did not fail to mention as a very important part of the happiness of a country life.

Without such touches of endearing absurdity, the portrait would not be complete. Perhaps we cannot fully love anyone we cannot, sometimes, laugh at. In the *Life of Savage* Johnson laughs at Savage, weeps over him, pleads for mercy for him, shares his sorrows and failings and admires his good qualities.

Is it fanciful to see a parallel between the place occupied by Savage in Johnson's life and that occupied by Hallam in Tennyson's or Synge in Yeats'? In each case, the ageing writer remembered his friend who had died much younger, before the back was bowed or the hair whitened, before there was any need to make compromises with the world or to suffer fools gladly. As a result, the dead man came to stand for a purity of endeavour, a refusal of shifts and expedients, so that each might have written, as Yeats in fact wrote of Synge, 'He did not speak to men and women, asking judgement as lesser writers do; but knowing himself part of judgement he was silent.'

Johnson threw himself at once and at white heat into the work of writing Savage's life, almost as if he wished to exorcise the man's ghost and then get on with his own life. But at a deep emotional level Savage stayed with him always, as a symbolic presence. He was the man who had lived intensely at all points, gulping down raw experience, confronting life directly and not through books or the opinions of others or cosy old proverbs worked on samplers. Behind Johnson's lifelong hostility to people in safe positions who theorized about life without knowing what went on in its dark alleys and on its raging oceans, there lay not only his own toilsome experience but that of Savage. So that the real theme of his noble Life of his friend is the rejection of armchair wisdom and conventional morality. 'Those are no proper judges of his conduct who have slumbered away their time on the down of plenty; nor will any wise man presume to say, "Had I been in Savage's condition, I should have lived or written better than Savage." '

CHAPTER 8

Stalemate

The *Life of Savage* produced no immediate increase in Johnson's fame; nor, since four years were to go by before another edition was called for, can it be said to have been a runaway bestseller. Still, such attention as it received was favourable enough. Indeed, it collected one highly enthusiastic notice, the kind of praise every writer dreams of in his Walter Mitty fantasies, in a paper called *The Champion*. Boswell, ever zealous for the fame of his hero, copied out a great chunk of it in his *Life*, all about the book's 'accuracy and spirit', its penetration to 'all the recesses of the human heart', its being hard to match 'in our own or, perhaps, any other language'.

Certainly it was a *succès d'estime*, and, in 1744 as today, those who were gripped by it were gripped very hard indeed. There is the famous story of Joshua Reynolds, who picked it up soon after it was published and began to read it one evening. As he started on the first page he was standing by his fireplace with one elbow on the chimneypiece, no doubt intending to sit down if the book proved to be worth going on with. In the event, he read on from page to page so intently that he did not try to move until he had finished the whole book, and then discovered that the arm he had been leaning on, and the whole of that side of his body, was benumbed.

Johnson had now, at thirty-four, two works to his credit which had won the praise of good judges of literature. Pope had read *London* with approval and predicted of the anonymous author that he would 'soon be *déterré*'. The *Life of Savage*, which might so easily have been a hack production rushed out to meet a journalistic demand, had blossomed into a deeply felt work with the strength to endure. Still a young man, Johnson had every reason to feel that he was acquitting himself honourably in his literary career, writing well above the standard demanded by Grub Street. Yet – 'this mournful truth is everywhere confessed' – there was no necessary connection between good work and high payment. He was still living from hand to mouth, working from one assignment to the next. Cave was doling out the money in shillings and pennies; in one document that passed between them, there is an entry in Johnson's hand, written on a separate piece of paper and carefully pasted in: '9 Sep, Mr Cave laid down 2s 6d.' Even with the purchasing power of money at roughly twenty times what it is today, the exact chronicling of half-a-crown is revealing Published, praised, highly regarded author as he was, Johnson could not afford a decent suit of clothes. From Edmund Malone, the careful and responsible scholar who gave Boswell so much help with the *Life*, we have a story that proves this melancholy fact. Soon after the *Life of Savage* was published, Cave entertained to dinner a man named Walter Harte, a poet and historian of some distinction who was also the tutor to Lord Chesterfield's son, the young man to whom the famous *Letters* were written. Harte, discussing recent books with his host, several times praised the *Life of Savage*. A few days later Cave met Harte in the street, and said, 'You made a man very happy t'other night.' 'How could that be? Nobody was there but ourselves.' Cave answered by reminding Harte that at one point a plate of food was sent behind a screen. There – he now explained – had sat Johnson, drinking in the good talk that reached his ears and glowing at the praise of his book; but too ashamed of his motheaten clothes to come and greet the respectable Mr Harte.

After five years of work Johnson was still a poor man. The house in Lichfield was mortgaged, and he and Tetty had to rely on what he could earn with his pen, and in that desperately meagre market. Yet there is a brighter side to the picture. Those five years had not been so totally wasted as they would have been at the equivalent level in our modern literary world. He had at least been engaged in work that involved using his mind and acquiring information. Already, in the late 1730s, he had worked for Cave on a project that must have extended his reading and thinking. Pope's *Essay on Man*, at that time still taken seriously as a philosophical poem, had been criticized on theological grounds by a Swiss scholar named Crousaz. Johnson and Elizabeth Carter shared the task of translating Crousaz's enormous Commentary and providing it with notes. That such a work could have appealed to Cave as a potential money-spinner is once again evidence that eighteenth-century readers spent their hard-earned assets on good solid fare as readily as on trash. It all helps to form the essential background to Johnson's remark in later life, 'No man but a blockhead ever wrote except for money.' The dictum has been so often quoted by literary cheesemongers who want to clothe themselves in a scrap of Johnson's respectability that it is worth reminding ourselves that to write for money, in those days, could mean doing things like translating Crousaz on Pope. The thought should be with us as we look over all Johnson's hack productions in these years. The Parliamentary Debates, as we have seen, were highly educative, forcing him to write on both sides of the most important questions of the day. The bulk of his contributions to *The Gentleman's Magazine*, in these years, were biographical. He contributed Lives of Father Paul Sarpi, the historian of the Council of Trent, and of the Dutch scientist Boerhaave; after getting back from his long visit to the Midlands in 1739–40, he wrote a life of the English admiral Blake, and followed it with accounts of Morin the French botanist, Burman the Dutch historian and scholar of poetry, and the English physician Sydenham. None of these was an original research job. He simply took the nearest standard authority and boiled it down, adding scraps of information from other sources, if they seemed apposite, and moral reflections drawn from his own observation of life and his strong religious belief. The result is never less than interesting. None of these lives has achieved the classic status of the *Life of Savage*, yet they show Johnson's wide range of interests, his curiosity about all sides of human life, and his strong grip on most of the knowledge available in his day. (He understood medicine, for instance, very well on its pragmatic side; only as a theoretical science did it begin to leave him behind.) And there was always the possibility of the self-identification which was to reach its deepest level of effectiveness in the account of Savage. In writing of Boerhaave, for instance, Johnson might almost have been describing himself; the great scientist, who had risen to eminence by his own efforts and against many difficulties, was

> of a robust and athletic constitution of body, so hardened by early severities, and wholesome fatigue, that he was insensible of any sharpness of air, or inclemency of weather. He was tall, and remarkable for extraordinary strength. There was, in his air and motion, something rough and artless, but so majestic and great at the same time, that no man ever looked upon him without veneration.

Johnson goes on to speak of Boerhaave's strength of mind; how he was never dejected by the detractions of those who envied him, nor overawed by the frown of the powerful, but persisted in an impartial search for truth, which truth he set firmly in a Christian framework. Obviously, the man was a Johnson among chemists. Johnson was not necessarily aware of producing a self-portrait as well as a portrait of Boerhaave, since anyone who has mixed with authors will know how often they are extraordinarily blind to self-reference which is obvious to any bystander. But he must have set before himself, quite consciously, the ideal of being a Boerhaave among writers.

Altogether, these were years of vast, miscellaneous activity. In later life, when he was no longer pressed for money, Johnson took up his pen very rarely. Friends who knew his love for the written word and his wealth of ideas found this puzzling. When Boswell, probingly, said that he 'wondered' that Johnson did not find writing more pleasurable than not writing, Johnson replied shortly 'Sir, you *may* wonder.' The explanation may lie in the years of ceaseless toil from 1738 to 1752, the scratch, scratch, scratch of the pen over the paper, the rustle of pages being turned as he consulted and compared, working, always working – not, indeed, steadily, for he could never do anything steadily, but in Gargantuan bursts in which he would cover over forty quarto pages with his strong, crabbed handwriting before stopping to rest. The quantity and variety of the work he produced in the first half of the 1740s, his hardest-driving decade, is astonishing, and its high standard, given the circumstances, is miraculous. At this point, a survey of his activities is in order.

From July 1741 to March 1744 Johnson was kept busy as sole author of the 'Debates in the Senate of Lilliput'; suddenly, one month after the appearance of the *Life of Savage*, he dropped them. He had, as he later told Boswell, moral scruples about producing imaginary speeches which were becoming more and more widely accepted as authentic. Most English people – or so Johnson hoped – took the Debates as a series of speeches that might well represent the opinions and attitudes of the politicians to whom they were attributed, without claiming to reproduce their words. But of late the speeches had begun to appear, translated, in Continental magazines. Johnson had the uneasy knowledge that the statesmen of his own country were being judged by foreigners on statements which he had put in their mouths. Furthermore, the initially harmless charade was taking in far too many people at home; since there was keen public interest in the proceedings of Parliament, volumes purporting to put the debates on record were published, and many of these made use of the speeches as conjecturally imagined by Johnson. From there they began to find their way into the official 'works' of the statesmen concerned. Years later, Johnson happened on a volume of miscellaneous works by Lord Chesterfield, and recognized several of the speeches as his own composition. Obviously the noble lord was not guilty of plagiarism; some anonymous compiler had lifted the speeches from the pages of *The Gentleman's Magazine*, not caring whom he deceived so long as he could make up the book and end his task. With this kind of thing happening, Johnson's rigorous honesty would naturally cause him to withdraw from the Debates, however much this might disappoint Cave, who had been gratified by the lift they had undoubtedly given to the magazine's circulation. Unwilling to drop a good selling line, Cave had the Debates carried on by someone else – probably a writer named John Hawkesworth with whom Johnson was friendly at this time – but the magic went out of them when they were no longer written by Johnson, and, running down in 1745, they ceased for ever in 1746.

The Debates and the series of Lives would have been enough for most men to do. But Johnson was working for survival and such work knows no limits. In 1741 and 1742 he lent a hand to his old Lichfield acquaintance Robert James, who was launching himself into the career of a fashionable physician. James had a project for an enormous medical dictionary, to be published in instalments; Johnson contributed some of the biographical entries which summarized the lives of famous physicians, and when the work came out in volume form he contributed the dedication by which James hoped to ingratiate himself with the celebrated Dr Mead, lavishing on it his full powers of elaborate formal compliment:

Sir

That the Medicinal Dictionary is dedicated to you, is to be imputed only to your reputation for superior skill in those sciences which I have endeavoured to explain and facilitate; and you are, therefore, to consider this address, if it be agreeable to you, as one of the rewards of merit, and if otherwise, as one of the inconveniences of eminence.

However you shall receive it, my design cannot be disappointed because this public appeal to your judgement will show that I do not found my hopes of approbation upon the ignorance of my readers, and that I fear his censure least, whose knowledge is most extensive.

I am, Sir,

Your most obedient humble Servant

R. JAMES

James's *Medicinal Dictionary* was published by a man named Thomas Osborne, a veteran bookseller who had earned the hostility of Pope and been pilloried in the *Dunciad*. Osborne, having come into contact with Johnson and registered him as a man of scholarly attainments who needed money, soon required such a man to work for him. In 1742 he bought the largest private library that had yet come into the market: the library of Edward Harley, Earl of Oxford. It was not unknown for an aristocratic bibliophile, in need of money, to sell off his books to a tradesman – and Johnson's mind must have gone back to the only high-flying business venture of his poor father, the purchase of the Earl of Derby's library three years before he himself was born – but this sale was on the colossal scale that makes news. Thirteen thousand pounds changed hands, and Osborne found himself with an asset that had to be exploited.

His first move, naturally, was to get a catalogue out. But this was to be no ordinary catalogue. It would contain a complete description of all the books that were for sale, with a summary indication of their contents, and a price would be charged for it. Osborne inserted a lengthy advertisement, doubtless written by Johnson, in the newspapers. This 'Account' made the point that even the catalogue of so great a library would be a useful tool of scholarship, for

> By the means of catalogues only can it be known what has been written on every part of learning, and the hazard avoided of encountering difficulties which have already been cleared, discussing questions which have already been decided, and digging in mines of literature which former ages have exhausted.

The advertisement published, Johnson got down to the task of examining the books and writing brief notes on them. He worked in harness with a lively-minded and well-informed man named William Oldys, who had been the Earl of Oxford's secretary and knew the books well. The work was endless. The first two volumes of the immense catalogue appeared in March 1743; the second and third in January 1744. The complete work lists some forty thousand volumes, and it is reasonable to suppose that Johnson handled and looked into virtually all of them.

It was hack work. But, like the Debates and the Lives, it was hack work that left something solid in a man's head. Adam Smith remarked years later that 'Johnson knew more books than any man alive'. And indeed it was always one of Johnson's tenets that the next best thing to knowing something is to know where it can be quickly and reliably found out. An accurate knowledge of any subject is based on its bibliography; Johnson's scholarship, founded on the early random investigations among the stock of his father's shop, developed during the thirteen months of rapid, omnivorous reading at Oxford, continued since in fits and starts as books happened to come his way, was now buttressed and filled in by three years of finding his way about this famous collection. Osborne, to be sure, was anxious for him to spend only the minimum of time on each book, just enough to be able to write a short description of its contents; but

Johnson was not the man, once he had a book in his hand, to lay it down until it had yielded up 'the precious lifeblood of a master spirit'. When the mood was on him, he could read and assimilate at an incredible speed; but even so it must have annoyed Osborne to see Johnson reading the books instead of entering up the catalogue. He grew impatient and on one occasion scolded Johnson for wasting time. Johnson did not care for his tone; words passed between them; Osborne forgot his manners still further. Johnson, though a fervent Christian, had always understood the injunction to turn the other cheek as what it is – a metaphor. He took a swing at Osborne and knocked him down.

The story of this little incident was afterwards built up until it became another of those Johnsonian anecdotes that 'everyone knows'. It has, of course, a deep human appeal. Johnson was a much greater man than his employer; his employer was insolent. We are all greater men than our employers and we should all like to have the spirit, and the muscle, to knock them down when they grow insolent. The story, once Osborne had unluckily let it out, mushroomed into some strange shapes. In one version, Johnson puts his foot on the body of the prostrate bookseller and delivers a speech. Others named the very instrument; a large, heavy volume (*Biblia Graeca Septuaginta*, fol. 1594, Frankfurt) was exhibited in a Cambridge bookshop in 1812 as the book which had felled Osborne. Et cetera. Johnson's own account, to Mrs Thrale, was simple and unvarnished:

> There is nothing to tell, dearest lady, but that he was insolent, and I beat him, and that he was a blockhead and told of it, which I should never have done; so the blows have been multiplying, and the wonder thickening, for all these years, as Thomas was never a favourite with the public. I have beat many a fellow, but the rest had the wit to hold their tongues.

If Osborne, as he got to his feet and dusted himself off, entertained any thoughts of sacking Johnson, he soon gave them up. There was no one else so well suited for the job, with the possible exception of his collaborator Oldys. Intent on milking the Harleian Library as completely as possible, Osborne also published a selection of the rare pamphlets it contained. For this 'Harleian Miscellany' Oldys did the selection and Johnson wrote the introductory essay, which was subsequently reprinted on its own as *An Essay on the Origins and Importance of Small Tracts and Fugitive Pieces*. As usual, Johnson made a piece of professional hack work the occasion of putting into circulation some real ideas. His essay shows his continuing interest in the ways and means of scholarship.

Poor Oldys! His intelligence and scholarship did not save him from the common fate of authors in that harsh time. He sank into indigence and debt; was thrown into the Fleet Prison; on his eventual release, suffering from the gaol rot that makes an ex-prisoner cling to the security of the place where he has been confined, he used to go round to the Fleet on his free evenings. He must have been like Dickens' John Dorrit.

Such tales remind one constantly of the fate that awaited Johnson if for any reason – for illness, for weariness, for domestic exigencies – his hand and brain

faltered in their ceaseless labour. Yet even during these years he must have had
some leisure, since no slave can live totally without it. He must have spent some
time at home with his wife; and we know that he spent many hours, probably
more than met with his self-approval, sitting in taverns and coffee houses with
friends.

What friends? In later life Johnson was a great former of clubs. He loved
the idea of a circle of friends meeting regularly for talk; and a simple procedure
of election or blackballing could control the membership of such a circle and
screen out the inevitable bores and hangers-on who scent out these gatherings
on the wind. The Ivy Lane Club, the Literary Club, the Essex Head Club of
his declining days – these are familiar to us. Through the artistry of Boswell we
know the friends of Johnson's heyday and old age as we know our own friends.
But this was long before Boswell's day: and, though Johnson was already
acquainted with one man who was to write his biography, John Hawkins, there
is little vivid portraiture in Hawkins' useful but monochrome pages. The men
with whom he passed evenings of conviviality and talk, in these early years,
emerge only fitfully from the shadows. There was Savage, of course; there was
poor Boyse, sitting up in bed with his arms poking through the blanket; there
were Tom Birch, and Oldys, and others with whom he worked. And there was
a reserve of regular friends, with whom Johnson met at stated times at a tavern
in Old Street in the city. Some of these friends have left only the faintest foot-
print; for instance, the 'metaphysical tailor', evidently one of those artisans
who have a taste for sounding off on big intellectual issues. The *doyen* of the Old
Street circle, deferred to even by Johnson, was an old man named George
Psalmanazar. At least, that was what he called himself; what his name had been
in the far-off eighties of the seventeenth century, when he was growing up in
the south of France, no one knew and perhaps even he had forgotten.

Johnson reverenced Psalmanazar. He always heard him out to the end of
every sentence, declaring that he would 'as soon have thought of contradicting
a bishop'. Yet the old man had a history that was far from respectable. Though
now reformed, he had been one of the most successful and shameless impostors
even in that century of splendid bare-faced rogues.

As a youth Psalmanazar had wandered from his birthplace, wherever that
was, to Avignon, where to draw favourable attention to himself he had pretended to be an Irish theological student who had quitted Ireland in order to
practise Roman Catholicism in peace. Finding this disguise too unremarkable to
get results, he moved to Germany and adopted the bolder policy of giving
himself out to be a Japanese convert to Christianity, a *persona* which he drama-
tized by observing 'Japanese' religious rites of his own invention and living on a
self-imposed regimen of roots and herbs. It was at this stage that he took from
the Bible (2 Kings xvii. 3) the name Shalmaneser, which he later altered to
Psalmanaazaar and finally to Psalmanazar.

At this point he was taken up by a rascally clergyman named Innes, chaplain
to a Scottish regiment which happened at that time to be in Germany. Innes
was not taken in by Psalmanazar's nonsense, but saw in it an opportunity for

self-advancement. He arranged for Psalmanazar to be 'converted' to Christianity and to undergo baptism, and the pair took off for London, where Psalmanazar, who had now shifted his ground slightly and was claiming to be a Formosan, was paraded as an interesting and conspicuous convert, brought into the Christian fold by the piety and persuasion of Innes. The plan worked perfectly. Innes was rewarded with the chaplaincy of the English forces in Portugal, and Psalmanazar remained in London to act out the part of a Formosan. He threw himself so zestfully into the role as to write a thick book about his imaginary birthplace, invented out of whole cloth and stuffed with hilarious absurdities. (Published in 1704, Psalmanazar's book was still going the rounds over a hundred years later, for in 1808 it was summarized by a French *savant* as part of the *Bibliothèque Universelle des Voyages*.) The astonishing leprechaun actually invented an entire language for his Formosans, written out in an alphabet that was also his own invention; he was sent to Oxford to teach this language to a group of young men who intended to go out as missionaries, and here too he threw himself into his role, burning a candle all night in the window of his room in Christ Church so that passers-by would picture him as incessantly studying.

Repentance, however, was at hand. Some time in the late 1720s Psalmanazar happened to pick up William Law's *Serious Call*, the book which had implanted religious thoughts in the nascent mind of Johnson, and under its influence he began to phase out the Formosan side of his life and look for less gainful but more honest employment in general literary work. In an autobiography designed to be published after his death he made a clean breast of his deceptions and gradually, with no sensational unmasking and no conspicuous breast-beating, sank from notice into a humble and useful life. (One would, though, rather like to know what happened to those Oxford missionaries when they first landed in Formosa and began talking to the natives in Psalmanazar's lingo.)

At the time Johnson knew him, Psalmanazar was a saintly old gentleman, living very simply in Ironmonger Row, Old Street, respected by the neighbourhood and by his colleagues. Probably he threw himself into this role as eagerly as he had posed as an Irishman, a Japanese and a Formosan. But his saintliness was genuine enough; Johnson was so impressed by his combination of piety and learning that he remembered him in later years as the best man he had ever known. When someone slyly asked him if the topic of Formosa ever came up in their conversations, Johnson replied that he never ventured to speak even of China. The whole subject of the Far East, clearly, was taboo in the tavern in Old Street.

Psalmanazar's accent in French was Gascon, and his English accent was that of the London working class. Johnson's own accent was Midland; to the end of his life he said 'poonsh' for 'punch' and 'woonse' for 'once'. So that the Old Street vignette is valuable in the same way as our glimpse of Johnson at Tissington is valuable. In his long progress through life he learnt that the specialized gifts of knowledge, erudition, originality, let alone the more evenly distributed quality of wisdom, are not the exclusive property of those on whom fortune has smiled. To be born into a good family, to go to the best schools, to have a large and comfortable library with a fire in the grate, to go on leisurely foreign tours and view masterpieces – these things are helpful, and when in later life Johnson came increasingly into contact with people who had them he showed no trace of a snarling, chip-on-the-shoulder attitude. On the other hand he always remembered that he had met with real clarity of thought in William Guthrie, a rich fund of anecdote in Tom Birch, genuine originality in poor monomaniac Savage, erudition and piety in old Psalmanazar. Johnson would have despised the type who, finding success in middle age, drops his old friends and considers that life is at last giving him his due. In every *milieu*, in every walk of life, he found people worthy of his respect and emulation.

Johnson's estimate of these people, of course, was always his own. In the poet William Collins, for example, he found a friend whose personality he loved but whose genius he rated substantially lower than subsequent generations have done. Collins had begun to send poems to *The Gentleman's Magazine* while still a schoolboy at Westminster; in his early twenties he went to London to live the literary life, arriving there at about the time Johnson published the *Life of Savage* and gave up the Debates. Gentle, enthusiastic, intensely creative but unable to settle down to steady work on any of his ambitious projects, Collins aroused all Johnson's warmth and loyalty. In his work, on the other hand, he seemed to the older man to be simply on a wrong tack. They started from different premises.

The adventure of the human spirit to which we have agreed to give the name 'Romanticism' was like any other seismic upheaval; it sent out preliminary tremors, noticed by some and unnoticed by others. Collins, unstable but deeply intuitive, was exactly the kind of man who receives these tremors and at once recognizes them for what they are. Very often, such men are not among the greatest of artists. Weight for weight, Johnson's poems are better than Collins' – if such comparisons have any meaning at all. In entirely objective terms, we might say that Johnson's poetry is strongly rooted in a culture that was shortly to pass away; that of Collins, of necessity more tenuously, is rooted in a culture which is slowly coming to birth. Unless we hold some simple-minded theory of literary evolution, whereby the later is inevitably the better, we shall not therefore assume that Collins is an improvement because he represents what is to come while Johnson represents what is doomed to go. But from where we are standing we can see one thing that was invisible to Johnson. Beneath their frail shell of mid-Augustan convention, the poems of Collins throb already with the sensibility that is soon to sweep the world in poetry, music, painting, fiction, philosophy – everything. To Johnson his friend was simply making a mistake. In a sketch of Collins which he contributed to a periodical in 1763, he summed it up with what seems like an affectionate and regretful shake of the head:

His poems are the production of a mind not deficient in fire, nor unfurnished with knowledge either of books or life, but somewhat obstructed in its progress by deviation in quest of mistaken beauties.

Faced with this kind of judgement – and we shall meet very similar judgements again and again, as Johnson comes into collision with writers who look forward to the nineteenth rather than back to the eighteenth century – we can do little but recall that facts are sacred but comment is free. If the 'beauties' for which Collins' imagination yearned were 'mistaken', and his quest for them a 'deviation', let us, instead of brushing Johnson aside with a sneer, simply register that this is how the poems of Collins appeared to a powerful and sensitive mind which had accepted Renaissance culture in its eighteenth-century form, rather than the culture of the modern world in its Romantic form. It is not a question of a 'correct' versus an 'incorrect' estimate. Under the eye of eternity the eighteenth-century attitude to human experience, and therefore to art, is as 'right' or as 'wrong' as that of the Romantics, or as our own.

But if modes of expression and angles of imaginative vision are subject to change, human nature is much less so. Johnson's view of Collins the man, as distinct from his view of Collins the poet, suffered no difficulties of perspective. He loved him, helped him, and, when madness came, visited and enquired after him and pitied him. Collins, in his way of life, was not very different from the other literary adventurers he met with in Grub Street or at St John's Gate. He dreamed; he planned enormous histories and tragedies; his actual achievement was limited to a few short poems – though these were, *pace* the judgement of Johnson, beyond the range of any but a few English writers of the 1740s. Hard up like all the rest, he was once besieged in his lodgings by a bailiff who patrolled the street outside, waiting to pounce on him for the payment of some small debt. Johnson, hearing of Collins' plight, hurried to the spot and suggested that Collins should raise the wind by getting an advance from a bookseller against some ambitious project – a method still widely in use today. The pair quickly outlined a scheme whereby Collins should freshly translate Aristotle's *Poetics*, 'with a large commentary'. The advance was handed over, the bailiff retired, and the shaken poet left town for the quiet of the country. Soon afterwards, on the death of an uncle, he received a legacy of two thousand pounds. The bookseller's advance was returned and Aristotle was for the time being left in peace. But poor Collins had no chance to enjoy his new-found security. His mind began to give way; he tried to buoy it up by travel and a change of scene, but in France his instability increased and he had to come home. Johnson visited him, and found the spectacle of his distress a painful one, the more so because it chimed in with his own secret fears of mental breakdown. He knew his mind to be not like the minds of other men; stronger in its bursts of powerful activity, entirely disabled during those dreadful interludes of melancholy and inertia. In the article of 1763 he reported that Collins during his madness

> languished some years under that depression of mind which enchains the faculties without destroying them, and leaves reason the knowledge of right without the power of pursuing it.

Did Johnson, as he wrote these words, grimly face the knowledge that the words would apply perfectly to his own case, during the bad times when he could not work, was not fit for company, and could do little but stare into the abyss? At such times he was capable of no activity; when his faculties returned he would throw himself on the mercy of his Creator, composing piteous appeals that his incapacity might not draw after it an eternity of punishment.

But the Johnson of 1763 could look back on Grub Street as on an evil dream. The Johnson of 1744 and 1745 was under the lash of immediate necessity. Years of slogging had done nothing to set him and his wife above poverty. For Tetty these years must have been tragically hard. From the few surviving glimpses of her we can tell that she was a highly developed specimen of the middle-class provincial lady who attaches great importance to clean, comfortable surroundings. Her husband, sunk in his thoughts and in any case myopic, was largely indifferent to his environment, but Tetty kept up the struggle, in year after year of dingy furnished accommodation. 'A clean floor is *so* comfortable,' she would say as she poked the broom round Sam's ankles, till he would growl that he had heard enough about the floor, and 'perhaps they might have a touch at the ceiling'. At other times he would grumble about her cooking, the only part of the domestic arrangements to which he was disposed to pay any attention; and on at least one occasion her annoyance boiled over while he was saying grace, and she interrupted him with 'Nay, hold – do not make a farce of thanking God for a dinner which you will presently protest not eatable'.

Poor Tetty, she must often have wondered during those years whether she would not have done better to accept her brother's offer and live on in Birmingham with plenty of money, a neat house and servants to do her bidding. She had declined the grey security of a placid widowhood, had reached out for happiness and adventure at a time when a less vivacious woman might have been content to begin the long, slow acceptance of age; and life had not, after all, been kind to her.

> Think now
> We have not reached conclusion, when I
> Stiffen in a rented house.

Such thoughts must often have been in her mind; the pleasant, easy-going life of her younger days in Birmingham, the good-natured and steady tradesman who had been her husband, that son who had now disowned her, the bright circle of friends now all gone from her except the faithful Elizabeth Desmoulins – these things must have troubled her dreams during the long evenings when she lay in bed while her husband talked away his time with strange, tatterdemalion companions whom she neither knew nor cared to know.

To be fair to that husband, he was beginning to face up to the knowledge that a supreme effort was needed while his strength held out: something that would lift him out of the ruck of Grub Street and put him high enough to be seen. He was sick of poverty. And his present way of life offered no escape from it. He was working as hard as a man could work, yet he was as far away as ever from ease and comfort; even the commonest necessities of life were sometimes elusive. Not many years earlier – in 1738, to be precise – he had signed off one of his letters to Cave with the word '*impransus*' – 'not having dined'. Whether Cave was to understand that on this particular evening Johnson was attending to his correspondence before eating dinner, or that he was out of funds and would have to go to bed hungry, is not clear. But the second alternative is at least possible. One thing is certain. Every object of value, everything that could realize a price, however modest, was sold off during these years. Sadly, Johnson had to part with the last relic of his childhood: the silver mug, inscribed SAM. J., that his mother had so carefully bought for him on that far-off visit to London in 1712, when the Queen had touched him. It was, he noted later, 'one of the last pieces of plate which dear Tetty sold in our distress'.

In his predicament he turned, as many have turned, to Shakespeare, that universal provider. Augustine Birrell once remarked that the supreme test of an English man of letters was his ability to write an essay on Shakespeare – a challenge which, generation after generation, the best of them have taken up. Birrell was right: to criticize an Elizabethan author needs a certain historical grasp; to criticize an author of Shakespeare's range and depth means standing on the tips of one's own toes; and, since Shakespeare was not a cloistered, bookish writer, but one who mixed with the world and had sympathy with people of every kind and every social class, and whose art was nourished in a popular tradition, to assess him is beyond the powers of a scholar who never ventures from the library. Characteristically, Johnson determined to work on the largest possible scale; he would issue an edition of the complete plays, with a running commentary that would explain all difficult passages and illuminate all profundities.

Such an edition would cost money to prepare and to publish. No bookseller would be willing simply to launch it as a gamble. The usual method of publishing such an ambitious work, in those days, was by subscription. But who would subscribe to an edition carried out by an unknown literary hack, a nobody? Johnson had to get himself noticed. He had already tried the subscription method, with Politian, and failed; he could not afford to fail again. So, in the early months of 1745, he sat down to write a pamphlet which should be a showcase of his ability as a Shakespearean critic and editor. He chose to concentrate on a single play, *Macbeth*; and his brilliant essay deals with the play in every kind of depth. It offers the relevant background knowledge, with an erudite discussion of attitudes towards witchcraft, both popular and learned, in the sixteenth century; it contains purely literary criticism of the play's tone and texture; and it plunges boldly into editorial problems, the highly expert business of sorting out what Shakespeare actually wrote, obscured as it has frequently been by the distortions of playhouse and printing office.

Writing to attract attention, Johnson had a stroke of luck just as his essay was being set up in type. From the Clarendon Press at Oxford, then as now the official scholarly press of the University, came forth a sumptuous edition of the bard's work, edited lightly and sketchily by a retired diplomat, Sir Thomas Hanmer. This decent and literate man evidently approached his task in the characteristic way of the eighteenth-century gentleman amateur. He enjoyed Shakespeare, he knew the plays well, he had definite notions as to what constituted elegance in poetry, and in seeing the text through the press he did not hesitate to alter words and phrases here and there, not on hard scholarly grounds but in accordance with his own confident taste. The result is nothing to sneer at; we in our century have just about witnessed the final demise of this kind of leisurely, cultivated gentleman of letters, and seen his place taken by hard-bitten career professionals; the work is undeniably now done more expertly, but something went out of English literary life when it ceased to be peopled by men like Hanmer. For Johnson, however, there was no time for these elegiac reflections. He needed the money and Hanmer didn't; he was a professional man of letters who had devoted much thought and much reading to these editorial problems, and Hanmer wasn't. As an extra motivation, he knew as every journalist knows that a controversy attracts attention faster than anything else. Accordingly, he set himself to rough up Hanmer in convincing fashion. Adding to the title-page of his pamphlet so that now it read *Miscellaneous Observations on the Tragedy of Macbeth: with remarks on Sir T. H.'s Edition of Shakespeare*, he provided a concluding section which rebuked Hanmer, in airily ironic vein, for venturing where his qualifications would not take him.

Johnson's case against Hanmer is, basically, that he has amused himself by fiddling about with Shakespeare's text, making numerous minor alterations for no better reason than to please his own ear, while neglecting serious difficulties which call for thought and scholarship. 'He appears', Johnson reports, 'to find no difficulty in most of those passages which I have represented as unintelligible, and has therefore passed smoothly over them, without any attempt to alter or explain them.' On the other hand, he goes on, Hanmer has made such unjustified emendations as

> This is the sergeant
> Who like a good and hardy soldier fought

emended to

> This is the sergeant, who
> Like a *right* good and hardy soldier fought

Or, again:

> Dismay'd not this
> Our captains Macbeth and Banquo?
>   —Yes

emended to

> Dismay'd not this
> Our captains *brave* Macbeth and Banquo?
>   —Yes

'Such harmless industry', Johnson comments with silky irony, 'may surely be forgiven if it cannot be praised; may he therefore never want a monosyllable, who can use it with such wonderful dexterity. *Rumpatur quisquis rumpitur invidia!*' The satirical Latin fragment – it is from Martial – means 'If anyone is going to burst with envy, let him do so!' Hanmer's prowess in the trivial pastime of improving Shakespeare's versification by the unauthorized injection of monosyllabic words is unlikely to arouse envy except in equally empty minds – that is the implication, and Sir Thomas and his Oxford publishers must both have found it irritating to be treated with this condescension by an unknown Grub Street writer. For unknown Johnson still was. Like his previous works, the pamphlet was anonymous. But the challenge was a real one. After flicking Hanmer with satire, Johnson moves on to a measured condemnation of his flimsy methods:

> The rest of this edition I have not read, but, from the little that I have seen, I think it not dangerous to declare that, in my opinion, its pomp recommends it more than its accuracy. There is no distinction made between the ancient reading, and the innovations of the editor; there is no reason given for any of the alterations which are made; the emendations of former editions are adopted without any acknowledgement, and few of the difficulties are removed which have hitherto embarrassed the readers of Shakespeare.

Having demonstrated that Hanmer's edition would not do, Johnson proceeded to offer Proposals for an edition that *would* do. Loosely inserted in each copy of the pamphlet was a large sheet (35 by 17 cm.) of

> Proposals for printing a new edition of the plays of William Shakespeare, with notes, critical and explanatory, in which the text will be corrected: the various readings remarked: the conjectures of former editors examined, and their omissions supplied. By the author of the *Miscellaneous Observations on the Tragedy of Macbeth.*

Nowhere does the name 'Johnson' appear. The essay demonstrates the fitness of the proposed editor for his task; the Proposals offer the author of the essay as the editor. The two derive support from each other, without the invocation of a name.

Was this the end of frustration and poverty? With a clear road ahead of him, Johnson was ready for a powerful burst of speed. But, once more, the chance was snatched away from him; the road was blocked. The edition of Shakespeare was to be published by Cave. And now, just as the work was to begin, Cave was threatened by a bigger publisher, the successful Jacob Tonson, with legal reprisals if he went ahead. For Tonson claimed that the copyright of Shakespeare's works belonged to him.

Cave immediately gave in without a fight. He was too cautious to argue the matter at law, though a clever advocate could probably have forced Tonson to back down. The law of copyright was, during the eighteenth century, in a state of confusion. During most of the preceding century the Licensing Act had provided a rough-and-ready protection against pirated editions from which the author could expect no profit. The authorities would not license the same book twice, and to issue a book without licence was to invite punishment. But in 1695 the Act lapsed and was not renewed. For fifteen years there was no protection at all for copyright; then, in 1710, an Act was passed which declared copyright to be the property of the author, or his assigns, for fourteen years, renewable thereafter for another fourteen years if he were still alive. But many publishers, while going along with the specific provisions of the Act, took the line that literary property, like other property, was inalienable. If a man owns a piece of land, it does not cease to belong to him after a certain date; it remains part of his estate until he definitely sells it or gives it away. So, they argued, with copyright. Johnson had his own moderate and sensible views on this question; our present-day compromise, whereby copyright belongs to the author or his assigns until fifty years after his death and then disappears into thin air, is not far wide of what he advocated. But, in the shadowy state of the law in 1745, a big publisher like Tonson would always win against a small publisher like Cave. If Tonson chose to crack down, that was the end of Johnson's projected edition, at any rate for the foreseeable future. Tonson did choose, and Johnson manfully faced one more in that series of disappointments which must have seemed endless.

Tonson's letter to Cave, which stopped Johnson's project cold, was dated 11 April 1745. The rest of that year was a gloomy one for Johnson. He wrote little; so little, indeed, that Boswell comments on his unproductiveness and mentions a belief, held by 'some', that the fateful Rising of that year, the last unlucky adventure of the House of Stuart, weighed heavily on his spirits and brought his mind to a standstill by 'sympathetic anxiety'. Boswell himself is careful to state that he himself believes no such thing; but the hint has proved a fruitful one for more enthusiastic and less responsible writers, and the celebrated John Buchan went so far as to perpetrate a novel (*Midwinter*) which depicts Johnson hastening north to give his services to the Jacobite cause. All good fun; but Boswell, whose concern was to represent Johnson accurately rather than to write romantic fiction, is more to be trusted:

> I have heard him declare that, if holding up his right hand would have secured victory at Culloden to Prince Charles's army, he was not sure he would have held it up; so little confidence had he in the right claimed by the House of Stuart, and so fearful was he of the consequences of another revolution on the throne of Great Britain.

No, the problems that Johnson faced during that dark year were surely nearer home. He had toiled for years, honourably giving a fair day's work for a less than fair day's pay; and when at last he had seen a chance to establish himself more firmly in the esteem of the public, the chance had been snatched away. What was to become of him? Would he meet a fate like that of poor Collins – dreaming, dodging the bailiffs, forming large plans which he never executed, and finally going mad? Would he sink into dissipation and paranoia like Savage? Outwardly he appeared, with his firm principles, to be the last man who would give way to vice and self-indulgence; but there must have been evenings when he felt desperately lonely and unhappy, evenings when the temptation to drink a bumper or two and forget his troubles with one of those 'women of the town' whom he now and then 'took to taverns' and questioned about their lives must have been strong upon him. Or would he just fizzle out like Birch and Oldys, working at full stretch year after year, till his overburdened brain cracked up into premature senility?

We know nothing, in detail, of these months. But Johnson would not have been human if he had not come very close to being crazed with frustration and bitterness. If only Corbet had kept those airy promises, he would be an Oxford M.A. by now, enjoying the easy living of a country schoolmaster or perhaps reclining in even greater comfort as a Fellow of Pembroke, like his contemporary and rival Jack Meeke. If only Michael Johnson had been luckier and more successful with the business, or if Nathaniel had been able to carry it on with more vigour! At least, then, there would have been a little money to live on while he wrote a major work that established him. Why had Dean Swift done nothing to help him get an honorary degree at Dublin? Why did Garrick move so slowly in the matter of *Irene*? Was there never to be a helping hand from anyone?

Not only were his own hopes frustrated. As things were turning out, he was also disappointing all the people who had believed in him and recognized his early promise. His mother, fretting alone in the mortgaged house in Lichfield, must be wondering what was happening to him; with her husband and younger son dead, she must have felt that the elder son, too, was lost to her – lost in poverty and obscurity in the jungle of London. Was Dame Oliver still alive? And Wentworth, the schoolmaster at Stourbridge who had kept copies of his early verses? Of his intellectual mentors Cornelius Ford was dead, but Walmesley was not; how did he feel about this failure of Johnson's to show his back above the water? That he was disappointed we know for certain, and so doubtless did Johnson, for in 1746 Walmesley wrote to David Garrick a letter which included a sad message:

> When you see Mr Johnson, pray my compliments, and tell him I esteem him as a great genius – quite lost both to himself and the world.

Did he voice his disappointment at that hospitable table where they had enjoyed hours of golden conversation? And if he did his feelings would be shared by his young wife, Magdalen – and she was Molly Aston's sister: and Molly, too, the beautiful and the clever, would know of his failure.

And so on, and so on . . . it would be easy, and in a melancholy way rather pleasurable, to go on adding brush stroke to brush stroke in the picture of Johnson's unhappiness at this time. One thing is certain – however black and deep we imagine his misery, we shall not be exaggerating. But fortunately, as we all know, help was at hand. The United States Cavalry was just over the next hill, in the shape of a posse of booksellers.

Johnson's reputation had, in fact, been growing. Though his work had been issued anonymously, though some of the most remarkable of it – the Debates, for instance – could not by their very nature have borne a signature, his fame had been rising; if not with the uninitiated reader, certainly with the inner circle of people who knew their way about the literary world. 'Some years' before this time (Boswell could not fix it more precisely) Johnson had had a conversation with Robert Dodsley, a respectable bookseller, in which Dodsley had dropped into his mind the idea of compiling an English dictionary. The idea seemed to strike Johnson, but after a moment's thought 'he said, in his abrupt, decisive manner, "I believe I shall not undertake it." ' Later Johnson insisted to Boswell that the notion was not, in fact, a new one to him ('I had long thought of it'). Be that as it may, whatever were the slow stages by which the idea took root, it was certainly Robert Dodsley who prodded Johnson gently but firmly into undertaking the vast project. In 1746 Dodsley brought up the matter again, in verbal negotiations with Johnson; this time Johnson agreed to take the suggestion seriously; he went away and wrote down his thoughts on how such a dictionary could best be carried out; by the end of April his *schema* was ready to be handed round among interested parties. In the end seven booksellers came together in what modern business would dub 'a consortium', and by June they had drawn up a contract and Johnson had signed it. Johnson was to write an English dictionary. And they were to pay him fifteen hundred and seventy-five pounds.

Boswell carefully copies out the names of all these seven men. And he is right. By getting together and resolving to employ Johnson on this colossal work, they were risking some of their capital in the hope of making a profit – which they duly did. But they were also providing a showcase example of the enlightened behaviour of which free enterprise is sometimes capable. France and Italy had academies, immense committees of learned men, financed by public money and private patronage, to do this kind of work. England had seven booksellers and Samuel Johnson.

So, following Boswell, let us honour Robert Dodsley; Andrew Millar; Charles Hitch; John and Paul Knapton; Thomas Longman and his nephew. They handed over their fifteen hundred and seventy-five pounds in larger and smaller lumps over the next nine years; and when, finally, they gave a dinner for Johnson at which, like careful tradesmen, they produced his total receipts, it turned out that they had paid him over a hundred pounds more than the stated sum. That is, in present-day money, over two thousand pounds. We shall not forget them.

June 18, 1746, is the date that marks Johnson's turning-point. From now on, he is no longer a hand-to-mouth hack-writer; he is subsidized by a group of responsible entrepreneurs; he has assistants whom he pays and in whose welfare he has an interest; he lives in a fine large house. For of course the undertaking cannot be carried on from the kind of hole-and-corner lodging that has been good enough for Sam and Tetty since they arrived in London. As in the days of his childhood, he lives now in a substantial dwelling, not because he is rich but because it has to be big enough to house the business.

Number 17, Gough Square, Fleet Street, needs no description, since, like the birthplace, it is still there to be seen, and in much the same guise as when he knew it. It was large, though not too large for the Johnsons, their servants, and the team of out-at-elbows literary men whom Johnson signed up to help with the lexicographical drudgery. It had three storeys and a spacious garret besides. And, what may give us food for thought, it was a few steps from Fleet Street – an area of London in which only a multimillionaire could own a house nowadays.

Ahead still lay years of back-breaking toil. But Johnson was not afraid of work. What he was afraid of, like all of us, was the leaden frustration that Coleridge had in mind when he wrote:

> Work without hope draws nectar in a sieve
> And hope without an object cannot live.

Now his work was sustained by hope, and his hope had a definite object: could it be that the Grub Street days were over?

PART III

The Dictionary Years

CHAPTER 9

Crossing the Bar

Number 17, Gough Square has a large garret (the word is defined in Johnson's Dictionary as 'a room on the highest floor of the house') which occupies the whole length and breadth of the building, has a decently high ceiling, and admits light through two windows at the front nowadays – three in Johnson's time – and two dormers at the sides. The existence of such a useful working space must have been one of the chief inducements to Johnson to rent the house. He now fitted it up with one of those long desks used in the counting houses of his day, at which several clerks could work standing up. The ship was ready. All he had to do was sign on a crew.

Johnson's Dictionary is, in the strictest sense, a one-man work. He chose the words, defined them, fitted them out with derivations, and illustrated the correct use of each one with a nosegay of quotations. For the entire colossal undertaking, from first to last, he accepted sole responsibility. But if the work was ever to be completed there must be help in the purely mechanical business of transcription. While he was reading and thinking, others must be writing and pasting up. Having decided that six was the most convenient number to employ (for he had to balance their wages, to be paid out of his own funds, against the probable speed of their work), Johnson looked round for suitable amanuenses. With his knowledge of the world of letters, it was no trouble to make enquiries in the right places and come up with six men literate enough to do the work and poor enough to be attracted by the wages.

As it happens, five of the six were Scotsmen. Probably this was no more than an accident. Johnson did not particularly go out looking for Scotsmen; he just happened to find them. Eighteenth-century London was in any case full of Scots. They had thrown in their lot with England in the Act of Union in 1707, a step taken only after prolonged heartsearchings and dubieties not at all unlike the crosscurrents of feeling that accompanied Britain's entry into the European Economic Community in 1973. The Scots were afraid of losing their national identity; the English were afraid that their country would be invaded by a swarm of job-hungry Scots who would work any hours and accept any wages rather than go home. To some extent both sets of fears were justified by events. Scotland, especially after 1745, declined into a provincial version of England, while many an Englishman had to endure being pushed off the ladder of his career by the sharp elbows of a hungry Scot. Both nations have by now accepted this situation as part of the normal order of things, but in the eighteenth century the Scots were definitely unpopular in England and especially in London.

That Johnson did not feel any hostility towards them is evidenced by his choosing to work, for years on end, with a six-man team of whom five were Scots. Indeed, Scotland was an enormous recurring fact in his consciousness. His closest disciple was to be a Scot; so was his most ferocious literary antagonist; his most memorable journey was to be made through Scotland. He enjoyed making anti-Scotch remarks, because he relished an argument, and any Englishman who makes an anti-Scotch remark is certain of a strong and immediate comeback. That is about as much as his celebrated 'prejudice' amounted to.

Naturally he got some fun out of teasing his North British employees. When the Dictionary reached the word 'oats', it amused him to define the word as 'A grain, which in England is generally given to horses, but in Scotland supports the people'. He knew well enough that in the upland parts of his own county of Staffordshire the shortness of the summer made it impossible for the hill farmers to put their whole trust in wheat, so that oats were regularly grown, and their flour baked into the delicious oatcakes which Staffordshire people still relish so much. The opportunity to have a dig at Shiels, at the Macbean brothers, at Stewart and Maitland, was too good to miss, that was all. Indeed, there is something affectionate about it. Johnson accepted responsibility for the men as much as for the book. He regarded them all as his dependants – Stewart who never lived to see the Dictionary completed, Shiels who died later of consumption, the Englishman Peyton whom Johnson helped again and again, and finally buried, and his wife too. As a team, they evidently fell far short of perfection. They did their share of gossiping, time-wasting, slipping out to the pub when Johnson's back was turned. On one occasion, as Johnson later told Boswell, they, or some of them, made a blunder that cost him a lot of money. The printer would only handle sheets that were written on one side only: too sleepy to realize this, they copied such a vast amount of material on to both sides that it cost Johnson twenty pounds – that is, four or five hundred pounds in modern money – to have the work redone.

But he was patient with them, as he always was with simple ordinary people, the common men and women who do the work of the world. To be among such people answered an emotional need in him. His combativeness, his determination not to be put down, came out when he was confronted by wealth, rank, brilliance, power of any kind; never among the poor and the humbly useful. As the years of toil brought them all closer together, they must have enjoyed many a pause for conversation. During one of these breaks Johnson played a prank he recalled years later. Among the Scots who had invaded England was James Thomson, one of the most successful poets of the day but not much to the taste of Johnson, who disliked his blank verse and rather inflated language. Shiels particularly admired Thomson and this made him a target. 'I took down Thomson', Johnson recalled to Boswell, 'and read aloud a large portion of him, and then asked – Is not this fine? Shiels having expressed the highest admiration, Well, Sir (said I), I have omitted every other line.'

With interludes like this, the work proceeded. Johnson's procedure was simple, though massively arduous. First of all he chose the words to be listed; sometimes from other dictionaries, sometimes from his reading or from conversational usage. He provided each word with a definition and an etymology, and this much of the material he seems to have written out in his own hand. I say 'seems' because the precise method followed by Johnson is not clear to me. Probably he did not follow one unvarying procedure during the whole nine years. According to an ex-employee of Strahan the printer, writing in *The Gentleman's Magazine* in 1799, the copy was written on separate sheets of the size known as 'quarto post', each sheet divided into two columns. Johnson wrote the words, with their derivations and etymologies, usually two or three to a column, and the intervening spaces were filled up by slips pasted in by his assistants. These slips contained the illustrative quotations. Presumably the man was remembering Johnson's process correctly; what puzzles one is how, in that case, the amanuenses came to copy large quantities of it on to both sides of the paper, when Johnson used only one side. Perhaps he arrived at that method after expensive trial and error, as something foolproof.

At all events, the work of the amanuenses was to write out the quotations which Johnson selected to illustrate the clearest and most correct use of each word. These quotations he provided from his vast reading, the bulk of which he did at an early stage in the work. Broadly speaking his method was to read first, and make word lists later. When he found a word used in the best way, he underlined it and wrote its initial letter in the margin, using a pencil; he also indicated, by vertical lines, the extent of the context to be quoted. The book was then handed to the nearest amanuensis, who copied out the relevant passage on to a slip, which was then arranged in correct alphabetical order and finally pasted up.

Johnson chose the quotations from what he considered the classic period of English, going back no further than Sir Philip Sidney, and coming forward, as a rule, no nearer than 1660. The provision of quotations, which enabled the reader to see each word on the hoof as well as in a bald definition, was Johnson's original contribution to lexicography. It has since become standard, particularly of course in the Oxford Dictionary; the difference being that in the Oxford Dictionary the examples are chosen with a view to charting the historical evolution of the word, whereas Johnson was concerned with setting a standard of correctness. Where the twentieth-century work follows each listed word through all its adventures, noting every significant use whether worthy of imitation or not, the eighteenth century was more interested in establishing a standard. Each reflects the characteristic preoccupation of its age.

Sometimes one reads the mis-statement that Johnson set out to fix the English language, to anchor it in a settled state. The best refutation of this is in Johnson's own Preface, where he gives a succinct enumeration of the reasons why such an attempt is impossible. Words, he remarks, are like the men who utter them:

When they are not gaining strength, they are generally losing it. Though art may sometimes prolong their duration, it will rarely give them

perpetuity; and their changes will be almost always informing us that language is the work of man, a being from whom permanence and stability
cannot be expected.

On the other hand, he shared with his age a general willingness to slow down
the rate of change as far as possible. The eighteenth-century aim was a language
which would not seem obsolete in two generations, and this aim was brilliantly
achieved. We nowadays can read eighteenth-century English with complete and
immediate comprehension. In spite of the colossal changes of the last two hundred years, we share with that epoch an English which, while it differs from ours
in many points of idiom and usage, is recognizably the same language. But if we
take a similar jump backwards from where they were standing, if we compare
the English of the eighteenth century with that of the sixteenth, we shall find
much greater differences. Elizabethan English grew so fast, putting on muscle so
swiftly and in such unforeseeable places, that it was both exciting and unpredictable. The English of Shakespeare is like a young racehorse just arrived at its
strength: very fast, very much a race-winner, but very hard to control. As Johnson was himself to write, 'The style of Shakespeare was in itself perplexed, ungrammatical, and obscure.' All three epithets are justified and all three apply to
sixteenth-century English generally. It is the same story with orthography.
Before the Civil War of the 1640s, which brought a rapid increase in printing
and made some kind of working convention a necessity in the training of
apprentices, there was no such thing as 'correct' or 'incorrect' spelling. Everyone
spelt a word in the way he thought it ought to be spelt. Printers would often
lengthen or shorten the form of a word to avoid breaking up the syllables with
hyphens, so that sixteenth-century books abound in oddities such as 'with' spelt
'wyththe'.

Thus, while Johnson was as well aware as we are that language cannot be
'fixed', he also understood that a reliable guide to usage, if it wins the confidence of a majority of readers, can do a great deal to prevent words from sliding
into one another, fading and blurring. The early part of his own century had
seen widespread anxiety about the instability of language; as Pope had put it,

> Our sons their fathers' failing language see,
> And such as Chaucer is shall Dryden be.

We are now as far away from Dryden as Dryden was from Chaucer, but we
understand his language much better than he understood that of the fourteenth-
century poet. Most of the credit for this must go to the determined eighteenth-
century effort at the regularization of English. It was a corporate work, undertaken by an entire society, but if there is one individual share that is demonstrably the largest that share is Johnson's. His work as a lexicographer fell out of
the national mind during the nineteenth century, when the rapid advance of
philology made some parts of his book seem amateurish. But his contemporaries
were almost pathetically grateful for what he did for them. They deferred to
him as 'Dictionary Johnson'; they bought up edition after edition of the book;
they based their usage on it, so that for a hundred years it was the chief authority

on English, passing through thousands of hands in stately two-volume editions or cheap one-volume abridgements.

In August 1747, just as he got fairly launched on to what he called 'this vast sea of words', Johnson put out a statement which was intended to publicize the venture and also to attract support and help. This was the masterly *Plan of a Dictionary of the English Language*, in which he defined the scope of the forth-coming work with his usual precision and clarity. It was, he announced, to be primarily a *useful* book; its aim would be to help the reader to clarify his thoughts and understand those of others, rather than to appeal to the doctrinaire and the purist. For instance, there was (in theory) an objection to admitting all those foreign words which had become lodged in English because they happened to have specialized meanings not covered by existing English words; obviously such terms were often jargon, and moreover they were not strictly 'English' words at all, though the English were glad enough to use them. A pure English dictionary would exclude such words, Johnson says, but 'in lexicography, as in other arts, naked science is too delicate for the purposes of life'. Whatever the theorist may decide, the ordinary man is going to look into the Dictionary when he meets a word he does not understand; and most of such words are technical terms, so in they must go, 'English' or not. At the other extreme we have those words which are so common that nobody needs to look them up. 'It seems of no great use to set down the words *horse, dog, cat, willow, alder, daisy, rose* and a thousand others, of which it will be hard to give an explanation, not more obscure than the word itself.' But it must be done, because it is impossible to fix the line between animals and plants whose names we know and cannot re-member not having known, and animals and plants we might not be able to name but which might be familiar to other people in other places; and he gives as examples 'the crocodile, the chameleon, the ichneumon and the hyena'.

The *Plan of a Dictionary* is an impressive statement, and if we compare it with the Preface that introduced the work when it finally appeared eight years later we find it more impressive still, for the two documents are substantially in line. The years of experience did not much alter Johnson's assessment of the job; his original forecast of its scope and nature had been remarkably accurate.

There is another aspect of the Plan which claims our attention. It is 'addressed' to 'the Right Honourable Philip Dormer, Earl of Chesterfield'. This circum-stance adds to the charm of the Plan, from a literary point of view, because it stimulated Johnson to introduce his argument with a page or two of high, stately compliment which yet manages to stay entirely clear of anything re-sembling the lickspittle. He addresses Chesterfield in a tone of magnificent hyperbole under which we can hear a distinct note of irony. The great ones of the earth do not often stoop to encourage dictionary-makers. The employment is regarded as too humble, too much a matter of mere drudgery. Johnson goes on, in a paragraph in which the note of sarcasm becomes for a moment uppermost:

I had read indeed of times in which princes and statesmen thought it part of their honour to promote the improvement of their native tongues; and in which dictionaries were written under the protection of greatness. To the patrons of such undertakings I willingly paid the homage of believing that they, who were thus solicitous for the perpetuity of their language, had reason to expect that their actions would be celebrated by posterity, and that the eloquence which they promoted would be employed in their praise. But I considered such acts of beneficence as prodigies, recorded rather to raise wonder than expectation; and content with the terms that I had stipulated, had not suffered my imagination to flatter me with any other encouragement, when I found that my design had been thought by your Lordship of importance sufficient to attract your favour.

Several things are being said here. In a back-handed way Johnson is asserting the importance of lexicography in the general scheme of life. (At a time when the army and navy are carrying British power to undreamt-of parts of the earth, it is time to put the language in order; nations yet unborn are going to have to use it, and it is our responsibility to teach it to them.) The 'princes and statesmen' who in remote times and regions understood and supported the making of dictionaries were rewarded with high rhetorical praise, as Johnson is even now rewarding Chesterfield; but they were doing no more than their duty, and that this duty has become forgotten is matter for the satirist. Perhaps most important of all, Johnson is staking a claim to independence. He had already decided on the work, already put thought and energy into it, when he 'found' that it had attracted Chesterfield's favour. There is a vigilant pride here. Johnson is very firmly making it impossible for anyone to believe that he went cap in hand to Chesterfield for his blessing before launching the Dictionary. No, he had started it and Chesterfield had subsequently 'thought it of importance'.

Johnson, indeed – and we might almost read as much between the lines – was unenthusiastic about dedicating the Plan at all. The idea had been Dodsley's. Chesterfield, as Secretary of State, was an important politician as well as a grand aristocrat. Moreover, he was an undeniably literate and cultivated man who looked favourably on art and letters. To associate his name with the project was bound to be good for business. So Dodsley urged, and Johnson had his own motive for letting him have his way. He had, as usual, procrastinated instead of getting down to work, and the Plan was not ready. If he went along with Dodsley's suggestion and dedicated it to the Earl, he could plausibly ask for a little more time to polish his paragraphs and weigh his adjectives. Dodsley agreed to the extra time, Chesterfield had his dedication, and Johnson remarked with sardonic satisfaction to his friend Bathurst, 'Now if any good comes of my addressing to Lord Chesterfield, it will be ascribed to deep policy, when, in fact, it was only a casual excuse for laziness.'

Meanwhile, domestic life went on. For the most part we can only guess at its day-to-day texture. But surely the new dispensation must have seemed to Tetty an enormous improvement. Working under the conjugal roof, her husband was less under the temptation to idle away his time in taverns and coffee houses with eccentrics and misfits like old Psalmanazar or poor Collins. Not that Sam quite gave up collecting the odd characters who must have been such a trial to Tetty. He never would. He was drawn to them, if only by the fact that he was an odd character himself, and she was resigned to it. About the time he signed the contract for the Dictionary, in fact, Johnson made the acquaintance of one of the most idiosyncratic figures in all his gallery: a man who was to be a lifelong friend, to live in his house for twenty years, and to inspire his finest utterance as a poet.

This was Robert Levet, a silent, morose northcountryman several years Johnson's senior. Like most of Johnson's *protégés* he had a strange history. Beginning as an apprentice to the wool trade in his native Hull, he had gone on to work briefly as some kind of upper servant in a nobleman's household, and saved enough money out of his wages to indulge a fancy for foreign travel. After wandering for a time in Italy and France, he had become a waiter at a Parisian café whose patrons were mainly medical men. Levet had always been interested in medicine, and the convivial doctors encouraged him by admitting him to lectures and demonstrations at the local hospital. Under their influence Levet gradually metamorphosed from a waiter to a physician. In this character he returned to England, and from then on eked out a regular, though meagre, living by mixing ointments and powders for the ailments of coachmen, fish-porters and bricklayers. For his services he accepted such payment as they could offer; if they had no money, he made it a principle to take his fee in kind, and Johnson noted with interest that Levet, though not a bibulous man, often staggered home drunk because a dram of some villainous brew was the only *quid pro quo* that was going.

Just how Johnson fell in with Levet we do not know. But the dour, mono-syllabic Yorkshireman had a story to tell, and somehow Johnson got it out of him. They became, and remained, inseparable friends. Together, they must have presented a strange appearance; the huge, heavy-featured Johnson with his peering, shortsighted eyes and rolling gait: the thin, swarthy Levet, whose face had a scorched appearance as of an alchemist who had stood too close to his own crucible.

One thing we know for certain: there was no great liking between Levet and Tetty Johnson. Her opinion of him is not on record, but it was certainly un-flattering. And his opinion of her? Levet was always very economical of words, and when, years later, Mrs Thrale asked him about Tetty, he replied that she was 'always drunk and reading romances in her bed, where she killed herself by taking opium'. Levet was never one to dress up a hard situation in soft words. Neither, on the other hand, was he a liar. The sad decline of Elizabeth Johnson's life is somewhere, like a plangent little melody played just out of earshot, in the spaces between those few and comfortless words.

CHAPTER 10

The Tragic Muse

David Garrick was now the young lion of the English theatre. After a faint-hearted show of joining his brother Peter in the wine business, he had been drawn increasingly towards the stage. As far back as 1740, when Johnson was still slaving at St John's Gate, Garrick had made an occasional visit to him at the office, and his talk of plays and roles had aroused the interest even of the phleg-matic Cave. Would Garrick, Cave asked, give them a demonstration of his powers? Seizing any chance to spread his wings, Garrick readily agreed. The large room over the archway was cleared and fitted up as a makeshift theatre, various of Cave's employees were brought in to read the subordinate parts, and Garrick gave a performance in the comic role of *The Mock Doctor*, Henry Fielding's adaptation of Molière's *Le Médecin Malgré Lui*. Johnson, watching, must have been reminded of the first time he had seen David act, in somewhat similar circumstances, at Gilbert Walmesley's house.

There was no holding back the fiercely dedicated youth. Some months later he joined a little fit-up company that went down for a few weeks to Ipswich, where he acted under the name of Lyddal. In October 1741, announced as 'a gentleman who never appeared on any stage', he took London by storm in his first appearance as Shakespeare's Richard III. He became a celebrity overnight, and was never for the rest of his life to be anything else, though there were to be difficulties enough with shifty managements, obstinate rivals, amorous and temperamental leading ladies.

The London stage was hedged about with legal restrictions. Plays, as such, could be put on only at those theatres which had managed to obtain a patent from the Lord Chamberlain, and Garrick's first resplendent success as Richard III was obtained by circumventing this law in a rather cumbrous way. Giffard, the licensee of the theatre at Goodman's Fields, advertised a concert of music, and slipped in a play between the two halves, the legal fiction being that the play was offered free of charge as a makeweight, much as the playhouse of the time offered a jig or a farce as an extra titbit. Once his name was made, Garrick was no longer content to perform in this hole-and-corner way. Besides, he had lofty ambitions, not only as an actor but as a manager; he dreamt of raising the whole standard of theatrical entertainment, and in particular of bringing a new seriousness to the production of Shakespeare, ridding it of the cobbled and vul-garized texts that had been common theatrical fare since the Restoration. No-thing would do but that he must become a manager, free to put on what he chose in his own theatre, and to this end he threw in his lot with one Lacy, the manager of Drury Lane, who had suffered severe financial losses during the troubled year of 1745 and was looking for a partner. Garrick, who reportedly paid the then very large price of £8000 for his share, became joint manager of this famous theatre in time to take control of the season for 1747–8.

One of his first actions was to set Johnson's pen to work. The first night of the season, under the ambitious new management, would obviously be an important occasion, and Garrick asked Johnson for a verse prologue, a verbal fanfare that he could recite from the stage as the first words spoken in the theatre in its new phase. Johnson obliged with a solid, closeknit, sonorously tolling sixty-two lines of verse, sketching the progress of the English drama from Shakespeare to his own day: strong, memorable, speakable stuff. Like everything Johnson wrote, the Prologue had a firm moral purpose; after commenting on the sad state of the theatre during the licentious times of the Restoration and then amid the frivolities and sideshows that had claimed attention since, he pointed out that the audience had it in their power to choose solid, nourishing fare and see that it was provided:

> Hard is his lot, that here by fortune placed,
> Must watch the wild vicissitudes of taste;
> With every meteor of caprice must play,
> And chase the new-blown bubbles of the day.
> Ah! let not censure term our fate our choice,
> The stage but echoes back the public voice.
> The drama's laws the drama's patrons give,
> For we that live to please, must please to live.

So that, as he went on to remind the glittering, fashionable crowd,

> 'Tis yours this night to bid the reign commence
> Of rescued Nature and reviving Sense.

The whole pronouncement was well in line with Garrick's lofty sense of mission; which made it all the more disappointing that when the great evening came – 15 September 1747 – Garrick was ill and unable to speak the lines in person.

Still, the opening was in every other respect a success, and now that his former pupil was so firmly established in a position of power in the theatrical world, Johnson's thoughts naturally began to turn back towards his own long-buried ambitions as a dramatic writer. *Irene* was brought out, dusted off, and handed to Garrick, who showed every sign of being co-operative. At last came the firm promise, one that this time would be kept. *Irene* would be seen on the stage of Drury Lane Theatre, not in the first winter's season but early in the second.

As Johnson toiled away in the garret in Gough Square, the promise must have been sweet. It helped him to keep alive his ideal of being a real man of letters, an imaginative writer, an artist, and not solely a lexicographer, 'a harmless drudge', 'without any higher quality than that of bearing burthens with dull patience, and beating the track of the alphabet with sluggish resolution'. The rueful words were Johnson's own. And of course they were uttered partly in a spirit of irony. They represent what the lexicographer was commonly thought to be, rather than what he was. Nevertheless, Johnson found the endless defining, compiling, deriving, ordering, listing a weariness of the flesh and still more of the spirit. Good scholar as he was, he had not been put on earth merely to settle the meanings of words and adjudicate questions of syntax and usage. He was a poet, a man of vision. Though older and a shade wearier, he was still the man of whom Gilbert Walmesley had once said, 'I have hopes that he will turn out a fine tragedy writer.' And now his tragedy was at last to be put on, by the finest actor and in the most dedicated theatre in England. Now, surely, he could keep his chin above the cold, heavy sea of dictionary-making. And to prove it he put his task aside for long enough to write a poem, a non-dramatic poem, one of his weightiest and in its sombre colouring one of his most moving and beautiful.

The Vanity of Human Wishes is, like *London*, an adaptation of Juvenal. But whereas the earlier poem took off from Juvenal's third satire, about Rome, Johnson turned now to the more stately and generalized tenth poem in the series, where the theme is not the corruption of a city but the shortcomings of human nature itself. The note has deepened; the liveliness, the virtuosity, of *London* are replaced by a density and gravity of language that is Johnson's particular contribution to English poetry. The lines are strong and weighty; the rhythms are emphatic, often antithetical yet with a steady forward beat: the language is vivid and concrete, but presses always towards generalization. To see all these qualities we need only take the first passage at which the book falls open:

> Unnumbered suppliants crowd preferment's gate,
> Athirst for wealth, and burning to be great;
> Delusive fortune hears the incessant call,
> They mount, they shine, evaporate, and fall.
> On every stage the foes of peace attend,
> Hate dogs their flight, and insult mocks their end.
> Love ends with hope, the sinking statesman's door
> Pours in the morning worshipper no more;
> For growing names the weekly scribbler lies,
> To growing wealth the dedicator flies,
> From every room descends the painted face,
> That hung the bright palladium of the place,
> And smoked in kitchens, or in auctions sold,
> To better features yields the frame of gold;
> For now no more we trace in every line
> Heroic worth, benevolence divine:
> The form distorted justifies the fall,
> And detestation rids the indignant wall.

Here we have a terse, economical sketch of what life has in store for those who stake everything on the climb to material success and social position. Their ambition is expressed in physical terms: they are 'athirst' for wealth, and like everyone tormented by thirst they are 'burning'. But they are not fully living beings, these ambitious people; two lines further on they are described in non-animate physical terms – they mount, shine, evaporate and fall in the manner of soap bubbles or vapours which are dispersed by the sunlight. To convey the degradation of their inevitable decline, Johnson first uses generalized words – 'hate', 'insult' – and peoples his lines with type figures, the sinking statesman, the morning worshipper, the weekly scribbler, each noun with its attendant epithet, conveying the impression of these people as cardboard cutouts and their life as an unreal charade. But these general terms become insipid and undramatic if continued over a long stretch, and soon Johnson moves in to the particularized, concrete image of the portrait being taken down from the wall: the very precise evocation of the smoky kitchen and the auction-room building up finally to the mingled abstract and concrete of the last couplet. Now that the important man is important no longer, people suddenly see meanness and stupidity in the features they formerly admired. The closeness in sound of 'form' and 'fall' forges a link between the two notions: and then, clinchingly, comes the detail that the very wall has become indignant at having, for so long, supported the weight of the portrait: the 'detestation' now felt for the fallen statesman has permeated the bricks and plaster – as our feelings do, indeed, permeate the world we live in.

If these qualities are so discernible in a passage chosen at random, they show to even better advantage in the famous set pieces: about the 'young enthusiast' whose ambition is to be a famous scholar, or about 'Swedish Charles', Charles XII of Sweden – an historical figure in whom Johnson had long been interested and about whom he had considered writing a play. True to the processes of 'Imitation', Johnson peoples his poem with characters whose impact was on his world and not that of Juvenal; for Juvenal's Sejanus he substitutes Cardinal Wolsey, for Hannibal Charles XII. The result is that he is free to cast a cold eye on the pretensions of worldly power and ambition as his society has known them. The poem levels down the human landscape remorselessly until it reaches the point where it can pose its ultimate question:

> Where then shall Hope and Fear their objects find?

One could hardly, in fact, ask a more fundamental question. And Johnson's answer is what, from our knowledge of his mind, we should expect it to be. Religious faith, the relinquishing of anguish and doubt in the unknowable, but undoubtable, providence of God – that is the only way.

> Still raise for good the supplicating voice,
> But leave to heaven the measure and the choice.

The Vanity of Human Wishes was published, like all Johnson's work so far, anonymously. But the inner circle of literary *cognoscenti* knew well enough that it was the work of that Mr Johnson who had made a strong impression with *London*, with the *Life of Savage*, with his work for Cave and on the Harleian catalogue, and who was now engaged in a prolonged wrestle with the language itself. Johnson was on the way up – though it was a slow and toilsome process compared with the series of bounds which had brought Garrick to his pinnacle. That Johnson was without jealousy of his ex-pupil it would be foolish to maintain. He knew that Garrick had not worked harder than himself, knew that he had no more to contribute to the common stock of wisdom and wellbeing than himself, yet there was the little man lording it over that city to which the pair of them had trudged a dozen years before. What was more, Garrick's personal life had a glow of pleasure and excitement that Johnson's had never known and obviously never would know. As they conferred on the matter of *Irene*, thrashing out various matters concerning text and production, Johnson often called at the theatre and became, briefly, a member of the privileged minority who could at any time wander backstage. He abandoned this privilege for a characteristic reason, which he voiced frankly to Garrick. The presence of so many attractive and bosomy young actresses put him into a disturbing state of sexual excitement. 'I'll come no more behind your scenes, Davy.' It was more than he could stand, who was committed to praying for 'obedient passions, and a will resigned'. The story is, of course, an implicit comment on Johnson's physical relationship with Tetty. If all had been reasonably well in that department, a certain degree of sexual arousal could have done nothing but good. But the probability is that by this time the sexual life of the Johnsons was already a thing of the past. For the powerful and virile Sam there was nothing for it but to champ on the bit. No wonder he avoided the proximity of Garrick's actresses, one of the most attractive of whom, Peg Woffington, had moved in with Garrick and was providing an agreeable, if unstable, domestic felicity.

No wonder Johnson was always slightly sour about Garrick. So many things that were beyond Johnson's dreams Garrick enjoyed effortlessly, as of right. Garrick, for his part, was a model of cheerfulness and steady goodwill. He put up with a lot from Johnson during these months. The play needed certain minor changes to make it fully actable, as every play does when it first leaves its author's desk. But Johnson was stubborn. He never believed in admitting 'the players' to the status of full collaborators. Their function was to get up on the stage and spout out whatever the author was pleased to write. In later years, as a critic of Shakespeare, it is noteworthy that Johnson never uses the words 'audience' or 'spectator'. When he discusses the effect of Shakespeare's work on its recipients, it is always 'the reader' of whom he speaks. His image of the public for Shakespeare is the image of a host of solitary readers, each turning the pages by his own fireside. Such a view of the drama is uncompromisingly literary. 'A dramatic exhibition is a book, recited with concomitants that increase or diminish the effect.' The definition is absurd unless we give so much weight to the 'concomitants' as to admit that they can make or mar the entire impression; and if we do it becomes meaningless.

Fortunately, Johnson's reluctance to allow Garrick to lay a finger on the text of *Irene* never hardened into a flat refusal. For this the credit should probably go to John Taylor, the stolid country lawyer turned parson who had known both of them since schooldays and could act as intermediary. Taylor, on his visits to London, used to come to evening performances at the theatre, and afterwards Garrick, fresh from the plaudits of the town, was not too proud to join his old Staffordshire mates in a tavern. Johnson, on these occasions, took a special pleasure in nit-picking criticism of Garrick's work. On one occasion Garrick brought along a professional colleague of his: Giffard, the same manager who had been responsible for launching him into his first successes. Johnson made his usual charge that actors had no idea how to respect the *nuances* of the English language. When Garrick and Giffard demurred at this, Johnson set them a test sentence. They were to pronounce the Ninth Commandment, 'Thou shalt not bear false witness against thy neighbour.' Both Garrick and Giffard uttered the words, but Johnson faulted them, maintaining, with an authority that recognized no court of appeal, that the emphases should run: 'Thou shalt *not* bear *false witness* against thy neighbour.' Years later, recalling the incident to Boswell, Taylor remembered the 'great glee' with which Johnson enjoyed his demonstration of superiority; which was, after all, a thin one enough.

But Garrick, in spite of these flickings, remained Johnson's unalterable friend. He threw himself into the business of staging *Irene*, omitting nothing that would help it towards success. Taylor noted that he spent an unusual amount of money on the production; and the cast included a number of star players – Garrick himself, Barry, who was one of his principal supporting actors, and two leading ladies, Mrs Cibber and Mrs Pritchard. (Eighteenth-century actresses were always called 'Mrs' this or that, whether they were married or not; an admirable convention.) With this glittering galaxy, *Irene* took the boards on 6 February 1749 – thirteen years after its composition.

Johnson decided to celebrate the event in style. Perhaps it was a reaction from the long, dusty hours of work on the Dictionary, but he was at this time in a mood to go into society, to appear in public, even to act the part of a celebrity in that gay and rather raffish world of 'players and painted stage'. Only a few years earlier, when Cave had invited Walter Harte to dinner and plied him with questions about Johnson's *Life of Savage*, the author of that book had been present, ears tingling, but his food had been sent to him behind a screen so that his ragged appearance should not cause genteel embarrassment. Johnson now determined to bury that kind of memory for ever. On the first night of *Irene*, he appeared in a box, wearing a scarlet waistcoat trimmed with gold lace, and with gold lace also on his hat. Tetty, we must assume, stayed at home. She would be in no mood to compete with such peacock finery.

The play went well, for four acts. Trouble came in the fifth, as the story wound up to its tragic *dénouement*. Mrs Pritchard, as the heroine, was to be executed onstage, and Garrick had determined that in accordance with high Turkish tradition she was to be strangled with a bowstring. The effect was disastrous: the audience shouted 'Murder, murder!' and fell about laughing. Finally the girl was led away to be despatched offstage. But the mood was broken. The high tragic experience had misfired.

Garrick, doggedly, held the play on the stage for nine nights, so that Johnson could get his three nights' benefit. (The standard Drury Lane contract was that the author of an original play received the profits from every third night, minus a deduction of sixty guineas for the expenses of the house.) Towards the end of the run he had to drag an audience into the theatre by means of the additional attractions of 'Scotch and Savoyard dances'. What Johnson thought of the Highland fling as a 'concomitant' to a Graeco-Turkish tale of high passion and noble virtue will never be known. But the result, financially, was welcome. He received £195 17s from the theatre, and an additional £100 when the publisher, Robert Dodsley, bought the copyright. All those months of writing in the big house at Edial, all the interviewing of managers, the scheming and fixing, the anxieties had been amply rewarded. Even the gold-laced waistcoat would come in handy if he were ever invited to the Lord Mayor's Show. Altogether, the situation had enough good features to enable him to keep his composure in the face of a certain amount of ridicule.

There was, also, a principle at stake. Johnson believed firmly that the public had a right to its own judgement. If a man approached his contemporaries with something designed to win their applause, they were to be the judges of whether it pleased them or not, and it was mean and foolish for an unsuccessful author to scold the very people whose taste he would have praised if they had approved his offering. 'We that live to please must please to live.' From first to last Johnson never took the pearls-before-swine attitude. He 'rejoiced to concur with the common reader'. Art, to him, was a matter of communication, and if it failed to communicate there should be no whining against the public. So that, when asked how he felt on watching the play bring the audience to laughter instead of tears, it was with a sense of living up to his own standards that he replied calmly, 'Like the Monument'.

And so ended the nine nights of *Irene*.

CHAPTER 11

Diversions of a Lexicographer

Johnson was still determined to try the strength of his pinions, to soar higher and higher. He was now three years deep into the Dictionary, loaded with work that filled up hours of each day and stretched far into the future. Yet he refused to give up his hold on life, his involvement in writing and talking and meeting people. His concern was to be not only with words but with the things that words were formed to express. Somehow, round the edges of the huge commitment, he kept his mind, and his pen, so active that a record of his activities during these years would read like a normal working schedule for most writers.

For instance, in 1748 Dodsley published a miscellany in twelve parts, offering 'a General Course of Education' for 'trying the Genius, and advancing the Instruction of Youth'. Johnson contributed a memorable preface, and also one of the pieces in the second number, 'The Vision of Theodore, the Hermit of Teneriffe, found in his Cell'. He remarked years later, in the hearing of Bishop Percy, that this was the best thing he ever wrote. Certainly it is a sombre and beautiful fable.

He was also involved with the fame of John Milton, that great craggy poet whose work and personality alternately attracted and repelled him. Johnson recognized in Milton a mind as powerful as his own, a learning even wider, a strength of character hardened under pressure into arrogance and inflexibility. He delighted in the majesty and beauty of Milton's verse and the loftiness of his conceptions, but was horrified by some of the liberties the poet took with the English language and with what Johnson considered the principles of good writing. Many years were to pass before, in his magnificently crusty life of Milton, he was to turn and face the whole bundle of contradictory feelings that Milton's work inspired in him. At this earlier period he stopped and started, adopted one viewpoint and then another, chipping away at the hard subject. In one mood, he felt simple reverence for a man so colossal and so gifted. *Paradise Lost*, very much under a cloud during the first few decades after its publication in 1667, had brightened steadily till it now blazed in the firmament of English poetry; and when it was discovered in the late 1740s that Milton's granddaughter and only surviving descendant was living in poverty Garrick immediately declared his intention of staging a benefit performance of *Comus* for her. Johnson, once again, wrote a reverberating prologue for Garrick to speak, and also published a letter in the Press, drawing attention to the performance in stirring terms:

> Whoever ... would be thought capable of pleasure in reading the works of our incomparable Milton, and not so destitute of gratitude as to refuse to lay out a trifle in a rational and elegant entertainment for the benefit of his living remains, for the exercise of their own virtue, the increase of their reputation and the pleasing consciousness of doing good, should appear at Drury Lane theatre tomorrow, 5 April, when *Comus* will be performed for the benefit of Miss Elizabeth Foster, grand-daughter of the author, and the only surviving branch of his family.
>
> N.B. There will be a new prologue on the occasion, written by the author of *Irene*.

The 'new prologue' paid resounding homage to Milton.

Johnson was certainly wholehearted in his efforts to better the worldly condition of Milton's grand-daughter. He renewed his appeals on her behalf, asking this time for subscriptions, in a postscript he contributed to a curious performance, William Lauder's *Essay on Milton's Use and Imitation of the Moderns in his Paradise Lost*. For this he also wrote a preface. Lauder's extraordinary essay thus appeared in a Johnsonian sandwich. Its object was, ostensibly, to demonstrate Milton's use of certain modern Latin poems as sources for his epic. Johnson, as we have already seen, was always interested in tracing the stages whereby some great effort of the human spirit had selected the channels into which it was finally to flow. He innocently recommended Lauder's investigation as an early example of *Quellenforschung*:

> Among the inquiries to which this ardour of criticism has naturally given occasion, none is more obscure in itself, or more worthy of rational curiosity, than a restrospection of the progress of this mighty genius in the construction of his work; a view of the fabric gradually rising, perhaps from small beginnings, till its foundation rests in the centre and its turrets sparkle in the skies; to trace back the structure, through all its varieties, to the simplicity of its first plan; to find what was first projected, whence the scheme was taken, how it was improved, by what assistance it was executed, and from what stores the materials were collected, whether its founder dug them from the quarries of nature, or demolished other buildings to embellish his own.

Unfortunately, Lauder's motives were not as pure as Johnson's, and without doubt Johnson was to blame for not looking into the matter far more carefully before dashing off his preface. Lauder was in fact a man with a pathological grudge against Milton. Exactly what was the matter with him must remain conjectural, but it is clear that his temperament was soured by misfortune and that his attitude to life in general had become paranoid. A Scot, Lauder had taken his degree at Edinburgh University, and soon afterwards had been watching a golf match when a ball struck him on the leg. The injury was not properly treated, and as a result the limb deteriorated and had to be amputated. Further trials were to follow. Lauder's repeated efforts to obtain a teaching post in Scotland were frustrated as he was passed over for one job after another. He wrote a preface for a Latin textbook by one Arthur Johnson, only to see it rejected in favour of an established one by the humanist Buchanan. Lauder tried to involve Pope in the controversy by sending him a copy of Johnson's book; Pope did not reply, but later, in *The Dunciad*, made an uncharitable reference to Johnson, comparing him unfavourably with Milton. This seems to have sown in Lauder's mind an unsleeping hatred both of Pope and of the unoffending Milton, who came to appear to his disordered vision as one of the barriers to his hopes of a successful career as a teacher of the classics.

Milton's poetry having become blended in a single hostile focus with the pretensions of Lauder's professional rivals, he began to cook up a vast hoax in which he would make fools of them and also discredit the English poet. Accordingly, he laid hold of a Latin translation of *Paradise Lost* by a man named Hog, and inserted passages of it into the works of earlier modern Latin poets, mainly those of Hugo Grotius, in order to make the charge that Milton had stolen some of his gems from them. Naturally the deception could not for long go undetected. Lauder based his pamphlet on some essays he had published in *The Gentleman's Magazine*, and already a Cambridge man, Richard Richardson, had exposed the imposture in a pamphlet which appeared in 1747. Samuel Johnson could not have read this pamphlet, or he would not, however absentmindedly, have given his support to Lauder's publication of 1750. In 1751, however, there appeared a refutation too weighty to be ignored. John Douglas, later Bishop of Salisbury, published a pamphlet entitled *Milton vindicated from the charge of plagiarism, brought against him by Mr Lauder, and Lauder himself convicted of several forgeries and gross impositions on the public.* Johnson immediately dictated to Lauder a confession, published within a few weeks of Douglas's exposure, and the publishers of Lauder's work advertised that they would thereafter 'sell his book only as a masterpiece of fraud'. All copies subsequently sold were provided with a disclaiming preface. But the spilt milk could not be entirely mopped up, and Johnson had to endure, for many years afterwards, the reputation of having made a *gaffe*.

Far more important and weighty than these casual commitments was the undertaking he hoisted up in March 1750. This was nothing less than to publish, twice a week, an essay containing serious reflections, usually on the conduct of life but sometimes also about literature, history, ideas in general. For this he was to get four guineas a week; if we go by our familiar rule of thumb in estimating the purchasing power of money as twenty times what it is today, it was an income on which he and Tetty could have lived, simply but without strain. But they already had a regular income from the Dictionary. It was not want that drove Johnson to his desk twice a week, to write those papers in which he expressed his deep and sombre convictions about the life of the human being in this dark and dangerous world. He could have done without the money, and no one could have accused him of idling or of failing to provide a decent home for his wife. No, it was a more profound emotional and intellectual hunger: the need to communicate with others, to pass on the lessons of his experience and the illumination that came to him in meditation and prayer. The second was as important as the first. Fervent Christian that he was, he clung to his faith the more tenaciously as life battered him more and more. Before beginning the series, he composed a gravely moving prayer that his work might be useful for ends higher than those of this world:

> Almighty God, the giver of all good things, without whose help all labour is ineffectual, and without whose grace all wisdom is folly, grant, I beseech thee, that in this my undertaking thy Holy Spirit may not be withheld from me, but that I may promote thy glory, and the salvation both of myself and others. Grant this O Lord for the sake of Jesus Christ. Amen. Lord bless me. So be it.

The idea of a periodical essay was, of course, no novelty. It had been strongly entrenched in English journalism since the success of Addison and Steele with *The Tatler* and *The Spectator* some forty years previously. As newspapers multiplied, and grew in size and scope, they swallowed the separately published periodical essay; just as many of them continued to be written, and for that matter continue to be written now, but they took their place alongside the news and editorial matter. During most of the eighteenth century, however, the essay of three or four pages, published on regular days, had a following. In the hands of Addison and Steele it had powerfully influenced the development of a new and gentler code of social behaviour – and also, incidentally, sunk the Tories still further in public esteem by representing Sir Roger de Coverley as a likeable but quaint old codger whose political views no modern-minded person could possibly share.

Johnson, as was his practice, related himself to the existing tradition, but with a difference. He envisaged a more weighty version of the familiar essay, with very little room for entertainment and none at all for flightiness. Neither now nor at any other time did he see himself as merely angling for the attention of the public with any attractive bait that would bring in the customers. He could take no satisfaction in a piece of work unless he could feel that it ministered to wisdom and helped his readers to see things clearly and put their values in order. To this end he marched steadily on, for the next two years, publishing two hundred and eight essays of which only five were in whole or in part by any other hand than his own. By the time he had finished, he had presented a complete view of the obligations, and rewards, of morality and piety, exhibited in just about every imaginable situation. For this stately procession it would be difficult to find a less appropriate name than the one Johnson came up with: *The Rambler*. (Though as Boswell, obviously choking with laughter, remarks, it is even more absurd in the Italian translation, *Il Vagabondo*.) Johnson, for his part, never pretended that *The Rambler* was a good name. It was simply the name he had been able to think of, when the job could no longer be put off. As he told Sir Joshua Reynolds, he sat down on his bed one night, determined not to go to sleep until he had found a name for the series, and *The Rambler* was the one that suggested itself and allowed him to blow out the candle.

The tiny incident catches one's attention because it anticipates the way in which so much of the work was to be carried out. By temperamental inclination and unbreakable habit, Johnson always produced his work at the last minute – was, indeed, scarcely capable of writing anything except under the lash of a deadline. He must have known, when he contracted for *The Rambler*, that this lash would be applied twice a week as long as the series went on. It was a perfectly deliberate means of forcing himself to write. He wanted to communicate with his fellow men, and he knew that this arrangement would make him do it. He wrote a hundred essays a year for the simple reason that he had to. The density and economy of the style gives the effect of deliberation; in fact, the majority of the pieces were written hurriedly and without revision. Sometimes, indeed, the 'printer's devil' – the ink-smeared, scruffy urchin employed to run to and from the printing house – would be standing by Johnson's desk as he wrote, carrying away each sheet as soon as he had finished it. In these punishing circumstances only one thing saved Johnson from loose writing, raggedness, imprecision. That was his lifelong habit of clear and precise expression on all occasions, even the humblest. He told Reynolds, who told Boswell, that he made it a rule to find the most lucid and effective way of expressing anything he had to say, so that 'by constant practice, and never suffering any careless expression to escape him, or attempting to deliver his thoughts without arranging them in the clearest manner, it became habitual to him'.

The Rambler is the triumphant justification of this rule. Even if Johnson had written and cogitated nothing else during these two years, it would still be an astonishing performance. The solidity of thought, the majestic harmonies of the prose, stride on through essay after essay; few, very few, are the descents into pomposity or platitude. And this achievement is the more remarkable inasmuch as Johnson was deliberately steering close to the obvious. Writing for the ordinary man who stood in need of instruction, he was determined not to wander off into the intricate mazes of speculation, nor leave the straight path to chase bright ideas that would immediately lose their novelty and become shabby. He wrote two hundred essays without a single page of specialist jargon, a single bright epigram, nothing but plain good sense and straightforward piety. The result, of course, does not suit everybody. Johnson knew well enough that his essays would hold no attraction for the reader who hankers always to be told something new. He disposed of this objection by remarking, in his vein of grand simplicity, that 'men more often require to be reminded than informed'. Almost every thought that we come across in *The Rambler* will have occurred to us before, in some guise or other. But we meet it again in these pages, cleaned, sharply focused, and glowing with the strong subdued light of Johnson's prose.

So much – in bald outline – for what *The Rambler* essays can do for us, the readers. On a more personal level, they have much to tell us about Johnson as man and writer. They illustrate two qualities: his compassion, and his belief in the absolute necessity of moral instruction.

The compassion is evident both in the opinions expressed in the essays, and in their tone and procedure. *The Rambler*, like Johnson's later series of essays, contains a number of papers on penal reform. On this topic, Johnson's thinking was considerably ahead of the general opinion of his time, as it was on the related issue of slavery. He was, frankly, aghast at the savagery he saw in the penal system, especially on two points: the treatment of debtors, and the reckless use of the death penalty. To be arrested for debt, in the eighteenth century, was considerably worse than being arrested for a criminal offence, except of the hanging sort. The debtors' prisons were among the worst for squalor and disease; those who survived beyond the first few weeks did so by means of an iron constitution and an iron will to live; this involved trampling on the weak and the infirm at mealtimes, when a hatch in the ceiling was opened and scraps of food, of a quality little higher than garbage, were showered in. In these circumstances, and given the fact that the debtor had no opportunity to engage in work that might pay off his debt – the only avenue to release – it followed that an arrest for debt was commonly regarded as a death sentence. As for the eighteenth century's notions on capital punishment, everyone has heard of Tyburn Tree, the public executions conducted in a holiday atmosphere, with all the paraphernalia of farewell speeches, the hawking of pamphlets recounting the sensational life-stories of the convicted men, the pushing and shoving to watch a fellow-creature choke to death. Johnson faces all these as resolutely as any other facts. With a human pity that never degenerates into sentimentality, with a rhetoric that tolls irresistibly without ever rising to stridency, he works earnestly at the task of awakening a public conscience in these matters. The essay on capital punishment (No. 114) is a good example:

> The learned, the judicious, the pious *Boerhaave* relates that he never saw a criminal dragged to execution without asking himself, 'Who knows whether this man is not less culpable than me?' On the days when the prisons of this city are emptied into the grave, let every spectator of the dreadful procession put the same question to his own heart. Few among those that crowd in thousands to the legal massacre, and look with carelessness, perhaps with triumph, on the utmost exacerbations of human misery, would then be able to return without horror and dejection. For who can congratulate himself upon a life passed without some act more mischievous to the peace or prosperity of others, than the theft of a piece of money?

Sometimes the compassion spills over from Johnson's subject matter to his method. Since the *Ramblers* offer moral instruction, which includes putting the reader on his guard against false premises and wrong behaviour, they resort frequently to satire. The length of the essay is exactly right for the satirical sketch of, say, a legacy-hunter or a sprightly widow with an attractive grown-up daughter. But satire, from a Christian point of view like Johnson's, has one great drawback. It encourages uncharitable feelings towards its object. By inviting us to ridicule a person or an institution or a foible, it gives a licence to our own feelings of superiority and complacence, which may be merely spite and envy in disguise. Hence Johnson sometimes blurs the satiric effect by suddenly pointing out that even the type he has been inviting us to laugh at is a man and a brother, who deserves our sympathy. Thus, in *Rambler* No. 59 he sets out promisingly to draw a portrait of 'Suspirius, the human screech owl'. This man is the inveterate grumbler with a determinedly pessimistic and negative view of the world, unable to see anyone enjoying anything without rushing in to point out all the dangers and drawbacks. Johnson sets about this lay figure with gusto, producing an outline that later served Goldsmith as a model for the character of Croaker in his successful comedy *The Good-Natured Man*. For several pages all goes spankingly, in this vein:

Another of his topics is the neglect of merit, with which he never fails to amuse every man whom he sees not eminently fortunate. If he meets with a young officer, he always informs him of gentlemen whose personal courage is unquestioned, and whose military skill qualifies them to command armies, that have, notwithstanding all their merit, grown old with subaltern commissions. For a genius in the church, he is always provided with a curacy for life. The lawyer he informs of many men of great parts and deep study, who have never had an opportunity to speak in the courts: And meeting Serenus the physician, 'Ah doctor', says he, 'what afoot still, when so many blockheads are rattling their chariots? I told you seven years ago that you would never meet with encouragement, and I hope you will now take more notice when I tell you that your Greek, and your diligence, and your honesty will never enable you to live like yonder apothecary, who prescribes to his own shop, and laughs at the physician.'

Suspirius has, in his time, intercepted fifteen authors in their way to the stage; persuaded nine and thirty merchants to retire from a prosperous trade for fear of bankruptcy, broke off an hundred and thirteen matches by prognostications of unhappiness, and enabled the smallpox to kill nineteen ladies, by perpetual alarms of the loss of beauty.

Johnson finishes by suggesting a solution; all these human screech owls should be debarred from normal company, and made to flock together in 'some proper receptacle, where they may mingle sighs at leisure, and thicken the gloom of one another'. One more paragraph, a closing flourish, and the essay is finished. And then, suddenly, it isn't. Johnson finds himself unable to lay down his pen without cautioning us against hardness of heart. After writing an entire essay against the compulsive grumbler, he softens the effect by reminding us that most of the people who complain have very genuine things to complain about, and that hardness of heart is a sin to be avoided:

To hear complaints with patience, even when complaints are vain, is one of the duties of friendship; and though it must be allowed that he suffers most like a hero that hides his grief in silence,

Spem vultu simulat, premit altum corde dolorem   Aeneid, I.209
His outward smiles concealed his inward smart   Dryden

yet, it cannot be denied that he who complains acts like a man, like a social
being who looks for help from his fellow creatures. Pity is to many of the
unhappy a source of comfort in hopeless distresses, as it contributes
to recommend them to themselves, by proving that they have not lost
the regard of others; and heaven seems to indicate the duty even of
barren compassion, by inclining us to weep for evils which we cannot
remedy.

The gentleness of that conclusion is something that no keen satirist would have
allowed himself. But Johnson is less concerned with writing a successful satire
than with expressing the truth about the human condition – a truth rarely as
clearcut as the satirist would make it. And since satire is a form of art we may
say that the moralist in Johnson has triumphed over the artist. This is a thought
we shall keep in mind when assessing Johnson as a writer. Though he had a
well-defined streak of the artist in him, his temperament was not entirely that of
the artist, who submerges himself in the medium and works by deep instinct.
Johnson has fundamental principles of action, arrived at emotionally and
imaginatively but formulated and codified in the head. These principles direct
everything. They are applied with all the strength of Johnson's powerful
ratiocinative intellect and they are dominant from first to last: which is not
exactly the way of art. The artist surrenders himself to the imaginative experience and lets its abounding current drive him where it will. Working very close
to the instinctual sources of experience, to the dream and vision which bypass
rationality, he touches the rock with his rod, and what gushes out is what is
there to gush out. It is too late, by that time, for ifs and buts:

> Our poesy is as a gum, which oozes
> From whence 'tis nourished.

Johnson is not this kind of imaginative writer. Deeply as he sees into life,
majestically as his harmonies and rhythms fall on the ear, he is essentially a
writer who uses art rather than one who allows art to use him. He belongs, that
is, with the great homiletic writers, the historians, the orators, the law-givers. It
would be fatal to underestimate such writers. Take them away from the literature of any nation and it becomes a heady but undrinkable fluid, wild, over-
volatile, uncontainable. But the imaginative artist in words, the seer and
utterer, the Shakespeare, the Blake, is made of a different stuff.

All this seems like a lot of effort to push away the idea that Johnson was a pure
artist, when nobody, as far as I know, has suggested that he was a pure artist.
But to raise the issue is to open the door to a central understanding of Johnson's
mind. That mind was aware of its own precarious balance, and all the more
determined to hold on to reason and clarity. No matter what went on in the
engine-room, the captain must always be on the bridge. If he left it even for a
moment, the ladder might collapse behind him and he might never get back.
Johnson had an immensely powerful reasoning intellect. He also had equally
powerful emotional and imaginative whirlpools just below the surface. In the

truly harmonious personality these forces are united and act together. To be truly alive is to give full scope to both, to avoid hampering or crippling either. So the theoreticians tell us. And perhaps, in one person out of every hundred thousand, such a harmony is achieved. Most human beings, however, achieve such balance as they have by starving one side or the other: the intellect, or the irrational forces. This principle works itself out not only in individual cases but in whole epochs. An age that puts its trust in the ordering intellect will distrust and underplay the instincts. An age like ours which worships the instinctual will become anti-rational. It is no accident that our age has seen reason and lucidity sink to their lowest level of esteem since man came down from the trees.

Johnson's trust was in reason. Not only did he come from a civilization that held this faith; he also endured a permanent inner turmoil that had to be held within bounds. He could, of course, have given way to that turmoil and let its waves carry him to some unknown shore. But to say this is to say that Johnson should have been Smart or Hölderlin and not Johnson. It is as if we should regret that Beethoven did not produce the physics of Newton instead of his own music.

The Rambler essays proclaim Johnson's trust in reason, in seeing things as they are, in thinking clearly and distinguishing justly. But they also, of course, mark the boundary line of that trust. Johnson believes in reasoning out everything that concerns conduct and the management of life. Deeper questions he resigns to faith. Above all the advice he offers there is one over-arching precept: resignation to the will of God. That will, he saw, was not knowable by reason, though God had provided man with certain clues and it was his duty to follow them up. Hence Johnson is preaching not rationality in the wide-open eighteenth-century sense, *à la* Voltaire or Hume, but a rationality strictly contained within the religious vision of life. This is a difficult balance to maintain and Johnson did, in fact, have difficulty in maintaining it. Because of his initial fear of mental disintegration, he clung fiercely to the two strongest things he knew – reason, and obedience to God. He did not dare let go of either. But the difficulty of reconciling them brought on fresh agonies and tensions; his very fear of madness drove him into a position where madness often seemed inevitable.

But Johnson fought back. His periods of gloom and exhaustion, his terrifying anxieties, rose now and then to a point of crisis at which he was unfit for work or for company, useless to himself and others. Whenever they were at a lower intensity he fought them off, and with a variety of weapons. He prayed; he wrestled with doubt; he studied; he shifted huge loads of work. And, whenever he got the chance, he talked. Conversation was immensely helpful to him because it took him away from the melancholy of solitude, and, what was even more important, confirmed him in his belief that his problems might be soluble by reason and discrimination. When he sat in a tavern, surrounded by highly intelligent companions who were obviously impressed by the power of his mind, who argued with him and had to admit that they had lost the argument, Johnson felt reassured and protected. The homage of a clever and well-informed circle provided objective evidence that the powerful brain with which God had chosen to endow him was functioning effectively – and that it might yet enable him to beat off the foul beasts who watched him from the shadows. With this end in view he had gathered together the friends who formed his immediate circle at that time, and set up, some months before beginning *The Rambler*, an informal club which met once a week at the King's Head, a tavern famous for its beefsteaks, in Ivy Lane near St Paul's. Here he regaled his leisure in talk that ranged over literature and life, in company with a group drawn from a number of professions. There was Hawkesworth, a writer who was later to score a resounding success with his account of Cook's voyages in the southern hemisphere; Johnson had known him since the days when they both worked for Cave on *The Gentleman's Magazine*. There was the staid, close-mouthed lawyer John Hawkins, later chairman of the Middlesex justices and a knight. Johnson did not like Hawkins much (nobody, indeed, liked him much), but some sort of friendship survived between them until Johnson's death, and Hawkins afterwards wrote his life. The most valued member of this circle was undoubtedly the kindly physician Dr Richard Bathurst, whom Johnson loved dearly. An easygoing, non-competitive man, Bathurst was not a success in his profession; he once told Johnson that after ten years' practice, he had never 'opened his hand to more than a guinea'. Gentle as he was, Bathurst had decided views and could express them with a trenchancy that delighted Johnson, who fondly re-called to Mrs Thrale, 'Dear Bathurst was a man to my very heart's content: he hated a fool, and he hated a rogue, and he hated a Whig; he was a *very good hater.*'

With this club Johnson must have passed some agreeable hours, and probably the cut and thrust of their conversation was helpful to him in arranging his thoughts for *The Rambler*. Meanwhile Tetty, we must suppose, stayed largely at home. The relationship between them cannot have been as close, these days, as it had once been. Johnson did, of course, spend more time at home than formerly, but he spent it either slaving away with his team of amanuenses or crouched over his desk feverishly writing the next *Rambler*. His leisure time, as ever, was spent largely outside. We know how Tetty spent many of the long hours; she lay in bed drinking and reading romances. But there must have been times when, like any middle-class lady, she presided over her tea-table. One guest in particular stands out. Johnson's odd collection of friends included an old Welsh physician named Zachariah Williams. Like most of the people Johnson enjoyed, he had a vein of originality, not to say eccentricity, which took the form in his case of a passion for scientific research, mathematical cal-culations and ingenious inventions. He had come to London originally in the hope that some of his original notions about navigation at sea would bring him fame and fortune. This had not happened, and never did happen, in spite of a powerful shove from Johnson, who listened attentively to the old man's rambling account of his discoveries and finally, in 1755, wrote them out in clear and incisive terms in a pamphlet entitled *An Account of an Attempt to ascertain the Longitude at Sea, by an exact Theory of the Variation of the Magnetical*

Needle; with a Table of the Variations at the most remarkable Cities in Europe, from the year 1660-1860. Zachariah Williams had a daughter, Anna, some three years older than Johnson, a gifted woman with literary ambitions; and Elizabeth Johnson made of Anna Williams a friend and a frequent visitor to the house in Gough Square. The time was to come when Samuel Johnson, too, was to enjoy her friendship; he always enjoyed the society of women, and his female friends contributed a very large share of such happiness as came his way. But at the moment Anna Williams was only on the fringe of Johnson's attention. Among his women friends pride of place was undoubtedly held by Charlotte Lennox, a young woman writer he had recently met.

Mrs Lennox, née Ramsay, was an interesting woman, who retained her liveliness and originality throughout a life of almost incessant misfortune. Born in America – the daughter, in fact, of the Lieutenant-Governor of New York – she was sent to England at about fifteen years old, to be educated under the care of a relative. By the time she got there, however, the relative had been overtaken by some unspecified calamity (death? lunacy?) and she could not return home because her father, Colonel James Ramsay, also chose this unsuitable moment to die, and made no provision for her. Charlotte had to shift for herself; it may be that she appeared briefly on the stage (Horace Walpole describes her as 'a deplorable actress') but mainly, and increasingly, she relied on her pen, especially after her marriage to a poor man plunged her into money difficulties from which she was never afterwards free. Beginning with a volume of poems, she passed rapidly to fiction, translation, editing. Her *Shakespeare Illustrated* was a pioneer work of literary scholarship, bringing into two substantial volumes all the sources Shakespeare had used for his plots, as far as these were known at that time; she translated Voltaire's *Le Siècle de Louis XIV* (1752) and also Brumoy's *Théâtre des Grecs* (*The Greek Theatre of Father Brumoy*, 1759). But her most memorable work, without doubt, was *The Female Quixote*, a novel still not quite forgotten. Obviously and self-confessedly derivative from Cervantes, the story tells of a young girl who forms her notions of life from seventeenth-century French romances, thus satirizing both the high-flown absurdity of the stories and the gullibility of the over-protected girls. Johnson much admired this book; it dealt with a theme, the relationship of appearance and reality, that was never far from his own thoughts, and did so with a wit and gusto that impressed him. He gave it a favourable review in *The Gentleman's Magazine* for March 1752, following hard on an equally good notice by Henry Fielding in the *Covent Garden Journal*. To be praised, first by the leading contemporary exponent of the picaresque novel, then by the foremost champion of morality and right thinking, must have been almost intoxicatingly encouraging for young Mrs Lennox; especially as Fielding gravely gave his judgement that her book was more convincing, in some respects, than the masterpiece of Cervantes: an old gentleman would be less likely to have his head turned by the reading of old romances than a young maiden.

Johnson's admiration for Charlotte Lennox, however, did not begin with the publication of *The Female Quixote* in 1752. It was already strongly implanted in the spring of the previous year, when she published her first novel, *The Life of Harriot Stuart*. (I have not read this book, nor met anyone who has, but it is said to be largely autobiographical, and certainly 'Harriot Stuart' is exactly the same kind of name as 'Charlotte Ramsay'.) Johnson proposed to his fellow-members of the Ivy Lane Club that they should mark the occasion by an all-night sitting.

It was agreed, and the members and their friends and womenfolk, to the number of about twenty, assembled at eight in the evening at the Devil Tavern near Temple Bar: a famous haunt of literary men – Ben Jonson, Swift, Addison, Steele. For what happened thereafter we are indebted to a delicious page or two in Hawkins's *Life of Johnson*. Here, in the only passage of his good grey book that has anything like the colour and *brio* of Boswell, the sobersides actually catches something of the conviviality of that evening in eighteenth-century Bohemia. His account is made all the more hilarious by its grudging tone, since Hawkins himself, who disapproved of all-night revelling and was in any case suffering from a raging toothache, obviously hated the whole affair.

'Our supper was elegant', he concedes, with the air of a man determined to be scrupulously fair, 'and Johnson had directed that a magnificent hot apple-pie should make a part of it, and this he would have stuck with bay-leaves because, forsooth, Mrs Lennox was an authoress, and had written verses.' That 'for-sooth' gives the game away; it conveys all the superiority and bad temper of the future Chairman of Magistrates among poets and ne'er-do-wells. 'Further', he goes on, '[Johnson] had prepared for her a crown of laurel, with which, but not till he had invoked the muses by some ceremonies of his own invention, he encircled her brow.' It is a pity that Hawkins evidently considered it beneath the dignity of his lawyerly pen to describe these 'ceremonies' of Johnson's 'own invention'. In any case, his attention was soon claimed by his aching tooth, which the kindly Bathurst endeavoured without success to soothe by one nostrum after another. Hawkins registered that the night passed 'in pleasant conversation and harmless mirth'. Johnson was at this time going through one of his periods of abstinence from alcoholic drinks, but he kept going on lemon-ade so buoyantly that at five in the morning, when most of the company were buckling at the knees, his 'face shone with meridian splendour', and he called for a fresh supply of coffee to revive his wilting friends. This woke them up enough to ask for the bill, but it was two hours before they could get it because 'the waiters were all so overcome with sleep'.

Hawkins, obviously, was glad to get out into the street. He felt ashamed, 'not by reflection on anything evil that had passed in the course of the night's enter-tainment, but on the resemblance that it bore to a debauch'. The man was a Victorian born before his time. Johnson, on the other hand, was an example of that rare species, the harmless, non-vicious Bohemian. He might keep his friends rather short of sleep, but he would never lead them into any more serious harm. Charlotte Lennox and her husband, it is safe to assume, went home through the early-morning streets in a pleased, unhawkinsian mood.

And how did Johnson get to know Charlotte Lennox in the first place? Because she had married one of Strahan's employees. And who was Strahan?

The printer of the Dictionary. The surface of life may have been variegated with new friends, new ideas, new enterprises; but its core was always the same, for nine years: the long garret with its counting-house desk, the scratch of quills and the snip of scissors, and the huge figure in the corner bent over his desk, reading, cogitating, racking his brain for definitions, consulting books, underlining passages, on and on as the seasons changed outside the window, for these were the Dictionary years.

CHAPTER 12

Alone

'Time, which puts an end to all human pleasures and sorrows', Johnson wrote, 'has likewise concluded the labours of the Rambler. Having supported, for two years, the anxious employment of a periodical writer, and multiplied my essays to four volumes, I have now determined to desist.' It was March 1752; he had proved his ability to keep the series going more or less indefinitely, but the effort was beginning to tell on him and, as he remarked in the last paper but one, 'He that is himself weary will soon weary the public.'

Not that the public had ever been particularly avid. *The Rambler* made so few concessions that Johnson neither expected nor wished that it should command a wide public, and in fact the only number to have a large sale was No. 97, one of the five that came from outside contributors – in this case the novelist Richardson, introduced as 'an author from whom the age has received greater favours, who has enlarged the knowledge of human nature, and taught the passions to move at the command of virtue'. Richardson was surrounded by a circle of female admirers, who bought this number in large quantities. Otherwise, the series went slowly enough, the average sale being something under 500.

Nevertheless it gained in public favour and, seen in perspective, was undeniably a success. As Johnson himself pointed out, the essays were not topical. 'I have never complied with temporary notoriety, nor enabled my readers to discuss the topic of the day.' But this very avoidance of the ephemeral ensured that *The Rambler* should not go out of date. The good sense, the clear vision of life, which were effective in the 1750s, went on being effective for the rest of Johnson's lifetime and well into the next century. Today, like most of Johnson's works, *The Rambler* is chiefly read by those with a specific interest in the eighteenth century; but for a hundred years it was read by ordinary English people who did not think of themselves as engaged in historical and literary study, but as learning directly about life. The number of reprints that were called for is a proof that Johnson's thinking made an impression. Most serial publications are not reprinted until the last one is written and the run is complete, but in the case of *The Rambler* the reprinting began immediately. A Scottish publisher named Elphinston began printing the essays twice a week, following the rhythm of London publication at three months' distance and, incidentally, at half the price – a penny instead of twopence. When completed, this edition bound up into eight handsome volumes, and Boswell speaks highly of its 'uncommon elegance'. This was only the beginning. The entire series was reissued no fewer than eleven times in the next thirty-six years. And each successive edition, one is pleased to note, put something into Johnson's pocket.

Some critics attacked *The Rambler* on stylistic grounds. One Archibald Campbell, a purser in the navy, brought out in 1767 a pamphlet ridiculing 'the affected style, hard words, and absurd phraseology of many later writers, and particularly of our English lexiphanes, the Rambler'. He was not alone in his objection to Johnson's 'hard words'. Over a century later Leslie Stephen, editor of *The Dictionary of National Biography* and (more surprisingly) father of Virginia Woolf, gave it as his magisterial opinion that '*The Rambler* marks the culminating period of Johnson's worst qualities of style. The pompous and involved language seems indeed to be a fit clothing for the melancholy reflections which are its chief staple.' 'Such literature', Stephen adds wonderingly, 'is often strangely popular in England.' Correct. The Anglo-Saxon is a great seeker after improvement, and no authors are more strongly rooted in the life of the English-speaking peoples than those who offer advice on how to live and what to do. Johnson's writing could hardly have been more 'pompous and involved' than that of many sociologists, political theorists, literary critics, who have in our time seemed 'charismatic' to the young: and where shall we find a more dusty, inky word than that? Johnson's 'adscititious' and 'equiponderant', which occur in the same sentence in the number for 26 May 1750, are certainly no worse.

We may concede, however, some justice in the criticism. Johnson's style in *The Rambler* is heavier, denser, more close-packed than in his more relaxed later writings. He seems, during these years, to be writing like a man on trial for his life: loading each statement with all available meaning in case he should not be able to make another. In later life Johnson looked back with pride on this strong, closeknit expression. 'My other works are wine and water', he said, 'but my *Rambler* is pure wine.' Many good judges have agreed. Ruskin tells us in *Praeterita* that his father always took 'four little volumes of Johnson', selections from *The Rambler* and the slightly later *Idler*, when he travelled on the Continent: finding in them 'more substantial literary nourishment than could be, from any other author, packed into so portable compass'.

This praise, could Johnson have heard it, would have pleased him. Even more gratifying was some praise he actually did hear. Tetty, sitting in her drawing-room or (more and more now) lying propped on pillows in her bed, was reading *The Rambler* and finding in it the strong good sense of the man who had won her heart. After the first few numbers had come out, she gladdened Sam by saying, 'I thought very well of you before; but I did not imagine you could have written anything equal to this.'

It is good that those words should be among the few remarks of Tetty's that happen to have come down to us. Not only because they show that her intelligence and perceptiveness did not leave her in her time of physical and nervous decline: but also because they are the last words we know her to have uttered. Three days after the final number of *The Rambler* was published, Tetty Johnson died.

The effect on Johnson was cataclysmic. In unbearable agony of mind he called at once on man and on God. Tetty died in the night; Johnson immediately sent a note to his old friend Taylor, who was then living in Westminster. Taylor did not preserve this message, but he remembered it ever afterwards as the strongest expression of grief he had ever read. It was then three in the morning: Taylor hurried round to Gough Square, and did what he could to comfort the weeping Johnson, who presently recovered enough composure to ask his friend to join him in prayer. By no stretch of the imagination could Taylor have been called a holy man; he was, though respectable enough, a coolly selfish materialist who had taken the cloth because it offered a comfortable life. Still, he was a man ordained by the Church and instructed in its manner of worship, and this always counted for a great deal with the orthodox Johnson. So, by the bedside of the dead wife, the two men knelt and prayed; now extempore, now according to the set practices of Anglican worship.

In the morning Taylor went home. Later in the day he received another note from Johnson, this time short, but poignant in its brief directness:

Dear Sir

Let me have your company and instruction. Do not live away from me. My distress is great.

Pray desire Mrs Taylor to inform me what mourning I should buy for my mother and Miss Porter, and bring a note in writing with you.

Remember me in your prayers, for vain is the help of man.

I am, dear Sir &c.

SAM: JOHNSON

And so Tetty leaves our story: not, surely, without the tribute of a salute. At the lowest estimate she was a woman who had the courage to take a throw of the dice: it rolled the wrong way, but still one cannot quite pity her, because she was too large a soul to be pitied, and because she saw clearly, towards the end, that if she could not manage to hold up the weight of her marriage there was no disgrace in crumpling under the pressure of a giant. Johnson had fulfilled the promise she had been one of the first to see in him. (Only Gilbert Walmesley had an obvious prior claim, and he had died the year before.) When she took him he was a raw-boned country youth, ugly in appearance and startling in his odd habits and gestures, marked out for failure if ever a man was. When death took her from him, he was the Rambler, 'Lexiphanes', a man already celebrated, his knowledge respected, his combativeness feared. His mother, still living out her twilight existence in the shop on the market square, had never understood what manner of being it was she had brought into the world, never known how to deal with him; she, Elizabeth Jervis, Elizabeth Porter, Elizabeth Johnson, 'Tetty', had seen him for what he was, taken him, been rejected by her family for his sake, endured poverty and neglect; she had been his mother as well as his wife, and before she died she had seen him launched into his maturity. In the last few years, when there was nothing much left that she could do for him, she took refuge in sedatives and pain-killers. But she stayed alert long enough to read *The Rambler*, and recognize its quality, and to know that her husband had grown up and made a life for himself. Peace be to her and to all good and loyal women.

Johnson's reaction to her death was both emotional and intellectual; naturally so, since it stirred him to his depths and involved his whole being. To begin with the obvious, there was his profound grief. Even if we split this up, as it were prismatically, and try to isolate that part of it which proceeded from guilt, we have to have a name for the whole bundle, and we might as well call it grief as anything else. Sometimes, at the death of a loved one, our suffering is increased by the suspicion that we have not loved as fully as we might; self-accusation adds another sting to the pain we already feel at missing the dead person. So it was, doubtless, with Johnson. Overburdened as he was, there were things he might have done to help Tetty through her melancholy last years, and he had not done them. John Hawkins, hard-faced man of the law, is being characteristically stony-hearted in that part of his *Life* of Johnson which deals with his marriage and widowhood:

> Those who were best acquainted with them both wondered that Johnson could derive no comfort [i.e. after her death] from the usual resources, reflections on the conditions of mortality, the instability of human happiness, resignation to the divine will, and other topics.

That Johnson 'derived no comfort' from meditation is not true. But such comfort is second-stage medication. It cannot work during the immediate onslaught of grief. When Hester Thrale was widowed, years later, Johnson wrote to her: 'I do not exhort you to reason yourself into tranquillity. We must first labour.' This excellent advice he followed, plunging into the work of the Dictionary, hiding himself in it until he felt able to surface and give shape to some thoughts on what had happened. Some seven years were to go by before he gave expression to these thoughts, in the gravely moving essay (*Idler*, No. 41) 'On the death of a friend'. There, the emotion is distanced and generalized; it is put into the form of a letter from an unspecified correspondent who has suffered an unspecified bereavement; it is a 'just representation of general nature'. As always in his best writing, Johnson himself is both involved and not involved; he stands both inside and outside the emotion that is re-created.

> Nothing is more evident than that the decays of age must terminate in death; yet there is no man, says Tully, who does not believe that he may yet live another year; and there is none who does not, upon the same principle, hope another year for his parent or his friend: but the fallacy will be in time detected; the last year, the last day, must come. It has come, and is past. The life which made my own life pleasant is at an end, and the gates of death are shut upon my prospects.
>
> The loss of a friend upon whom the heart was fixed, to whom every wish and endeavour tended, is a state of dreary desolation, in which the mind looks abroad impatient of itself, and finds nothing but emptiness and

horror. The blameless life, the artless tenderness, the pious simplicity, the modest resignation, the patient sickness and the quiet death are remembered only to add value to the loss, to aggravate regret for what cannot be amended, to deepen sorrow for what cannot be recalled.

The whole essay deserves to be read. It should finally silence those who still entertain doubts about Johnson's status as a writer. Solemn and majestic thoughts in solemn and majestic language: the emotions which a man relives in the silence of his own mind, over a greying fire at midnight, conveyed not as disjointed musings but as fully clothed, logically connected sentences: these are what Johnson offers. Our age, which prefers its writers to shriek, grunt and babble, will naturally turn away from such ordered writing. The loss is ours. 'We need art', writes a modern critic whose name I will not put down on the same page as Johnson's, 'that screams, roars, vomits, rages, goes mad, murders, rapes, commits every bloody and obscene act that it can to express only a shred of the human emotions that lie prisoner beneath the sanitary tiles here in adman's utopia.' There were emotions lying prisoner, if we want to put it that way, under the polished parquet of eighteenth-century rationality and courtesy. But its writers still managed to produce a literature intended for grown-up people.

To come back to our thread. So much for Hawkins's blundering statement that Johnson 'could derive no comfort' from philosophical reflection. But then Johnson's feelings were opaque to Hawkins, whose version of it seems to have been that since he himself couldn't have loved Mrs Johnson he found it perverse in Johnson to pretend to have done so. ('I have often been inclined to think that if this fondness of Johnson for his wife was not dissembled, it was a lesson that he had learned by rote, and that, when he practised it, he knew not where to stop till he became ridiculous.') To most of us, there will be nothing 'ridiculous' in the spectacle of Johnson's perfectly sincere grief over the death of his wife. Nor in the deep meditation and speculation it provoked in him. For the first time he found his mind turning towards the idea of the intervention of spirits in human life. What became of the souls of the departed? The wicked, no doubt, were in torment (a thought from which his own fears caused him to shy violently away), but what of the blessed? Could they not intercede with the Almighty, beseeching help and comfort for those still struggling on earth? These thoughts came to the surface in a prayer he composed scarcely a month after his bereavement:

April 26, 1752, being after 12 at night of the 25th.
  O Lord, Governor of Heaven and Earth, in whose hands are embodied and departed spirits, if thou hast ordained the souls of the dead to minister to the living, and appointed my departed wife to have care of me, grant that I may enjoy the good effects of her attention and ministration, whether exercised by appearance, impulses, dreams, or in any other manner agreeable to thy government; forgive my presumption, enlighten my ignorance, and however meaner agents are employed, grant me the blessed influence of thy Holy Spirit, through Jesus Christ our Lord.   Amen.

He did not, however, allow these speculations to bulk too large in his think-ing and feeling. Already, his mind had taken on the cast it was to retain. Orthodoxy was its life blood. Johnson was at the farthest possible remove from that typically English figure, the harmless eccentric with the home-made religion, convinced that his own inner light enables him to see truths that have been veiled from the profound theologians and grave prelates. Never – except by harsh necessity – a solitary man, he had no relish for proclaiming that everyone was out of step except himself. As he saw it, the Church to which he belonged had elaborated its doctrines and worked out its procedures through centuries of trial and error and debate, and had achieved a consensus on which the individual mind could repose. Just as, in his historical writings, he shows impatience with the preaching tinkers and tailors of the seventeenth-century Commonwealth, so he wishes also to show obedience to central custom and tradition. A year after Tetty's death he observed the anniversary solemnly and tenderly:

> 28 March 1753. I kept this day as the anniversary of my Tetty's death with prayer and tears in the morning. In the evening I prayed for her condition-ally if it were lawful.

'If it were lawful.' Johnson's version of the Christian religion did not admit of any notion of rushing, naked and howling, into the presence of the Creator. He seems to have envisaged a majestic decorum even in one's supplications for mercy. The Church of England did not have a precise ruling on whether the dead could still benefit by the prayers of the living or whether, having lived their lives and reaped their reward, they were beyond reach. And since there was no definite line laid down by orthodoxy Johnson declined to take the decision on himself. His prayers for Tetty, though doubtless fervent, were 'conditional'. It is this kind of thing that makes one say that Johnson's religion was one of piety rather than of blazing vision and hosanna. In his Dictionary he defines the word 'pious' as 'Careful of the duties owed by created beings to God'. His own religious attitude could hardly be more neatly formulated.

In these ways did the death of his wife afflict, torment, exercise and extend Johnson's mind. But sooner or later he had to turn back to ordinary cares and responsibilities. On 6 May he wrote in his diary that he proposed to 'return to life tomorrow'. Though in some ways it would be much the same life as before, it would lack something that had been at its centre. Tetty, who had been with him since Edial, who dated back in his life to the old Birmingham days of Warren and Edmund Hector, who had known David Garrick as a schoolboy and shared the hopes and fears of those early advances to Cave, left a gaping hole in the continuity of his life. Somehow that crater must be filled. He needed people about him: not just coming and going but always there, unquestioned, taken for granted. Gradually, from this time forward, Johnson assembled that household whose strange, unprepossessing inmates were to be the wonder and exasperation of his friends. Already he knew Robert Levet and Anna Williams. And of course Elizabeth Desmoulins, his godfather's daughter, long since

widowed by her husband, the Huguenot writing-master, had been a frequent
guest since the Hampstead days. In due course they would all find a home under
Johnson's roof. But at the head of the procession came Frank, the Negro boy
whom Johnson took into his service, and under the protection of his care,
about a fortnight after Tetty's death; whom he instructed, bore with, rescued
from scrapes, and to whom he finally bequeathed most of his few worldly
possessions.

It was Bathurst who set the matter in motion. His father, Colonel Bathurst,
had owned Frank Barber as a slave in Jamaica, and on his return to England had
sent the lad to school in Yorkshire. When the Colonel died, his son evidently
asked Johnson to take the seven-year-old Frank as his servant. There was no
question of handing him on like a piece of property, since Colonel Bathurst's
will bequeathed Frank his freedom; and, in fact, during the years that followed,
he several times left Johnson's house to try his hand at other occupations. He
worked for a time with an apothecary in Cheapside; on another occasion he
joined the navy, and Johnson had to work hard to get him out again. There was
also a period, near the beginning of their association, when Johnson sent Frank
to continue his education at a school in Northamptonshire. But, with these few
interruptions, they were a part of each other's lives from then on.

Not that Johnson intended to take on a manservant and settle down to a
celibate existence. Far from it. With due deliberation, after keeping the matter
in his thoughts and prayers for many months, he decided to 'seek a new wife'.
On Easter Day 1753 he made a special journey to the church at Bromley in
Kent where Tetty was buried. There he attended service; he prayed, both
according to the set forms and with a prayer of his own, on Tetty's behalf,
which he had composed before going down. During the sermon, finding that
he could not catch what the vicar was saying, he occupied his thoughts by composing another prayer, 'against unchastity, idleness, and neglect of public
worship'. (These were all failings of which he considered himself guilty, even
if the 'unchastity' was a matter of thoughts rather than deeds.) Then, in tears,
he stood beside Tetty's grave, bidding her a solemn farewell before betaking
himself to the choice of another wife.

And the choice itself? Johnson never made it. If he had, the rest of the story
would have been very different, since it is impossible to imagine a married
Johnson adopting the pattern of life with which we associate him during the
years of his fame and influence. When we picture the mature Johnson, the
Johnson of Boswell's *Life*, it is always as a bachelor – not even as a widower –
that we picture him. He lived a life of inns and taverns, of journeys and visits.
His 'home', though he found it an indispensable sheet anchor and always kept it
up, was not a place in which he could find much peace or comfort. We think
of him as a man always going out; and so reluctant to be left alone with his
thoughts that it was generally very, very late before he came home.

Yet in some obvious ways marriage – to the right woman – would have
suited Johnson very well. At forty-four he had certainly not outgrown his
sexual desires; it is doubtful whether he ever did, except at the very end when

he was hopelessly ill and infirm. And even at that stage he did not outgrow his passionate need to love and be loved. Then, again, he liked women. He enjoyed arguing with an intelligent woman quite as much as with an intelligent man. Like many roughly masculine men, he had a strong feminine streak in his nature, and this made him at ease with women, able to see their point of view.

All this he recognized well enough. And there it is, the diary entry: 'I purpose on Monday to seek a new wife' – 'without', he adds characteristically, 'any derogation from dear Tetty's memory.' What women did he pass in review, during those long hours of meditation? And why did his quest come to nothing?

In 1753 Johnson numbered among his friends and acquaintances a fair number of women of suitable age and attainment to make him a good wife. Not all of them, of course, were attractive to him, or he to them. Hester Mulso, a girl of twenty-six of whose mind he thought highly enough to accept her as one of his few collaborators in *The Rambler*, showed no sign of responding to him as woman to man. Nor did Catherine Talbot, another young (thirty-two) lady of letters. Elizabeth Carter, his old friend and co-worker on *The Gentleman's Magazine*, certainly had his warmth and esteem; but for reasons which are now past recovering he made no approach to her. Charlotte Cotterel, a lively and attractive girl, daughter of an admiral, may have been on his list; she was un-married until 1756, when she was snapped up by a clergyman. Johnson always maintained an interest in Charlotte, and in the last year of his life was still on good enough terms to ask her to dine with him; but, for one reason or another, he made no approach to her during this crucial time.

Probably the simple reason is the true one: Johnson considered love an essential ingredient in marriage (*pace* some of his rather cynical later remarks on the married state, squeezed out of him by the pressure of Boswell's relentless interviewing), and he simply did not love Miss Cotterel or Miss Carter or Miss Mulso, though he esteemed and admired them. He certainly knew what it was to be in love: he had been in love with Molly Aston, back in that brief Arcadian period at Ashbourne and Tissington and Appleby, and he stayed in love with her all his life, treasuring the memory of the few meetings he had had with her. But Molly Aston had married her sea captain, and Johnson's firm morals would not allow him to look in the direction of a married woman. Molly had become a beautiful memory; he had lost touch with her, and he had no intention of looking her up now.

Elizabeth Desmoulins? From some points of view she would have been a logical choice, younger than Johnson and yet bound to him by old associations. He did, in fact, make a lifelong friend of her; she lived in his house, till driven away in later years by ceaseless feuding with Anna Williams, and she was at his bedside when he died. But marriage? She was a woman of narrow views, not intelligent enough to delight him in talk; the relationship would have been a purely physical one. And that in turn might have exposed Johnson to attack from his phenomenally active conscience. For, as we saw earlier, his relations with Mrs Desmoulins had at one time taken on a tinge that could almost be called amatory. She it was who, responding to his desperate emotional need, had allowed him to fondle and caress her during those late-night conversations in Hampstead, while Tetty snored in the next room. To Johnson's harshly self-critical eye, this must have seemed perilously close to a breach of his marriage vows. To marry the woman who had, however momentarily and however marginally, seemed to be supplanting his wife might have appeared an insult to her memory.

Whether these were the reasons or not, Elizabeth Desmoulins was out. So was Anna Williams, three years Johnson's senior and peevish in temper – though she was intelligent and characterful enough for any man. Who else? Charlotte Lennox, whom he had delighted to honour, whose friendship he sought, whose career he helped, whose gifts he admired, was stuck down in her unfortunate marriage to that printing-house drudge.

All these women, some available, some not, had their good qualities. But there was one, placidly living out her life in faraway Derbyshire, whom Johnson admired more than any of them, who stirred his heart more than any-one except lovely Molly. This was Hill Boothby, whom Johnson had met at the house of the intelligent Mary Meynell and her husband, William Fitzherbert. If Johnson had married Hill Boothby! As things turned out, she died only three years later – and Johnson reacted to her death with an outburst of grief that almost paralleled his feelings at the death of Tetty – and may therefore have been in frail health: still, marriage usually changes a woman's health one way or another, and if Hill Boothby had married Johnson, one year younger than her-self, she might have outlived him. It is tempting to suppose that Johnson was working up his nerve to go and visit Miss Boothby and make her a proposal of marriage, though whether she would have been prepared to leave her pleasant and secure country existence and launch herself into the kind of life that Tetty had had to endure is another matter. But Johnson made no step in her direction. And for a good reason. News reached him that made him realize that the enter-prise was hopeless. Almost exactly a year after Tetty's death, Mary Meynell also died; 'in the flower of her age', as a writer in *The Gentleman's Magazine* put it, 'distinguished for her piety and fine accomplishments'. The pleasant and amiable William Fitzherbert was left a widower with six children. 'Miss Sainthill' at once honoured an old promise that she would move in and run Fitzherbert's house and look after his children. Having given her word, she would not take it back for Johnson or any man. He understood this, and continued for the short remainder of her life to love her at a distance.

So Johnson's second marriage, so seriously purposed, so long meditated, never happened. And 'the courts and alleys about Fleet Street' resounded, in the still night, with his solitary tread, and the deep murmur of his voice as he talked to himself, turning over the ideas, the memories, the speculations that jostled unceasingly in his capacious mind.

CHAPTER 13

'I Now Begin to See Land'

The summer of 1754 saw a pleasant diversion. At last, after eight years of toil on the Dictionary, Johnson felt able to make a long-planned visit to Oxford. He needed to consult books in the libraries there; besides, it was a sentimental pilgrimage for him to revisit the haunts of learning and poetry from which poverty had driven him in 1729. There was also an urgent need for some kind of intellectual stimulus. Johnson had the very human habit of leaving till last the part of an undertaking that he found least welcome. In the case of his Dictionary, this meant that part which approached the purely philological. Johnson was, to be blunt, an indifferent philologist. He had a sound grip on the derivation of any English word that came from the Greek or Latin, but his knowledge of Anglo-Saxon and Middle English was shaky. These areas of study were of course far less cultivated in the eighteenth century than they are today. But still there were scholars then living who had studied them very effectively; and some of them were to be met at Oxford. To talk with these men might well revive Johnson's interest, always faint and now flagging almost unto death, in 'Saxon', as he called it, and mediaeval language generally. In a diary entry for 3 April 1753 he noted: 'I began the 2nd vol. of my Dictionary, room being left in the first for preface, grammar and history, none of them yet begun. O God who hast hitherto supported me enable me to proceed in this labour.' If, at this late stage in the work, he had not begun the 'history' (i.e. of the language), he might well quail before the work that still lay ahead. Fortunately there were people at Oxford who could give him informed advice. One of them was Thomas Warton, a Fellow of Trinity College, who had recently sought Johnson's acquaintance by sending him a copy of his book on Spenser, *Observations on the Færie Queene*. Johnson wrote to him in a vein of high, handsome compliment:

> Sir
> It is but an ill return for the book with which you were pleased to favour me, to have delayed my thanks for it till now. I am too apt to be negligent; but I can never deliberately show my disrespect to a man of your character; and I now pay you a very honest acknowledgement, for the advancement of the literature of our native country. You have shown to all who shall hereafter attempt the study of our ancient authors the way to success; by directing them to the perusal of the books which those authors had read.

Of this method, Hughes, and men much greater than Hughes, seem never to have thought. The reason why the authors, which are yet read, of the sixteenth century, are so little understood is that they are read alone; and no help is borrowed from those who lived with them, or before them. Some part of this ignorance I hope to remove by my book, which now draws towards its end; but which I cannot finish to my mind, without visiting the libraries of Oxford, which I therefore hope to see in a fortnight. I know not how long I shall stay, or where I shall lodge; but shall be sure to look for you at my arrival, and we shall easily settle the rest.

I am, dear Sir, Your most obedient, &c

SAM: JOHNSON

Within a fortnight of writing this letter Johnson was in Oxford; full, as usual, of good resolutions about getting on with work. In the event, Oxford drowned him in its cultured *accidie*; Warton, who delighted in his company and conversation, noted that 'during this visit at Oxford, he collected nothing in the libraries for his Dictionary'.

Still, Johnson had never put his whole trust in reading as a means of acquiring learning. There were hours of convivial talk with Warton and with other dons to whom Warton introduced him; besides, he doubtless felt, as many have felt, that the very stones of Oxford seem gently to smooth away the rough edges of one's ignorance. (A dangerous illusion, for you and me. But less so for a Johnson.) And there was the pleasure and reassurance of finding that Oxford welcomed him back; that a man like Warton, who had been two years old when Johnson's undergraduate career came to its sad and lonely end, regarded him as a scholar and critic to be deferred to. Not everyone was as welcoming, of course; Oxford never opens all her doors at once. Johnson was particularly wounded by the cool reception he had from Dr Radcliffe, Master of his old college, Pembroke. Full of pious enthusiasm, Johnson went round to Pembroke on the first morning after his arrival. Many of the College servants remembered him, 'particularly a very old butler', and this gave him a keen pleasure; but Radcliffe, who had been Bursar in Johnson's undergraduate days and now presided over the College, was cool and distant. When Johnson rose to go, Radcliffe did not ask him to dine or even to call again before he went back to London. Outside, Johnson turned, looked up at the Master's lodgings, and said vehemently to Warton, 'There lives a man who lives by the revenues of literature, and will not lift a finger to support it. If I come to live at Oxford, I will take up my abode at Trinity.' Later, the breach with Pembroke was healed, but Trinity still remained a favourite college with Johnson. During this stay, which lasted some five weeks, he lodged at Kettel Hall, a small building near Trinity and under its aegis.

Altogether, it is clear that the ripening friendship with Tom Warton was the brightest jewel of this Oxford visit. Warton was admirably fitted to be a friend of Johnson and his chief academic ally. He was a literary man to his fingertips, both by inclination and family tradition; his father had been Professor of

Poetry, and his elder brother, Joseph, also to become one of Johnson's circle, was a poet and an influential critic. Thomas Warton's appetite for the printed word was insatiable, and his literary activities ranged from profound scholarly works to the editing of a collection of comic verses, *The Oxford Sausage*, which enjoyed a prolonged vogue. He wrote poetry, which was at any rate good enough to win him, in later years, the office of Poet Laureate; but his real achievement was in literary history, and particularly in his enquiries into mediaeval and Renaissance poetry. At this time, still a young man, Warton was only slowly working towards the majestic *History of English Poetry* he would one day publish, and which, though he never finished it, took the story from the earliest records down to the sixteenth century and broke ground that was not to be fully cultivated for a hundred years. But, as Johnson said in his letter, Warton had already given a showcase example of how earlier English poetry should be studied. And all this at a time when there was, of course, no 'Faculty of English Literature'; apart from the doubtful privilege of being Professor of Poetry, a post he held for two five-year terms, Warton could hope for no material reward for his indefatigable labours of research and writing. It was done out of love for poetry and a scholar's passion. With all this, Warton had endearingly simple tastes. He liked his glass of beer, and if he was not to be found in his rooms or in the Bodleian he could usually be flushed in one of the taverns along the riverside, for he delighted particularly in the company of watermen. Since the Thames ceased to be an artery for trade and travel, this doughty race has vanished, so that no modern person can say with authority whether Warton's taste for their company was creditable or not; I suspect it was highly creditable, and a salutary change of intellectual diet. On a summer evening Warton could often be seen in a boat, rowed by one of his muscular friends, puffing contentedly at his pipe; knowing perfectly well that his simple pleasures would not escape criticism in university circles, he evidently cared not a fig.

In Warton's company Johnson blossomed. They went for long walks in the surrounding countryside; to Elsfield, for instance, to see Mr Wise, Bodley's librarian, 'with whom Johnson was much pleased'. (On their way back from that excursion, Warton kept up such a relentless pace that Johnson cried out *Sufflamina*, for which Warton found an English equivalent, 'Put on your drag chain.') They also explored mediaeval buildings, both intact and ruined. Warton was as much in love with old buildings as with old poems; his vacations were devoted, invariably, to archaeological tours, and he was a foremost authority on what his age called 'the Gothick'. The two of them walked through the Thames-side meadows to examine the ruins of two abbeys, Oseney and Rewley. The stark, crumbling walls, monuments to piety and learning stamped down under the heel of government, stirred Johnson to deep emotion; as they walked away, he was silent for a full half-hour, then burst out, 'I viewed them with indignation!' Today, even the ruins have gone.

Altogether, it was a sunny five weeks. Warton was Johnson's mainstay for company and the sharing of ideas, but he met and talked with a number of other dons, including Jack Meeke, his fellow-undergraduate at Pembroke. Meeke had stayed on at the college, enjoying the placid life of a don, with no need to exert himself; and Johnson noted, with a grim satisfaction, that while his own life had been far more effortful than Meeke's he had at least something to show for the effort. 'About the same time of life', he remarked to Warton, 'Meeke was left behind at Oxford to feed on a Fellowship, and I went to London to get my living: now, Sir, see the difference of our literary characters!' There was also Robert Chambers, of Lincoln College, a man of a very different type from either Warton or Meeke. A shrewd, ambitious young lawyer whose acquaintance Johnson had already made in London, he had come to Oxford to take up a Fellowship as part of a planned, step-by-step career which ultimately won him fame, wealth, rank. Johnson, in a kindly and courteous letter written a few weeks after his Oxford holiday was over, expressed the hope that Chambers did not 'regret the change of London for Oxford', and passed on the good wishes of friends they had in common.

So the pleasant summer visit extended itself until Gough Square, the counting-house desk, and the treadmill of the dusty bookshelves called him back. He settled down, and that winter it was work, unremitting work. The history of the language got itself written somehow, the last slips were pasted in, the last derivations worked out, the last definitions clarified and subdivided. Then, in the middle of December, Johnson received the most welcome Christmas present imaginable. Warton and Wise had been pulling strings on his behalf. The University of Oxford was going to confer on him the degree of Master of Arts – *honoris causa* – for his services to literature. This would look very good on the title-page of the Dictionary, and in his letter of thanks to Warton he expressed his intention of holding back the printing until he knew for certain that the magic letters M.A. could accompany his name. The last few weeks of labour were sweetened by the thought of the reward his efforts had already earned him, whether the Dictionary had a good reception or not; and on 1 February he was able to write to Warton: 'I now begin to see land, after having wandered . . . in this vast sea of words.'

But before the book saw the light there was to be another episode, one that has become famous wherever English books are read. Six days after writing to Warton that he could 'see land', Johnson sat down to write a letter of very different import. 'My Lord', he began,

> I have been lately informed by the proprietor of *The World* that two papers in which my Dictionary is recommended to the public were written by your Lordship. To be so distinguished is an honour which, being very little accustomed to favours from the great, I know not well how to receive, or in what terms to acknowledge.

The letter was to Lord Chesterfield. It is not only the most superbly dignified snub ever administered but also a signpost in social history, since it is usually taken to mark the end of the system of patronage. This, as we shall see in a moment, is a slight simplification of a complex historical and social chain of events: still, once that letter was delivered, patronage was never the same again, and every impoverished but proud man of letters could look any grandee squarely in the eye, knowing that he had the authority of Johnson for so doing.

Chesterfield, as we saw, accepted the dedication of Johnson's *Plan of a Dictionary* in 1748. In those early days they met and talked a few times; asked about these conversations, Johnson was courteous enough to concede that Chesterfield had allowed him the choice of ground; they had talked of literature and philology, subjects in which Johnson naturally had the advantage. Whether their conversation ranged more widely we have no means of knowing, but it is at least probable that they spoke of Parson Ford, Johnson's early friend and instigator, whom Chesterfield had known and to whom at one time he had presented a living.

But that was at the beginning. Chesterfield rewarded Johnson for his dedication of the 'Plan' with a little of his time and ten pounds in cash. Then silence descended. From the beginning of 1748 to the end of 1754 Chesterfield ceased to be conscious of Johnson's existence. Later, he tried to excuse his neglect by saying that he had heard Johnson had changed his lodgings, and did not know where to send for him. As if he could not have found out in a few minutes, by sending one of his servants round to enquire of their original go-between, Robert Dodsley! One does not, however, wish to be too hard on Chesterfield. He was a busy man, and Johnson, though on the threshold of his wider fame, was during these seven years buried under a mound of books, rarely showing 'his back above the element he lived in'. What nettled Johnson was not so much His Lordship's neglect as the belated interest, the last-minute help when help was no longer needed. Chesterfield sent two essays to a fashionable paper, *The World* (28 Nov and 5 Dec 1754), and leaked the information that they were of his writing. Boswell says rather breathlessly that 'they contain some studied compliments, so finely turned, that if there had been no previous offence, it is probable that Johnson would have been highly delighted'. But then Boswell was a bit of a snob, as distinct from Johnson, who believed that 'subordination' was necessary to society, that distinctions of rank ought to be observed, but who in practice never allowed anyone to pull rank on him. Chesterfield's performance, in these two essays, is on the whole rather foolish. He protests that he has not been bribed; 'neither Mr Johnson, nor any bookseller or booksellers concerned in the success of it have ever offered me the usual compliment of a pair of gloves or a bottle of wine'. More unfortunately still, he tells a silly story about 'a fine gentleman and a fine lady' who had an assignation, but missed each other through a spelling mistake; the letter arranging details was wrongly addressed and the would-be lovers went to different houses. 'Such examples', the anonymous Chesterfield simpers, 'really make one tremble; and will, I am convinced, determine my fair fellow subjects and their adherents to adopt and scrupulously conform to Mr Johnson's rules of true orthography.' Johnson had not toiled nine years to be rewarded with such backstairs compliments. Chesterfield had asked for it, and he got it. The first paragraph of the letter I have just quoted. Here is the rest:

> When upon some slight encouragement I first visited your Lordship I was overpowered like the rest of mankind by the enchantment of your address, and could not forbear to wish that I might boast myself Le Vainqueur du Vainqueur de la Terre, that I might obtain that regard for which I saw the world contending, but I found my attendance so little encouraged, that neither pride nor modesty would suffer me to continue it. When I had once addressed your Lordship in public, I had exhausted all the art of pleasing which a retired and uncourtly scholar can possess. I had done all that I could, and no man is well pleased to have his all neglected, be it ever so little.
>
> Seven years, My Lord, have now passed since I waited in your outward rooms or was repulsed from your door, during which time I have been pushing on my work through difficulties of which it is useless to complain, and have brought it at last to the verge of publication without one act of assistance, one word of encouragement or one smile of favour. Such treatment I did not expect, for I never had a patron before.
>
> The shepherd in Virgil grew at last acquainted with Love, and found him a native of the rocks. Is not a patron, My Lord, one who looks with unconcern on a man struggling for life in the water and, when he has reached ground, encumbers him with help? The notice which you have been pleased to take of my labours, had it been early, had been kind; but it has been delayed till I am indifferent and cannot enjoy it, till I am solitary and cannot impart it, till I am known and do not want it.
>
> I hope it is no very cynical asperity not to confess obligation where no benefit has been received, or to be unwilling that the public should consider me as owing that to a patron, which providence has enabled me to do for myself.
>
> Having carried on my work thus far with so little obligation to any favourer of learning, I shall not be disappointed though I should conclude it, if less be possible, with less, for I have been long wakened from that dream of hope, in which I once boasted myself with so much exultation, My Lord, Your Lordship's most humble, most obedient servant
>
> SAM: JOHNSON

This famous salvo has been quoted, admired, dissected so many times that there is nothing left to say about it. Except, perhaps, that it is no mere wallop such as Johnson was later to administer to, say, James Macpherson, but a centrally Johnsonian performance, bringing out all his powers. It has all the qualities we associate with the man and his mind: wit, terseness, grandeur and beauty. The sentence that always pulls me up is, 'The shepherd in Virgil grew at last acquainted with Love, and found him a native of the rocks.' Not only is this a superbly cadenced piece of writing, reminding us that we are dealing with a poet; it also signals a change of tone in the letter, moving from the particular grievance of

Johnson against Chesterfield to broader and deeper considerations. It introduces what is in fact the central paragraph of the letter, and its most miraculous piece of writing.

Examining the matter at leisure, from a safe ringside seat, we may well feel that Johnson's reaction was out of proportion to any affront that Chesterfield had actually offered him. Certainly Chesterfield's behaviour had been inconsiderate, but it was well within the normal bounds of the treatment given by men of wealth and rank to poor and friendless writers. The power and intensity of the rebuke made the letter a masterpiece of literature, but judged simply as a response to Chesterfield's neglect they made it seem like an over-reaction. Certainly some of Johnson's friends thought so. The exact contents of the letter were not at first widely known, but it was common knowledge that Johnson had rebuffed the Earl in stinging terms, and Adams, his old tutor at college, went so far as to 'expostulate' with him (the word is Boswell's). Chesterfield, he insisted, was a man of easy good manners, approachable by all and especially by men of letters. Johnson denied this, calling Chesterfield 'the proudest man this day existing'. 'No', Adams replied; 'there is one person, at least, as proud; I think, by your own account, you are the prouder man of the two.' Quickly, Johnson countered: 'But mine was defensive pride.'

Defensive, yes; and self-medicating. We shall misunderstand Johnson at this period of his life unless we see him as a man deeply exhausted, worn down nervously, mentally, physically, by nine years of almost inhuman labour. George Orwell rightly observed that 'Writing a book is a horrible, exhausting struggle, like a long bout of some painful illness'. This is true of any book, of whatever kind, except a collection of bits and pieces put together at odd times. A sustained book, of which the whole weight has to be carried during every hour of its composition, is as hard to weather as an illness, so that most authors would admit to being exhausted, by each book, to the point of prostration. And if this is true of ordinary, run-of-the-mill book-writing, what depths of strain and fatigue must be involved in an undertaking like Johnson's Dictionary is scarcely imaginable. He bore up against it, like the heroic caryatid that he was, but the cost was terrible, compounded as it was by grief at the death of his wife, and at the time of the book's completion and publication he was in a bad state: nervously spent, with his deeper feelings explosively near the surface. The terrific mule-kick at Chesterfield is partly a desperate counterattack against the darkness and drudgery that had enveloped Johnson's own life; and Chesterfield is to some extent a symbolic target, for when we are keeping ourselves above water by brutally hard work it is always irritating to see some smiling fellow stroll by with his hands in his pockets, placed by the mere injustice of life well above the tide that threatens our own survival. Johnson's resentment of Chesterfield had been smouldering for a long time; in the Dictionary itself he had defined 'Patron' as 'One who countenances, supports or protects'; then, remembering his own patron who had countenanced but not supported or protected him, he added savagely, 'Commonly a wretch who supports with insolence, and is paid with flattery.' And there is another, even more conspicuous, indication of the gloomy and indignant feelings that the word awoke in him. The first edition of *The Vanity of Human Wishes* contains the couplet,

There mark what ills the scholar's life assail,
Toil, envy, want, the garret, and the jail.

In a revised edition published in the same year as the Dictionary, the word *garret* is replaced by *patron*. It might happen to anyone to have to work in a garret; but a man who depends on a patron is really unfortunate. Years later Johnson quoted these lines amid the solid comfort of Henry Thrale's house, and 'burst into a passion of tears'. Those tears were the marks of no facile self-pity. Johnson had suffered, and suffered deeply, from the evils enumerated in his tolling lines. We may say of him what he said of Savage: 'Those are no proper judges of his conduct, who have slumbered away their time on the down of plenty.'

The 'celebrated letter', then, is, like most of Johnson's writings, a highly personal utterance. But, again like most of Johnson's writings, it is couched in a dignified, generalized manner that is a standing temptation to give it as wide an application as possible. To this we may attribute the tradition that uses the letter as a bookmark in the volume of English social history. 'The End of Patronage' – where else can it be so conveniently located? And of course that end had been in sight for some years. Johnson was born at the time when the trading middle class, all over Europe but especially in England, had just about got rid of its feudal competitors. Many forces had contributed to this enormous liberation of energy. Most conspicuously, the improvement in manufacturing techniques (so that a greater volume of goods was produced), and in transport (so that the goods could reach a cash-paying public). It is arguable that the canal system, by itself, did more to modernize western Europe than anything dreamed up by political theorists. The same year, 1755, that saw Johnson's letter to Chesterfield also saw the Act of Parliament which authorized the cutting of the St Helen's Canal, generally reckoned the first modern canal in England; the French had enjoyed the benefits of the Canal du Midi for over half a century. Since a horse can pull a maximum of two tons on a road, and then only if it is dead level, and the same horse can move anything from fifty to a hundred tons floating on water, the heavy materials needed for the second phase of the industrial revolution were already being moved into place well within Johnson's lifetime. The stagecoach was also of prime importance; when books and periodicals can be carried to any corner of the kingdom within ten or fifteen days of their issuing from the press, it becomes possible for the author to appeal directly to the public and be paid directly by them.

The situation of the literary man did, therefore, undergo a rapid and total change during the eighteenth century. For many centuries previously – as far back, indeed, as we can trace the art of literature – the writer had been firmly cemented into his place in a rigid social structure. The nature of that place had varied with time and situation. In a tribal society the writer is bard or chronicler; the two functions tend to merge into each other, but in either case the essential function is the same, to celebrate the deeds of the ruling dynasty and to memorialize the achievements of the nation. In the Middle Ages the writer is usually somewhere inside the Church. At the Renaissance the great private patrons appear – or rather reappear, since they had been a feature of the culture of ancient Rome and were to some extent conscious of their role in a revival of classical *mores*. The new element in the eighteenth-century situation was mobility. Given that books could be printed quickly and cheaply, it was imperative that the book-buying public should be reached with a matching pace and promptness. Michael Johnson had ridden the miry lanes with his saddle-bags stuffed with books; now the stagecoach spanked along made-up highways. The writer need no longer provide servile dedications to his books, angling for a few guineas from some overlord.

In view of this, it is easy to see a landmark in the dignified rebuff delivered by the bookseller's son to the stately aristocrat. But every such landmark is to some extent a simplification. It was indeed during Johnson's lifetime, and under his presidency, that the literary man, like the actor, became a member of the professional class rather than a needy and suspect adventurer. The eighteenth century, with its material improvements in respect of transport and manufacture, put the author into a direct, trading relationship with his public. Since it was now possible for books to be offered for sale over the length and breadth of the kingdom within a few days of their publication, it was no longer necessary for a writer to depend on the immediate source of cash represented by a patron. He could be supported by the small sums that could be spared by ordinary readers, now that those sums could flow in by the thousand. But Johnson, as we noted earlier, never quite crossed this bridge. In the early days he worked at beggarly piece-rates for booksellers; his Dictionary, and later his *Lives of the Poets*, were commissioned jobs; and there was always the factor of his pension, which, as we shall see, released him from financial care after the age of fifty-two.

In this matter of literature and patronage, Johnson was, in fact, in an interesting middle position. And this should not surprise us. The same could be said of his standpoint on political, social and constitutional matters. The broad comprehensiveness of his views prevented his taking a clearcut stance on anything except the great questions of religion and morality. On any topic that arose out of the fertile tangle of human life his attitude was pragmatic, which means that it took account of the contours of experience. He might choose to walk down one road, but always with an eye to the avenues he had not, but might have, followed. When in the name of learning and independence he clobbers Chesterfield, Johnson stands out in silhouette as a champion of that middle-class freedom which expressed itself in the mobility of money and the flow of goods and services. When he advocates 'subordination' or confesses to Boswell 'I have the old feudal notions', he seems a man of the old order. He is the reverse of the doctrinaire whose position on everything has been blueprinted ahead of time. As a critic of literature and as a practitioner, he took his stand on the Augustan qualities of poise, economy, lucidity, irony. This involved being highly critical of the incoming taste for the mediaeval, the romantic, the uncombed and rhapsodic. Yet the Johnson who clambered about the ruins of Oseney and

Rewley with Tom Warton, whose help is acknowledged in the Preface to Bishop Percy's *Reliques of Ancient English Poetry*, is (to put it no higher) capable of understanding, and contributing to, the new impulse. It is better to face the fact that Johnson was a profound and many-sided man. There is no simple grab that will take hold of him.

As if to caution us not to over-simplify the literary, social and economic significance of the 'Letter to Chesterfield', genealogy itself takes a hand. It is a striking illustration of the closeknit texture of English life that Johnson and Chesterfield were, though neither of them knew it, related. As we can see by consulting A. R. Wagner's *English Genealogy* (1960), table 38 on page 184, the two families were connected by a thin, tensile web of ties by blood and by marriage. As James L. Clifford has succinctly boiled it down, 'Chesterfield's younger brother was married to Johnson's cousin's wife's great-niece'.

Because of his complex many-sidedness, Johnson has for two hundred years been largely underestimated. We may say that Chesterfield was a notable pioneer in the expanding field of underestimating Johnson. He showed good sense in his immediate reaction to the famous letter. Well aware that personal antagonisms are best dealt with by employing the principle of judo – throwing the opponent with his own strength – he left the letter lying open on a table, showing it to visitors and pointing out the most telling passages with such comments as, 'This man has great powers.' Unfortunately for himself, in his eagerness for a *rapprochement* with Johnson he went further. He sent an emissary to smooth things over, and the emissary seems to have been as badly chosen as the terms of praise in his *World* essays. Sir Thomas Robinson, a notorious bore and hanger-on, and something of a toady, a Yorkshireman with more than his share of that crassness which seems to afflict Yorkshiremen when they fall below their natural standard, was known as 'long Sir Thomas', as if the only remarkable thing about him was the tallness of his bony frame. He seems to have made a rare mess of his embassy to Johnson. Throwing down a thick layer of flattery across which he hoped to advance dry-shod, he declared that if his circumstances permitted it he would settle five hundred a year on Johnson. 'And who are you', Johnson asked, 'that talk thus liberally?' 'I am Sir Thomas Robinson, a Yorkshire baronet.' 'Sir,' said Johnson, 'if the first peer of the realm were to make me such an offer, I would show him the way downstairs.'

At that, Chesterfield gave up. He made no further attempt at a reconciliation with Johnson. As for Johnson, his pride was assuaged. Never a vengeful man, he allowed the matter to rest. The famous letter was not passed from hand to hand, to gratify vulgar curiosity. Over a quarter of a century was to pass before he finally yielded to Boswell's importunity and dictated it to him from memory. Later still, he unearthed a copy which he had dictated to his Italian friend, Baretti, when it was fresher in his mind; this copy, too, he gave to Boswell, who published it, the year before his *Life*, as *The celebrated letter from Samuel Johnson, LL.D., to Philip Dormer Stanhope, Earl of Chesterfield: Now first published, with Notes, by James Boswell, Esq.* With an astute sense of market values, Boswell priced this titbit at half a guinea.

But to put the letter into the public domain was Boswell's idea, not Johnson's. In fact, Johnson showed considerable delicacy, springing from his usual inability to bear a grudge. One surviving story bears this out. Dr Douglas, the Bishop of Salisbury, had come by a copy; and, at some date which Boswell merely gives as 'many years ago', he asked Johnson if he might have permission to show it to Lord Hardwicke, a peer with literary proclivities. Johnson seemed flattered by the request; but, after thinking it over for a few minutes, he said with a smile, 'No, Sir; I have hurt the dog too much already.'

CHAPTER 14

Word-Hoard

At last the work was over. The longed-for, dreamed-of, impossibly unattainable day had really come, when there was nothing more to do on the Dictionary. Johnson, the money long since spent, everyone's patience long since rubbed thin, despatched the last sheet of copy to Millar, the bookseller in the Strand who was in charge of the physical production of the work. When the messenger returned, Johnson asked what Millar had said. Not surprisingly the answer was, 'Thank God.' 'I am glad', said Johnson, 'that he thanks God for anything.'

The presses rolled, the binders stitched and glued, the wagons rumbled through the streets, and at last the two enormous volumes lay on the table. 'Johnson's Dictionary' was a reality. It has remained one ever since. If Johnson had died in 1755, his name would still be illustrious among literate Englishmen and users of English throughout the world. When the young Robert Browning decided that his destiny was to be a poet, he prepared himself for the work by sitting down and reading Johnson's Dictionary from beginning to end. If modern young poets would do the same, we should have to endure far less shoddy thinking and approximate writing.

Johnson's was not, of course, the first English dictionary. He knew and used his predecessors. Edward Phillips, nephew of the poet Milton, had published a dictionary in 1658, and this had held its place through the generations, achieving a seventh edition in 1720. In the following year Nathaniel Bailey brought out his *Universal Etymological English Dictionary*, a most creditable work; in its later expanded version, re-titled *Dictionarium Britannicum*, it contained more words than Johnson's relatively modest forty thousand. In citing his source for an etymology Johnson often simply writes *Dict.*; it is usually safe to assume that *Dict.* is Bailey, though for technical terms he also used a number of specialized collections: the *Universal Dictionary of Trade and Commerce*, the monumental work of two Frenchmen, translated into English; Edmund Stone's *Mathematical Dictionary*; John Harris's *Lexicon Technicum*; the *Builder's Dictionary*, the *Farrier's Dictionary*, the *Military Dictionary*.

That part of any lexicographer's work in which he most needs the help of others is, naturally, in establishing etymologies; no one is familiar with all the languages that have been drawn on in the forming of a nation's speech. Johnson was well able to take care of the derivation of those words that came from Latin and Greek, even in cases where the intermediaries had been French, Provençal, Italian, Spanish. But, as he correctly pointed out, English had been formed partly from these languages and partly, at a deeper level, from 'the Teutonic range', i.e. 'the Saxon, German, and all their kindred dialects'. In these languages Johnson was, as we remarked earlier, more or less completely at sea. For 'Teutonic' etymologies he relied, as he told Adams, on 'Junius and Skinner'. Both Francis Junius (1589–1677) and Stephen Skinner (1623–67) were pioneer scholars whose massive labours could have been faulted in detail by many critics then living. But they were good enough for Johnson. The purely etymological part of dictionary-making was what interested him least, and is the least valuable part of his work.

What is the most valuable? Johnson's Dictionary has two great strengths. The definitions are masterly, and the illustrative quotations are aptly and beautifully chosen so as to bring together many diverse kinds of interest. We will take these in order.

Everyone who reflects for a few minutes on the making of a dictionary realizes the unremitting attention, the incredible effort of mental concentration and alertness, involved in defining a national vocabulary word by word. It is easy enough to define words like 'expostulation' or 'wardrobe', but how does one define 'put' or 'take' or 'sour'? Confronted by a word like 'set', how does one sort out which of its meanings are literal and which metaphorical? In all these departments Johnson is brilliant. He is especially good at the very difficult task of distinguishing the 'head' sense of a word from its secondary senses. This came naturally to that part of his mind that was lawyerly, with its instinct to approach a problem by breaking it down into its component parts and tackling each part separately. Even so, it was, all the way through, a formidable difficulty, to which he drew attention in the Preface. 'Kindred senses may be so inter-woven, that the perplexity cannot be disentangled, nor any reason assigned why one should be ranged before the other. When the radical idea branches out into parallel ramifications, how can a consecutive series be formed of senses in their nature collateral?' Nevertheless he soldiered on with remarkable success. The clarity of Johnson's thinking, on every issue that came up in everyday life as well as in his work, arose from this habit of distinguishing and shredding-out, the refusal to take hold of a question in a tangled heap.

Naturally there are some of Johnson's definitions which have become famous for other reasons. Now and then he relieved the tedium and impersonality of the work by sewing in some bright, conspicuous thread of his own – a sudden defiant intrusion of individuality, of memory or feeling, of prejudice even. 'Everybody knows' the definition of 'oats' with which, as we have seen, he twitted his Scotch assistants. Or of 'pension': 'An allowance made to any one without an equivalent. In England it is generally understood to mean pay given to a state hireling for treason to his country.' Sometimes a prejudice of Johnson's which drew tolerant chuckles from his comfortable Victorian editors will arouse a more sympathetic response in our hard-pressed times. As I write, the English people are groaning under the fresh burden of Value Added Tax, which is diabolically rigged so as to put the onus of collecting the tax on to the payers of it, and is extorted not by the ordinary Revenue authorities but by the

Customs and Excise. Brooding over this situation, I happened on Johnson's definition of 'excise': 'A hateful tax levied upon commodities, and adjudged not by the common judges of property, but wretches hired by those to whom excise is paid.' Again, I write this at a time when the world's currency system is tottering on the brink of collapse because of the activities of speculators who juggle with wealth without producing anything themselves – which puts me just in the mood for Johnson's 'stockjobber'. 'A low wretch who gets money by buying and selling shares in the funds.'

Sometimes the prejudice is more apparent than real. 'Whig', understandably, is 'the name of a faction'. A cool description of the party which held, and was to go on holding, invincible power! 'Tory', after a bad start etymologically ('A cant term, derived, I suppose, from an Irish word signifying a savage'), swells to 'one who adheres to the ancient constitution of the state, and the apostolical hierarchy of the church of England, opposed to a whig'. Here, we think, is Johnson at his old game of seeing that the Whig dogs do not have the best of it. But it is a mistake to read any of his definitions without going on to the illustrative quotations. And under 'Whig' we find a wise remark of Swift's. 'Whoever has a true value for church and state, should avoid the extremes of whig for the sake of the former, and the extremes of tory on the account of the latter.'

Some of the definitions have become standing jokes. Johnson himself foresaw that people would find things to laugh at; as he says loftily in the Preface, 'a few wild blunders, and risible absurdities, from which no work of such multiplicity was ever free, may for a time furnish folly with laughter, and harden ignorance in contempt'. The contempt, if ever it existed, has long since died away, but we can cheerfully admit to the folly which finds a good laugh here and there in Johnson's stately pages. 'Network' is one of the most famous: 'Any thing reticulated or decussated, at equal distances, with interstices between the intersections.' (But then, how would you define a net? A collection of holes tied together with string?) 'Dross' is 'The recrement or despumation of metals'; 'blister' 'a pustule formed by raising the cuticle from the cutis, and filled with serous blood'. But merely to cite these amusing instances can give no idea of the pleasure and interest of browsing through the Dictionary. (My own cherished copy of the third edition of 1765, which I bought in 1943 and trundled back to my college room on a handcart, has made the greatest single contribution to such understanding of eighteenth-century life and literature as I have attained.) How comely it is, and how reviving, to learn (for instance) that a 'drudging-box' is 'the box, out of which flour is sprinkled on roast meat'. (Johnson spells it 'flower', which intensifies the Arcadian associations.) Henceforth, no kitchen of mine will be complete without a drudging-box. These things alter the flavour of one's life. Interesting, too, to find that in this compendium of the language of pre-imperial England the word 'jungle' is not listed. Dominion over palm and pine had not yet altered the Englishman's view of the world. Failing to find 'jungle', one's eye moves to 'jump'. Johnson's third sense for this, as a noun, is (from French *jupe*) 'A waistcoat; a kind of loose or limber stays worn by sickly ladies'. (Put on your jump, my dear, the weather is inclement.) Obviously this is the word that died a temporary death and reappeared in the nineteenth century as 'jumper'. *Und so weiter.* I resist the temptation to go on. It is one's own browsing, not other people's, that is delightful.

As well as defining the words, Johnson often passed judgement on their suitability, firmly taking the attitude that the presence of a word in his columns did not imply approval of its correctness or elegance. A reader who looked for a word was entitled to find it, but not necessarily to go away and employ it. Thus 'fuss' is 'a low cant word'; 'fib' is 'a cant word among children'; 'flirtation' 'a cant word among women'. 'Cant', by the way, is '1. A corrupt dialect used by beggars and vagabonds', 2. 'A particular form of speaking peculiar to some certain class or body of men', 3. 'A whining pretension to goodness, in formal and affected terms', 4. 'Barbarous jargon', and 5, surprisingly enough, 'Auction' ('offering to sell their leases by *cant*'). When Johnson told Boswell to clear his mind of cant, he meant 3, with overtones of both 2 and 4. In any case, to list a word as 'cant' was to alert the reader not to use it if he, or she, wished to be taken seriously. Similar warnings abound. 'Shatterbrained' ('Inattentive; not consistent') is 'a low word'. Sense no. 4 of 'Dab' is '[In low language.] An artist; a man expert at something. This is not used in writing.' With prohibitions fore and aft, the word is heavily put in its place. On the other hand 'cully', which I should have thought a real piece of eighteenth-century slang or cant, is glossed without comment as 'A man deceived or imposed upon; as by sharpers or a strumpet'. Which leads in turn to the fact that Johnson considered 'sharper' a respectable word, fit to be used in a definition; and indeed he glosses it in the appropriate place with authority from L'Estrange, Arbuthnot and Pope.

Years earlier, Johnson had said in one of his pert back-answers to kind old Jorden of Pembroke, 'Sir, you have sconced me twopence for non-attendance at a lecture not worth a penny.' Perhaps he remembered the remark, and disapproved of his younger self, as he wrote the gloss on 'sconce': 'To mulct; to fine. A low word which ought not to be retained.'

There is, in one way and another, an enormous amount to be learnt from Johnson's Dictionary. Much of it is linguistic, naturally; when he says that 'deft' is obsolete, we find it interesting to note that this useful word appeared at that time to be going out of use, and has since come back and stayed. It is interesting, too, that the word 'civilization' had a strictly limited meaning for Johnson; it was a technical process in law, by which a criminal trial was turned into a civil action; for our modern use of 'civilization' he used 'civility'. We know, from other sources, that the change was already happening, but Johnson resisted it, and would not admit the modern sense of 'civilization' into the revised edition of the Dictionary seventeen years later, though Boswell tried to persuade him to do so.

In the case of 'civilization' it is clear that a contemporary usage, becoming conventional within his lifetime, appeared to Johnson as something to be resisted. In general, though, it is quite impossible for us to look back and say whether, when he blacklisted a word, his condemnation was based on his sense of the best contemporary style or whether it reflected a purely personal decision. He signified his dislike of (among other words) *belabour, cajole, dumb-found, gambler, ignoramus, pat* (in the sense of conveniently to hand), *simpleton, touchy* and *volunteer*, all of which have gone on their long march completely unaffected. Johnson's dislike of these words is less reliable as information about the history of the English language than as information about *him*. And this is another area of interest in the Dictionary. It brings its author so vividly before us. He complains of the backbreaking, inhuman work to which he is giving his life; whenever the occupation of dictionary-making is mentioned, the tone is rueful. 'Lexicographer' is 'A writer of dictionaries; a harmless drudge, that busies himself in tracing the original, and detailing the signification of words'. 'Grub Street' is 'Originally the name of a street in Moorfields in London, much inhabited by writers of small histories, dictionaries and temporary poems; whence any mean production is called grubstreet'. And underneath the definition Johnson quotes two lines of Greek verse, which have been translated as

> Hail Ithaca, after strife and bitter trials
> Gladly I approach thy threshold.

At other times the personal note is softer. In glossing 'Lich', 'a dead carcase', he goes on to 'Lichfield, the field of the dead, a city in Staffordshire, so named from martyred christians. *Salve magna parens.*' The sudden interjection – hail, great parent – is touching; one pictures him hunched over his desk in Gough Square,

> long in populous city pent,
> Where houses thick and sewers annoy the air

and suddenly seeing the gentle valley, the streams, the moggs, the trees and the three graceful red spires. It was a long time since he had been home, and for all his sturdy self-sufficiency in London, home sometimes tugged at his heart. Glossing 'Shaw', 'a thicket; a small wood', he feels a pleasant boyhood memory jog stealthily at his elbow, and adds, 'A tuft of trees near Lichfield is called Gentle shaw.' The trees have gone but Gentleshaw Common still exists.

Not only the definitions, but the illustrative quotations, are full of information about Johnson; his tastes, his standards of judgement, even the progress of his reading (some authors are quoted more often in the later sections than in the earlier, thus showing that he became more familiar with them over the nine-year period; others – Donne, for instance – are quoted consistently throughout, showing that he was solidly familiar with them before he started).

The quotations are, from every point of view, one of the glories of the Dictionary. To begin with, the idea of illustrating – and, by implication, enforcing – definition and usage by citing authorities was Johnson's most important original contribution to lexicography, and would have remained so even if he had made a mess of the selection. In fact, he made a brilliant success of it. The Dictionary is one long fascinating anthology. He consciously chose the quotations not only to illustrate the words but to convey valuable thoughts or interesting information. This part of the work attracted him (he wanted to 'relieve the labour of verbal searches, and intersperse with verdure and flowers the dusty deserts of barren philology'). Accordingly, he flung himself into it, selecting

> from philosophers principles of science; from historians remarkable facts; from chemists complete processes; from divines striking exhortations; and from poets beautiful descriptions.

The result was such a plethora of material that Johnson hastily cut back his programme, lest he produce a dictionary in twenty volumes rather than two. If we look at a copy of the Dictionary we can actually see the cut-off point; the words under 'A' are far more copiously illustrated than those under the remaining twenty-five letters. Moreover, he had a strong and consistent policy about the choice of authors to be quoted. He believed, as we have had occasion to note earlier, that there had been a classic period of English, when it became a fully developed language, able to express any idea, while still remaining in touch with its pristine purity and vigour. This lay behind his decision to go back no further than Sir Philip Sidney:

> From the authors which rose in the time of Elizabeth, a speech might be formed adequate to all the purposes of use and elegance. If the language of theology were extracted from Hooker and the translation of the Bible; the terms of natural knowledge from Bacon; the phrases of policy, war, and navigation from Raleigh; the dialect of poetry and fiction from Spenser and Sidney; and the diction of common life from Shakespeare, few ideas would be lost to mankind for want of English words, in which they might be expressed.

As a forward limit, he fixed on the years immediately before his own working lifetime:

> My purpose was to admit no testimony of living authors, that I might not be misled by partiality, and that none of my contemporaries might have reason to complain; nor have I departed from this resolution, but when some performance of uncommon excellence excited my veneration, when my memory supplied me, from late books, with an example that was wanting, or when my heart, in the tenderness of friendship, solicited admission for a favourite name.

If we dig into the matter and find out whose the 'favourite names' were, we come up with some interesting discoveries. Charlotte Lennox, she of the hot apple-pie and the sprigs of myrtle, is quoted under 'talent' in its sense of 'faculty; power; gift of nature'; it is tempting to see this as a graceful compliment; but, if we do so see it, how shall we interpret the fact that David Garrick is quoted just once, and that under 'giggler'? Richardson is given as an authority, but Fielding never. Johnson quotes himself several times; 'lacerate' from *The Vanity of Human Wishes*, 'intimidate' from *Irene*. Under 'dissipate' he gives two illustrations from his own work. Under sense 2, 'To scatter the attention', we read,

> This slavery to his passions produced a life irregular and *dissipated*. (*Savage's Life*.)

And under the next sense,

> 'To spend a fortune':
> . . . the wherry that contains
> Of *dissipated* wealth the small remains. (*London*.)

The first passage refers to Savage in his own person, the second to the indignant poet in *London* who shakes the dust of the metropolis from his feet, and who, though not originally conceived as a portrait of Savage, inevitably brings him to mind. Was the connection automatic, an example of 'free association'? Or was it perfectly deliberate, Johnson's way of dropping an unnoticed tear on Savage's grave?

Each of these details is an important brush stroke in our picture of Johnson as a living man. Dictionary-making involves thousands upon thousands of small decisions, many of which reveal the character behind them. His choice of authors to be quoted, contemporary or otherwise, naturally reflected also his strong religious and ethical principles. Throughout the whole vast range of the work he quoted no writer who might exert a bad moral influence. He was determined not to be the means of introducing some unwary mind to a book that might undermine faith or conduct. Not that he was prudish in the Bowdlerizing, Victorian sense. He refused to quote Hobbes, out of disapproval of Hobbesian doctrine; he has no quotation from any of the licentious comic writers of the Restoration, though well aware that Congreve, for instance, is an exemplary writer of English; but his most frequently quoted author is Shakespeare, whose unexpurgated writings were considered unfit for young readers until well into the mid-twentieth century. All in all, the moral intention of this vast anthology is more often evinced positively than negatively. It was not so much a matter of screening out writers who might do harm as offering the reader good thoughts – page after page of wise reflections on morality, politics, religion. The word 'God', for instance, under its primary sense of 'The Supreme Being', is illustrated by just one quotation, from the Gospel According to St John:

> God is a spirit, and they that worship him must worship him in spirit and in truth.

Then of course there is the great preface. In assessing what the Dictionary reveals to us about its author, we should never underestimate this, one of the most profound statements he ever made – about his profession, about his way of life, about himself. It deserves to be read entire, and with total attention, by anyone interested in coming to terms with Johnson. It is not only a statement of his methods and principles but an account of the way he understands language and its functions; and as such it is the utterance not only of one man but of a society that pinned its faith on language, on verbal and written utterance, as we pin ours on technology. To Johnson, as to his age, language was the essential instrument of thought. In this view, sloppy and imprecise use of words, a habit of shovelling them about contemptuously as if they were so much gravel instead of a collection of living entities each with its history and personality, can produce only half-baked thinking which blurs distinctions and fails to get to the heart of anything. (Some of us still hold the same belief, even now, though most of the 'thinkers' in vogue in our society – sociologists, e.g. – seem to have either abandoned the belief in clear and precise language or never heard of it.) Johnson believes that a language, and by extension a literature, is the fullest and best expression of the selfhood of any civilization – to use two words in rapid succession that certainly don't find a place in his Dictionary. In the most natural way, he expresses his own faith in this ideal, and aligns his personal situation with it:

> The chief glory of every people arises from its authors: whether I shall add anything by my own writings to the reputation of English literature must be left to time: much of my life has been lost under the pressures of disease; much has been trifled away; and much has always been spent in provision for the day that was passing over me; but I shall not think my employment useless or ignoble, if by my assistance foreign nations, and distant ages, gain access to the propagators of knowledge, and understand the teachers of truth; if my labours afford light to the repositories of science, and add celebrity to Bacon, to Hooker, to Milton and to Boyle.

The miniature painting of Johnson's own life – struggling against ill health, against the fits of sluggish idleness that arose from the disabling conflicts within his own nature, against the ever present threat of want and destitution – is, if we like to put it so, the importation of personality into an area normally reserved for the impersonal. But it is no merely gratuitous intrusion of the personal into a place where it has no business. I once took part in a radio panel discussion with a famous historian who was, and had made it his business to be, a 'character'. The issues we were talking about were general, concerning the society at large, bearing on us as individuals only inasmuch as we necessarily shared the fate of our society. But this distinguished gentleman could not forbear introducing, every few minutes, the sort of coat-trailing or picturesque remark that was supposed to make the listener chuckle and remark once again that he was a 'character'. Each time he did so, he gave a little smirk and looked up to the ceiling, obviously from force of habit, since the small and unresponsive audience around the table could not have seemed to him a gallery worth playing to. This display of irrelevant vanity came near to ruining the discussion, and certainly made no contribution to it. I tell the unimportant story as the quickest way of indicating what Johnson's self-portrait in the preface to the Dictionary is *not*, what Johnson's habitual introduction of the personal note never is. Johnson is engaged in the impersonal task of compiling a dictionary; but he has made that task personal to himself, has rooted himself in the centre of the work that is to be done, partly by the length and arduousness of his labours but even more so by his unreserved acceptance of his own destiny as an English man of letters. Language, essential to the life of the nation in all its aspects, is the particular care and responsibility of literary men. It is they who involve themselves with the language, study it, use it professionally, pour their individual lives into its collective life. It is they who devote thought and skill to style, *nuance*, and distinction. Not all of them, of course. At any given moment there are writers who, popular for one reason or another, obviously care nothing for the language that serves them and that they should serve reciprocally. As Johnson put it in this same Preface,

> illiterate writers will, at one time or other, by public infatuation, rise into renown, who not knowing the original import of words, will use them with colloquial licentiousness, confound distinction, and forget propriety.

The responsibility of the true man of letters is all the more serious. And here we see how natural and right it is for Johnson himself to step on to the stage. He comes before us as a man who has identified his own life with the life of his country as it is expressed in language, the shared creation of thousands of minds but shaped and focused by the individual minds of writers who use it at its highest point of meaning and intensity. 'The chief glory of every people arises from its authors; whether I shall add anything by my own writings to the reputation of English literature must be left to time . . .' But, however modestly presented, this is his aim. He knows that his life will stand or fall by what he has been able to achieve in this sphere of words, of expression, as far as earthly judgement is concerned; standing right with his Creator is another matter, separable from his artistic and professional endeavours though never entirely apart from them. And this is why he can, without self-pity and without arousing our impatience, present himself as a sad man, who has lost most of the earthly happiness he ever knew, who lives in a 'gloom of solitude'; the personal note we find in the noble paragraph which closes the Preface, and which is perhaps the best known and most quoted of Johnson's writings, is moving and inspiriting, not in the least embarrassing or factitious, because it is the voice of a man who is saying to us, *Here, in this work, in this pursuit of meaning and understanding, I have invested my hopes.*

> If the lexicons of ancient tongues, now immutably fixed, and comprised in a few volumes, be yet, after the toil of successive ages, inadequate and delusive; if the aggregated knowledge, and co-operating diligence of the Italian academicians, did not secure them from the censure of Beni; if the embodied critics of France, when fifty years had been spent on their work, were obliged to change its economy, and give their second edition another form, I may surely be contented without the praise of perfection, which, if I could obtain, in this gloom of solitude, what would it avail me? I have protracted my work till most of those whom I wished to please have sunk into the grave, and success and miscarriage are empty sounds. I therefore dismiss it with frigid tranquillity, having little to fear or hope from censure or from praise.

PART IV

'True, Evident and Actual Wisdom'

CHAPTER 15

'Toil, Envy, Want...'

The nine years of effort that went into the Dictionary had brought even the Herculean Johnson to a state bordering on breakdown. He had the right to a long rest if ever a man had a right to anything. But his material circumstances made even the briefest holiday an impossibility. On the morning after the publication of the Dictionary he had no choice but to take up his pen and 'provide for the day that was passing over him'. For years past, and for years to come, the only periods of rest in his overdriven life were those intervals when he sank into a stupefied dejection that paralysed his mind. Apart from these grim holidays, he found his only leisure in the convivial evenings of argument and counter-argument that switched his brain from one kind of activity to another.

In 1756, the year after the Dictionary, a torrent of miscellaneous work came from Johnson's pen. He wrote Prefaces to Rolt's *Dictionary of Trade and Commerce* and Payne's *Introduction to the Game of Draughts*; he brought out an edition of Sir Thomas Browne's *Christian Morals* with a life of the author; he wrote two important essays, 'Further Thoughts on Agriculture' and 'The Political State of Great Britain'; since the Dictionary was already proving itself to be a success and a more portable edition was called for, within this year he produced an abridgement. As if this were not enough, he served as an editor of, and frequent contributor to, *The Literary Magazine or Universal Review*.

It is true that his editorial method, during the two years' life of this periodical, was mainly conversational, not to say Socratic. With the Dictionary, *The Rambler* and his two long poems to back his reputation, Johnson was already seen as a lawgiver in all matters concerning literature. Aspiring and struggling authors, old and young, came to him literally in crowds, and for the editorial office he substituted the tea-table. Arthur Murphy's biographical essay contains a vivid picture of Johnson at this time, lying in bed all morning and rising in the early afternoon to preside over a non-stop informal seminar with the aid of gallons of tea. 'Authors, long since forgotten, waited on him as their oracle, and he gave responses in the chair of criticism. He listened to the complaints, the schemes, and the hopes and fears of a crowd of inferior writers.' Small wonder that, as Murphy adds, Johnson 'believed that he could give a better history of Grub Street than any man living'. If this brigade of scribblers drew solid benefit from Johnson's learning and judgement, he also took something from them. Their anecdotes and reminiscences flowed into the enormous vault of his memory and remained there. As a boy he had heard from Cornelius Ford what it was like to be a man of letters in the early years of the century; Savage had filled in the outline with lurid colours; Johnson himself had known Grub Street in the thirties and forties; and now the endless succession of callers each contributed his grain of information, an anecdote here, a reminiscence there, keeping him *au courant* with the literary life of the city.

This buzz of activity did not yet satisfy Johnson's intellect. There was, besides, the ever-pressing question of money. Inevitably, his mind moved back to that large scheme he had been forced to abandon over ten years earlier: the complete edition of Shakespeare. Established as he was, he was safe now from any jealous publisher who wanted to play tricks with copyright. All that was necessary was to issue the appropriate 'Proposals' and get on with the work while the subscriptions flowed in. Accordingly, this same year of 1756 saw Johnson's pamphlet *Proposals for printing by subscription the dramatic works of William Shakespeare, corrected and illustrated by Samuel Johnson.* As an incisive, economical and complete statement of the nature of a large task, this deserves to stand beside the Proposals for the Dictionary. There is no better statement of the reasons why Shakespeare needs to be edited, and what aims an editor can reasonably set himself. In such passages as Johnson's summary of the causes of obscurity in Shakespeare, we see his characteristic blend of the scholar's learning and the writer's sensibility with the lawyer's flair for clear and concise presentation of evidence.

Johnson was in confident mood, secure in the strength of his grip on Shakespeare's work and in the proof he had given of being able to move mountains. When preparing the Dictionary, he had read carefully through Shakespeare and quoted him more often than any other writer. His knowledge of the text must have been very intimate. From this position of strength, he allowed himself to make a rash promise: the edition would be available to subscribers by Christmas of the following year.

Anyone who has ever undertaken to edit a text – to compare the various copies, estimate their order of authenticity, sort out contradictions, and then go on to explain obscurities, gloss obsolete words and phrases, and generally package it for the modern reader – will agree that Johnson was being unusually confident in arranging to polish off Shakespeare's plays at the rate of about two a month, not counting any time for tidying up and writing a critical preface. He seems to have been relying on the fantastic speed at which he could work when not interrupted by his fits of helpless inertia. Doubtless if he left these spells out of his calculations, the deadline could be made to seem plausible. He had underestimated the time it would take him to do the Dictionary by exactly two-thirds, expecting to manage it in three years when in the end it took nine. But this, as anyone knows who comes into contact with authors, is just about normal in a literary man. If a writer announces that he will finish a book in a year, a wise publisher will always allow three. To budget for less would be optimistic: for more over-cautious. So perhaps the year and a half which Johnson allowed for the edition of Shakespeare might reasonably amount to no more than five. His friends in the world of scholarship and literature, men like the Wartons, John Hawkins, Arthur Murphy, were hopeful of his good speed while sceptical of his self-imposed timetable.

Meanwhile he continued, as always, to move from task to task. Just as, during the years of work on the Dictionary, he had found it refreshing to undertake even such day-labour as turning out *Rambler* essays, so now he devoured books of every kind and gave the world his opinion of them. He reviewed, for the *Literary Gazette*, works on theology, philosophy, geography, politics, history, military training; a treatise on distilling sea water, and on 'curing an ill taste in milk'; a pamphlet about tea. And to everything he brought that close attention to reasoning and evidence, that intensive scrutiny of detail that were the recognizable marks of the Johnsonian mind. 'No man', Sir Joshua Reynolds was later to write, 'had like him the faculty of teaching inferior minds the art of thinking'; and Reynolds was not referring to mere vulgarization, for one of the 'inferior minds' he was thinking of was his own; inferior, that is, not to the common standard of minds but to Johnson's. The cast of Johnson's mind was forensic; he liked to make clear distinctions, and was irritated by confusions; he carried the habit of examining evidence into everyday life. When we add to this the nine years of sorting out shades of meaning within the definition of single words, we understand why it was that he could contribute usefully to the discussion of almost any subject. Even where his own knowledge was amateurish (and it was never very safe to assume that), he could bring the discussion under logical headings and state each problem in its final terms.

This gift for cross-examination ought to have made Johnson a formidable controversialist. And so, of course, he was, when the occasion arose. But nearly always in conversation. In his writings he was, though firm in his opinions, remarkably peaceable towards individuals. Very seldom in his long career did he use his great strength to knock down another writer. There are a few deft jabs at rival editors in the notes to his Shakespeare, and there are the famous bombshell letters to Chesterfield and (as we shall see later) James Macpherson; but on the whole Johnson's voluminous works are not blemished by attacks on other writers. He was at the opposite extreme from those writers who appear to feel a need every so often to launch a venomous attack on some rival practitioner, as a kind of emotional release. No man who held such definite views, and was so fearless in upholding them, ever trod on so few individual toes as Johnson.

There is, however, one important exception to this, and it dates from his period on the *Literary Magazine*. In 1757 he was given for review a book by one Soame Jenyns, *A Free Enquiry into the Nature and Origin of Evil*. The argument struck him as pernicious. He read it with mounting anger, then sat down and composed a review so long that it was serialized in three numbers of the magazine. Having decided that Jenyns' book ought to be slammed, he slammed it, three times, very hard.

One of Soame Jenyns' acquaintances described him as 'a male bluestocking' – an assiduous frequenter of polite assemblies, a cultivated amateur. In philosophy, he was of the school of Leibnitz, whose doctrine of cosmic optimism was widely diffused in the eighteenth century, both from his own writings and by means of disciples such as Wolff in Germany and Shaftesbury in England. Leibnitz's starting-point was the ontological method of proving the existence of God, which maintains that, if we imagine a being possessed of every possible kind of perfection, this being must necessarily exist, since non-existence would be a lack, a failure to realize its full potentiality. Leibnitz agreed with this, and proceeded to the view that existence is an embodiment of perfection not only for God but for the lesser creation. Everything fulfilled itself by existing and the greater the number of diverse modes of being that came into existence, the more the Divine creativity manifested itself and the more perfect the universe became.

Leibnitz further maintained that the universe was logically coherent, that for everything that existed or happened there was a 'good and sufficient reason'. In its popular form this gave rise to the rather fatuous optimism expressed in Pope's *An Essay on Man* ('whatever is, is right') and (negatively) to Voltaire's figure of fun in *Candide*, the foolish philosopher Pangloss with his motto that 'everything is for the best in the best of all possible worlds'. In fact the theory as Leibnitz developed it is quite consistent with experience and has a pleasing logical stringency; he did not exempt even God from the demands of the 'good and sufficient reason'; even the Divine Will was governed by the principle it had itself created. Hence, when God was confronted with the infinite variety of choices inherent in the creation of a universe, he harmonized them along the lines of the Great Chain of Being, calling forth a multitude of modes of existence, from the humblest sand-worm to the most resplendent archangel, each with its allotted station. In the universe as Leibnitz envisioned it, the most widely different beings were related in so far as they were following the laws of their own nature, and thus co-operating in the working out of God's master plan. This applied not only to those elements in the universe which human beings found benevolent and reassuring but also to those from which they recoiled with horror; a cancer cell or a hungry shark was as fully justified in existing and in acting out its role as the man whose life it claimed. Leibnitz's optimism is philosophical and lofty, taking cognisance of the tragic destiny of individual human beings; it is not easy or fatuous, though its opponents projected it as such because that was the easiest way to discredit it.

Soame Jenyns accounted for the presence of suffering and evil along Leibnitzian lines, though his immediate source seems to have been Pope's poem. It was not a doctrine that Johnson cared for; while not being in head-on collision with his own penitential version of Christianity, it smacked a little of complacency; in its popular form, certainly, it encouraged a certain indifference to suffering (the man, or animal, whose agonies arouse our pity could cheer up by reflecting that he is fulfilling God's benign purpose). Johnson was so achingly aware of the vast quantity of suffering that went on around him, and the gratuitousness of so much of it, that he always preferred to draw people's attention to the plight of the victims than to encourage them to be complacent

1 Samuel Johnson in 1770, by Joshua Reynolds.

2 A view of Lichfield in 1785, showing the house where Johnson was born (now the Johnson Birthplace Museum).

3 Lichfield Grammar School in the late eighteenth century.

4 Michael Johnson,
  Samuel Johnson's father.

5 Gilbert Walmesley, 'one
of the first friends [whom]
literature procured me'.

6 A letter in which Walmesley recommends the young Johnson and David
Garrick to a clergyman friend in Rochester. Johnson is described as 'a very good
scholar and poet and I have great hopes will turn out a fine tragedy-writer'.

*He & another Neighbour of mine one Mr Johnson,
set out this morning for London together: Davy
Garrick to be wt You early & next week, & Mr
Johnson to try his Fate wth a Tragedy & to see to get
himself employ'd in some Translation either from
ye Latin or ye French. Johnson is a very good
Scholar & Poet & I have great hopes will turn out a
fine Tragedy-Writer. I am ever, Dear Sir*

*To
The Revd Mr. Colson
at his house in
Rochester.
Kent*

*by way of
London*

*Your most oblig'd &
most Affecte. hum Servt
Gilb Walmesley.
Lichfield,
Mar. 2. 1736/7*

7 (*above left*)
Elizabeth Porter,
Johnson's 'Tetty'.

8 (*above right*) Lucy Porter,
his stepdaughter, in later
years.

9 David Garrick.

10 Edial Hall, Staffordshire, where the Johnsons kept a short-lived private academy.

11, 12 Ashbourne Hall (*left*), the home of John Taylor (*right*), a lifelong friend of Johnson's, with whom he attended Lichfield Grammar School.

13 Lord Chesterfield.

14 (*below*) 'Doctor Johnson in the Ante-Room of Lord Chesterfield, waiting for an audience 1748', a reconstruction by E. M. Ward, painted in 1845.

(*right*) 17 Gough Square, where Johnson lived from 1748 to 1765.

(*below, left*) George Psalmanazar.

(*below, right*) Edmund Cave, founder of *The Gentleman's Magazine*, Johnson's earliest London employer.

18 Sir Joshua Reynolds; a self-portrait, 1753-4.

19 (*above*) Bennet Langton.

20 (*left*) Samuel Johnson in 1756, by Joshua Reynolds

21 (*right*) Johnson's Court,
off Fleet Street, where
Johnson moved in 1765.

22 (*below*) A literary party at Sir Joshua Reynolds'. *Left to right:* James Boswell,
Samuel Johnson, Joshua Reynolds, David Garrick, Edmund Burke,
Pasquale Paoli, Charles Burney, Thomas Warton, Oliver Goldsmith.

23 (left) No. 8 Bolt Court

24 Francis Barber,
attributed to James
Northcote.

25 Anna Williams.

26, 27 James Boswell, painted by George Willison in 1765, three years after meeting with Johnson . . . and (*below*) caricatured by H. Bunbury, eating with Johnson in a chophouse.

28 Hester Thrale, by
R. E. Pine.

29 Johnson in 1775, by
Joshua Reynolds.

30 (*above*) A nineteenth-
century painting of
Streatham Place.

31 (*right*) Johnson in the
summerhouse at
Streatham.

32 (*above*) Vauxhall Gardens. In the box on the left Johnson sits with a party that includes Hester Thrale and Oliver Goldsmith.

33 (*left*) Johnson in the Highlands.

34 (*opposite*) A page from the manuscript of Johnson's *Prayers and Meditations*.

Aug 13... after 1 in 100w...

O God, most merciful Father who
by many diseases hast admonished me of
my approach to the end of life, and by this
gracious addition to my days hast given
me an opportunity of appearing once more in
thy presence to commemorate the Sacrifice
by which thy Son Jesus Christ has taken away
the Sins of the world, assist me in this com-
memoration by thy Holy Spirit, that I may
            of my life past
look back upon the Sinfulness, with holy pious
Sorrow, and efficacious Repentance, that my
resolutions of amendment may be rightly formed
and diligently exerted, that I may be freed
from vain and useless Scruples, and that I may
serve thee in with Faith, Hope, and Charity so

35 John Opie's portrait of
   Johnson, for which he
   on the day of his strok

36 Joshua Reynolds' last
   portrait of Johnson,
   1782–4.

about it. Jenyns, then, would hardly be a candidate for Johnson's favour. But to make matters worse he had allowed himself two small embroideries on the familiar Leibnitzian theme. The first was that every state of existence has its advantages and consolations which tend to cancel out its pains and handicaps; the second that the sufferings of humanity may be to the advantage of other beings higher up the scale, as the sufferings of animals in the slaughterhouse may be held to be for the benefit of mankind, and that – further – these sufferings may even 'entertain' the higher beings, as mankind takes pleasure in tormenting animals by such diversions as hunting, fishing and bull-fighting.

Both these suggestions revolted Johnson. He went for them with a cold, concentrated fury that is unique in his work and ranges him, for the moment, with the great demolishing ironists of his century, Swift and Voltaire. It is tempting to refrain altogether from quotation, for the essay ought to be read entire by anyone interested in Johnson's powers of thinking, feeling and expression. But the counter-temptation, to enrich my pages with some of his nobly indignant and trenchant sentences, is too strong. Here are a few extracts. Jenyns has been arguing that the poor are exempt from many annoyances that beset the rich; that to be ill is to know certain kinds of enjoyment denied to those who are well; that to be foolish, or even mad, may be quite pleasant when seen from the inside; that ignorance is a positive advantage in people born to a low station, since the poor are made comfortable by ignorance, and ought not to be robbed of it: 'It is a cordial administered by the gracious hand of providence, of which they ought never to be deprived by an ill-judged and improper education.' Johnson deals with these points in turn. On poverty, he begins by censuring Jenyns' preferred euphemism, 'want of riches':

> In that sense almost every man may in his own opinion be poor. But there is another poverty which is *want of competence*, of all that can soften the miseries of life, of all that can diversify attention or delight imagination. There is yet another poverty which is *want of necessaries*, a species of poverty which no care of the public, no charity of particulars, can preserve many from feeling openly, and many secretly.

Jenyns, it seems to Johnson, is another of those well-to-do, comfortably protected people (usually Whigs!) who find the misfortunes of others all too easy to theorize away:

> Life must be seen before it can be known. This author and Pope perhaps never saw the miseries which they imagine thus easy to be borne. The poor indeed are insensible of many little vexations which sometimes embitter the possessions and pollute the enjoyments of the rich. They are not pained by casual incivility, or mortified by the mutilation of a compliment; but this happiness is like that of a malefactor who ceases to feel the cords that bind him when the pincers are tearing his flesh.

When he gets to the subject of madness, which Jenyns airily thinks of as probably rather pleasant, Johnson again brings in a note of sombre realism: he has not, thank God, any direct experience of being insane, but has Jenyns ever looked closely at a madman?

> On the happiness of madmen, as the case is not very frequent, it is not necessary to raise a disquisition, but I cannot forbear to observe that I never yet knew disorders of mind increase felicity: every madman is either arrogant and irascible, or gloomy and suspicious, or possessed by some passion or notion destructive to his quiet. He has always discontent in his look, and malignity in his bosom. And, if we had the power of choice, he would soon repent who should resign his reason to secure his peace.

Moving on, Johnson punctures Jenyns' theory that ignorance is a God-given comfort to the poor and should be left alone. Who, he asks, are the poor? Those who lack the competence to make a good living? Or, as Jenyns seems to assume, all those who happen to be born in poor homes?

> To entail irreversible poverty upon generation after generation only because the ancestor happened to be poor is in itself cruel, if not unjust, and is wholly contrary to the maxims of a commercial nation, which always suppose and promote a rotation of property, and offer every individual a chance of mending his condition by his diligence.

And he concludes, in words that deserve to be engraved in marble,

> I am always afraid of determining on the side of envy or cruelty. The privileges of education may sometimes be improperly bestowed, but I shall always fear to withhold them, lest I should be yielding to the suggestions of pride, while I persuade myself that I am following the maxims of policy; and, under the appearance of salutary restraints, should be indulging the lust of dominion and that malevolence which delights in seeing others depressed.

So much for what might be called the social implications of Jenyns' thesis. When he comes to the more purely philosophical part of the argument, Johnson is – it is only fair to admit – partly biased by his dislike of speculation. Though he believed that every man had a duty to use his intelligence, Johnson did not therefore regard intellectual curiosity as a virtue. To him the supreme questions had been settled by God and the answers given to man in Holy Writ. To be dissatisfied with this situation, to be too hot for answers and certainties, bordered on impiety. Anecdote after anecdote testifies to Johnson's distaste for speculative philosophy. The best known concerns Bishop Berkeley's *Three Dialogues Between Hylas and Philonous* (1713), which subtly argues the case for 'subjective idealism' against the commonsense view that our perceptions bring us into contact with a world of objects that exist independently of our perceiving them. Asked how he would set about refuting such a view, Johnson went up to a large stone, kicked it hard, and said 'I refute Berkeley thus'. As an answer it was

both unceremonious and unphilosophical, and Johnson intended it to be both.
A bishop ought to be on his knees praying, or in his study reading the theologians and trying to comprehend the nature of God – not spinning theories which question the validity of the senses given to us by God to be our guide through experience.

In much the same spirit, he lays it down in the Soame Jenyns review that the business of every writer is to help us to live our lives, to bring us nearer to the hope of heaven and in the meantime to put up with what happens to us. Speculations like those of Jenyns do neither; besides, they are morally repugnant.

> He might have shown that these hunters whose game is man have many sports analogous to our own. As we drown whelps and kittens, they amuse themselves now and then with sinking a ship, and stand round the fields of Blenheim or the walls of Prague as we encircle a cock-pit. As we shoot a bird flying, they take a man in the midst of his business or pleasure, and knock him down with an apoplexy. Some of them, perhaps, are virtuosi, and delight in the operations of an asthma, as a human philosopher in the effects of the air pump. To swell a man with a tympany is as good sport as to blow a frog. Many a merry bout have these frolic beings at the vicissitudes of an ague, and good sport it is to see a man tumble with an epilepsy, and revive and tumble again, and all this he knows not why. As they are wiser and more powerful than we, they have more exquisite diversions, for we have no way of procuring any sport so brisk and so lasting as the paroxysms of the gout and stone which undoubtedly must make high mirth, especially if the play be a little diversified with the blunders and puzzles of the blind and deaf. We know not how far their sphere of observations may extend. Perhaps now and then a merry being may place himself in such a situation as to enjoy at once all the varieties of an epidemical disease, or amuse his leisure with the tossings and contortions of every possible pain exhibited together.
>
> The only end of writing is to enable the readers better to enjoy life, or better to endure it: and how will either of those be put more in our power by him who tells us that we are puppets, of which some creature not much wiser than ourselves manages the wires: that a set of beings, unseen and unheard, are hovering about us, trying experiments upon our sensibility, putting us in agonies to see our limbs quiver, torturing us to madness that they may laugh at our vagaries; sometimes obstructing the bile, that they may see how a man looks when he is yellow, sometimes breaking a traveller's bones to try how he will get home, sometimes wasting a man to a skeleton, and sometimes killing him fat for the greater elegance of his hide?

Such writing – fluent, sinewy, with the speed and lightness of good talk combined perfectly with the accuracy and lucidity of a written language carefully pondered – is an example of how Johnson could write when the strength and solidity of his mind were suddenly mobilized by the trumpet call of strong emotion. Everything comes into play at once – the emotion canalizes the thinking, and the thinking orchestrates and dignifies the emotion.

Jenyns' essential offence, in Johnson's eyes, was that he skated over the depths of darkness and suffering in human life. Johnson was always deeply affronted by any attempt to whitewash the realities of existence. To him the beginning of wisdom was to accept the human condition as tragic, and mortal life as a time of trial and suffering. And never more so than in this period, when his outlook was sombre indeed. To be honest about his own experience of life – and he was always that – was to report a half-century of almost continuous suffering. The brief happiness he had known with Tetty had evaporated long before her death; and if he searched his memory further back, to the earliest years, when he might have been fondled and protected, he recalled chiefly the gloom of the house, his father's melancholy and his mother's nagging. Even the innocent vanity of youth had been denied him; loaded with physical disabilities, an ugly appearance made more offensive by his convulsive nervous twitches and peering short sight, he had never been able to preen himself. His only solid comfort, in these drab and hard-pressed middle years, was the knowledge that his unusual powers were recognized and that he was respected by people whose respect meant a great deal. From this point on, the register of Johnson's friends begins to read like a roll-call of the names that make up the fairest fame of eighteenth-century England.

Some of his friendships began as chance encounters, but more often they were won for him by his work, when those who had been deeply impressed by his writings came to seek his acquaintance. In these years Johnson began his long and steady friendship with Charles Burney, famous in his day as the distinguished historian of music, who was so delighted with *The Rambler* essays and the Proposals for the Dictionary that he wrote and introduced himself to Johnson from his country home in Norfolk, where he had retired for a few years in an attempt to better his health. He was, he explained, very anxious to possess a copy of the Dictionary, and a few extra copies to give to his friends, as soon as it was published. Could Johnson advise him? Was it to be published by subscription? He begged for Johnson's directions as to how to lay hold of the book at the first possible opportunity. Johnson's reply is a rare combination of stately courtesy with spontaneous warmth. There was no question of flattering a man who might prove an important customer; Burney was younger than Johnson, he had as yet no reputation, he wrote from an obscure address. But something in his letter had touched Johnson, and aroused that liking for Burney which never afterwards failed.

Sir

If you imagine that by delaying my answer I intended to show any neglect of the notice with which you have favoured me, you will neither think justly of yourself nor of me. Your civilities were offered with too much elegance not to engage attention; and I have too much pleasure in pleasing men like you, not to feel very sensibly the distinction which you have bestowed upon me.

Few consequences of my endeavours to please or to benefit mankind have delighted me more than your friendship thus voluntarily offered, which now I have it I hope to keep, because I hope to continue to deserve it.

I have no Dictionaries to dispose of for myself, but shall be glad to have you direct your friends to Mr Dodsley, because it was by his recommendation that I was employed in the work.

When you have leisure to think again upon me, let me be favoured with another letter; and another yet, when you have looked into my Dictionary. If you find faults, I shall endeavour to mend them; if you find none, I shall think you blinded by kind partiality: but to have made you partial in his favour, will very much gratify the ambition of, Sir, Your most obliged and most humble servant

SAM: JOHNSON

Another valued friend Johnson made at this time was Thomas Percy, later a bishop, who like Thomas Warton was a deep student of mediaeval poetry. This was a taste Johnson did not share, and no doubt he irritated Percy now and then, as he certainly irritated Warton, by poking fun at his mediaevalizing verses; but when Percy finally brought out his monumental *Reliques of Ancient English Poetry*, which played a major part in revolutionizing English literary taste and made the way smooth for such achievements as Coleridge's 'Rime of the Ancient Mariner', his preface acknowledged Johnson's very real help.

But Johnson's deepest friendship, in these years, had already been formed for some time. Joshua Reynolds, already climbing to his great eminence as a painter, had met Johnson back in the days when he and Tetty were living in Cavendish Square. It had been a chance encounter, at the house of Charlotte Cotterel and her sister. They met at the tea-table, began to talk, went off to supper together, and became and remained devoted friends. Reynolds stood by Johnson in the crisis of grief that followed Tetty's death in 1752; he was to share griefs and joys while life lasted, and to visit Johnson on his deathbed.

Then there was the Italian scholar Giuseppe Baretti, like himself a linguist and lexicographer, like himself troubled with weak eyesight, whom Johnson had known since about 1751. Baretti was an irascible man, but Johnson saw good qualities in him and was always ready to help him – a letter of introduction here, a dedication there. Another friendship dating from the 1750s was with the actor and writer Arthur Murphy a man in whose wit and charm Johnson delighted. Their acquaintance began in what might have been an awkward manner, but for Johnson's fundamental modesty and the ease with which he forgave minor offences. Murphy, as a young man, had undertaken the sole responsibility for a paper called *The Gray's Inn Journal* in much the same way as Johnson had undertaken responsibility for *The Rambler*. One day when he was staying in the country with the actor Foote, Murphy mentioned to Foote that he had to go to London to prepare material for the next issue. Foote said that this would not be necessary, and showed him a recent number of a French periodical containing a short and effective 'oriental tale'. 'Translate that', he urged him, 'and send it to your printer.' Murphy read the story, liked it, translated it into English, and earned himself a little extra holiday. Only afterwards did he find out that the French magazine had, without advertising the fact, translated a tale by Johnson (*Rambler*, No. 190). Murphy, feeling that he owed Johnson an explanation of why he had translated into English a French translation of his English, called to see him. Far from resenting the incident, Johnson welcomed the pleasant new friend it had brought him. In later life Murphy, who was obviously a *raconteur*, would make a good story of his first meeting with Johnson, saying that he had found him in the middle of a chemical experiment, covered with soot like a chimney sweep, in a small room full of heat and smells. Johnson would interrupt him with, 'Come, come, dear Mur, the story is black enough now; and it was a very happy day for me that brought you first to my house, and a very happy mistake about the *Ramblers*.'

After Johnson's death Murphy wrote an interesting *Essay on the Life and Genius of Samuel Johnson*, LL.D., which gives us a few sidelights not in Boswell. In one of these we have a testimony to the growth of Johnson's reputation. One evening – Murphy does not date the incident, but presumably it was in the 1750s – a group of people who included Johnson, Murphy, and a man named Francis, author of a celebrated translation of Horace, were dining at Foote's house. They had been reading the *Debates in the Senate of Lilliput*, and Francis remarked that one of Pitt's speeches, in an important debate towards the end of the Walpole administration, was the finest he had ever read. He had, he went on, spent eight years in the study of Demosthenes, and completed a translation of his orations, generally regarded as the best in the world; but nothing he found there had equalled that particular speech of Pitt's. Others present remembered the speech in question, and began to quote passages from memory, and praise them. Johnson sat silent until their talk slackened its pace; then he suddenly said, 'That speech I wrote in a garret in Exeter Street.' The entire company sat silent, in amazement. At last Francis found his voice and asked for the circumstances. Johnson outlined Cave's procedure on *The Gentleman's Magazine* and his own part in it. Francis's reply is worthy of a great age of stately compliment. 'Then, Sir', he said, 'you have exceeded Demosthenes himself; for to say that you have exceeded Francis's Demosthenes would be saying nothing.' Of such stuff, it seems, was the dinner-table conversation made, in the literary London of those days; we, who live among the scorched and blackened ruins, can only hope to imagine what such talk must have been like.

In friendship, Johnson's arduous and impetuous nature could flow towards a fellow human being and feel an answering return. It was, moreover, a strip of firm ground amid the ghastly quicksands of existence. Sexual relationships, at any rate in so far as they involved physical contact, were treacherous ground to him. He had known some happiness in his marriage, in the early days at least, and he was pathetically grateful to Tetty in memory; but the much stronger sexual desires he experienced outside marriage were represented by his religion as leading straight to hell-fire, and he did everything he could to smother them. In a mind more happily constituted, religious belief might have provided the emotional sustenance it forbade him to seek in women. As a religious man Johnson had in theory the possibility of a comforting and up-lifting relationship with his God. But this relationship, for various reasons, was associated in his mind with guilt and terror. Whatever Johnson's religion did for him, it did not make him happy in this mortal life. No wonder, then, that he turned so eagerly to an evening of good talk with his friends, and felt so rich in their company and the warmth of their interest in him.

This pleasure in his friends, in the colourful variety of their temperament and idiosyncrasy, is reflected in the series of essays he wrote in the two years between April 1758 and April 1760. *The Idler*, like *The Rambler*, was a regular series of miscellaneous essays, but lighter and less ambitious. Unable, or unwilling, to bind himself to a second undertaking as strenuous as the first, Johnson wrote now at only half the speed – one essay per week instead of two – and instead of challenging the attention of the public with an individual paper he was content for the essays to appear within the sheltering covers of *The Universal Chronicle or Weekly Gazette*, an eight-page miscellany issued from Paternoster Row. He had already come down from the gravity and density of *The Rambler* with some essays of a rather lighter kind in a paper called *The Adventurer*, edited by his friend Hawkesworth in 1753 and 1754. But now we see him relaxing still further. The firm moral purpose is as evident as it always was, but there is more sense of holiday and fun. *The Rambler* had occasionally admitted portraiture, invariably in the interests of pointing a moral, as in the fictitious or composite sketch of Suspirius, the 'human screech owl', or the satirical sketch of 'Prospero', the actor whose head has been swollen by popular success, usually taken to be a cut at Garrick. But the rogues' gallery in *The Idler* – Jack Sneaker, Tom Tempest, Dick Minim the little critic, or Jack Whirler, whose original was John Newbery the publisher – is made up of pictures only in-cidentally satiric or cautionary. Johnson is relaxing and enjoying a new-found skill in the drawing of deftly witty thumbnail sketches. The novelist in him is coming out.

This matter deserves a word in passing. As a critic Johnson was always rather unresponsive to the realistic novel, the most important new form to arise in his lifetime. He found it insufficiently attentive to the duty of teaching a sound moral lesson. 'Realism' was all very well, but, as he put it in an early *Rambler*, 'If the world be promiscuously described, I cannot see of what use it can be to read the account; or why it may not be as safe to turn the eye immediately upon mankind, as upon a mirror which shows all that presents itself without discrimination.' But in these *Idler* essays he shows that his lack of response to the lighter fictional fare of his day was not caused by inability to relish a *soufflé*. He could, if he saw fit, turn out such a dish himself. Number 71, for instance, which takes the born-and-bred Cockney Dick Shifter into the country in search of the Arcadian bliss and calm he has read about, and (of course) involves him in a chain of farcical disillusionments, is quite up to the standard of most eighteenth-century comic fiction. The yokels put the city man through the customary mill:

> He enquired for a newspaper, and was told that farmers never minded news, but that they could send for it from the ale-house. A messenger was despatched, who ran away at full speed, but loitered an hour behind the hedges, and at last coming back with his feet purposely bemired, instead of expressing the gratitude which Mr Shifter expected for the bounty of a shilling, said that the night was wet and the way dirty, and he hoped that his worship would not think it much to give him half-a-crown.

The little story concludes with an incident of slightly darker tinge:

> Finding his walks thus interrupted, he was inclined to ride, and, being pleased with the appearance of a horse that was grazing in a neighbouring meadow, enquired the owner, who warranted him sound, and would not sell him but that he was too fine for a plain man. Dick paid down the price, and, riding out to enjoy the evening, fell with his new horse into a ditch; they got out with difficulty, and, as he was going to mount again, a countryman looked at the horse and perceived him to be blind. Dick went to the seller and demanded back his money, but was told that a man who rented his ground must do the best for himself, that his landlord had his rent though the year was barren, and that, whether horses had eyes or no, he should sell them to the highest bidder.

Here (we may fairly say, without overpraising Johnson's light performance) we have a momentary glimpse of the harsh penury of a country life: in a world where man is greedy and God does not always send the right growing weather, one cannot afford generosity – 'a man who rents his ground must do the best for himself'. The point is made without strain or emphasis, but it does its work, leaving in our minds the picture of a rural suspicion of town ways that is not confined to comic horseplay but comes out of the decidedly un-comic hardness and narrowness of the peasant who knows what it is to be hungry.

Yes, Johnson might easily have been a novelist. But the novel, as a form, failed to attract his interest or gain his confidence. When he wrote fiction, it was not – except for these brief gambols – in the mode of realism, but in the more stately vein of the fable, with roots going back to those romances he loved from childhood on, and beyond that to the folklore of the world and the great exemplary tales of Scripture. As a critic of literature, he remained cold to the novel, dismissing Sterne impatiently ('Nothing odd will do long: *Tristram Shandy* did not last') and grossly under-rating Fielding, the only contemporary writer whose breadth of vision, good sense and humour equalled his own. Later in life he was to dote on Charles Burney's gifted daughter Fanny, but the only novelist of his own sex and generation to win his praise was Samuel Richardson, whose strongly didactic histories of triumphant virtue seemed to him preferable to Fielding's picaresque tapestry. He appreciated Richardson's very genuine, if limited, perceptiveness, and he was reassured by the tone of unremitting high-mindedness. In the Postcript to his *Clarissa, the History of a Young Lady*, Richardson had made a statement of intention that must have seemed to Johnson the ideal programme for a novelist: explaining that 'he', the writer,

> imagined, that if in an age given up to diversion and entertainment, he could *steal in*, as may be said, and instigate the great doctrines of Christianity under the fashionable guise of an amusement, he should be most likely to serve his purpose.

Richardson, as we saw, gave Johnson practical evidence of his goodwill by contributing a paper to *The Rambler* – the only one, in fact, that sold well. He was now to be given an opportunity for even more decisive aid. On 16 March 1756 Johnson penned him a hurried note:

> I am obliged to entreat your assistance. I am now under an arrest for five pounds eighteen shillings. Mr Strahan from whom I should have received the necessary help in this case is not at home, and I am afraid of not finding Mr Millar. If you will be so good as to send me this sum, I will very gratefully repay you, and add it to all former obligations.
>
> I am, Sir, Your most obedient and most humble Servant
> Gough Square, 16 March   SAM: JOHNSON

Richardson obliged with the money and a few shillings over. In view of the fate that awaited a man imprisoned for debt in those days, it is fortunate that Johnson had one or two solvent friends. Worse was to come. In February 1758 he was again under arrest, and for the much larger sum of forty pounds. He was bailed out this time by the publisher Jacob Tonson, the third of that name, who had an interest in his edition of Shakespeare. Obviously this could not go on. In *The Vanity of Human Wishes* Johnson had written feelingly of the evils of the scholar's life: 'Toil, envy, want, the patron and the jail.' He had had plenty of the first three (whether one takes 'envy' as meaning the cloak-and-dagger attacks of other people who are envious of one's gifts, or one's own smarting envy of the more successful, or – most probably – both); he had had quite enough of the fourth; now even the fifth, it seemed, was a constantly looming danger. The author of *The Rambler* in prison! The author of the Dictionary compelled to listen to the argot of thieves and desperadoes! It would make a subject for the pen of Fielding. None other would be equal to it.

Fortunately, the matter remains within the realm of speculation. Johnson, no doubt, would have suffered imprisonment and even death with his customary stoicism. But another and different blow awaited him: one he must have seen coming, but which yet found him unprepared and pathetically vulnerable.

CHAPTER 16

A Death; and a Journey in the Mind

All these years, the three ladies in Lichfield had been living out their lives as quietly as the three spires of the cathedral. But now the three were to become two. Sarah Johnson was ninety and her life was over. In January 1759 Lucy Porter wrote to Johnson with the news that she was gravely ill.

Johnson's letter of response is dated 13 January. By 23 January he was writing to Lucy about 'the loss of my mother'. It took her, then, some ten days to die, and during those ten days Johnson wrote her four letters in whose rapid, burning sentences he breathed out the poignant sensations of grief and loss which bade fair to overwhelm him. All these letters have been quoted and reproduced innumerable times, and could well be reproduced again now, but that they are so personal, so agonized, that it seems an intrusion to set them up in cold print for any casual eye to read. We will choose one, the last of the four.

Dear honoured Mother
Neither your condition nor your character make it fit for me to say much.
You have been the best mother, and I believe the best woman in the world.
I thank you for your indulgence to me, and beg forgiveness of all that I have done ill, and all that I have omitted to do well. God grant you his Holy Spirit, and receive you to everlasting happiness, for Jesus Christ's sake. Amen. Lord Jesus receive your spirit. Amen.
I am, dear mother, Your dutiful son

SAM: JOHNSON

There is no mistaking the strength of feeling here. The exact nature of the feeling is more difficult to judge. I spoke of 'grief' and 'loss': why not of love?

Because, sadly, I do not think that love, in any sense in which I understand the term, was effectively present among the bundle of emotions which Johnson felt for his mother. He had tried to love her; the attempt had proved impossible, for neither in his infancy nor later did she put herself within the reach of his love. Since the frustration that resulted was deeply painful to him, he did the only other possible thing – absented himself from her for the last twenty-one years of her life. During those years he appears to have thought of her as little as possible, once he had done his best to ensure her material comfort. This indeed was no light matter. After mortgaging the Lichfield house to Theophilus

Levet for eighty pounds in 1739, as we noted, Johnson made himself responsible for paying Levet the 4½ per cent interest, and also set himself to repay the principal. This he finally achieved, not without struggle and sacrifice, in 1757.

It is, I think, incontestable that Johnson avoided an actual interview with his mother. He was short of money, yes; loaded with work, yes; the roads were bad and travel uncertain, yes; but he did get himself as far as Oxford in 1754, and spent week after week there doing very little, and Lichfield could have been reached easily enough from there if he had really wanted to reach it.

Shortly after the publication of the Dictionary in 1755, Bennet Langton wrote to invite Johnson down to the family house in Lincolnshire; Johnson replied that he would have dearly loved to go, but did not feel free to accept the invitation because 'I have a mother more than eighty years old, who has counted the days to the publication of my book in hopes of seeing me, and to her, if I can disengage myself here, I resolve to go'. The resolve came to nothing.

Even during his mother's brief terminal illness he could, if he had been determined enough, have got to her bedside before she died, and a short note to Lucy Porter, despatched at the same time as the letter to Sarah which we have quoted, talks of coming down 'if it is possible' and adds, 'If I miss to write next post, I am on the road.' But he stayed in London.

Everyone who saw Johnson at this time is agreed that the effect of his mother's death was shattering to him. Hawkins, in his dry, unsympathetic way, remarks that the philosophic poise Johnson had acquired with advancing years was useless to him in this crisis; he 'was as little able to sustain the shock as he would have been had this loss befallen him in his nonage'. Indeed, Johnson was dazed. His letters to Lucy Porter are pitiful; he leans on her, begs for her help and comfort, asks that she shall stay on in the house and let the little business go on as it can, and is content to leave all the details to her and take her word for everything. 'You will forgive me if I am not yet so composed as to give any directions about anything. But you are wiser and better than I and I shall be pleased with all that you shall do.'

The declaration is sincere enough. Johnson could not bear to turn his thoughts in the direction of the house in Breadmarket Street. Yet it is interesting to note that he was perfectly well able to 'give directions', perfectly well 'composed', when the matter in hand was anything apart from his relationship with his mother. On the same day as the grief-stricken letter of farewell to her, he wrote a calm and businesslike letter to William Strahan.

Sir

When I was with you last night I told you of a thing which I was preparing for the press. The title will be

The Choice of Life

or

The History of   Prince of Abyssinia

It will make about two volumes like little Pompadour that is about one middling volume. The bargain which I made with Mr Johnston was seventy five pounds (or guineas) a volume, and twenty five pounds for the second edition. I will sell this either at that price or for sixty the first edition of which he shall himself fix the number, and the property then to revert to me, or for forty pounds, and share the profit, that is retain half the copy. I shall have occasion for thirty pounds on Monday night when I shall deliver the book which I must entreat you upon such delivery to procure me. I would have it offered to Mr Johnston, but have no doubt of selling it, on some of the terms mentioned.

I will not print my name, but expect it to be known.

I am, Dear Sir, Your most humble Servant

SAM: JOHNSON

The matter-of-fact tone of this letter is remarkable. Johnson's distraught grief at Sarah's death apparently rolls away for long enough to allow of sober calculations about editions and format and copyright. It is true that he makes a point of asking for immediate payment ('thirty pounds on Monday night') and we know that he needed this money for the expenses of Sarah's funeral and a few small debts she had left. It is clear, nevertheless, that his emotions overwhelmed him only when he thought directly of her rather than of the duty he owed to settle her affairs.

No wonder his mind was convulsed with pain. For years he had not willingly thought of his mother, and for the rest of his life he took no comfort in remembering her. We can say this categorically because there is evidence that his inability to face the thought of her led him to contravene one of his own excellent principles for dealing with the suffering of bereavement. Some nine years previously Johnson's Scottish publisher, James Elphinston, wrote that he had lost his mother and that the blow was a heavy one. Johnson's letter of consolation (25 September 1750) is masterly. He brings together all the thoughts that can possibly strengthen a man in that situation, and goes on to give some sound practical advice.

There is one expedient, by which you may, in some degree, continue her presence. If you write down minutely what you remember of her from your earliest years, you will read it with great pleasure, and receive from it many hints of soothing recollection, when time shall remove her yet farther from you, and your grief shall be matured to veneration. To this, however painful for the present, I cannot but advise you, as to a source of comfort and satisfaction in the time to come; for all comfort and all satisfaction, is sincerely wished you by, Dear Sir, Your most obliged, most obedient, and most humble servant

SAM: JOHNSON

Yet what Johnson so sagely recommended to Elphinston he did not himself practise. There is no evidence that he ever sat down to put on paper every scrap of detail about his mother that memory offered. Whatever it was that had held him back from visiting her continued to inhibit him from visiting her in memory.

Meanwhile, it was at least a relief to go on undertaking the financial responsibility. What hard work and material sacrifice could do should be done. Johnson's letter to Strahan, as we saw, mentioned the immediate need for thirty pounds, to be paid in a week's time on the delivery of a work that was then in progress. In the end he negotiated a total price for the new work of a hundred pounds, with a further seventy-five for the second edition.

The book thus rapidly brought out was *The History of Rasselas, Prince of Abyssinia*. Johnson knew that he must work quickly; he could, indeed, hardly work in any other way, but this time the pace had to be fantastic. He later told Sir Joshua Reynolds that he had written the whole story in the evenings of one week, and his word in such matters is entirely reliable. Under these conditions, it was inevitable that he should turn to a blend of the 'oriental tale', at which he was already a practised hand, and the moral essay. Searching his mind for usable material, he remembered Father Lobo's *Voyage to Abyssinia*, the book he had borrowed from Pembroke College and translated with Hector's help in the old Birmingham days.

Johnson's mind always delighted to wander in far and mysterious places; it was the other side of the coin of his down-to-earth realism. Beside Lobo's book, he also knew Ludolph's *New History of Ethiopia* (1681), of which he possessed a copy, and he also dipped into an early seventeenth-century travel book, *Purchas: His Pilgrimage*, which mashes together observation and legend. Abyssinia, or Ethiopia, is very much the kind of place about which Johnson would daydream. It was, until the development of aircraft, the most mysterious country in the world: a range of high mountains, separated by unscaleable gorges so that one isolated community had no chance of contact with the next and the whole surrounded by a belt of desert that is one of the hottest places on earth. Very few travellers could get there, and those who did found it more or less impossible to move about.

No wonder Johnson read accounts of this never-never land with fascination. In Lobo he found the character of 'Rassela Christos', Lieutenant General to the Sultan; and in every book he consulted he read that the princes of Abyssinia were kept in retired seclusion until the day of their accession – presumably to keep them from being influenced by rival power-groups. In Lobo he read that the prince was confined on the summit of a barren mountain, but Purchas had it that the mountain top was covered with 'many fruitful and pleasant valleys'. An earthly paradise, perched on top of an impregnable mountain! The setting offered a challenge both to the poet in Johnson and to the moralist. What strange shapes would the human mind assume, and particularly the young, developing mind, during the years spent in such a place? Would the result be happiness, or discontent? Would the prince naturally seek to escape, or would he dread the day when his father's death would summon him into the world of troubles and dangers below?

So Johnson's story begins with the prince, Rasselas, and his sister Nekayah,

living in the 'happy valley'. Nekayah is attended by her 'favourite', a girl named
Pekuah; Rasselas by a philosopher of mature years, Imlac, who to some extent
represents Johnson himself. Rasselas is possessed by a craving to escape from the
happy valley and see the world; he imparts his desire to the others; they contrive their escape, and the story tells of their wanderings and ultimate return.

Rasselas of course presents a moral – to 'point a moral' and 'adorn a tale' were
to Johnson the two inseparable tasks of the serious writer – and its moral is one
that will cause us no surprise: the vanity of human wishes. To Johnson, here
as everywhere, happiness is not to be looked for in strictly human terms.
Momentary pleasure, yes; but settled, predictable contentment, no. To search
for happiness on earth and in earthly terms is to fall into serious error, since
it distracts our attention from the eternal life to come, in which our hopes of
happiness must be centred. Accordingly the prince and his party wander from
scene to scene, always in search of people who could be called happy and always
failing to find them. The loosely contrived plot is for the most part nothing but
a series of situations in which new aspects of human disappointment can be
revealed. Surely the rich are happy with their abundance and power? Surely
the poor are happy in their simplicity? Surely the wise and learned are happy?
Surely the simple and ignorant are happy? Surely the young are happy in the
vigour of their bodies? Surely the old are happy in the quietness of their garnered
experience? Surely the married are happy? Surely the single are happy? And so
the party conduct their long march of disillusion, as the disadvantages of each
state of life are revealed.

Put like this, it sounds as if *Rasselas* were a depressing book. Actually it is
the reverse. Pithy, economical, fast-moving, written at a very high level of
energy, it leaves one feeling challenged, stimulated and generally keyed up for
life. The wisdom of *Rasselas* lies not so much in the central message, which after
all is a commonplace of Christian homiletics, as in the acuteness and depth of
the descriptions of disillusion in its various forms, and the brilliance of the
incidental remarks. Merely to discover that human beings are discontented
wherever you find them takes no penetration: to see so clearly the essential
nature of their discontent in each case, and its essential causes, is an enterprise
worthy of Johnson's sagacity and deeply felt experience.

An example might be the party's meeting with the learned astronomer
(Chapters 50–4). They hear much of the fame of this savant, and assume that
he must have found happiness in a life spent in peaceful seclusion, studying the
movements of the heavens. Imlac gets to know him and, as their acquaintance
improves, begins to realize that there is something wrong. Finally, the astronomer confesses his trouble. During the long years of study and the refusal of
human contact, his mind has become possessed by a delusion. He thinks it is in
his power to control the movements of the sun, to bestow light and warmth on
one part of the earth in proportion as he denies it to another. This responsibility
– for as such he accepts it, not of course as a delusion – weighs him down with
an intolerable pressure for, as he points out, the power of a king is trivial in
comparison; what he must control is the good or ill of an entire world. Feeling

himself sinking towards the grave, he begs Imlac to learn his secrets and inherit the responsibility, so that he can die in the knowledge that he has left his awful gift in the hands of a good and wise man. Imlac gravely goes along with this, knowing that the astronomer cannot be helped by a frontal attack on his delusion, and promises co-operation.

When he rejoins his young companions, Imlac describes the astronomer's madness. The two girls give way to the impulse to laugh at the story, whereupon Imlac rebukes them with Johnsonian sternness:

'Ladies', said Imlac, 'to mock the heaviest of human afflictions is neither charitable nor wise. Few can attain this man's knowledge, and few practise his virtues; but all may suffer his calamity. Of the uncertainties of our present state, the most dreadful and alarming is the uncertain continuance of reason.'

On reflection, the princess and Pekuah determine to visit the astronomer and get into contact with him. Since he is not in the habit of receiving ladies in his retired abode, their first problem is to find admission; they have the notion of introducing themselves as strangers in distress, which will ensure at least one interview with a man of his benevolence; but the question soon occurs to them, how will the acquaintance be carried on after the imaginary problem is solved? And Rasselas adds that he has an even stronger objection to such a subterfuge; he has 'always considered it as treason against the great republic of human nature to make any man's virtues the means of deceiving him, whether on great or little occasions'.

The ladies in the end introduce themselves as would-be students of astronomy; Nekayah has already acquired the rudiments of it, and she intends to give the impression of knowing more than she actually does 'by concurring always with his opinions'. Having delivered herself of this little stroke of irony about male human nature, she betakes herself to the astronomer, accompanied by Pekuah, both of them dressed to kill. The astronomer soon discovers in them the unusual aptitude for study that learned men can always find in beautiful girls, especially those who turn up dressed with a fortune on their backs. He welcomes their visits and soon begins to propose excursions that will involve him also in their leisure. This has the happy effect of drawing him out of the solitude that has turned his wits, and soon he is sane enough for Imlac to discuss frankly with him the nature of his delusion and encourage him to see it for what it is. There follows a remarkable passage in which Imlac talks to the astronomer like a psycho-analyst, illuminating the nature of his illness and pointing out the particular difficulty of curing any mental unreality-state that has managed to entwine itself with guilt and self-accusation. Because the astronomer has accepted that his power over the sun is an awesome responsibility laid on him by God, his momentary impulses of sanity, during which he longs for normal relationships and ordinary diversion, appear to him as temptations.

'No disease of the imagination', answered Imlac, 'is so difficult of cure as that which is complicated with the dread of guilt: fancy and conscience then act interchangeably upon us, and so often shift their places that the illusions of one are not distinguished from the dictates of the other. If fancy presents images not moral or religious, the mind drives them away when they give it pain, but, when melancholic notions take the form of duty, they lay hold on the faculties without opposition, because we are afraid to exclude or banish them. For this reason the superstitious are often melancholy, and the melancholy almost always superstitious.'

The episode sheds a powerful light on Johnson's own mental and emotional troubles, and the steps he took to fight against them. The astronomer is hauled up from the depths not by reasoning, not by the wisdom of Imlac (that comes into operation only when he is already on the way to recovery) but by the gay and pleasing presence of the two girls, who lead him by easy steps from the gloom of solitude to the sparkle and gaiety of company. Johnson, deeply interested in ideas though he was, never overestimated what ideas will do for a man. In particular, he never imagined that we are to be reasoned out of subjective states of mind. When melancholy lays siege, repel it with the methods that work best, not with those that sound most impressive. Where you cannot win, it is no disgrace to run away – such was his constant advice, to himself and others; as Imlac counsels the astronomer, 'when scruples importune you, which you in your lucid moments know to be vain, do not stand to parley, but fly to business or to Pekuah, and keep this thought always prevalent, that you are only one atom of the mass of humanity, and have neither such virtue nor vice as that you should be singled out for supernatural favours or afflictions'.

'Fly to business or to Pekuah' – the admirable advice could hardly be given in fewer words. And indeed the shortness of *Rasselas* is a miracle of compression, arising from the same source as that other miracle, the speed of its composition. Johnson was able to write so fast, and encapsulate his wisdom so perfectly, because he was dealing with material that had, for many years, lain about his heart. The loose structure of the story – the characters move from conversation to conversation as much as from incident to incident – allows him to bring up any topic that has a bearing on the great over-arching question of how to live and what to do, and to put into the mouth of Imlac the thoughts that his own meditation has matured through the years. (For one example out of many, we might instance the terse but thorough discussion of the advantages of a monastic life in Chapter 47.) The story is frankly a device for projecting the maximum quantity of Johnsonian wisdom. As such, it hits a high level and never drops below it. Every page of *Rasselas* is on a level with the best passages of *The Rambler*. The density and force of the writing that we recognize in *The Rambler* is here, but the fact that Johnson is not simply laying essay on top of essay, but constructing a longer work, gives him the advantage of being able to set out his wisdom strategically. He makes each point when he judges that the reader is most open to it. For instance: Rasselas mixes for a time among the gay young blades of Cairo; he finds them agreeable, but their way of life is shallow and unsatisfying because they live entirely in the present and make no provision, either materially or spiritually, for later years when their physical vitality shall have ebbed away. He tries to point this out to them, and they drive him away with mocking laughter. His next acquaintance is a philosopher who gives notable lectures on 'the government of the passions'. This man utters excellent wisdom; from Johnson's summary of his teachings, we conclude that they are substantially the same as the teachings of the Rambler himself. Rasselas is delighted by this philosopher's steadiness and good sense; 'I will', he tells Imlac, 'learn his doctrines, and imitate his life'; Imlac as usual is sceptical. On his next visit Rasselas finds the sage plunged in hopeless grief: 'My daughter, my only daughter, from whose tenderness I expected all the comforts of my age, died last night of a fever. My views, my purposes, my hopes are at an end: I am now a lonely being disunited from society.' Rasselas tries to comfort him by repeating back to him his own precepts about truth and reason, but he replies pathetically, 'What comfort can truth and reason afford me? Of what effect are they now, but to tell me that my daughter will not be restored?' The obvious moral of the episode is that those with theoretical wisdom are no better at bearing misfortune than those without it; but the story gains an extra effect from its placing in the overall plot. The young sparks of Cairo made no provision for the future; the philosopher did and his suffering was all the more cruel.

All this sounds very sombre, but in fact there is a good deal of humour in *Rasselas*. Johnson's way of seeing life, and his way of expressing what he saw, were so shot through with humour that we should expect no other. In tone the story is ironic; we are never far from a play of fancy, as in the 'dissertation on the art of flying' in Chapter 6, or from a lightly indicated inconsistency or contradiction, as when the hermit in Chapter 21, who has set an example of retirement from the world and taken to a cave in the woods, decides that he has had enough and, volunteering to accompany them back to the city, digs up 'a considerable treasure which he had hid among the rocks'. In similar vein is Imlac's lofty exposition of the art of poetry (Chapter 10), which is entirely in line with Johnson's own views and those of the neo-classic culture generally, but is conducted on such a relentlessly high level, with so few concessions to human fallibility, that Imlac at last interrupts the catalogue of essential poetic qualities with 'Enough! Thou hast convinced me that no human being can ever be a poet.' Or again there is the self-satisfied philosopher who teaches that happiness is found in 'a life lived according to nature'; Rasselas, impressed, asks him to explain, which he does with a tissue of meaningless platitudes; the prince decides not to waste his breath in arguing, but bows and is silent, whereupon the philosopher infers that he has made another convert: '. . . the philosopher, supposing him satisfied and the rest vanquished, rose up and departed with the air of a man that had co-operated with the present system'. We know that air.

Yes, *Rasselas* has its humour, though it appears stuffed with *gravitas* by comparison with the knockabout atmosphere of Voltaire's *Candide*, which by an odd coincidence came out in the same year and also tells of a journey in quest of happiness and a continuous disillusionment. As Johnson himself realized, there were many points of resemblance between the two books; the youthful Candide and his travelling companions form a party not unlike that of Rasselas; the philosophers Pangloss and Martin correspond to Imlac and the astronomer, and the lady Cunégonde to Nekayah. Widely different as they are in tone and in immediate intention – for Voltaire's tale is a fighting controversial pamphlet designed, as we saw, to combat Leibnitzian 'optimism' of the kind that Johnson had already swatted in the review of Soame Jenyns, whereas Johnson's is a straight contribution to the literature of wisdom – the two stories come very close together in their endings. Candide's party decide that the best recipe for contentment is to settle down on a small farm which they cultivate by their own efforts, thus leaving themselves no time for metaphysical speculation or for melancholy; *il faut cultiver notre jardin*. In Johnson's brief last chapter, 'the conclusion, in which nothing is concluded', the party 'return to Abyssinia'. Critics have debated the exact meaning that should be attached to these words. Do they return to Abyssinia because their quest for happiness has been futile and they might as well never have left in the first place? Or have they, in their wanderings, gained some wisdom and now have the elements of contentment to hand: the habit of resignation, the knowledge that the grass is not, after all, greener on the other side of the fence? My own preference is for the second of these views; I feel Johnson viewed with kindly (though ironic) indulgence the natural wish of Rasselas to be out of the Happy Valley and seeing life for himself. In the end he returns to the state of quiet and secluded preparation that will, in due course, reach its end when he inherits the throne.

Considered strictly as a work of literature, *Rasselas* is in some ways a strange work to come from the later 1750s, just when the realistic novel was at take-off point. When most writers of prose fiction were turning to realistic action in credible settings, and cultivating a representational style of dialogue which went further towards straight reporting of everyday rhythms and turns of phrase than the stage had ever gone, *Rasselas* turns resolutely away from these tendencies. It is, in its way, as mannered as *Tristram Shandy*; as in some novel by Ivy Compton-Burnet, the *personae* all speak in the same manner, and it is the manner of the author; after the initial gesture towards historicity, the action is deliberately imbued with the fragile unreality of a soap bubble. Johnson had shown, in a number of his essays which took the form of sketches of life, that he could handle realistic dialogue and everyday settings as well as any of the emergent realists; but in this book he chose to play by different rules. The result is a work that puts one in mind of a dragonfly – a purposeful and powerful body moving on wings of gauze.

Rasselas enjoyed a very high reputation in Johnson's own day and for half a century after his death. This in turn led to a reaction, so that some have regarded it as over-rated and used against it Johnson's own deprecating reference in a letter of 25 March 1759, 'I am going to publish a little story book.' But Johnson was a modest man who never cried up his own wares. Boswell, who gave so much of his life to the study of Johnson and his works, tells us that he made a point of reading *Rasselas* every year and found it so impressive that he could hardly believe he had once enjoyed the friendship of the man who wrote it. I used to think Boswell's tribute slightly over-stated, until I myself took to reading *Rasselas* every year. Since then, I have found it easy to understand why Boswell, and not only Boswell, found it such a miraculous performance; and why Johnson himself, happening over twenty years later to come across the book when travelling in a carriage, and having scarcely thought of it in all those years, 'seized upon it with avidity' and read it with his attention 'intensely fixed'.

CHAPTER 17

The Machine Stops

Johnson's fame was now assured. In arranging with Strahan for the publication of *Rasselas* he had written, 'I will not print my name, but expect it to be known'. And indeed it was known. A new work by Johnson was regarded as an event. People sought his acquaintance: less in the spirit in which modern people seek out a celebrity, to pester him with irrelevant questions, than in the spirit in which the ancient Greeks visited the oracle. His fame was national and was soon to be international. *Rasselas* was translated into French in 1760, into Italian in 1764, into German in 1785, into Russian in 1795.

Still, as Johnson was neither the first nor the last to discover, one can have an honourable literary reputation and still be a poor man. Several sketches of his appearance and habits date from this time, and they all agree as to the shabbiness of his attire and the discomfort of his surroundings. Perhaps the liveliest vignette comes from Sir Joshua Reynolds' sister, Frances, who loved and revered Johnson and set down her recollections of him, intending to publish them but never getting round to it. Aware that Johnson's physical peculiarities and extraordinary get-up might excite some quantity of barren spectators to laugh at him, Miss Reynolds refused to give a detailed description of his appearance, and for a good reason; such a description might give some scurrilous cartoonist the idea of drawing a picture of the great Johnson in ludicrous guise, 'and I might have the mortification of seeing it hung up at a print shop as the greatest curiosity ever exhibited'.

That Johnson's appearance was unforgettably 'curious' is obvious. It was also strikingly at variance with his stately and courteous manner. Except when he was demolishing an opponent in verbal warfare, Johnson was unfailingly polite, and to ladies in particular his manner could only be compared with that of a courtier of the *ancien régime*. Miss Reynolds reports that if a lady visited him at Gough Square he would never allow her to leave without coming down in person and seeing her into her carriage. This involved him in walking through Bolt Court to Fleet Street, where a mob invariably gathered within seconds of his arrival. Of his clothes Miss Reynolds says only, in cautiously general terms, that they would 'excite the utmost astonishment in my reader, how a man in his senses could think of stepping outside his door in them, or even to be seen at home in them'.

But then Johnson had lived for so long without the conveniences of life, even without many of its ordinary decencies, that he had accustomed himself to very modest demands. Broken furniture, dusty books, his meals taken at some chop-house round the corner and his social life at other people's houses or in a tavern – all this had come to seem normal. Certainly he never complained about his comfortless life, nor even appeared to notice it much. Miss Reynolds again:

> Before he had the pension, he literally dressed like a beggar; and from what I have been told, literally lived as such; at least respecting common conveniences in his apartments, wanting even a chair to sit on, particularly in his study, where a gentleman who frequently visited him whilst writing his Idlers always found him at his desk, sitting on one with three legs; and on rising from it, he remarked that Mr Johnson never forgot its defect, but would either hold it in his hand or place it with great composure against some support, taking no notice of its imperfection to his visitor. Where he sat, whether on the window seat, on a chair, or on a pile of folios, or how he sat, I do not remember to have heard.

That he should have been without a chair to sit on seems unlikely; Miss Reynolds, whose own surroundings were elegant and comfortable, probably had an exaggerated reaction to Johnson's less couth habitat. But the essential impression remains: even at this first high crest of his fame, he was needy. However, that very account has already indicated that this was about to be remedied, for in its opening sentence it drops the word 'pension'.

George III, who came to the throne in 1760, has had a mixed press from English historians; perhaps it is true that, as John Richard Green put it, George 'was wretchedly educated, and his natural powers were of the meanest sort'. But in one respect he stands out well. He was open-handed towards men of genius and learning. Obviously there had always been royal patronage of the arts and sciences, but George III initiated the policy of making public money available, as a matter of principle, to prevent distinguished men from starving and to help them with their work. This decision, some time in the early summer of 1762, was made in respect of Johnson.

Naturally there were other aspects to the matter. The State pension had notoriously been a method of buying political support, and it was this that Johnson had in mind when he wrote the surly definition of 'pension' in the Dictionary. That definition was to be many times thrown in his face after his own acceptance of a pension; and Johnson himself was sufficiently worried, after hearing the news of the King's intention, to hurry round to the house of his trusted friend Reynolds. What did Reynolds think? After saying that in England the word 'pension' usually signified 'money given to a State hireling for treason to his country', would it be fatal to his reputation for honesty if he now accepted one? He asked Reynolds to think calmly and not to hurry his answer; he would call again the next day, and wanted no decision before that. Reynolds unhesitatingly replied that he could give his considered answer there and then: that a pension to Johnson was a pension to literary achievement; that no one could possibly consider him a hireling, then or thenceforward. This answer satisfied Johnson, for he did not go back to Reynolds until he had accepted the pension and written his letter of thanks to the immediate agent in the matter, Lord Bute – a letter which for its combination of manly dignity with warm gratitude deserves to be given entire:

My Lord

When the bills were yesterday delivered to me by Mr Wedderburne, I was informed by him of the future favours which his Majesty has, by your Lordship's recommendation, been induced to intend for me.

Bounty always receives part of its value from the manner in which it is bestowed; your Lordship's kindness includes every circumstance that can gratify delicacy, or enforce obligation. You have conferred your favours on a man who has neither alliance nor interest, who has not merited them by services, nor courted them by officiousness; you have spared him the shame of solicitation, and the anxiety of suspense.

What has been thus elegantly given, will, I hope, not be reproachfully enjoyed; I shall endeavour to give your Lordship the only recompense which generosity desires – the gratification of finding that your benefits are not improperly bestowed.

I am, my Lord, Your Lordship's most obliged, most obedient, and most humble Servant

SAM: JOHNSON

Surely that is a deeply moving letter. There could be no more perfect example of how to accept a favour without falling into one of the two ever present dangers of servility or arrogance. Lord Bute had evidently shown instinctive courtesy in his manner of conferring the gift, and the matching courtesy with which Johnson thanks him completes the dialogue in an entirely satisfying way. One notes, too, that even at the moment of expressing gratitude – and without in the least jarring against that expression – Johnson conveys firmly that the money is not going to buy his services. He has 'neither alliance nor interest'; he has nothing to give and will not have it assumed that, if he had, he would necessarily give it.

Later, as we shall see, Johnson did turn his pen to polemical use on the government side; and once more there was a flurry of accusation. We shall examine the motivation of that episode when we come to it. In 1762 Johnson had no thought of working for his pension. Working for it directly, that is. In fact, he put it to the best possible use. By taking away the intolerable strain of day-to-day necessity, it undoubtedly lengthened his life; by enabling him to study and improve his mind, instead of incessantly reading in order to write, it gave a relaxed, spacious quality to his later writings, notably the *Lives of the Poets*. And of course it liberated him as a talker. It is arguable that the benefit of this was confined to the small circle who knew him personally, whereas his writings would have benefited the nation at large. But time has taken care of that problem. Headed by the incomparable Boswell, a whole string of Johnson's friends gathered and published their recollections of his talk. So even the words he sent forth upon the air were not lost to posterity.

The amount of the pension was £300 a year – by any standards a generous sum. Maecenas gave Horace his Sabine farm, on which he resided in comfort for the rest of his life, when the poet was in his early thirties. George III's ministry did not quite reach that all-time standard. But Johnson, quite rightly, considered the income a handsome one. In the *Life of Savage* he had written of the time when Savage had been granted, by some benefactor, an income of fifty pounds a year (before his impossible behaviour inevitably caused him to forfeit it again); and while, says Johnson, fifty pounds a year is not wealth it is a sum on which 'families are supported above the fear of want'. That being so, a single man should be able to do very well on six times that amount. It is difficult to fix a modern equivalent, writing as one is in a period of inflation when the value of money is going down all the time, but at a very conservative estimate Johnson's three hundred would buy what six thousand buys today – and it was free of tax.

And so, at last, the sun came out on the whole of that side of Johnson's life. His difficulties of a more intimate nature remained; he still dreaded the judgement of God, his sexual needs were still unslaked, he still had to use the powers of his mind to win respect as a hopelessly inelegant person in an age that valued elegance. But at least the grind to earn his daily bread was over.

Immediately he celebrated by taking a holiday. Since the spring of 1741, when he dragged himself back to London after that carefree time at Appleby and Ashbourne and Lichfield, he had been fettered in the smoke for twenty years, apart from three visits to Oxford, which he was able to justify on professional grounds. Then, just before the award of the pension, he had paid a visit to Lichfield. (This in itself is significant; his financial circumstances were no better than they had been for years, but his mother was safely dead.) After so long an absence, he had been slightly appalled at the littleness and provinciality of the place; as he wrote to Guiseppe Baretti,

> Last winter I went down to my native town, where I found the streets much narrower and shorter than I thought I had left them, inhabited by a new race of people, to whom I was very little known. My play-fellows were grown old, and forced me to suspect that I was no longer young. My only remaining friend has changed his principles, and was become the tool of the predominant faction. My daughter-in-law, from whom I expected most, and whom I met with sincere benevolence, has lost the beauty and gaiety of youth, without having gained much of the wisdom of age. I wandered about for five days, and took the first convenient opportunity of returning to a place, where, if there is not much happiness, there is at least such a diversity of good and evil, that slight vexations do not fix upon the heart.

This sounds rueful but a great part of the trouble was that Johnson on this first visit was not yet re-absorbed into the life of the neighbourhood; as he made more regular visits, and picked up the threads with this person and that, Lichfield began to reflect back to him the warmth he felt for it, and he remained faithful to his 'great parent' for the rest of his life; so that one of his last acts, when he knew himself to be dying, was to go and look upon it once more.

For the moment, however, he was in search of new experiences. With this great wealth of time on his hands, he was like a child in a toyshop. Where to go, what to do? Reynolds came up with the best idea; he was about to pay a visit to his native Devonshire, and he offered to take Johnson along. They set out in mid-July and for six glorious weeks wandered about Devonshire, meeting with generous hospitality and enjoying each other's company.

We know very little, in detail, about these six weeks, but they must have been one of the few spells of unclouded happiness in Johnson's life. To be free at last from the years of drudgery; to feel that his freedom had been fairly earned, that it came from fame he had merited and a character he had kept unspotted; to ramble in one of the most delectable regions of a country that was beautiful as no part of the earth is beautiful now; and to have beside him a loving, unalterable friend – life does not often make up such a bouquet. Reynolds, as well as suggesting the trip, must have been the cause of a great part of its happiness; he understood Johnson's mind and heart perfectly, and the proof is in the five portraits he painted of him over the years – marvellous paintings which show a developing sense of Johnson's personality as that personality itself developed. The earliest shows Johnson a year after the publication of the Dictionary, sitting at a table with pen and paper. His upholstered chair is covered in cloth with a bright check pattern, but everything else is drab and sober, including his plain suit of black; the immense bushy wig frames a strong, brooding face. One hand holds a pen, the other rests on the paper on which he is writing – but 'rests' is not quite the right word, for the hand is tense, the first two fingers splayed out; perhaps he is making a conscious effort to mark the place at which he left off writing; he could be revising or proof-correcting. It is above all things the portrait of a man *at work*: the spirit of the Dictionary years is there. The next portrait, thirteen years later, is completely different; there is no evidence that Johnson sat for it, and obviously Reynolds was working from imagination and memory, painting his idea of Johnson. With no wig, his own short hair brushed back from the high forehead, Johnson stands beside a high desk or shelf on which are books, pen and ink, and a roll of paper, the implements of his trade, but he is not working. Or rather he is working at a deeper level, for this is Johnson the poet, lost in reverie, wearing a loose robe-like garment and with his shirt open at the throat, like a Romantic poet of a hundred years later. Again one particularly notices the hands, held up in front of his chest, one above the other, fingers tensely crooked as if to pluck some elusive idea out of the silence of the room. I have seen the statement in print that this picture shows Johnson 'enforcing argument by gesticulation', but this is not a picture of a man arguing in company; he is alone, intensely occupied in exploring the depths of his mind; the eyes, deep-set and almost closed, indicate not merely Johnson's myopia but the deep concentration of a gaze turned inward:

> Such thought, that in it bound
> I need no other thing,

Wound in mind's wandering
As mummies in the mummy-cloth are wound.

In 1775 Reynolds painted Johnson again; this time the Johnson of the Streatham years, the mature critic of literature and society. Like the first portrait it shows him working; not sitting at a desk producing a daily stint of words but holding up to his fierce, near-sighted gaze a book that in the rapture of attention he is grasping and forcing out of shape, the covers back to back (it will never be the same again). Once again one notices the hands: large, strong, actively participating in the thrust towards knowledge and ideas, as if wisdom were a juice that could be literally squeezed out of dry paper and ink.

In the portrait of 1778 we have the Johnson of the Club: full-wigged, dressed for company, staring straight at us, the lips parted as if in the act of speaking, one hand across his waistcoat in a position suggesting that the arm is resting on the arm of a chair, no doubt that 'tavern chair' that was 'the throne of human felicity'; *this* is the Johnson who is enforcing argument.

Finally, some time between 1782 and 1784, we have Johnson at the end of his life, his head drooping slightly to one side as if the neck muscles have no longer the strength to hold it up straight. Indeed, loss of strength is everywhere in the picture; the skin hangs loosely around the chin and neck; one almost senses the difficulty in breathing, so that I would expect a doctor to know that this was the portrait of an asthmatic. But the eyes under their dark brows are still enquiring, the mind is still questing.

No wonder that Boswell should have dedicated the *Life of Johnson* to Reynolds, and prefaced it with that letter of dedication in which he says, 'You, my dear Sir, studied him, and knew him well: you venerated and admired him. Yet, luminous as he was upon the whole, you perceived all the shades which mingled in the grand composition; all the little peculiarities and slight blemishes which marked the literary colours.'

To return to the Devonshire trip: of what the two friends did and said very few fragments have survived, though we do know that a large part of their time was spent at Plymouth, and that Johnson was impressed by the naval dockyard with the colossal scale and complexity of its operations. It was his first sight of the sea (at fifty-two!) and, though London river had accustomed him to the sight of ships, the Thames was nothing to this. The Commissioner of the Dockyard courteously made a sailing vessel available for Johnson and Reynolds, and this conveyed them to visit the Eddystone lighthouse; another time they spent a few nights on board a man-of-war, entertained by a Captain Knight. From this visit one fragment remains but it is too good to lose. Johnson asked one of the seamen what was the function of something or other on the ship, and received the reply, 'That's where the loblolly-man keeps his loblolly.' According to Mrs Thrale's account, he regarded this answer as 'disrespectful, gross and ignorant'; and so it is, but one would not have it otherwise. Dignified and venerable as he was, Dictionary Johnson, Rambler Johnson, Rasselas Johnson, Johnson honoured with a royal pension, to this sailorman he was just another landlubber who kept asking questions, and the situation has in it a dash of the kind of humour Johnson himself so relished.

And there, on the deck of H.M.S. *Belle-isle*, in the aura of the loblolly-man, let us, for the moment, leave him.

CHAPTER 18

'You dogs,
I'll have a frisk with you'

One morning in 1754 or thereabouts, a tall young man knocked on Johnson's door and introduced himself as Bennet Langton. He added that he had consulted Mr Robert Levet as to the possibility of calling on Mr Johnson, and Mr Levet had indicated that it would not be considered an intrusion.

Langton had, in fact, manœuvred carefully towards this interview, on which he had long set his heart. As a boy he had read through *The Rambler* essays with a mounting admiration for the wise and humane character he sensed behind them. He was little more than a boy even now; he had not yet entered Trinity College, Oxford, where he was to complete his elaborate education under the guidance of Thomas Warton; but he was old enough to come up to London from his home in the country, and one of his chief motives for doing so was to seek the acquaintance of the Rambler. Luck guided his feet to a lodging-house where Levet was known; he asked the landlady to introduce him, and asked Levet in turn to sponsor his plan of getting to know Johnson; and now the wished-for day had come.

Langton was admitted, presumably by Frank Barber, and asked to wait. When Johnson came down and greeted him, the youth's first reaction was one of amazement and shock. As he later told Boswell, he had formed a mental picture of Johnson as a 'decent, well-dressed, in short, a remarkably decorous philosopher. Instead of which, down from his bed-chamber, about noon, came, as newly risen, a huge uncouth figure, with a little dark wig which scarcely covered his head, and his clothes hanging loose about him.'

This disconcerting impression was something Langton shared with virtually everyone meeting Johnson for the first time. The artist Hogarth, happening to call on Richardson at a time when Johnson was also visiting him, was shown into a room where Johnson was standing by the window, absorbed in his thoughts; as usual when in this state, he was twitching, rolling his frame about, and making strange *sotto voce* noises, and Hogarth assumed that this was a poor idiot to whom the charitable Richardson was giving shelter. When their host arrived, the 'idiot' moved forward and began to speak, so forcefully and eloquently that the thought crossed Hogarth's startled mind that he was witnessing a case of divine inspiration of the insane.

Bennet Langton now had a similar experience. Johnson began to talk, and at once the flow of his ideas, and the strong grasp with which he marshalled them, took away attention from his appearance. Surprise and dismay gave way to admiration and, increasingly, to affection. Johnson, on his side, was curious to know something about the young man who had sought him out. What he learnt pleased and reassured him. Langton ('of Langton, Lincolnshire') belonged to a squirearchical family which traced its lineage back to stirring times in English history. His ancestor was that Stephen Langton who, as Primate of England, was the first to put his signature to Magna Carta; the family's right of free warren had been granted by Henry II; the mild youth could show a pedigree engrossed on a piece of parchment ten inches wide and between twelve and fifteen feet long. Johnson, with his love of tradition, relished such things – a relish which, as he remarked, was commendably free of any personal vanity, since he himself 'could hardly tell who was his grandfather'.

Not that Langton's pedigree was Johnson's reason for liking him; it was merely a spice to his good qualities. Gentle, unassuming, benevolent, he seems fully to have merited Johnson's judgement that 'the earth does not bear a worthier man than Bennet Langton'. Johnson went further and paid Langton the highest tribute he could possibly have paid anyone – 'I know not who will go to Heaven if Langton does not.'

Johnson commonly abbreviated the names of his friends, addressing them as Bozzy, Goldy, Mur and the like. His name for Langton, 'Lanky', is more like a nickname in the usual sense, for Langton was immensely tall, and the more facetious members of their circle never tired of making jokes about his height. He would sit on a chair, leaning forward as if lacking the strength to hold his long body upright, and twine one leg round the other in a seeming effort to minimize the space he had to take up. One acquaintance, a Mr Best, said that he looked like the stork who stands on the shore, one leg raised, in Raphael's cartoon for his tapestry 'The Miraculous Draught of Fishes'. (In a picture alive with dramatic movement, the stork stands, its back towards us, in an irresolute stance that seems to convey the humble amazement of animal creation witnessing a miracle.) In conversation, Langton would take out a gold-mounted snuff-box which at other times he never used. His face was handsome, his smile uncommonly sweet.

Johnson soon discovered that there was depth under this amiability. Langton had firm principles and knew his own mind. He was also an excellent scholar, particularly in Greek. In an effort to attain a pure style in Greek composition, he had learnt by heart the Epistle of St Basil. He had also studied Clenardus's Greek Grammar. ('Why, Sir', said the impressed Johnson, 'who is there in this town who knows anything of Clenardus but you and I?') To Thomas Warton, when Langton was an undergraduate, Johnson wrote, 'I see your pupil sometimes: his mind is as exalted as his stature. I am half afraid of him; but he is no less amiable than formidable.' As a concise portrait of Langton, those two sentences will do as they stand.

Johnson recognized in Langton an instinctive goodness, deepened and strengthened by meditation and learning. Those qualities which he, Johnson, strove so hard to achieve, he felt Langton had by natural right. Convinced as he was of his own bad qualities, severely as he judged himself for sloth, wandering thoughts, fleshly temptations, tormented as he was by guilt and fear of the wrath to come, he deferred to Langton as a man God had chosen to make effortlessly good. Some faults Langton had, and Johnson did not hesitate to remark on them; he was a bad manager of his income, a poor family disciplinarian (he had his children 'too much about him', in Johnson's opinion) – but these were secondary matters, and never came anywhere near to touching Langton's solid virtues of heart and head. So that Johnson was always ready (or as ready as he could force himself to be) to accept advice and even correction from this lad nearly thirty years his junior.

There is an interesting example of this, early in their relationship. Langton contributed a paper to *The Idler* (No. 67, 28 July 1759) in which he sketched a fanciful, but not wildly exaggerated, picture of Johnson's working habits under the title 'A Scholar's Journal'. The entries begin with a stern resolution:

> The following three days I propose to give up to reading; and intend, after all the delays which have obtruded themselves upon me, to finish my essay in the Extent of the Mental Powers; to revise my treatise on Logic; to begin the epic which I have long projected; to proceed in my perusal of the Scriptures with Grotius's Comment; and at my leisure to regale myself with the works of classics, ancient and modern, and to finish my Ode to Astronomy.

Already we see Johnson, in amusing parody, but recognizably – the Johnson who was perpetually forming ambitious schemes of disciplined study, too rigorous for any human being but particularly too much so for him, with his irregular, stop-and-start habits and his perpetually hungry mind which tore and devoured whatever came within its field of attention. In entry after entry of Johnson's private journal, we read pathetic resolutions to work methodically, to bring his thoughts under control, to march steadily forward along a high road and ignore side turnings. This, for instance, from January 1772:

> I hope to cast my time into some stated method.
> To let no hour pass unemployed.
> To rise by degrees more early in the morning.
> To keep a Journal.
> I have, I think, been less guilty of neglecting public worship than formerly. I have commonly on Sunday gone once to church, and if I have missed, have reproached myself.
> I have exerted rather more activity of body. These dispositions I desire to improve.
>
> I resolved, last Easter, to read within the year the whole Bible, a very great part of which I had never looked upon. I read the Greek Testament

without construing and this day concluded the Apocalypse. I think that no part was missed.

My purpose of reading the rest of the Bible was forgotten, till I took by chance the resolutions of last Easter in my hand.

I began it the first day of Lent, and for a time read with some regularity. I was then disturbed or seduced, but finished the old Testament last Thursday.

I hope to read the whole Bible once a year as long as I live.

What Langton realized, and what Johnson could never bring himself to acknowledge, is that such rigorous method can be hampering as easily as rewarding; the brilliant flash of intuition, the sudden turn of the thoughts in a new direction, can often be more productive than hard, regular pounding. Langton brings out the point well in the 'Scholar's Journal'; a succession of comically described interruptions comes between the scholar and his projects; in the fragments of time left to him, he aimlessly picks up one task after another, blaming himself all the time for not sticking to his lofty programme; but by the end of the three days he has done just as much work as he had planned to, though of a different kind. The only originally blue-printed job to be finished is the Ode to Astronomy, which comes to him late at night when he has calmed his mind with a quiet reading in the Bible, and induced benevolent thoughts: 'As I observed the moon shining through my window, from a calm and bright sky spangled with innumerable stars, I indulged a pleasing meditation on the splendid scene, and finished my Ode to Astronomy.'

Clearly, Langton was (in the gentlest possible way) preaching a little at Johnson. Clear-sighted man as he was, he had brought into focus one of Johnson's weaknesses – the constant striving for method and the nagging self-accusation. When we stand back and survey Johnson's work, it seems to us not only remarkably copious but remarkably consistent. He has certain themes which engage his attention, and he comes at them again and again, from different angles. Morally, the conduct required of a Christian and the duty of charity; intellectually, the most advantageous use of the Western intellectual heritage as revealed and garnered by the scholars of the Renaissance; in literature, the search for enduring excellence and the resisting of vogues and false novelties; historically, the exploration of the nature of civilization and the potentialities of civilized man; politically, the nature of an emerging democracy, the limits of democratic power and the responsibilities of expanding nations. Virtually everything that Johnson wrote turns on one or other of these subjects; much of it (the Shakespearean criticism, for instance) has implications for all of them. That such a mind, so intent on hammering away at its major themes, should torment itself with accusations of aimlessness, seems almost incredible – or would do if we did not have other, supporting examples. George Orwell, for instance, who resembled Johnson in more ways than one, but especially in his preoccupation with a relatively small number of themes and his determination to put first things first, lived the same kind of frenziedly hard-working life as Johnson (he did not, of course, live to the age at which Johnson received his pension) and experienced the same kind of guilt. In a notebook found at his death, Orwell wrote:

> It is now (1949) sixteen years since my first book was published, and about twenty-one years since I started publishing articles in the magazines. Throughout that time there has literally been not one day in which I did not feel that I was idling, that I was behind with the current job, and that my total output was miserably small. Even at the periods when I was working ten hours a day on a book, or turning out four or five articles a week, I have never been able to get away from this neurotic feeling that I was wasting time. I can never get any sense of achievement out of the work that is actually in progress, because it always goes slower than I intend, and in any case I feel that a book or even an article does not exist until it is finished. But as soon as a book is finished, I begin, actually from the next day, worrying because the next one is not begun.

No doubt if Orwell had been fortunate in having a friend as perceptive as Langton he might have received a similar warning against this corrosive habit of mind. And no doubt if he had it would have made as much difference as Langton's admonition to Johnson – viz., none at all.

Langton's friendship meant a great deal to Johnson, on every level. It was, once, broken off for a time over a senseless wrangle, but knitted up more strongly than ever, and never again interrupted; Langton sat by Johnson's deathbed and was one of the comforters of his last hours. Through him, too, the celibate Johnson had one of his welcome glimpses of family life. He made several happy visits to the house in Lincolnshire and developed a respect for 'old Mr Langton', who at one time made him the offer of a substantial living that lay within his gift. But Johnson, who at one period of his life had struggled so hard and so unavailingly to become a country schoolmaster, had no ambition now to be a country clergyman. Besides, he had enough self-knowledge to know that his unconquerably Bohemian habits would be no good example to set before his rustic flock.

When Bennet Langton went up to Trinity College, Oxford, he made the acquaintance of a fellow-undergraduate, Topham Beauclerk, and presently there sprang up one of those odd friendships which can sometimes exist between people of very different character and outlook, as if each of them supplied his deficiencies from the other. Topham Beauclerk was worldly, witty and fashionable; his conduct was less innocent than Langton's; his tongue markedly less so.

Johnson met Beauclerk, in Langton's company, when he paid a long visit to Oxford in 1757. At first, he wondered to find the gentle Langton associating with a young man of the world like Beauclerk but presently he, too, fell under the spell of Beauclerk's extraordinary charm and wit. (When Garrick heard of the association, he said that from now on he expected to have to bail Johnson out of the lock-up.) Perhaps the attraction is not so hard to explain. Beauclerk was the great-grandson of Charles II and Nell Gwyn; and Johnson, strict moralist though he was, always confessed a regard for Charles II ('the last English monarch who was a man of parts') and would not hear him decried. His fondness for Beauclerk seems to have had a similar foundation. Though he disapproved of the malicious tone of Beauclerk's conversation ('You never open your mouth but with intention to give pain,' he once scolded him), he was diverted by its wit, and he recognized the very real warmth of Beauclerk's attachment to himself. He did not, however, as in the case of Langton, draw into the circle of his affection all those connected with his original friend. Beauclerk was the cause of a divorce between the eldest daughter of the Duke of Marlborough and her husband, Viscount Bolingbroke; two days later he made an honest woman of her, but Johnson was not mollified by this; to Boswell, who tried to justify her conduct in abandoning her first husband, he replied dismissively, 'My dear Sir, never accustom your mind to mingle virtue and vice. The woman's a whore, and there's an end on't.'

What Johnson seems particularly to have admired in Beauclerk was a quality of style. 'Everything comes from him so easily,' he said. 'It appears to me that I labour when I say a good thing.' Beauclerk would bring out his most brilliant *mots* with no suggestion in his face or manner that he was about to say something unusually good, nor any suggestion afterwards that he had done so. Obviously he was a higher specimen of that type Johnson had already admired in Henry Hervey and to some extent in Cornelius Ford. Such men, elegant and worldly, appealed deeply to the Johnson who had described himself in the letter to Chesterfield as 'a retired and uncourtly scholar'.

In both Langton and Beauclerk, then, Johnson delighted as men whom he could admire, and who yet looked up to him as a figure of authority. It was a happy relationship and they all found happiness in it. One famous story in particular stands out. Quite early in their acquaintanceship, Langton and Beauclerk dined together one evening in London and sat over their wine till three in the morning. Then the idea suddenly occurred to them that Johnson, if they could wake him, might be prevailed on to join them in a dawn frolic. He was then living in the Temple, and they thundered on the door of his chambers until he lurched out of bed, snatched up a poker and came to the door in his night-shirt to repel invaders. When he recognized his callers he lowered the poker and said, 'What, is it you, you dogs? I'll have a frisk with you.'

Quickly Johnson threw on some clothes and the three of them were at large in the streets as daylight came up. The fruit and vegetable market at Covent Garden lay close by, and Johnson tried to give the countrymen a hand as they unloaded their wagons and set up their stalls; but his appearance caused them so much amazement that the work came to a standstill. The trio adjourned to a tavern, where they called for a bowl of a punch that Johnson particularly liked, called 'Bishop', and as they quaffed it he repeated a festive invocation to Sleep:

> Short, O short then be thy reign,
> And give us to the world again!

The story is touching and delightful as an illustration of Johnson's unbounded appetite for harmless pleasure. When the punch was finished, they took a boat and had themselves rowed down the river to Billingsgate. Langton there left them because he had an appointment to breakfast with some young ladies ('leaving his social friends', Johnson grumbled, 'to go and sit with a set of wretched un-idea'd girls'), but Johnson and Beauclerk kept up their junketing for the rest of the day.

We owe that story to an unforgettable page or two in Boswell. And now, at last, we must make way for Boswell to appear onstage in his own person. His voice has been heard often enough. Everyone with an interest in Johnson is very much in debt to Boswell not only for the years of devotion he invested in the study of Johnson's life – he is far and away the most important source for the facts in this book, for instance – but for the uncanny skill with which he conveyed the quality of Johnson's personality and his effect on the people about him. If there had been no Boswell, Johnson would have been one of the most famous names in English literature; but that he has become a household name, known to millions who will never read a line of his writing, is due to the chance that brought Boswell into his company in the back parlour of Tom Davies's bookshop on the afternoon of Monday, 16 May 1763.

One says 'chance', but chance, in fact, entered into the matter only in so far as they happened to meet on this occasion and not some other. Boswell had been making determined efforts to get to know Johnson for some time. He had, like Langton, received his first impression of Johnson from his writings; asked about the possibility of meeting him; been indulged with hopes by various minor figures who had some degree of acquaintance with him; and at last, after repeated disappointments, brought it off.

What kind of young man was it who leapt to his feet in mingled joy and terror as he saw Johnson's majestic form moving towards him from the shop to the parlour? If we want a full character-analysis and case-history, we need only apply to Boswell himself. His collected journals make up the most extraordinary biography, the most determined effort of a human being to put himself totally on record, to be found anywhere. Compared with Boswell, Rousseau is evasive, Henry Miller reticent. For our present purposes it should be enough to remark those features of Boswell's character that impinged on his relationship with Johnson and equipped him to give us the one indispensable biography.

Boswell was thirty years younger than Johnson, and this gap, which in itself is not so very great, turned out by an accident of historical pattern to be all-important. If Johnson had been born in 1680 and Boswell in 1710, the difference between them would merely have been the difference between youth and middle age; but since Johnson's birth date was 1709 and Boswell's 1740 they are separated by one of those seismic cracks in the historical surface. Boswell is a new man in Johnson's world; he belongs to the epoch of Rousseau; all the attitudes that we associate with the end of the eighteenth century – the onset of 'sensibility', the obsession with the individual and the curious, the swelling tide of subjective emotion – are strongly present in him. Where Johnson still belongs to the world of Aristotle and Aquinas, the world of the giant system-builders, Boswell inhabits the ruins of that world. Where Johnson instinctively proceeds

by erecting a framework and then judging the particular instance in relation to
that framework, Boswell is the sniffing bloodhound who will follow the scent
of individuality into whatever territory it leads him. The fascination of their
dialogue, that dialogue of mind, heart and voice round which Boswell organized
his great *Life*, is that it is not merely between two very different men but
between two epochs. In its pages, Romantic Europe speaks to Renaissance
Europe, and is answered.

Boswell was typical of his age in taking a passionate interest in the self. He
was, besides, not altogether untypical in the fact that the self in which he took
the most intense interest was his own. He saw his own personality not only as a
labyrinthine mystery but also as the chaotically heaped material for a great
work of art. The prime objective of his life was to define his identity and in so
doing to shape it: to make himself into a being fit to bear the proud name of
James Boswell. At the age of twenty-four, having scraped acquaintance with
Jean-Jacques Rousseau, he sat down and dashed off a self-portrait and sketch of
his history up to that time, mentioning the unsteady graph of his emotions and
opinions, his grievous temptations of the flesh and his joyful surrender to those
temptations, his pride and his self-doubt, and concluded with the fervent appeal:

> Sir, I have given you in haste an account of all the evil in my nature. I
> have told you of all the good. Tell me, is it possible for me yet to make
> myself a man?

For Boswell the process of making himself a man involved inhabiting a hall
of mirrors. It was impossible for him merely to *be*. He had to be in relation to
another personality. Whatever he thought or did must be observed from outside
and the observation must be reflected back. It hardly mattered whether the
outside observer was another person or another part of his own nature. When
he poured his self-analysis and self-observation on to paper, he was addressing
that part of his own personality that could stand aside and watch with detach-
ment as the panting, sweating, involved self pushed on through thicket after
thicket. 'I should live no more than I can record,' he wrote once; thoughts and
actions that escaped the record were not fully real to him.

Boswell's thirst for self-observation was matched by his need to measure himself against others. He was, in that sense, a natural parasite, living from one
intense relationship to the next and always drawing a great deal of his energy
from the host. His doglike hero-worship and his equally doglike sexual promiscuity were opposite sides of the same coin. Whether he was coupling his
mind with that of some man of unquestioned achievement, or coupling his body
with that of some attractive girl, he felt a relief from the intolerable burden of the
unmitigated self, and in this sense his whole life was one long act of copulation.

From the moment of their first meeting, the relationship with Johnson was
the most important in Boswell's life. But even that did not take up the full slack
of his needs and interests. Within a few weeks of that meeting, Boswell was off
on an extended tour of Continental Europe, in which he introduced himself to
(among many others) both Voltaire and Rousseau. The meeting with Voltaire,

especially, reads like something out of a great comic novel; their talk, in Voltaire's drawing-room at Ferney, turned on the truth or falsity of the Christian religion, and they sat there with the Bible open between them and argued away until Voltaire could stand it no longer:

> The daring bursts of his ridicule confounded my understanding. He stood like an orator of ancient Rome. Tully was never more agitated than he was. He went too far. His aged frame trembled beneath him. He cried, 'Oh, I am very sick; my head turns round', and he let himself gently fall upon an easy chair. He recovered. I resumed my conversation, but changed the tone. I talked to him serious and earnest. I demanded of him an honest confession of his real sentiments.

If Voltaire thought that an assumed, or even a real, fainting fit was going to get him off the hook of a Boswellian cross-examination he had another think coming. Nothing shook Boswell off; he was impervious to snubs – would, indeed, record those snubs for the interesting sidelights they offered on the character of his interlocutor and his own character. This is the Boswell who sometimes pestered Johnson out of his mind, the Boswell of whom Johnson said, when the question came up of how a stay-at-home man might be dislodged, that they should send Boswell to him – if that didn't drive him out of his house nothing would. On another occasion, as Boswell records,

> I was once present when a gentleman asked so many [questions], as, 'What did you do, Sir?' 'What did you say, Sir?', that he at last grew enraged, and said, 'I will not be put to the *question*. Don't you consider, Sir, that these are not the manners of a gentleman? I will not be baited with *what* and *why*; what is this? what is that? why is a cow's tail long? why is a fox's tail bushy?' The gentleman, who was a good deal out of countenance, said, 'Why, Sir, you are so good, that I venture to trouble you.' Johnson: 'Sir, my being so *good* is no reason why you should be so *ill*.'

It is, of course, Boswell himself who acts the role of gadfly here. And though 'a good deal out of countenance' he no doubt forgave himself readily enough. After all, no question is too absurd or too trivial if the point of asking it is to stab a beam of light into some out-of-the-way corner of the personality. Boswell's questioning seemed to his contemporaries marvellously eccentric; to us, living in the age of psycho-analysis, it will appear to have its own logic.

But Boswell did not always, or even often, annoy Johnson. He very frequently cheered and uplifted him. The younger man's egotism was unaccompanied by any prickliness or ill-temper; necessarily so, perhaps, since a man interested in every ebb and flow of his own temperament will see even his *gaffes* and blunders, even his inadequacies, as interesting in their own right. It was all very well for Macaulay to write, with the severity of a fellow Scot, 'Everything which another man would have hidden, everything the publication of which would have made another man hang himself, was matter of gay and clamorous exultation to his weak and diseased mind.' This, like so many of

Macaulay's remarks, begins from a base of sound understanding and slices into the rough because of Macaulay's journalistic propensity for exaggeration. That Boswell revealed, to himself and to others, everything that most men try to keep out of sight is true; but that such revelation was 'a matter of clamorous exultation' is sheer journalese. It was, rather, a matter of absorbed poking and prying and analysis, in which there was often an element of fascinated revulsion. But then Macaulay, with his direct and high-stepping mind, was the last man in the world to have understood Boswell: though even he can see Boswell's most immediate virtues, good humour and the absence of vindictiveness. 'An ill-natured man', he says, 'Boswell certainly was not.' He pleased Johnson from the beginning by taking in good part some very rough teasing. There is no need to give once more the details of their first conversation in Tom Davies' parlour – if ever a passage of English literature was too well known to need rehearsing, it is that one – but everyone remembers the Punch and Judy quality of the encounter; every time Boswell ventures a remark, Johnson fetches him a box on the ear. At the end of the interview Boswell felt sore all over; but the friendly Davies followed him to the door and sent him off comforted: 'Don't be uneasy. I can see he likes you very well.' And Davies was right. Boswell called on Johnson at home a few days later; they talked freely and, as the gratified Boswell reports, 'as I took my leave, [he] shook me warmly by the hand'. In June, Johnson says, 'I have taken a liking to you'; in July, 'My dear Boswell, I do love you very much.' By the end of the same month Boswell is all packed to go to Harwich on his way to Utrecht, where he is to study the law; Johnson is so pleased with the new friendship that he says, 'I must see thee go; I will go down with you to Harwich.' And then follows that delightful description of their two-day journey, the other occupants of the stagecoach, and Johnson's relaxed, genial conversation:

A fat elderly gentlewoman and a young Dutchman seemed the most inclined among us to conversation. At the inn where we dined, the gentle-woman said that she had done her best to educate her children; and, particularly, that she had never suffered them to be a moment idle. Johnson: 'I wish, Madam, you would educate me too; for I have been an idle fellow all my life.' 'I am sure, Sir (said she), you have not been idle.' Johnson: 'Nay, Madam, it is very true; and that gentleman there (pointing at me) has been idle. He was idle at Edinburgh. His father sent him to Glasgow, where he continued to be idle. He then came to London, where he has been very idle; and now he is going to Utrecht, where he will be as idle as ever.' I asked him privately how he could expose me so. Johnson: 'Poh, poh! (said he) they knew nothing about you, and will think of it no more.'

They parted with mutual expressions of regard. Boswell's description of the moment is touching and deserves to be quoted.

My revered friend walked down with me to the beach, where we embraced and parted with tenderness, and engaged to correspond by letters. I said, 'I hope, Sir, you will not forget me in my absence.' Johnson: 'Nay, Sir, it is more likely you should forget me, than that I should forget you.' As the vessel put out to sea, I kept my eyes upon him for a considerable time, while he remained rolling his majestic frame in his usual manner; and at last I perceived him walk back into the town, and he disappeared.

Johnson continues to roll his majestic frame through the pages of Boswell's incomparable *Life*, which gives us not only the best portrait of Johnson but vivid glimpses of Goldsmith, Burke, Gibbon, Reynolds, Garrick, that whole brilliant society. The achievement is all the greater in view of the fact that Boswell did not, when we come to reckon it up, spend very much time in Johnson's company. As we saw, they met a number of times in the early summer of 1763, but after that Boswell was away for three years; first in Holland, then on a whirl through Germany, Switzerland, Italy, Corsica and France. His return to England was made in characteristically Boswellian circumstances; he had escorted Rousseau's mistress, Thérèse Le Vasseur, to England sc that she might join the philosopher, who had been hounded from the Continent and was at present living in Chiswick; and on the way he had taken the opportunity to involve himself even more closely with Rousseau's thought processes by investigating the girl's charms for himself. They reached England in February and, having unloaded Thérèse, Boswell hastened round to visit Johnson, who received him with affection and assured him that his, Johnson's, failure to write letters had been due to laziness and not to any lack of regard. Then, after a few days, Boswell was off to Scotland. His mother had died during his absence; his father was ill; he had to get down to work as a lawyer, and he had also ambitious literary projects on hand. For two years London saw him no more. This fairly suggests the pattern of Boswell's contacts with Johnson. During the twenty-one years in which Boswell knew Johnson they spent, as nearly as can be computed, two hundred and seventy days, or parts of days, in one another's company. Of these, a hundred were spent in one continuous three-month stretch when they travelled in Scotland. Boswell made use of the opportunities he got; but he spent far less time in Johnson's company than Reynolds or Goldsmith or the other regular, London-based members of the Club; and certainly far, far less than blind Miss Williams or old Levet or Frank, the Jamaican boy. Johnson reminisced with him much less than he did with John Taylor or Edmund Hector, and confided in him much less than he did in Hester Thrale. But with that last name we come in sight of Boswell's only real competitor as a source of our knowledge of Johnson, and she is important enough to await her own place in the story.

Johnson liked Boswell for the same reasons for which he liked Langton and Beauclerk, and he was clear-sighted about those reasons. As he put it to Boswell: 'Sir, I love the acquaintance of young people; because, in the first place, I don't like to think myself growing old. In the next place, young acquaintances must last longest, if they do last; and then, Sir, young men have more virtue than old men; they have more generous sentiments in every respect. I love the young dogs of this age.'

'Who's for Poonsh?'

Reynolds continued to be a good friend. He had so much enjoyed the six weeks of Johnson's company in 1762, and in particular the pleasure of hearing him in conversation with the long and varied roster of their West Country hosts, that he cast about for some means of hearing Johnson talk more often. The idea naturally occurred to him of an informal club of friends, meeting regularly in an agreed place, and electing its own members democratically. According to Edmond Malone, it was at Johnson's own fireside that Reynolds put to him the idea of such a club, to revolve round himself; and in the winter of 1763–4 it became a reality.

During the two decades of Johnson's greatest fame, the Club played a central part in his life. Since he had so largely abandoned writing for talking, it was important that he should have friends he might talk *with* rather than merely admirers to talk *at*. The membership of the circle, accordingly, was from the first drawn from among people who were in some sense Johnson's intellectual equals, rather than just people he liked. (Johnson liked, after all, many people whose warmest defenders would not have called them intellectual giants – old Levet, for instance, or Sastres, the teacher of Italian, or 'good Mrs Gardiner, the tallow-chandler on Snow Hill'.) The eight original members of the Club were, apart from Johnson himself, Reynolds, Burke, Nugent, Beauclerk, Langton, Goldsmith, Chamier and Hawkins. Most of these names will need no footnote. It is impossible to think about the civilization of eighteenth-century England without thinking of Reynolds, Burke, Goldsmith, men whose achievement, in their several spheres, is in every way worthy to stand beside Johnson's. Nugent, a physician, was Burke's father-in-law. Chamier, a well-read and cultivated man, had made a fortune in the City and retired from business to pursue his literary and intellectual interests; but he did not choose a completely leisured life, for in 1764 he was Secretary to the War Office, and in 1775 Under Secretary of State. Beauclerk and Langton we know; Hawkins was rather wished on the other members by Johnson, who was so tenacious of old friendships that merely to have known a man for a long time was to him a sufficient reason for liking him. Hawkins, however, behaved in a characteristically surly and unsociable manner. He refused to pay his share of the cost of supper on the grounds that he ate no supper at home; at one meeting he was so aggressively rude to Burke that 'all the company signified their displeasure', and the next time Hawkins showed up he was treated so coldly that he never came again. Johnson passed the matter off by remarking that Hawkins was 'unclubable' – a soft synonym for curmudgeonly, tight-fisted and Pecksniffian.

The Club was from the beginning held in high esteem. Election to it was regarded as at least the equivalent of election for Parliament. From the original eight members it had grown to sixteen in ten years, and ten years further on still, at the time of Johnson's death, it had reached its peak at thirty-five. At first they met for a weekly supper on Mondays; after 1772, for a fortnightly dinner on Fridays. The atmosphere was one of frank and free competition in the exchange of ideas; but there was no throat-cutting. It was a circle of men who liked and trusted each other. Not that these evenings of conversation were mere recreation. The range of topics discussed, and the knowledge and experience which collectively these men brought to bear on them suggest that they thought of debate and discussion as part of the essential business of their lives. So, of course, does every sensible human being. But most human beings do not live in a social setting which permits of debate and discussion, on any level high enough to extend their minds and add to the stock of their thoughts. Moving about incessantly as we nowadays do, we are nearly always with strangers, and settled, purposeful talk is best conducted among people we know well. Again, the talkers must be capable of disinterested intellectual curiosity, which presupposes the willingness to think seriously about matters that do not directly involve one's own interests. And here most social *milieux* are useless. Fashionable society is too empty and frivolous, mercantile society too anchored to buying and selling; while the conversation of closely knit professions, such as the medical or the legal, consists either of shop or of certain permitted topics of non-shop (where did you go for your holidays?). It is an important fact about eighteenth-century England that it could not only give birth to a man like Johnson but also produce a circle among whom he could feel at home and be himself while using the full powers of his mind.

Before considering what happened when Johnson used the full power of his mind, let us look once more at the nature of his circle, the Club. Not only was it such a gathering as only a civilized society could produce; it also sheds some interesting light on the structure of power and influence within that society. The eighteenth century was, by comparison with the later developments of democracy, frankly an age of privilege. A poor boy could climb to the top, or very near the top, but he had to have a great deal of luck as well as a great deal of talent. There was no built-in *carrière ouverte aux talents*, no scholarship ladder, no upward spiral which a gifted youth could claim to follow as a matter of social right. Yet, given this, one is struck by the enormous contribution made to English life in that age by men who started with no advantages. Johnson himself is an obvious example. So is Captain Cook, the working seaman who started his career carrying seacoal on Tyneside, and whose famous voyages of exploration still used the same design of craft because of its tested weight-carrying capacity. Cook's rule-of-thumb methods raised him to command over men who had every advantage of wealth and rank, for no better reason than that the eighteenth century knew a good thing when it saw one. The same would be true of the career of, say, Clive of India. Of the industrial barons of the later century there is no need to speak; such men have their own avenues to power, which are independent of the previously existing structure. A Wedgwood or a Boulton does not wait for the nod from Whitehall or St James's. But the career of a politician, even to some extent of an artist or writer, depends to some extent on finding a relationship with the society as it exists independently of him. An industrialist produces goods which people are free to buy or not; if they buy he becomes rich, but his relationship is primarily to *things* – to raw materials, means of transport, balance sheets – rather than people. But anyone working within the sphere of ideas, and this applies equally to administrators, artists, teachers, mobilizers of opinion, has to take up an attitude towards his fellow-beings as they exist in social organization. He recognizes certain points of agreement among society generally and he has to make up his mind which of those points he feels able to agree with, and which he must oppose and attack.

These decisions the members of the Club, collectively and individually, had taken. Though they were predominantly men of the new middle class rather than the hereditary aristocracy, and though they recognized that they had a duty to apply their intelligence to the problems facing their society and if necessary criticize its current solutions, as Johnson criticized the harshness of the penal system, they were not an association of rebels, but rather of men who felt their lives to be contiguous with the life of the society. They were even patriotic, in the sense that they wished their country well and were glad to be thought well of by it. Which is not to say that they were infected with the evil nationalism that sees its own nation as a mechanism for seizing power and wishes to see it go on and on, blindly seizing more and more power until the day comes of the inevitable conflict with some rival expression of a collective will. Johnson, conspicuously, was free of jingo patriotism, being anti-expansionist and anti-imperialist. In wishing his country well, he primarily wished it to be a civilized place where people could be happy.

Of the forty-four members of the Club in Johnson's lifetime, nineteen, by the end of their lives, were the bearers of some kind of title: seven by inheritance and twelve on merit. The proportion is neatly illustrative. The Club laid down no rules which would discriminate against a man because he happened to come from the hereditary aristocracy. On the other hand, by its very nature as an association of free intelligences, it weighted its membership on the side of pure talent, energy, distinction. Among the later members, one has only to think of Gibbon, the Wartons, Garrick, Sir William Jones, the Orientalist, to realize that the Club gathered in all professions. There was no subject that could not be illuminated at its discussions. One day when Boswell and Johnson were on their Scottish journey, the notion occurred to Boswell that the Club could form a university at St Andrews, to take the place of the existing one which had fallen into such doldrums. Johnson relished the idea, and they immediately began distributing the various subjects among its members. Boswell was to teach 'civil and Scotch law'; Burke, politics and eloquence; Garrick, the art of public speaking; Langton, Greek; Colman, Latin; Nugent, medicine; Vesey,

Celtic antiquities; Jones, Oriental studies; Goldsmith, poetry and ancient history; Chamier, commerce; Reynolds, painting, 'and the arts which have beauty for their object'; Chambers, English law. And Johnson? At first he said, 'I'll trust theology to nobody but myself,' but recollecting that Percy was a clergyman he decided to assign 'practical divinity' (as well as 'British antiquities') to him, while he himself took over 'logic, metaphysics, and scholastic divinity'. Johnson remarked that since the death of a member named Dyer, who seems to have been a prodigiously learned man, they had no one who understood mathematics; but for everything else they could get along very well.

In this respect, of course, the Club was fortunately placed by history. The mid-eighteenth century was the last moment at which a man of intelligence and energy could hope to be fairly abreast of the whole range of knowledge. Not, indeed, to carry all the available information in his own head – that was already impossible – but to be sufficiently *au courant* to have the feel of every subject, to estimate what he did not know by what he did know, to keep some kind of finger on the pulse. This situation was changing as new knowledge mounted; it was, in fact, the tremendous intellectual thrust of this generation that changed it, and in that sense it could be said that the Club were sawing away the branch they were sitting on. But all great moments of civilization are necessarily fleeting, since by seeking perfection they are contriving their own decadence.

The range of subjects covered in a typical evening by the Club is fairly indicated by Boswell's account of the meeting on 3 April 1778 – the only formal attempt he ever made to plot the course of their talk for an entire session. The conversation begins with sculpture. Of a marble statue of a dog, valued at a thousand guineas, Johnson remarks that what we chiefly prize is not the object itself but the skill needed to produce it. One of the company mentions the marble boar in the Uffizi at Florence, and Johnson declares that the first boar accurately fashioned in marble should be preserved as a landmark in human progress; to learn to model realistically in so hard a stone is a step forward for the whole species. Obviously Johnson is deficient in aesthetic appreciation of sculpture; he sees it almost wholly as a triumph of man's contrivance and skill rather than of his imaginative vision; he consistently held that a sculpture would not be of so much interest if it were cut out of a lump of soap or a carrot. That a man should be able to carve very exactly in so resistant a medium as marble is to him the remarkable thing. Short-sighted as this view is, it is not nonsense; it is exactly the kind of consideration that our modern art appreciation keeps out of sight; it takes us back to the world in which 'art' meant any kind of specially acquired skill, so that Milton could refer to Galileo as 'the Tuscan artist'.

The subject of art is now dropped for that of emigration, introduced by Burke. The company begins by kicking about the proposition that emigration actually increases the population of a country, as the export of manufactures increases the volume that is produced, by encouraging an expanding market. Fordyce, the chemist, then puts in: 'It is remarkable that the most unhealthy countries, where there are the most destructive diseases, such as Egypt and

Bengal, are the most populous.' Johnson at once corrects the logical error: 'Countries which are the most populous have the most destructive diseases. *That* is the true state of the proposition.'

A little later there is another abrupt change of topic, when R. B. Sheridan congratulates Burke on his Parliamentary oratory, and in particular finds it admirable that Burke takes as much trouble over a speech that cannot possibly achieve any practical result, the votes being certain to go the other way, as over one that might really sway the house. Burke replies that a speech may have an effect without influencing the pattern of voting; it may drop certain ideas into the minds of Ministers and members who, before hearing it, were entirely convinced of being in the right; it may prepare the ground for getting rid of an unsuitable measure at a later opportunity. The company then embark, under the direction of Burke and Johnson, on an extremely interesting discussion of the nature of Parliament, the part played in its activities by self-interest and the part by disinterested public spirit. Cool, realistic, moderate, the debate neither blunders into cynicism nor reaches after an impossible idealism.

Another switch takes them to philology. Burke volunteers that the Irish language is not 'primitive' but 'Teutonic'. Johnson goes along with this only up to a point. Gaelic may be 'radically' Teutonic but that does not make it resemble English; High Dutch is Teutonic and an Englishman cannot understand it. The two of them bandy philological examples for a while, during which one imagines the rest of the company recharging their glasses with claret.

Johnson then moves from languages to travel. He has been reading Thicknesse's *Travels*, a forgotten book which evidently followed the irascible example of Smollett, who in his *Travels through France and Italy* grumbled his way robustly round those countries finding fault with everything. Johnson remarks mildly that 'there has been, of late, a strange turn in travellers to be displeased'. This leads on to the whole topic of judging men's actions and forming an estimate of human nature generally. Burke opens with, 'From the experience which I have had – and I have had a great deal – I have learnt to think *better* of mankind.' 'From my experience', says Johnson, 'I have found them worse in commercial dealings, more disposed to cheat, than I had any notion of; but more disposed to do one another good than I had conceived.' 'Less just and more beneficent,' puts in Gibbon, quietly. Johnson goes on, 'And really it is wonderful, considering how much attention is necessary for men to take care of themselves, and ward off immediate evils which press upon them, it is wonderful how much they do for others. As it is said of the greatest liar, that he tells more truth than falsehood; so it may be said of the worst man, that he does more good than evil.' But when Boswell hopefully tries to take this a step further with 'Perhaps from experience men may be found *happier* than we suppose', Johnson's stern view of life asserts itself quickly – 'No, Sir; the more we enquire, we shall find men the less happy.' They go on to speak of virtue and temptation, and Johnson makes some wise observations on how far a man has the right to subject another to temptations which may prove too strong for him. The evening concludes with a general resolution that Johnson shall write a letter, on behalf of the Club, to a gentleman who has offered them a hogshead of claret when their present supply shall have run out.

As Boswell's account occupies no more than four or five pages, it is unlikely to cover anything like the full range of thoughts that found expression even in this one evening. But one is grateful for it as the record of a freely unhampered conversation and in particular as indicating its positive, constructive tone. If this evening was typical, the Club seems to have wasted very little time on bemoaning the evils of the times or head-shaking over the depravity of human nature. That Johnson and Burke, who had looked on life from every angle, should be able to report that they had found men better than might be expected is comforting; that Burke, particularly after the fantastic way he had been for years libelled and insulted by hired party-writers, should have discerned good sense and principle in the cut and thrust of Parliamentary conflict is positively uplifting.

The formation of the Club was a great landmark in Johnson's life. It ushered in that period in which he built a second reputation, as a great talker, on the basis of his first one as a writer and scholar. Of course, just as he continued to write during the years of talk, he had always talked, whenever opportunity offered, during the years of writing. Before ever leaving the Midlands he had enjoyed those evenings at Gilbert Walmesley's house, with golden hours of disputation during which he had begun to put on muscle as a debater. With Cornelius Ford, with Hector and the Birmingham circle, doubtless with the tough-minded and sharp-witted Tetty during the early years of their marriage, before she began to break up, he had talked to his heart's content, moving by easy association from one topic to another, developing that quickness of adaptation and that matchless retrieval system which, as they matured, were to become the astonishment of a later generation. What evenings of literary talk lie buried in the early London years! We have no record of what Johnson and Collins said to one another; no word that fell from the lips of the saintly old Psalmanazar or his neighbour, the 'philosophical tailor'. Yet they were all, in their way, good value; they gave to Johnson as much as they took from him. And in these early Bohemian years he learnt to associate good talk with the idea of meeting his friends in a tavern. For various reasons he never entertained in his own home, and his friends, for the most part, had nothing much in the way of a home to ask him to. Even Richard Savage, though he was not averse to entertaining friends at someone else's house, if the man had a good enough cellar, seems to have been more at home at an inn. The habit formed thus early remained with Johnson a lifelong preference. The French, whose literary and artistic interchange is largely conducted in cafés, would see nothing strange in Johnson's way of life, though the more domestic English have generally regarded it as quaint or even slightly disreputable. But Johnson's love of tavern life was unshakeable. He had enjoyed most of his happiest hours in such places and was not above testifying to the fact. Sir John Hawkins has recorded one characteristically warm utterance:

I have heard Johnson assert *that a tavern chair was the throne of human felicity.*
'As soon', said he, 'as I enter the door of a tavern I experience an oblivion of

care and a freedom from solicitude: when I am seated I find the master courteous and the servants obsequious to my call, anxious to know and ready to supply my wants: wine there exhilarates my spirits, and prompts those whom I most love: I dogmatize and am contradicted, and in this conflict of opinions and sentiments I find delight.'

In that passage, short as it is, there are several points which claim our attention. One, which should perhaps be got out of the way here, is the reference to wine as 'exhilarating' Johnson's spirits. His attitude to alcohol varied at different times of his life, but underlying it was the consistent fact that, like most people of strong appetites, he found abstinence easier than moderation. When Hannah More, late in his life, invited him one evening to 'take a little wine', he replied candidly, 'I can't take *a little*, child, and therefore I never touch it.' He was, however, by no means a total abstainer. Roughly speaking, he abstained from 1736 to 1757, and again from 1765 to the end of his life. During his drinking periods, he performed some creditable feats of ingestion. At the age of sixty-nine he remarked to Boswell, 'I did not leave off wine because I could not bear it; I have drunk three bottles of port without being the worse for it. University College has witnessed this.' We should remember, of course, that an eighteenth-century bottle of port was only about half the size of a modern bottle, and the wine much less heavily fortified. On his celebratory trip to Devonshire with Reynolds, he once drank in an evening three bottles of an unspecified 'wine', probably claret; on that occasion, as Reynolds noted, he was decidedly glassy-eyed.

Going back to that paragraph of Hawkins, another sentence that catches the attention in Johnson's testimony to tavern conversation is 'an interchange of discourse with those whom I most love'. It is entirely characteristic of Johnson to bring in the word 'love' in this context. He cared deeply for his friends, and in leisurely conversation, on the neutral ground of a tavern, he savoured their individualities and idiosyncrasies. Much as he enjoyed the play of ideas, he never saw his friends as walking intelligences; their small habits and casual associations were to be treasured as much as their learning and wit. Nugent, for instance, being a Roman Catholic, always ordered an omelette when the Club dined on a Friday, in order to fast from meat. Some years after Nugent's death, Johnson happened to catch sight of an omelette, and was moved to tears by the association with Nugent: 'Ah, my dear friend', he lamented, 'I shall never eat omelette with *thee* again.'

Still on the same passage, we pause again at the words, 'I dogmatize and am contradicted.' The point is of capital importance because Johnson has so often been accused of dogmatism, of shouting down the opposition and enforcing authority when what was called for was the give and take of opinion. The reputation is unjust; it dates from the Victorian period when Johnson's own writings, like all eighteenth-century literature, fell completely out of fashion and he was scarcely known outside the pages of Boswell. Not that Boswell's account of Johnson is untrue. It is too scrupulous and too sensitive for that. But we all see what we want to see, and Boswell, who hero-worshipped Johnson, delighted to show him in the guise of unconquerable gladiator. This side of Johnson undoubtedly existed. He frankly owned that conversation, to him, was competitive. By showing his intellectual mastery, by establishing a dominant position, he could put himself beyond the reach of ridicule or contempt, of both of which he had had to endure more than his share in early life. Besides, there was the love of the game. Johnson regarded the last word in an argument as a legitimate prize, to be tilted for. After all, with interlocutors of such quality as he enjoyed, a great deal of truth would inevitably be discovered on the way to the last word; it hardly mattered who 'won' the argument, when the argument itself produced so much illumination. So that Johnson had no hesitation in pulling the rug out from under his opponent, by some irrelevant or personal remark if there was no other way. This is what Goldsmith had in mind when, adapting an expression from the playwright Cibber, he remarked that there was 'no arguing with Johnson: if his pistol misses fire, he knocks you down with the butt-end of it'. Some of the people who were 'knocked down' resented it. But Johnson never meant to give offence. 'The cup of life', as he wisely remarked, 'is bitter enough, without squeezing in the hateful rind of resentment.' He liked a dispute, but he hated a quarrel. Anyone who once gained Johnson's friendship had it for ever afterwards in his power to wound him deeply by coldness or neglect. When Thomas Warton published some verses in which he aimed at the poignant simplicity of the late mediaeval ballad, Johnson amused himself by extemporizing a parody or two, and dashed off a short set of satirical verses. Warton was offended; he avoided Johnson for some years; and Johnson, deeply sorrowing, declared that Warton had no heart.

Sometimes, in the heat of debate, Johnson said things he would not have written down deliberately, let alone sent to the printer. This does not mean that he said what he knew to be untrue, or went against his deeply held convictions. He was, if anything, obsessional about the need to be truthful even in the smallest matter. He would not, for instance, allow Frank Barber to say that he was out when the truth was that he was in but did not want to receive visitors. To accustom a servant to telling lies on one's behalf, even small white ones, might set his feet on an evil path. Much less would he be guilty of saying one thing and thinking another. It was more a question of selection and highlighting. Sometimes he said more than he would have said in a published essay, sometimes less. An example of his saying less would be his retort to 'one of the company' (probably Boswell) who interposed, when he was praising Pope's *Dunciad* and repeating its magnificent concluding lines, 'Too fine for such a poem: – a poem on what?' Johnson, 'with a disdainful look', swept him aside: 'Why, on *dunces*. It was worth while being a dunce then. Ah, Sir, hadst *thou* lived in those days! It is not worth while being a dunce now, when there are no wits.' This is a resort to mere rudeness; Johnson wanted to shut the man up (and if it was indeed Boswell who is cloaking his identity under 'one of the company' he had every justification). But it is noteworthy that though Johnson overturned the table to avoid the trouble of finishing the game, he did not say anything that went against the true state of his opinions. He did admire Pope; he did admire the *Dunciad*; he could easily, at no notice, have explained fully his grounds for the admiration, pointing out that the *Dunciad* was a great satire in defence of certain positions which Pope thought essential to civilization, and which he felt were under heavy attack. But such a lecture would have held up the flow of conversation, and this would have been a discourtesy to the company. Johnson therefore chose the lesser discourtesy of slapping Boswell down.

An example of the opposite – of Johnson's saying *more* than he would have said in a printed essay – is provided again by a retort to Boswell, who had been loudly singing the praises of his beloved Corsicans. 'Why, Sir', Johnson broke out, 'what is all this rout about the Corsicans? They have been at war with the Genoese for upwards of twenty years, and have never yet taken their fortified towns. They might have battered down their walls, and reduced them to powder in twenty years. They might have pulled the walls in pieces, and cracked the stones with their teeth in twenty years.' 'It was in vain', says poor Boswell, 'to argue with him upon the want of artillery; he was not to be resisted for the moment.'

'I dogmatize and am contradicted.' The words recall those of a celebrated passage in Johnson's essay on Shakespeare: 'What I have here not dogmatically but deliberately written . . . .' To be dogmatic could produce one kind of useful result, by stimulating the other side to bring up effective counter-arguments. To be deliberate was Johnson's invariable practice when left to himself, without such stimulus to competition. 'When there was an audience', Boswell writes on one of the last pages of the *Life*, 'his real opinions could seldom be gathered from his talk; though when he was in company with a single friend, he would discuss a subject with genuine fairness.'

Given that Johnson's conversation, like all conversation, was adapted to time and place and occasion, and thus very rarely embodied 'his real opinions' in all their depth and complexity – given that, what were the marks of a Johnsonian conversation? How would we describe Johnson as a talker?

The first hint comes, once again, from the invaluable Boswell:

> His superiority over other learned men consisted chiefly in what may be called the art of thinking, the art of using his mind; a certain continual power of seizing the useful substance of all that he knew, and exhibiting it in a clear and forcible manner; so that knowledge, which we often see to be no better than lumber in men of dull understanding, was, in him, true, evident, and actual wisdom.

The tribute is a noble one. And it shows, if by this time such a thing needed to be shown, that Boswell was not the fool that Macaulay and others have made him out to be. His admiration for Johnson was based on a very accurate perception of where Johnson's greatness lay. Intellectually, as Boswell pinpointed it, Johnson's great gift was not merely that he knew a great deal but that he had such superb control over what he knew. This control was probably innate in him, but in any case he had had to strengthen it as a matter of survival. All his experience, all his training, had demanded it. When writing the Dictionary, for instance, it had been necessary to marshal such a colossal range of information, to bring to bear such power of memory, that the task would have been beyond the reach of most men, even of most learned men. On the simplest level, when he was selecting the quotations to illustrate a word, what guarantee had he that he had not used the same quotation, somewhere or other, already? Again, in the unrelenting assembly-line work of composing two *Rambler* essays a week, his mind had been required to turn up, with a readiness that would not halt his hurrying pen, quotations and anecdotes and concrete instances of this and that. In the 208 numbers of *The Rambler* he quotes from a staggeringly wide range of authors, ancient and modern, English and Continental. The scholars at Yale University have produced an interesting breakdown of Johnson's quotations and allusions in *The Rambler*, which can be consulted in Volume III of their edition of his Works, pages xxxi–xxxiv. From it we learn that the essays contain 669 quotations or allusions, over half of them from Latin or Greek; that modern literature (in its broadest sense, i.e. post-mediaeval) is cited 251 times, and that all but 37 of these references are to writers before the eighteenth century. Johnson's interest in the Renaissance, which was life-long, comes out in the roll-call of European writers from the fifteenth to the seventeenth century whose work he had at his fingertips: the Yale editors list Bellarmine, Camerarius, Cardano, Castiglione, Cornaro, Cujacius, Descartes, Erasmus, Fabricius, Gassendi, Grotius, Julius Libri, Lipsius, Politian, Pontanus, Quevedo, Sannazaro, the Scaligers and Thuanus.

In his search for knowledge and understanding Johnson read incessantly, and what he read was always active in his mind. Yet, vividly present as his reading was, it never dominated his horizon. An important aspect of Johnson as a talker is indicated by his remark to Boswell in the Hebrides, 'They call me a scholar; and yet how little literature is there in my conversation.' It is true that he said this when looking through some pages of Boswell's journal, which recorded chiefly their conversations with simple people, and that Boswell immediately replied, 'You would not give literature to people who could not relish it. Stay till we meet Lord Elibank.' Even so, the point is valid. Johnson is far from being one of those literary men whose talk never gets out from under the bat shadow of literature. He talks from life, and he uses his literary and historical knowledge to reinforce his judgements – which is surely the right way round. As Boswell says in the very next sentence after those given above,

> His moral precepts are practical; for they are drawn from an intimate acquaintance with human nature.

Correct. Johnson's wisdom was masticated by experience as well as leavened with knowledge of 'the best that has been thought and said in the world'. Take, as one example out of a thousand possible, his *aperçu* that 'to help the ignorant commonly requires much patience, for the ignorant are always trying to be cunning'. This, in fact, could have been learnt from literature; the bumpkins in Shakespeare's comic sub-plots are united in their unshakeable belief that cunning and deviousness are the answer to all life's problems. But Johnson obviously got it from life, as he did all his perceptions; with the result that, when he met them in literature, he had the reassuring sense that there was no dissonance between the wisdom of great men and the path of common experience; they were both part of 'general nature'.

The result of all this was a force and freshness in Johnson's utterances that made the men and women of his day crowd to hear him; and we may take 'crowd' in the most literal sense. Bennet Langton once wrote Boswell a letter, which he duly prints in the appropriate place (May 1780), describing an evening at the house of a Mrs Vesey. Those present included a raft of hereditary aristocrats, the Duchess Dowager of Portland and half a dozen others, whom he names; there were also Pepys, the Master in Chancery, and Barnard, the Provost of Eton; a distinguished enough company, as distinction is usually reckoned. Langton goes on:

> As soon as Dr Johnson was come in and had taken a chair, the company began to collect round him, till they became not less than four, if not five, deep; those behind standing, and listening over the heads of those that were sitting near him.

It is a vivid picture of homage. Indeed, a few years earlier, the King himself had set an example. Having heard that Johnson was in the habit of dropping in to the library at Buckingham House, a royal residence on the site of the present Buckingham Palace, he asked his librarian, Mr Barnard, to let him know when Dr Johnson came next to the library. This Barnard duly did, one day in 1767, with the result that Johnson was sitting quietly by the fire, deep in a book, when Barnard came up to him with 'Sir, here is the King'. Johnson quickly rose, and stood waiting as the King approached. There followed a conversation on which Johnson afterwards looked back with a good deal of satisfaction. It followed a fairly conventional pattern; the King asked about the libraries at Oxford, and whether there was any interesting work being done there; whether Johnson was writing anything; what was Johnson's opinion on the controversy between Warburton (who had attacked the University of Oxford) and Lowth (who had defended it); what he thought of the medical theorist Dr Hill; whether there were any literary journals published in England except the Monthly and Critical reviews, and other such questions. To each, Johnson returned a measured and informative reply. On the subject of Hill, who was commonly held to be a quack, he said that the man lacked veracity, and quoted in illustration an easily verifiable mis-statement about the use of the microscope. But then, remembering to whom he was speaking, he decided that it was unfair to depreciate the man in the opinion of his King, and quickly added that Hill was 'a very curious observer' – a typical Johnsonian afterthought.

The interview seems to have pleased both men. Johnson, though his attitude was one of profound respect, made no attempt to speak in the hushed undertone that people usually adopt on these occasions; his voice was 'resonant' (Boswell's word); he evidently showed his habitual blend of respect for hierarchy and degree with sturdy self-esteem. The King, for his part, took the trouble to pay Johnson a compliment. On Johnson's remarking of himself that he 'thought he had already done his part as a writer', George replied, 'I should have thought so too, if you had not written so well.' This, Johnson remarked afterwards, was a compliment 'fit for a King to pay. It was decisive.' Asked whether he had made any reply, he said firmly, 'No, Sir. When the King had said it, it was to be so. It was not for me to bandy civilities with my Sovereign.'

The event is of more than trivial importance because it marks the end of Johnson's lingering hostility towards the Hanoverian dynasty. The King was, henceforth, described as 'the finest gentleman I have seen'. 'Sir', Johnson said to Bennet Langton, 'his manners are those of as fine a gentleman as we may suppose Lewis the Fourteenth or Charles the Second.' And, again harking back to Charles the Second, he described George as the first English monarch for a hundred years who had seriously identified his interests with those of the English people, and seriously tried to make friends with them.

Within five years Johnson was to do what he had earlier declared his intention of not doing: use his gifts as a writer in the service of the government. Did King George's compliment help to soften him? Perhaps; and perhaps, also, the Whig-dominated government appeared to him, as George III's reign lengthened out, to wear a less hostile face. In contrast with his two previous namesakes, George was a constitutional monarch; he ruled very much with the consent of Parliament, and it was an anti-royal faction within Parliament, determinedly hostile to the King and 'the King's friends', who in 1780 tabled the celebrated motion that 'the influence of the monarchy has increased, is increasing, and ought to be diminished'. Johnson might well have felt that to undermine the power of the King was merely to put more power into the hands of rich and aristocratic Whigs, who were no more democratic than the King and far less accountable to public criticism.

With all this fame and favour, Johnson never developed the pride that puts a man above the reach of his fellow-creatures. Dr Maxwell, the assistant preacher at the Temple, wrote down some reminiscences of Johnson in which he called him 'the most accessible and communicative man alive'. Giving a vivid description of Johnson holding a levee over his morning tea, and then going on to another set of company, and then another, Maxwell decided that Johnson was 'considered as a kind of public oracle, whom everybody thought they had a right to visit and consult'. Only one thing Johnson would not tolerate: the thought that he was being made a show of. If he suspected that an invitation was motivated not by a rational desire to enjoy his conversation but merely to attract company and give people something to gossip about, he refused it. When Boswell, who loved to stage-manage Johnson's conversations so as to produce the liveliest exchanges, unguardedly remarked, 'I wish I saw you and Mrs Macaulay together' – Mrs Macaulay being a lady of decidedly Whiggish views – Johnson 'grew very angry; and, after a pause, while a cloud gathered on his brow, he burst out, "No, Sir; you would not see us quarrel, to make you sport. Don't you know that it is very uncivil to *pit* two people against one another?" Then, checking himself, and wishing to be more gentle, he added, "I do not say you should be hanged or drowned for this; but it *is* very uncivil." '

Johnson, then, talked for victory but never talked *merely* for victory, remaining true to his deep convictions; enjoyed his fame but never consented to be sought out *merely* for his fame; consorted from choice with those whom he 'loved best'. What else should we bear in mind, when we try to get close to him and hear the authentic accents of his talk?

One remark by an acquaintance stands out. 'Johnson is like a ghost,' said Thomas Tyers. 'He never speaks unless he is spoken to.' And indeed it is remarkable that in the whole range of his conversations as recorded by Boswell, by Hester Thrale, by Fanny Burney, by Arthur Murphy Johnson never initiates a topic. He was at the furthest possible remove from the studiedly 'clever' talker who before going out to a party works up a suitable subject and polishes a few epigrams. Johnson's mind was so well stocked, his thoughts so immediately available, that whatever subject was proposed to him he could immediately set in a new light.

This new light was sometimes a matter of information; he was always ready with an illustration, as he had been on that far-off first evening at Pembroke College, when he had intervened in the conversation of his elders with an apt reference to Macrobius. But it was equally likely to be a matter of distinguishing, of shredding out the secondary features of a subject from the primary; of moving to one side the accidental and the incidental, to get at the heart of the matter. All who came into contact with him felt the bracing effect of this. When Reynolds published his *Discourses on Painting*, he paid therein a glowing tribute to the influence of Johnson's mind on his own – Johnson, who knew nothing about painting! But, as Reynolds said, that was not the point; the point was rather that the habit of rigorous thinking, as inculcated by Johnson, was transferable to any subject:

> Whatever merit they [the Discourses] have must be imputed in great measure to the education which I have had under Dr Johnson. I do not mean to say, though it would certainly be to the credit of these Discourses if I could say it with truth, that he contributed even a single sentiment to them: but he qualified my mind to think justly.

It is true that Reynolds wrote these words in a first draft and took them out before the *Discourses* actually saw print. But this was understandable enough; the malicious whisper was already going round that Johnson had ghosted the book for him. How otherwise would Reynolds, a mere painter, a man who had never been to a university, have written so lucidly and with such range and polish? And then Johnson's generosity with his pen was well known. In taking out such an overt testimony to Johnson's influence, Reynolds was only guarding himself against the ill-nature of a certain kind of reader. But as a statement on the nature of Johnson's help in forming his mind we may take the passage at face value.

One of Johnson's ways of encouraging clarity and honesty – 'qualifying the mind to think justly' – was to wage unremitting war on what he and his age called 'cant'. 'My dear Sir,' he said to Boswell, 'clear your *mind* of cant.' We may note the italicization. Boswell is making it clear that Johnson is prepared to tolerate a certain amount of cant in the mouth as long as it does not 'ascend me into the brain'. He goes on: 'You may *talk* as other people do: you may say to a man, "Sir, I am your most humble servant." You are *not* his most humble servant. You may say, "These are bad times; it is a melancholy thing to be reserved to such times." You don't mind the times. You tell a man, "I am sorry you had such bad weather the last day of your journey, and were so much wet." You don't care sixpence whether he is wet or dry. You may *talk* in this manner; it is a mode of talking in society; but don't *think* foolishly.'

The willingness to make a gesture towards social usage is characteristic of the Johnson who considered himself 'a very polite man' – even remarking to Mrs Thrale that he was 'well bred to the point of needless scrupulosity'. He was entirely free of the essentially egotistic surliness of the man who disdains ordinary politeness on the grounds that it does not reflect the true state of his feelings, who refuses to write to the bank manager as 'Dear Mr So-and-so' because the bank manager is not in fact dear to him. Such foolishness would soon make all social life impossible, and Johnson was well aware of the need for social life. What he insisted on was the duty always to see things as they are, no matter how, for the sake of oiling the social wheels, one chose to describe them.

So much for cant at its lighter, shallower level. But there is a deeper form of cant, the habitual use of misleading language which arises partly from a wish to deceive others and partly from a deeper need to deceive ourselves. In this sense cant is always with us, and the more so as we allow propaganda and advertising a larger share in our lives. The kind of political trained parrot who refers to the slave states of Eastern Europe as 'people's democracies' is indulging in cant; so is the person who uses the word 'gay' to mean 'homosexual', as if heterosexual people were incapable of gaiety.

Perhaps, by now, our picture of Johnson as a conversationalist is coming into less bleared focus. Wide-ranging, instantaneously marshalling information, weighing evidence, exploding cant, never initiating a subject . . . we may add two negatives. Johnson was not a *raconteur*. By contrast with all those famous talkers who base their talk on reminiscence and anecdote, he introduced both sparingly, though his friends were agreed that he could tell a good story when he wanted to. Second, Johnson was not an epigrammatist. Most of his remarks are pithy and memorable, to the extent that they lose something if we quote them in paraphrase rather than in his own fresh and concrete idiom. But they are not epigrams.

To make the point clear I should state my own idea of an epigram. Here are two examples. The first, inevitably, is from Oscar Wilde: 'If you tell the truth, you are certain sooner or later to be found out.' The second is G. K. Chesterton's description of Cardinal Newman as 'a naked man with a naked sword'. The first expresses an important truth in a new way by standing it on its head; the

second gives a brilliant impressionistic summary of the character of a great
man, catching both his incisiveness and his vulnerability in a brief phrase. Each
example is entirely natural to its author, an habitual mode of utterance. There is
no straining for effect; we feel, in each case, that this is the way the mind
spontaneously expresses itself.

Except in its spontaneity and naturalness, the typical Johnsonian utterance is
like neither of these. His remarks are not feathered shafts in swift motion
through the air; they are interestingly shaped stones lying on the ground, where
the careless passer-by is apt to fall over them. And they are stones which lie
about in the landscape, not on glass shelves in a geological museum. The quotable Johnsonian remark always occurs in a texture of argument or closeknit
reasoning; it is not, like the examples from Wilde and Chesterton, equally
effective in isolation. Consider the conversation reported by Boswell on 10
April 1778:

> We talked of war. Johnson: 'Every man thinks meanly of himself for not
> having been a soldier, or not having been at sea.'   Boswell: 'Lord Mansfield
> does not.' Johnson: 'Sir, if Lord Mansfield were in a company of General
> Officers and Admirals who have been in service, he would shrink; he'd
> wish to creep under the table.' Boswell: 'No, he'd think he could try them
> all.' Johnson: 'Yes, if he could catch them: but they'd try him much sooner.
> No, Sir: were Socrates and Charles the Twelfth of Sweden both present
> in any company, and Socrates to say, "Follow me, and hear a lecture in
> philosophy"; and Charles, laying his hand on his sword, to say, "Follow
> me, and dethrone the Czar"; a man would be ashamed to follow Socrates.
> Sir, the impression is universal: yet it is strange. As to the sailor, when you
> look down from the quarter deck to the space below, you see the utmost
> extremity of human misery: such crowding, such filth, such stench!'
> Boswell: 'Yet sailors are happy.' Johnson: 'They are happy as brutes are
> happy, with a piece of fresh meat – with the grossest sensuality. But, Sir,
> the profession of soldiers and sailors has the dignity of danger. Mankind
> reverence those who have got over fear, which is so general a weakness.'
> Scott: 'But is not courage mechanical, and to be acquired?' Johnson:
> 'Why yes, Sir, in a collective sense. Soldiers consider themselves only as
> part of a great machine.' Scott: 'We find people fond of being sailors.'
> Johnson: 'I cannot account for that, any more than I can account for other
> strange perversions of imagination.'

Here is a three-minute snatch of Johnson's talk, and in it there are several remarks which approach the epigrammatic, at least in so far as they encapsulate
Johnson's opinion in a form that can be lifted out and quoted: 'Every man thinks
meanly of himself for not having been a soldier'; 'Mankind reverence those
who have got over fear'; 'Soldiers consider themselves only as part of a great
machine.' Just as Johnson's writing drives always towards generalization, so
his talk naturally moves from proposition to proposition. Or take another
snatch of Boswell (11 April 1776):

A journey to Italy was still in his thoughts. He said, 'A man who has not been in Italy is always conscious of an inferiority, from his not having seen what it is expected a man should see. The grand object of travelling is to see the shores of the Mediterranean. On those shores were the four great empires of the world; the Assyrian, the Persian, the Grecian and the Roman. All our religion, almost all our law, almost all our arts, almost all that sets us above savages, has come to us from the shores of the Mediterranean.'

Here is one of Johnson's most often quoted remarks, 'The grand object of travelling is to see the shores of the Mediterranean.' By being put back into context, it gains colour and density without losing its quasi-epigrammatic force. The same is true of the clinching, summarizing phrases in his writing. For instance: 'Liberty is to the lowest rank of every nation little more than the choice of working or starving: and this choice is, I suppose, equally allowed in every country.' By itself this is a just and memorable remark; but in its place it has a settled strength which deserves not to be disturbed.

The parallel between Johnson's talk and his writing does not stop there. Everyone who knew him remarked that he talked in the same way as he wrote, and most of them understood that the incredible speed with which he could write was related to his habit of shaping his sentences and selecting his words in even the most trivial talk. Brook Boothby remarked that Johnson, when a topic was presented to him, would 'utter upon it a number of *The Rambler*'.

Johnson's talk, like his writing, is built on strong, vivid concrete detail. It uses abstract words but always in juxtaposition to the earthy, everyday imagery. His habit is to state something in general terms and then add the clinching, defining image. An example from his writing would be, from the Life of Dryden:

Learning once made popular is no longer learning; it has the appearance of something we have bestowed upon ourselves, as the dew appears to rise from the field which it refreshes.

And a parallel example from his talk (Boswell, 12 April 1776) would be:

Talking of a penurious gentleman of our acquaintance, Johnson said, 'Sir, he is narrow, not so much from avarice, as from impotence to spend his money. He cannot find it in his heart to pour out a bottle of wine; but he would not much care if it should sour.'

That is as near as I can come to a description of Johnson's talk. But of course the best way to render anyone's talk is to report it. Open Boswell, read a few pages, and all attempts at a formal description fade into irrelevance: the man is *there*. In the united judgement of uncounted readers, those successive English generations who have taken Boswell's book to their hearts, read it, quoted it, lent it, borrowed it, lost and stolen it, we may fairly, as Johnson did in another connection, 'rejoice to concur with the common reader'.

To Boswell, then: remembering as we read that Johnson to the end of his life spoke with a Staffordshire accent; so that, as Boswell tells us – and on this detail let our description of Johnson's talk come to rest –

Garrick sometimes used to take him off, squeezing a lemon into a punch-bowl, with uncouth gesticulations, looking round the company, and calling out, 'Who's for *poonsh*?'

PART V

Turtle and Burgundy

CHAPTER 20

Effort and Collapse

All this time Johnson's health had been far from good. Large and strong as he was, he was under continual attack both mentally and physically. Towards the end of his life he was to write, to his old friend Hector in Birmingham, 'My health has been, from my twentieth year, such as has seldom afforded me a single day of ease'; and John Hawkins, in his *Life*, records Johnson's statement that he 'knew not what it was to be totally free from pain'. Exactly what pain he suffered it is difficult to say with certainty, but the likelihood is that in such general statements Johnson was including mental anguish and restlessness as well as more purely physical sensation. The reference to 'my twentieth year' of course goes back to the depressive melancholia into which he sank during the dark months of 1729 after his retreat from Oxford; and his ill health at that time was certainly more mental than physical – if, as seems unlikely, the two can ever be clearly distinguished. Johnson's childhood attack of scrofula had left him blinded in one eye and myopic in the other; he had scars from an early bout of smallpox; apart from these symptoms, his physical disabilities seem to have been more or less purely nervous in origin. He moved clumsily; when he walked along he seemed to be putting his whole body into the effort, as much swimming as walking; in later years his limbs frequently shook as with a palsy, but even in his prime he was subject to more or less continual twitches and convulsive starts; it has been conjectured by some medical men that he was a mild form of spastic. In addition, his inner tensions expressed themselves in a number of compulsive habits. Going along a street in which there were posts, he would carefully lay his hand on each one as he passed, and if inadvertently he missed one he would go back a considerable distance in order to touch it. He also, as Boswell noticed, made a ritual of entering or leaving a door or passage in such a way as to take a certain number of steps to reach a certain point. At least, Boswell was never quite sure whether the important thing was the number of steps or the compulsion to start or finish the series with his left foot or his right, as the case might be; and he never ventured to ask Johnson the reason for the strange but never-omitted ritual. All he knew for certain was that it was too important to be neglected. 'I have, upon innumerable occasions, observed him suddenly stop, and then seem to count his steps with a deep earnestness; and when he had neglected or gone wrong in this sort of magical movement, I have seen him go back again, put himself in a proper posture to begin the ceremony, and, having gone through it, break from his abstraction, walk briskly on, and join his companion.'

These small peculiarities were in themselves harmless enough; most of us have something of the same kind; but obviously in Johnson's case they were linked with deep emotional and nervous malaise. He told Boswell, in the Hebrides, that he regarded his neurotic condition as hereditary. 'I inherited (said he) a vile melancholy from my father, which has made me mad all my life, at least not sober.' Boswell considered this expression 'too strong', but Johnson was perfectly consistent in his opinion; looking back on his life in old age, he saw it as a journey along the frontier of madness. 'When I survey my past life', he wrote in his diary on Easter Day 1777, 'I discover nothing but a barren waste of time with some disorders of body, and disturbances of the mind very near to madness.'

With all these burdens it is amazing that Johnson should have struggled on as effectively as he did, producing an enormous volume of work and making such a large general contribution to life. During his years of poverty he had no choice but to work or starve; after 1762 he might have been forgiven for letting drop his pen and spending his whole time in pursuit of those diversions which he allowed himself – conversation and travel. In fact, he produced an impressive amount of work after that date – particularly impressive in view of what it cost him to shut himself up in a room and write.

Of the works that Johnson produced after the award of his pension, the first, the most laborious and the most nearly shipwrecked was his edition of Shakespeare. He had, as we have seen, started out in a vein of sturdy confidence, engaging himself to edit the plays at the rate of about two every month. Each volume was to contain, besides the text and Johnson's own annotations, the most valuable comments from the previous editions of Rowe, Pope, Theobald, Hanmer and Warburton. He was determined to produce a definitive Shakespeare that should supersede all others.

Johnson's original contract stipulated that the complete edition should be published by Christmas 1757. On 24 December of that year he wrote to Burney, 'I shall publish about March.' On 8 March he wrote again to Burney, making no reference to his earlier prediction, but saying that he would publish 'before summer'. This can only mean that he regarded the task as very nearly completed. Notes, and scraps of information that would go towards notes, were coming in all the time, for Johnson was not bashful in asking his friends to contribute any sidelights that might arise from their reading or specialized knowledge; as he wrote to Thomas Warton, 'a commentary must arise from the fortuitous discoveries of many men in devious walks of literature'. But he proposed to gather in all such miscellaneous items in an appendix, to be printed last of all, so that 'nothing comes too late'.

After the confident prediction of 1758, however ('before summer'), some of Johnson's optimism seems to have ebbed away. We hear no more predictions, only of work in sullen fits and starts. In 1763 a young bookseller brought in a subscription, and asked that the subscriber's name should be included in the printed list, as was conventional. Johnson replied that he would print no list of subscribers, adding in explanation, 'Sir, I have two very cogent reasons for not printing any list of subscribers; one, that I have lost all the names, the other, that I have spent all the money.' The admission was all the more handsome inasmuch as Johnson was already under attack, already the target of satire, for his slowness in delivering the goods. Charles Churchill, satirist and man about town, well aware that he was the kind of man of whom Johnson disapproved, had published in 1762 a poem, *The Ghost*, in which Johnson is ridiculed as 'Pomposo', and his pocketing the subscribers' money referred to in a vein of gleeful hostility:

> He for subscribers baits his hook,
> And takes their cash; but where's the book?
> No matter where; wise fear, we know,
> Forbids the robbing of a foe;
> But what, to serve our private ends,
> Forbids the robbing of our friends?

Doggedly, Johnson toiled on. As the years go by we catch occasional glimpses of him battling with the enormous task. At the end of 1763 he is staying at Joshua Reynolds' house in Twickenham, working on Shakespeare. In the summer of 1764 he is staying with Percy at Easton Maudit, Northamptonshire, working on Shakespeare. In the summer of 1765 he is working on Shakespeare, but now the edition is almost finished and he is writing the noble preface which sums up the findings of all those years. And at last, on 10 October, the monumental edition – eight volumes, a thousand copies – is on sale.

Now, if ever, he could sit back with a sense of achievement. The edition of Shakespeare is a gigantic labour, in every way worthy of Johnson's stature, among his professional achievements second only to the mighty Dictionary. It is comprehensive in the true Johnsonian fashion; he worked over Shakespeare as a textual editor, an annotator, a critical interpreter. When he sat down to write the preface, which naturally he did last, he had behind him nine years of minute examination of the text. At that time Johnson must have come close to knowing the entire text of Shakespeare by heart. The strongly confident generalizations of the preface are rooted in the line-by-line analysis of particular passages. Having commented on, explained, as a last resort even conjectured, thousands of times, he is ready with a grand over–all view which is like the summing-up of some great judge.

Johnson's starting-point in the preface is the same as that of Dryden, in the well-known passage of the *Essay on Dramatic Poesy* which praises Shakespeare's 'comprehensive soul'. What Dryden admired was Shakespeare's breadth of human understanding – the deep intuition, the quick imaginative sympathy, which enabled him to get inside the skin of any kind of human being in any situation. Johnson was later to endorse Dryden's judgement in the most emphatic terms, in his Life of that poet, calling it 'a perpetual model of encomiastic criticism, exact without minuteness, and lofty without exaggeration'. He takes the same line himself; Shakespeare is pre-eminently the poet of nature, of life as it is demonstrably lived; he draws directly from experience:

> His persons act and speak by the influence of those general passions and principles by which all minds are agitated, and the whole system of life is continued in motion.

So that, in a very real sense, to study Shakespeare is to study life:

> This therefore is the praise of Shakespeare, that his drama is the mirror of life; that he who has mazed his imagination in following the phantoms which other writers raise up before him, may here be cured of his delirious ecstasies by reading human sentiments in human language, by scenes from which a hermit may estimate the transactions of the world, and a confessor predict the progress of the passions.

This way of appreciating Shakespeare's genius is of course squarely in conformity with the neo-classic view of literature and art; it starts from the premise of 'general nature'. The peculiar, the singular, the perverse, so valued by a later generation, have no place in this scheme of values. Johnson, here as elsewhere, writes from well within the neo-classic tradition. But, characteristically, he resists its narrower applications. Johnson grew up in a world in which the neo-classic culture was unquestioned and supreme, and lived on into a world in which it was undermined and soon to be toppled. With his invariable policy of stating the objections to the most widely held view, his instinctive preference for the outs over the ins, Johnson in his later criticism reasserts the neo-classic values very strongly in a world that has grown neglectful of them; but in 1765 the seismic warnings of this upheaval were barely perceptible, and the preface to Shakespeare shows him restraining the excesses of neo-classicism, protesting forcefully against its high priests who would legislate against Shakespeare in the name of a literary theory distilled from Aristotle's *Poetics* by French and Italian critics of the Renaissance. Such critics disapproved of Shakespeare's neglect of the three Unities of action, time and place. So much the worse for the Unities, is the essence of Johnson's retort. Similarly with the demand for decorum, the rigid distinction between 'high' and 'low', between tragic and comic or satiric. It is all very well for critics to amuse themselves by dividing human experience into tragic and comic, and then expecting the imaginative writer to arrange his material in separate showcases; the trouble is that in life, and therefore in the drama of Shakespeare, everything happens all the time:

> Shakespeare's plays are not in the rigorous and critical sense either tragedies or comedies, but compositions of a distinct kind; exhibiting the real state of sublunary nature, which partakes of good and evil, joy and sorrow, mingled with endless variety of proportion and innumerable modes of combination; and expressing the course of the world, in which the loss of one is the gain of another; in which, at the same time, the reveller is hasting to his wine, and the mourner burying his friend; in which the malignity

of one is sometimes defeated by the frolic of another; and many mischiefs and many benefits are done and hindered without design.

The neo-classic theory of generality had likewise been turned against Shakespeare by its narrower exponents. Such critics interpreted the Aristotelian canon of general nature to mean that in literature all kings should be kingly, all soldiers soldierly, all senators grave and dignified – a demand which would reduce the drama to a procession of cardboard cutouts. Johnson tersely disposes of this hampering pedantry:

> His adherence to general nature has exposed him to the censure of critics, who form their judgements upon narrower principles. Dennis and Rhymer think his Romans not sufficiently Roman; and Voltaire censures his kings as not completely royal. Dennis is offended that Menenius, senator of Rome, should play the buffoon; and Voltaire perhaps thinks decency violated when the Danish Usurper is represented as a drunkard. But Shakespeare always makes nature predominate over accident; and if he preserves the essential character, is not very careful of distinctions superinduced and adventitious. His story requires Romans or kings, but he thinks only on men. He knew that Rome, like every other city, had men of all dispositions; and wanting a buffoon, he went into the senate house for that which the senate house would certainly have afforded him. He was inclined to show an usurper and a murderer not only odious but despicable; he therefore added drunkenness to his other qualities, knowing that kings love wine like other men, and that wine exerts its natural power upon kings. These are the petty cavils of petty minds; a poet overlooks the casual distinction of country and condition, as a painter, satisfied with the figure, neglects the drapery.

Johnson's preface, then, is neo-classic in its largeness, its demand that literature shall make the generally applicable statement; but rebellious with regard to those aspects of the theory that tended to tie the writer's hands, or deny to a great poet the fullness of his just fame. When we turn to the notes on particular passages, we find another facet of Johnson on Shakespeare: the keenness with which he appreciated Shakespeare's naturalistic skill in character-drawing.

Criticism before Johnson had concerned itself little with Shakespeare's skill in portraiture. The change came during Johnson's lifetime. At the time he was born hardly any attention was paid to characterization in Shakespeare; by the time he died hardly any attention was paid to anything else. The impulse that made itself felt in the rise of the novel, putting emphasis on realism, credibility, and three-dimensional characters, appeared likewise in criticism. That Johnson was fully responsive to this need is proved by his brilliantly economical thumbnail essays in the interpretation of character. For instance:

> Polonius is a man bred in courts, exercised in business, stored with observation, confident of his knowledge, proud of his eloquence and declining into dotage. His mode of oratory is truly represented as designed to ridicule

the practice of those times, of prefaces that made no introduction, and of method that embarrassed rather than explained. This part of his character is accidental, the rest is natural. Such a man is positive and confident, because he knows that his mind was once strong, and knows not that it is become weak. Such a man excels in general principles, but fails in the particular application. He is knowing in retrospect, and ignorant in foresight. While he depends upon his memory, and can draw from his repositories of knowledge, he utters weighty sentences, and gives useful counsel; but as the mind in its enfeebled state cannot be kept long busy and intent, the old man is subject to sudden dereliction of his faculties, he loses the order of his ideas, and entangles himself in his own thoughts, till he recovers the leading principle, and falls again into his former train. This idea of dotage encroaching upon wisdom, will solve all the phænomena of the character of Polonius.

Very often, as he works through the plays, Johnson's attention is caught by some instance of Shakespeare's profound knowledge of the emotions and the subtle strokes by which he conveys this knowledge to us. And, fortunately, he considered it within the bounds of an editor's duty to draw attention to them now and again. When Leonato, in *Much Ado*, says

> Being that I flow in grief,
> The smallest twine may lead me,

Johnson is ready with the comment:

> This is one of our author's observations upon life. Men overpowered with distress eagerly listen to the first offers of relief, close with every scheme, and believe every promise. He that has no longer any confidence in himself, is glad to repose his trust in any other that will undertake to guide him.

Not that everything in his notes, or all of the preface, is congratulatory. Adam Smith called Johnson's preface the most manly piece of criticism to have been produced in any country, and part of the manliness consists in Johnson's bluntly laying a finger on the weaknesses of Shakespeare's work – the hasty writing, the loose constructions, the instances of carelessness and inconsistency. Very little escapes Johnson's watchful eye. Two lines in the last act of *Measure for Measure* reveal Shakespeare hurriedly at work:

Lorenzo: Who comes with her?
Messenger: None, but a holy hermit, and her maid.

> I do not perceive the use of this hermit, of whom nothing is seen or heard afterwards. The Poet had first planned his fable some other way, and inadvertently, when he changed his scheme, retained something of the original design.

An unconvincingly assigned metaphor in *The Winter's Tale* opens a window momentarily on the poet's mental associations:

> How would he look, to see his work, so noble,
> Vilely bound up!

It is impossible for any man to rid his mind of his profession. The authorship of Shakespeare has supplied him with a metaphor, which rather than he would lose it, he has put with no great propriety into the mouth of a country maid. Thinking of his own works his mind passed naturally to the Binder. I am glad that he has no hint at an Editor.

When Shakespeare seems to him indefensible, Johnson simply gives up the defence. Of the plot of *Cymbeline*,

> To remark the folly of the fiction, the absurdity of the conduct, the confusion of the names and manners of different times, and the impossibility of the events in any system of life, were to waste criticism upon unresisting imbecility, upon faults too evident for detection, and too gross for aggravation.

Obviously in a rapid survey we cannot begin to do justice to the interest and variety of Johnson's edition of Shakespeare. It is one of the glories of English criticism, and a work of literature in its own right. Not that it is without faults. As in the case of the Dictionary, Johnson tended to scamp that part of the work which he found least congenial, and in this case it was the purely textual side of the edition that suffered. Johnson knew that the text of Shakespeare needed a good deal of sorting out – he gave, indeed, a brilliant summary of the reasons why it was so corrupt – and in particular he knew the importance of collating every variant copy, both folio and quarto, that he could lay hands on. He pursued this part of the work with much less energy than the part which could be done by the pure attentive intelligence, and offered the somewhat feeble apology that 'I collated such copies as I could procure, and wished for more, but have not found the collectors of these rarities very communicative'.

Still, if Johnson's edition is weak on its purely textual side, it makes up for the weakness, as the Dictionary makes up for its occasionally amateurish philology, by the strong and logical grasp of his mind on particular points. With him, the eighteenth-century habit of altering Shakespeare's text at will, on the grounds that he 'must have' intended to comb out some of the logical tangles and metaphorical inconsistencies, finally dies the death. Bishop Warburton, a very learned man and the only one of Johnson's six predecessors for whom he had much respect, had been still in this tradition of reckless conjectural emendation. As a result even the respect due to a Bishop does not prevent an occasional snort from the Johnsonian nostrils.

> A gentlewoman of mine,
> Who falling in the flaws of her own youth,
> Hath blister'd her report.

Who does not see that the integrity of the metaphor requires we should read Flames of her own youth? (*Warburton*)

Who does not see that upon such principles there is no end of correction?

It is time to leave Johnson's edition of Shakespeare. But, before we do so, one more parallel with the Dictionary. Within a framework of large impersonality, Johnson manages to make the work strongly individual. In hundreds of tiny details, amounting to an overwhelming general impression, he gives us the sense that this work could only have come from him, Samuel Johnson. Occasionally, as in the Dictionary, he allows himself the expression of a personal opinion for its own sake. His low view of the theatrical profession finds expression in considering the character of Bottom:

> In this scene Shakespeare takes advantage of his knowledge of the theatre to ridicule the prejudices and competitions of the players. Bottom, who is generally acknowledged the principal actor, declares his inclination to be for a tyrant, for a part of fury, tumult and noise, such as every young man pants to perform when he first steps upon the stage. The same Bottom, who seems bred in a tiring-room, has another histrionical passion. He is for engrossing every part, and would exclude his inferiors from all possibility of distinction. He is therefore desirous to play Pyramus, Thisbe and the Lion at the same time.

This is in sportive vein. The diatribe against vivisection, however, which finds a place among the notes to *Cymbeline*, is written in a cold fury, reminding us how deeply Johnson hated all forms of cruelty:

> Queen: I will try the forces
>   Of these thy compounds on such creatures as
>   We count not worth the hanging, but none human.
> Cornelius: Your Highness
>   Shall from this practice but make hard your heart.

> There is in this passage nothing that much requires a note, yet I cannot forbear to push it forward into observation. The thought would probably have been more amplified, had our author lived to be shocked with such experiments as have been published in later times, by a race of men that have practised tortures without pity, and related them without shame, and yet suffered to erect their heads among human beings.

The sanity and centrality of Johnson's criticism, as evinced so strongly in his work on Shakespeare, undoubtedly sprang primarily from his belief in general and impersonal truth, a belief he shared with the whole neo-classic culture. But the impulse to find such a centre, to screen out the idiosyncratic and reach a broadly acceptable basis of agreement, must have received a powerful impetus from his own inward fears of disintegration and madness. The Romantic critics of the nineteenth century, who commonly expressed themselves in rhapsodic hyperbole, were misled by the firm, no-nonsense tone of Johnson's criticism to conclude that he lacked sensibility, that he sat calmly in judgement on great poetry instead of vibrating to it. The reverse is true. Johnson's emotional reaction to all his experience was extremely strong, and literature was an important part of that experience. As a boy he had been terrified by the ghost scenes in *Hamlet*; as a mature man he could not bear to read through the last scenes of *King Lear* or *Othello*, until he had to work over them as an editor. Of the scene in which Othello strikes and insults Desdemona he remarks feelingly, 'I am glad I have finished my revisal of this dreadful scene. It is not to be endured.'

To anyone who has fears for his own mental stability, great literature can be dangerous in much the same way that certain kinds of X-ray are dangerous for the surgeon. Literature indeed orchestrates the emotions and ultimately calms them by importing order into the nervous system; but it begins by stirring them up. Johnson's work on Shakespeare probably exhausted him almost as much as his Gargantuan toil on the Dictionary; it also involved his emotions much more nearly. Admittedly this is no more than speculation, but perhaps we may see some connection between those years of fierce, intermittent work and vibrant emotional response and the illness which overwhelmed him in 1766, the year after the Shakespeare was published. This illness was evidently something in the nature of a nervous collapse. Johnson's will deserted him; he lay on his bed for weeks on end, and gloomy forebodings gnawed incessantly at his mind.

One day, as he sweltered in his misery, he received a visit from two friends he had recently made. Henry Thrale and his wife, Hester, had got to know Johnson in 1765, through the good offices of Arthur Murphy. Johnson had gone down to Streatham to dine with the Thrales at their house there, and the evening had been a decided success. It is true that their rapidly ripening friendship had met with a setback when, in that first summer of their acquaintance, Johnson had gone down to join the Thrales at their house in Brighton, and found that owing to a misunderstanding they had returned to London without letting him know. He was annoyed and expressed his annoyance in a letter, but Murphy was brought in as peacemaker and explained that Henry Thrale had decided to stand for Parliament on the sudden death of one of the sitting members, and that Hester, who was pregnant, needed to consult her doctors; so they had returned sooner than they had expected. Johnson was entirely mollified by the explanation and the new friendship expanded more rapidly than ever. Now, the Thrales visited him in the close and stifling air of Johnson's Court. As they arrived, already alarmed by what they had heard of his condition, they found Johnson taking his leave of a friend named John Delap, who had been visiting him and was just departing. He begged Delap's prayers so urgently that his new visitors were much moved; and, when Delap had gone, broke into lamentations and self-accusations so violent that Thrale, a stolid and unimaginative man, could stand it no longer and clapped his hand over Johnson's mouth. Presently, Thrale left to attend to his manifold business; but he charged Hester to persuade Johnson to come down to the house at Streatham and stay there, in clean air and tranquillity, till he was recovered.

So began the closest relationship of Johnson's life, with the single exception of his relationship with Tetty. Left alone with him, Hester Thrale spoke consolation and encouragement, offered help and companionship, and very soon had Johnson in a coach, travelling towards Streatham and the comfort of a large, well-run house.

Next to the award of his pension, getting to know the Thrales was the greatest piece of material good fortune in Johnson's life. For seventeen years this wealthy couple unstintingly shared with him their material advantages. Indeed, their friendship benefited him in much the same ways as his pension. It prolonged his life, improved his health, smoothed away some of his worries, provided him with a good library, a good table and good company. For all these things Johnson was ungrudgingly grateful. The contribution that he could make to the life of the household – and it was no mean contribution – he made without reserve. And when, in the end, the relationship crumbled and his comfortable world fell about his ears, he accepted the suffering of that loss in the same spirit.

But on that first afternoon, in the coach jogging towards Streatham, Johnson cannot have looked so far ahead. All he knew, for the moment, was that he had fallen bruised and exhausted beside the hard road of life, and that kind hands had picked him up.

CHAPTER 21

The Two Families

Henry Thrale belonged to a type familiar enough in England, the prosperous tradesman with the education of a gentleman. Like many such men he had political ambitions, which his money enabled him to indulge. His father, Ralph Thrale, was the archetype of the industrious apprentice who rises to wealth and influence; he went into the family business, which was brewing, and proved so capable that in early middle life he bought the brewery for £30,000 and proceeded to make a large fortune out of it. His only son, Henry, and Henry's three sisters, grew up with all the advantages that money could buy. After Oxford he went on the Grand Tour, his companion being William Henry Lyttelton, later Lord Westcote; thereafter, for some years, he devoted himself to the pursuit of enjoyment until, on his father's death in 1758, he suddenly threw himself into the business of managing the large brewery at Southwark, with a wholeheartedness that took by surprise some of the friends who had known him only on the tiles.

At the time of his marriage Thrale was thirty-three or thirty-four years old, reasonably good-looking and personable and with a firm and decided manner. He was selfish but no more so than most young men from a moneyed background who have never been encouraged to be anything else. Virginia Woolf spitefully calls him 'a cold, callous, conventional man of business who aped the habits of the aristocracy but was without their distinction, who had the grossness of the middle class but lacked their geniality'. But this is very much a Bloomsbury verdict and about as reliable as such verdicts generally were. The gay and witty Arthur Murphy found Henry Thrale an acceptable companion, and not merely because of his money-bags; and Johnson always expressed respect for him. Thrale was, indeed, one of the very few people who could shut Johnson up. In the middle of a disquisition at table he would break in with 'There, that will be enough for one lecture, Dr Johnson' – and get away with it.

The choice of a wife was not an easy business for Henry Thrale. He needed a woman of good social background, and the intelligence and vivacity to make a hostess; yet she must not be too proud to spend some of her time at the house he owned in Southwark, next door to the brewery with its noise and smell – even if she spent most of it in the statelier atmosphere of Streatham. In the end he chose fortunately and wisely. Hester Lynch Salusbury was a Welsh girl of high descent. She traced her lineage on both sides to Henry Tudor, 'the Rose of Anglesey', and (also on both sides) to Katherine de Beraine, whose fertility with a rapid succession of husbands earned her the proud title of 'Mam Cymru', the Mother of Wales. With all this, Hester had a simple country upbringing and had never been accustomed to riches. Her parents, and a doting grandfather, had encouraged her precocious literary tastes, and she was educated far beyond the usual female standard of her day, reading widely in Latin, French and Italian – though not, it seems, in Welsh.

At the time of her marriage Hester was twenty-two years old; tiny (not quite five feet tall, and of slight build); vivacious; eager for life. Her existence, however, was narrow and rather dull. Thrale did not allow her to concern herself with the running of the household; he paid people to do that. He also forbade her favourite outdoor amusement of horse-riding, as being too dangerous; though we know she took it up in later years because in 1774 she was heavily thrown and carried a scar on her face for ever afterwards. Frustrated, she turned to her books and her children. The latter soon began to arrive. Her first, Hester Maria, was born in 1763, and for the next dozen years she was more or less continually pregnant.

Pregnancy, however, is a poor amusement for a young woman who spends a lot of time at home, and there can be no doubt that the irruption of Johnson into her household was a blessing to her and that she regarded it as such.

As for Johnson, the benefit to him was immediate and enormous. Not since the golden days when Walmesley had made him free of the magnificent Palace in Lichfield Close had he been familiarly in and out of such a splendid home. The meaningless jumble which is today known, with appropriate hideousness, as 'Tooting Bec' was then the quiet country village of Streatham. Some six miles from the centre of London, it was reached by traversing wide commons, on which highwaymen lurked. (One of them had had the temerity to rob Henry Thrale and had been caught and hanged for his pains.) There, amid an estate of a hundred acres, stood Henry Thrale's handsome and comfortable residence, variously known as 'Streatham Place' and 'Streatham Park'. By either name it was a very dear place to Johnson. He had his own room there; he was consulted on the purchase of books for the library (for which Reynolds painted a series of portraits); he kept a patriarchal eye on the growth of the family, forming a specially close link with the eldest child, Hester Maria, whom he nicknamed 'Queen Hester' and then 'Queeney', which became her family name from then on. In the Thrales' kitchen garden he indulged his passion for 'wall fruit'; at their table he did himself well; he joked and laughed and was affectionate. People who knew him only at Streatham found him relaxed, benign, humorous. Fanny Burney met him there in 1777, and left a portrait of him in her diary which is almost entirely sunny. Without it, we should scarcely guess at the prolonged spells of ease and geniality when Johnson's melancholia and irritability seemed like a bad dream.

The Thrales were perfect hosts. Everything that could be done for Johnson's comfort and convenience was done without question. They also had the sense to spare themselves, where possible, the drawbacks of having so incorrigible a Bohemian in their house. Johnson's short sight caused him to read with a candle perilously close to his forehead; his wigs, as a result, were always scorched in front. The Thrales soon trained a footman to wait beside the door with a fresh wig, and, when the Doctor came down to dinner, put it unobtrusively into his hand.

Streatham also meant family life. Johnson loved children, and concerned himself in every detail of the upbringing of the Thrale family – those who survived, that is, for Hester was even more unlucky than most women of that epoch in the number of her children who died in infancy. He took part in all those domestic celebrations and giggling family games that seem nothing much at the time but, when they are gone past recall, tug so hard at our heartstrings. One day they amused themselves by deciding which animal each member of their circle most resembled, and Johnson was not at all put out when they cast him as the elephant.

The Thrales did more. They improved Johnson's health by encouraging him to take exercise. From their house in Brighton, he sallied forth to bathe in the sea and even to ride to hounds. The latter, he maintained, was a poor sort of entertainment; he found the dogs stupid and the men hardly less so; still, like most literary men, he was glad to be praised for any kind of active prowess, and was pleased when one gentleman remarked, 'Why, Johnson rides as well, for aught I see, as the most illiterate fellow in England.'

Thus, as if by magic, the circumstances of Johnson's life were transformed. Not that even the kindly ministrations of the Thrales could altogether turn his bad health into good. By the time he met them it was too late for that; the destructive nervous patterns were too deeply ingrained, and his years were advancing. His diaries, during the 1770s, revert again and again to his physical sufferings. In Easter Week 1770 he records that he has lately been tormented by 'lumbago, or rheumatism in the loins, which often passes to the belly, where it causes equal, if not greater, pain'. In warm, sunny weather the pain eased but it generally recurred at night; he would lie wrapped in flannel and with a 'very great fire' burning near his bed, but even this would not prevent his having to get up every couple of hours and roast his belly in front of the flames. He records the various methods by which he fought back at his affliction – blister poultices, opium, blood-letting. For all his piety, there was in Johnson no trace of the mystical resignation of the mediaeval saint, who accepted sores and diseases as part of God's mysterious bounty. Johnson, offspring of the English Midlands, believed firmly that God helped those who helped themselves. If a remedy existed it was ungrateful not to use it. Not all the ills of frail humanity could be remedied, but some of them could, and it was up to every man to keep himself healthy and active. So the battle went on, with a running commentary in his diary.

Either the hot bath or the derivation by the cups eased me for two nights, but last night the pain was great and the necessity of rising frequent.

There follows a typically Johnsonian reflection:

The pain harasses me much, yet many have the disease perhaps in a much higher degree with want of food, fire, and covering, which I find thus grievous with all the succour that riches and kindness can buy and give.

Just as Johnson's increasing importance in the world never made him less appreciative of old friendships dating from humbler days, so the opulence and comfort of his surroundings at the Thrales never caused him to forget that the mass of humanity lived in sweat and poverty. Always Johnson kept the poor and the unfortunate in his thoughts. Indeed during the Streatham years he gave striking proof of this by the protective and patient care he took of his 'family'.

The Thrales would have been only too glad if Johnson had given up his house in Fleet Street and resided permanently with them. But this he never even contemplated. After leaving the house in Gough Square which still stands and is familiar as 'Dr Johnson's house', he had lived for some years in rooms or in chambers in the Inns of Court, but in 1765 he took a house, No. 7 Fleet Street, otherwise known as Johnson's Court. (The name is not due to his residing there; it is a simple coincidence.) Here, he took back Anna Williams, whom he had accommodated elsewhere during his years without a house; and with her a miscellaneous crowd of pensioners who had nothing in common except that they were all poor and all quarrelsome. Apart from Frank Barber, who was young and sprightly and increasingly a ladies' man, everyone in the house was old and broken-winded. Blind Miss Williams, the widow Desmoulins, morose old Levet, and a woman named Poll Carmichael whom Johnson tersely characterized as 'a stupid slut' lived in a state of ferocious mutual hostility. As Johnson wrote once to Hester Thrale, 'Williams hates everybody, Levet hates Desmoulins and does not love Williams; Desmoulins hates them both; Poll loves none of them.' He was, he declared, positively afraid to go home, because of the storm of complaints that greeted him on the doorstep. Nevertheless, he went. Every Saturday he left Streatham, gritted his teeth and entered the dingy, gloomy house, to preside there until Monday. In this way he saw to it that his pensioners had three good dinners in the seven days. The rest of the week they got by on a fixed allowance that he left with them.

Johnson never made the claim that his dependants were more than ordinarily deserving people. They had drifted into his life by one route or another, and they stayed there because – excellent reason! – he could not imagine how else they could be provided for. As Hawkins put it, wonderingly:

When asked by one of his most intimate friends how he could bear to be surrounded by such necessitous and undeserving people as he had about him, his answer was, 'If I did not assist them, no one else would, and they must be lost for want.'

The picture was not altogether black. Though the household was a gloomy one ('There is as much malignity amongst us', wrote Johnson once, 'as can well subsist, without any thoughts of daggers or poisons'), he took genuine pleasure in Levet's company; the two men breakfasted together and this made Johnson's habitual point of departure for the day. Anna Williams, too, had a well-stocked and lively mind which went far to compensate for her fiery temper.

We may go further. Johnson's patient care for these ailing and peevish fellow-creatures answered a profound instinctive need within him. We are not in the least detracting from his disinterested generosity if we recognize the fact. He enjoyed and accepted the blessings which his fame had brought him, financial independence and the comfort of living in the bosom of a rich, lively and interesting family. But poverty, illness and misfortune were to him bedrock facts of life, and he felt saner and stronger as long as he kept bedrock facts well in sight. He was Michael Johnson's son, Nathaniel Johnson's brother, the friend of Savage and Collins. His goodness of heart needs no further demonstration than the bare facts of his life provide. The sheer number of people he helped and the variety of ways in which he helped them easily entitle him to be called one of the most benevolent men who ever lived. From the young men for whom he tried to get jobs, and the needy writers for whom he wrote prefaces and dedications, to the fever-ridden prostitute he found slumped in a doorway in the early hours of one morning, and slung across his shoulders and carried home and nursed back to health Johnson gave his resources of time, of energy, of money, with no sparing hand. No one is in any doubt about that. But it is also true that if his helpless, bickering dependants needed him he also needed them. Hester Thrale saw it clearly enough. She knew that the comforts of Streatham, the conversation of the learned and polished, did not fully meet the demands of Johnson's nature. Years later, when Boswell's *Life* came out, she read it eagerly and annotated her copy; and by the side of one of the many passages which show Johnson's faithfulness to old and undistinguished friends, she wrote, 'Ever sighing for the tea and bread-and-butter of life, when satiated with the turtle and burgundy of it.'

One way and another a good deal of Johnson's time and energy, during these middle years, went on helping those about him who got themselves into scrapes. Frank Barber was a worry; he ran away and joined the navy, and Johnson had to write a letter to one of the Lords of the Admiralty begging for his discharge; he went with Johnson into the country one winter, and cut such a swath among the rustic beauties that one of them followed him back to London and made difficulties; after his marriage to an English girl named Betsy, he threw tantrums because the footmen at Streatham flirted with her. Even crabbed old Levet was not beyond the reach of the softer emotions, though in his case, as befitted his years, they were intermingled with the love of a guinea. He fell into the company of a woman whom Johnson, in a letter, described laconically as 'a street walker'. Despite the fact that their habitual place of tryst was a small coalshed in Fetter Lane, the wench managed to get Levet to accept her story that she was closely related to a wealthy man who refused to hand over her rightful share of his money; while Levet, not to be upstaged, represented himself, despite his fondness for coalsheds, as a physician in a flourishing way of business. They were married; within four months Levet was served a writ for debts incurred by his wife. He managed to avoid paying anything, and soon afterwards Mrs Levet was arrested for picking pockets at the Old Bailey. Levet declared his intention of going to her trial in the hope that she would be hanged; was with difficulty dissuaded; and the couple parted for ever.

Even worse befell Johnson's friend Baretti. One October evening in 1769 he was on his way back to Soho from the Orange coffee house, Haymarket, when a woman who was sitting on a doorstep jumped up and struck him. The choleric Baretti hit her back, whereupon three ruffians who were lounging nearby set upon him. He tried to escape but, being clumsily built and extremely short-sighted, made poor headway, and meanwhile the cry had gone up that a damn'd Frenchman had insulted a woman, and a crowd was gathering. One man made repeated grabs at Baretti's pigtail; in desperation Baretti struck at him with a small knife he carried for peeling fruit. The blow was an unlucky one, inflicting a wound from which the man later died. Baretti escaped by rushing into a shop and saying that he wished to give himself up to the police.

He was imprisoned in Newgate to await trial. Johnson and Burke visited him there, and in sturdy eighteenth-century fashion cautioned him against being optimistic of acquittal. 'Why', said Baretti, standing between them and taking a hand of each, 'what can he fear, that holds two such hands as I do?' Another visitor was a rival teacher of Italian, who asked Baretti to write letters of recommendation to his pupils, explaining that he meant to take them on after Baretti's execution. 'You rascal,' was the reply, 'if I were not *in my own apartment*, I would kick you downstairs directly.'

When the trial took place at the Old Bailey on 20 October, the defence called an extraordinary array of character witnesses who testified to Baretti's peaceable and humane nature. Burke, Garrick, Beauclerk, Johnson, Reynolds and Goldsmith went in turn into the box. Johnson, speaking in a loud, deliberate voice, described Baretti as 'a man of literature, a very studious man, a man of great diligence. He gets his living by study. I have no reason to think that he was ever disordered with liquor in his life. A man that I never knew to be otherwise than peaceable, and a man that I take to be rather timorous.' Garrick and Beauclerk, in their testimony, emphasized particularly that Baretti had not been carrying an offensive weapon; everyone on the Continent carried such knives, for in foreign inns only forks were laid with the food. 'When you travel abroad', Garrick was asked, 'do you carry such knives as this?' 'Yes', he replied, 'or we should have no victuals.' Baretti was acquitted and discharged.

Johnson's abundant kindliness and benevolence were manifested inside the Streatham household as well as outside it. He took an affectionate interest in the family; Henry Thrale he called 'Master', Hester 'Mistress'; Hester's mother, who lived there, was 'honoured Madam', Queeney was 'little Miss'. He encouraged Hester's literary ambitions, composed extempore verses for her, gave her hours of companionship and talk. Undoubtedly she found happiness in the relationship. She had no time to be bored; not only Johnson but Johnson's friends were perpetually about her; Streatham became a second base for the Club. And yet . . . there is always a yet. She was a young woman; her husband did not love her, and though she was a dutiful wife it cannot be said that she loved him. Children kept arriving, but all the good medical attention that money could buy seemed powerless to prolong their little lives. Out of eleven only four survived their infancy, and each death was a new heartbreak. Two babies died of mastoid infection; a young boy suffering from appendicitis was treated by being immersed in water as hot as he could bear; he died within a few hours. Johnson did what he could to console her. He shared with her all the experience that life had brought him in the art of coping with grief. Almost, it was enough.

But it was not quite enough. She hungered and thirsted so much for life, and her deeper needs were not met. Good friend though Johnson was, the wise old elephant from whom she drew much comfort and strength, she could never confide in him the emptiness she carried in her heart. He would console her on the death of a child; but, childless himself, he could hardly sound the depths of her woman's agony. As for her other recurring sorrow, Thrale's want of love for her and his habit of keeping mistresses, she could hardly confide this to Johnson, who took a very eighteenth-century view of marriage. When Boswell, on 10 October 1779, mentioned 'a friend' (himself, perhaps?) who had had a dispute with his wife on the subject of infidelity, 'which my friend had maintained was by no means so bad in the husband, as in the wife', Johnson replied, 'Your friend was in the right, Sir. Between a man and his Maker it is a different question: but between a man and his wife, a husband's infidelity is nothing. They are connected by children, by fortune, by serious considerations of community. Wise married women don't trouble themselves about infidelity in their husbands.' And in a cancelled earlier draft of his book Boswell went on to record how Johnson confided in him, 'My wife told me I might lie with as many women as I pleased, provided I loved her alone.' When Boswell doubted whether Tetty had been in earnest, Johnson insisted, 'But she was. Consider, Sir, how gross it is in a wife to complain of her husband's going to other women, merely as women; it is that she has not enough of what she would be ashamed to avow.' With sentiments like these, Johnson was perfectly prepared to allow to Henry Thrale a licence that he certainly would not, with his tender conscience, have allowed to himself. Thrale's being a whoremaster seems to have made no difference at all to Johnson's regard for him. The pain of being neglected for a succession of girls was one that Hester had to bear alone.

More: she had to conceal her grief and depression as much as she possibly could. All men, in the end, make impossible demands on women, and Johnson's demands on Hester Thrale were no exception. He told her of his own anxiety and misery, but he did not like having to hold still while she told him of hers. He clutched at her hand while walking through the valleys of his own private Inferno; she had to walk through hers alone. This is the great contrast between Johnson's relationship with Hester Thrale and his relationship with Boswell. Johnson listened for hours at a time to Boswell's confessions and emotional outpourings. But when he was with Mrs Thrale it was his turn to do the talking. When he was in one of his fits of depression, he resented it if she was slow to pull him out. Once, when he was lying in bed in a state of gloom, she came into the room in a gown of some drab colour. He snarled at her, asking if she were trying to depress him still further. Later, half ashamed, he tried to turn the matter aside with a joke. 'What', he growled, 'have not all insects gay colours?'

All insects do not, of course, have gay colours. The remark is useful in indicating the role that Johnson wanted Hester to play in his life. He wanted her to be a butterfly, or perhaps a gaily spotted ladybird to walk over the back of his hand and bring him luck. She was neither; she was a woman, crying out in the silence of her own mind against the frustration of her deep needs.

This demand that Johnson made on Hester – that while he might be sometimes in the darkness she must be perpetually in the sunshine – probably had deeper and darker roots in his emotional relationship with her. We shall probe those roots at the appropriate point in our story. For the moment, what concerns us is that the relationship he imposed on her was one that she found, in the end, impossible to sustain. She was a deeply suffering woman; he failed to respond to her suffering or to recognize the emptiness at the centre of her life. Years later, this failure of perception was to isolate him in an irremediably false position *vis-à-vis* her, and the result was to be the greatest emotional shock of his life.

But that was in the future. Meanwhile, the good meals and the good talk went on, the bright fires danced in the grates, the footman attentively handed him his fresh wig at the dining-room door, and the sun shone on the lawns and flowerbeds and fruit trees of Streatham Place, and peered in at the windows of the summerhouse where Johnson sat talking so memorably to his friends; and the disaster that was to come, the disaster that in all unconsciousness he was preparing for himself, slept in its causes.

CHAPTER 22

'The Great Republic of Human Nature'

Johnson was easy at the Thrales'. Which is not to say that he was idle. During the late sixties and seventies of the century, which were his own late fifties and sixties, he got through a respectable amount of work. By smoothing his path materially, Hester and her husband released a great deal of energy which went into thinking and writing as well as into enjoying himself.

Already, in the year in which the Thrales took him up, Johnson was involved in an undertaking which called out his full powers and took up the slack of his extraordinary erudition. The origin, as so often, was a good-natured impulse to help someone. Robert Chambers, one of Johnson's Oxford friends, whom he remembered as a seventeen-year-old undergraduate at Lincoln College, had pursued the academic study of the law to such purpose that the University had appointed him Vinerian Professor. (Viner, a scholar who published an encyclopaedic abridgment of the laws of England, gave his name to a professorship, which has survived, and to a course of lectures, which has not.) It was the lectures that worried Chambers. He knew he had to make a success of them; but his predecessor was the famous Blackstone, and he shrank from the inevitable comparison. Johnson gave him timely encouragement. 'Come up to town', he wrote in December, 'and lock yourself up from all but me, and I doubt not but lectures will be produced.' Indeed they were, and with such a massive contribution from Johnson that the work can be regarded as a collaboration.

The Vinerian Lectures delivered by Chambers run to sixteen hundred pages. The extent of Johnson's involvement in this enormous work was never guessed until an American scholar, Mr E. L. McAdam, in his *Dr Johnson and the English Law* (1951), performed the invaluable service of working through the whole mass and extracting those passages which were, on internal evidence, obviously from Johnson's pen. In addition, of course, to writing large sections, Johnson must have discussed with Chambers the range and scope of the series and its overall plan.

The lectures generally, and Johnson's identifiable contributions in particular, shed a wonderful light on the strength of Johnson's mind and the richness of his knowledge. At every turn there are passages which give his basic position on important issues of law and government. Almost at random we may select two. The first concerns kingship. Johnson was entirely rationalistic about this; he considered the monarchy, as it had developed in his own day, as merely a sensible bargain. His opinion of 'divine right' may be inferred from a passage in the lecture 'The King and his Coronation Oath':

> In that age of prejudice and ignorance, when the civil institutions were yet few, and the securities of legal obligation were very weak, both because offences against the law were often unpunished and because the law itself could be but little known, it was necessary to invest the king with something of a sacred character that might secure obedience by reverence and more effectually preserve his person from danger of violation. For this reason it was necessary to interpose the clerical authority, that the crown being imposed by a holy hand might communicate some sanctity to him that wore it. And, accordingly, the inauguration of a king is by our ancient historians termed consecration; and the writings, both fabulous and historical, of the Middle Ages connect with royalty some supernatural privileges and powers.

Such as touching for the King's Evil! This was the mature Johnson's verdict on his confused but solemn childhood memory of the 'old lady in black, wearing diamonds', who had laid royal hands on his diseased infant body. The other quotation concerns not a historical survival but an urgent contemporary problem, the rights and obligations of colonists. To the lecture on the government of Ireland and the American provinces, Johnson contributed some memorable passages; for instance:

> No man has a right to any good without partaking of the evil by which that good is necessarily produced; no man has a right to security by another's danger, nor to plenty by another's labour, but as he gives something of his own which he who meets the danger or undergoes the labour considers as equivalent; no man has a right to the security of government without bearing his share of its inconveniences.
>
> Those who increase the expenses of the public ought to supply their proportion of the expenses increased. The payment of fleets and armies may be justly required from those for whose protection fleets and armies are employed. No state intends to place its colonies in a condition superior to its own, to afford protection without the return of obedience, or to be satisfied with obedience so easy and unexpensive as every man suffered to be his own judge would prescribe to himself. If by forsaking our native country we could carry away all its happiness and leave its evils behind, what human being would not wish for exile?

But to convey the breadth of Johnson's thinking in these lectures, we should have to quote for pages. As Mr McAdam sums it up,

> The range of subjects which he touched on is highly characteristic – revealed law and human, customary law, the disappearance of ancient British law, origins of feudalism, the codes of Alfred and Edward the

Confessor, the general character of feudal law and of common law, scepticism a requisite for historical inquiry, the implications of the coronation oath, royal power and medieval trade, the maxim that the king can do no wrong, forfeiture of estates for treason, the origins of the Commons and the Privy Council, courts of equity, local magistracy, civil rank and precedence, the Union with Scotland, taxation of colonies, the general nature of punishment, the medieval clergy as preservers of civilisation, the laws against exportation of specie, forgery, divorce, villenage, recoveries, and the use of books by a law student.

On all this astonishing range of topics he gave Chambers the fruit of his thinking and reading, and many pages of his writing too; partly out of pure goodness of heart, and partly as a labour of love. And this was the Johnson who said, 'No man but a blockhead ever wrote for anything but money'!

Not that he neglected paid work. Another substantial task to which he sat down in the early years of his domestication with the Thrales was a complete revision of his Dictionary. He was working on this from the summer of 1771 to the autumn of 1772, and the revised edition – the fourth – was published in 1773. Johnson celebrated the completion of the work, in December, with a poignantly confessional poem in Latin, in which he put into stately verse his inward doubts and misgivings. But that was a private utterance. The public side of his mind, during these years, was confident and strong. It was, also, more relaxed than formerly. There was no longer any need for Johnson to be a hungry fighter, intent always on establishing a reputation and outclassing the opposition. The marks of this relaxation can be seen, charmingly, in the fourth edition of the Dictionary. As David Nichol Smith remarked, 'No doubt the first edition of the Dictionary will always command the higher price in the auction-room; but the fourth has more to tell us than the first.' In particular, it shows Johnson relaxing the severity of his self-imposed rule not to quote from his contemporaries. In the preface to the first edition he had explained that to avoid the appearance of partiality he had decided to quote from no author of his own day except 'when some performance of uncommon excellence excited my veneration, when my memory supplied me from late books with an example that was wanting, or when my heart, in the tenderness of friendship, solicited admission for a favourite name'.

As we saw, he allowed several contemporaries, including himself in a few instances, through this mesh. But in the fourth edition the roll-call of contemporaries is much wider. He had made new friends during the intervening years, and his heart 'solicited admission' for several of them. Beattie of Aberdeen, a lively minded philosopher who, like Tom Warton, also demonstrated his sensibilities in verse, had the pleasure of seeing his *Essay on Truth* quoted, and his poem *The Minstrel* used to illustrate the word 'no', though it had already been illustrated quite sufficiently. Under 'bosom' Johnson quoted from Gray's *Elegy*; under 'sport' he quoted no fewer than six lines from a poem called *Boulter's Monument*, by one Samuel Madden – a poem which had never achieved fame in the world but which stuck in Johnson's memory for the very good reason that Madden had consulted him as to how it should be improved, and paid him ten guineas for his pains at a time when a guinea was a rarity with him. (This notion of having a consultant critic and paying him as one pays a doctor or dentist has always seemed to me an excellent one.) Perhaps the most endearing of Johnson's new quotations is the one that occurs under 'grater'. In the first edition he had provided no illustration at all for his definition of this humble domestic implement, 'a kind of coarse file with which soft bodies are rubbed to powder'. Now he gave in its entirety a pleasant little poem by Aaron Hill, familiar to many generations of English children:

> Tender-handed touch a nettle,
>   And it stings you for your pains,
> Grasp it like a man of mettle,
>   And it soft as silk remains.
> So it is with human natures,
>   Treat them gently, they rebel
> But be rough as nutmeg graters,
>   And the rogues obey you well.

Clearly, there was no utilitarian reason for giving all this space to illustrate 'grater'. Johnson simply yielded to the amiable temptation to plant a little flower beside the dusty highway of lexicography.

During these years, however, most of the ideas that issued in rapid succession from Johnson's 'quick forge and working-house of thought' were not literary or scholarly, but political. He allowed himself, during the seventies, to be drawn more and more directly into political discussion. Some of this may have been due to the proximity of Henry Thrale, who had political ambitions and was, as we noted, a Member of Parliament for fifteen years. Johnson wrote election publicity for him and no doubt listened to his accounts of what went on in the House. There was even talk, at one stage, of Johnson's standing for Parliament himself. His friend Strahan the printer, who was himself a Member, wrote a letter to one of the Secretaries of the Treasury in which he recommended Johnson to the Government as a Parliamentary candidate; and he gave a copy to Boswell, who inserted it under the appropriate date, 30 March 1771. The affair has remained something of a mystery; as Boswell remarks, Strahan would hardly have taken such a step unless Johnson had been willing to proceed; but Boswell never heard Johnson allude to the matter, and the whole business seems to have gone quietly to sleep. But his interest in political matters continued high, and in the 1770s he wrote four political pamphlets, which we shall come to in a moment. First, a few words on his general position.

When Johnson remarked in Boswell's presence (31 March 1772) that he 'would not give half a guinea to live under one system of government rather than another', he was hardly to foresee that this throw-off, duly recorded by his disciple, would become one of his most often quoted sayings and would give many people the impression that the art of government was one in which he took no interest. In fact, he took an alert interest in all political and social matters. No primitivist, he cared little about the picturesque habits of men in undeveloped societies; it was the large, complex, wide-ranging systems of government that he wanted to know about, as they existed in Christendom and Islam. (He seems, like most of his contemporaries, to have had very little sense of the Far East.)

Not that the remark about half a guinea was altogether without meaning. Johnson believed that good government was important, but that great areas of human life lay outside the scope of any government, good and bad. In the lines he contributed to his friend Goldsmith's poem *The Traveller* occurs the couplet,

> How small, of all that human hearts endure,
> That part which laws or kings can cause or cure.

In this, he was merely being honest. One of the ways in which human beings can be divided up is that some of them are capable of pinning their total faith in a 'system' and others are not. All of us know the man (or, just as frequently, the woman) who maintains, and appears sincerely to believe, that if only this or that political system were to swallow all its rivals and prevail the millennium would arrive immediately. What makes the rest of us faintly suspicious is not that we have cut-and-dried counter-arguments but merely that we do not believe that any political system, by itself, can make humanity entirely fulfilled and contented. Some forms of government, obviously, are better than others; now and then tyrannies arise which are too bad to be changed and simply have to be escaped from or overthrown; but, over most of the earth at most times, the difference is not all that great. No matter who is in power at the top, one's own struggle goes on.

The notion of Johnson's sturdy indifference to political niceties is simply part of the caricature of him that has been current for some two hundred years. A similar fate has befallen his historical thinking. We know that Johnson was impatient of certain kinds of niggling historical discussion; he is on record with several trenchant and colourful expressions of impatience with people who bored him in this manner; how one man insisted on talking to him about the Catiline conspiracy until he 'withdrew his attention, and thought about Tom Thumb'; how he 'never wished to hear about the Second Punic War as long as he lived', etc., etc. In fact Johnson's attitude to the study of history was much the same as Tolstoy's. The mere scribble of historical fact and anecdote irritated Tolstoy into that entertaining grumble quoted in Sir Isaiah Berlin's *The Hedgehog and the Fox*:

> History is nothing but a collection of fables and useless trifles, cluttered up with a mass of unnecessary figures and proper names. The death of Igor, the snake which bit Oleg – what is all this but old wives' tales? Who wants to know that Ivan's second marriage, to Temryuk's daughter, occurred on 21 August 1562, whereas his fourth, to Anna Alekseyevna Koltovskaya, occurred in 1572. . . ?

Tolstoy's essential concern with history, with the backward look that modifies the object, is of course obvious in his novels. Similarly with Johnson. From the noble defence of historical study in *Rasselas* (Chapter 30), and the intimate acquaintance with English historians such as Knolles and Raleigh shown in *The Rambler* and the Dictionary, his concern with growth and development, with the way a society puts itself together and the ideas that slowly accumulate to make up its instinctive, scarcely conscious view of itself, lasted all his life. In old age he gave to Bennet Langton, who gave it to the King, a list of his projected studies: themes and topics in which he had a special interest and into all of which he had enquired at one time and another. The list, which Boswell prints under November 1784, should be pondered in its entirety by anyone interested in taking the measure of Johnson's mind; but for our present purposes we may note particularly those items which Johnson's lifelong concern for historicity, his interest in the way a nation, or a civilization, or a set of conventions in literature and art, forms itself by adding cell to cell. Thus:

> History of Criticism as it relates to judging of authors, from Aristotle to the present age. An account of the rise and improvements of that art; of the different opinions of authors, ancient and modern.

And:

> History of the Revival of Learning in Europe, containing an account of whatever contributed to the restoration of literature; such as controversies, printing, the destruction of the Greek empire, the encouragement of great men, with the lives of the most eminent patrons and most eminent early professors of all kinds of learning in different countries.

These are not the schemes of a man indifferent to history. Johnson saw his own epoch in historical terms, as having been brought into being by the Renaissance – what he called 'the Revival of Learning' – that great event or series of events which had altered everything and from which he dated his world as the Romantics of the nineteenth century dated their world from the French Revolution or as we date ours from 1914.

Johnson was interested, then, in politics, in history, in everything that goes to explain the way men get themselves together in societies. He enquired; he compared; he put these matters into perspective; in a word, despite the caricature of him as an amusingly irascible bundle of prejudices, he approached political and social issues very much with his mind rather than with his passions. (Though where the mind was the passions very readily followed.) His view of government was remarkably cool, even prosaic. To him, it was a matter of convenience. Men banded together in societies because by so doing they could the more easily supply their wants, protect their property, and defend themselves against outside enemies. He was equally without a trace of the mystique of the conservative or of the progressive. Not for him the rosy myth that man is perfectible, that nothing is needed save to throw off the yoke of outworn institutions and mistaken policies, and allow the natural goodness of man to take over. On the other hand, neither did he believe in the divine right of kings nor in the quasi-mystical forms of authoritarianism. He was a Tory in the sense that he believed in obeying the existing power rather than leapfrogging into an undefinable future. A devout Christian, he channelled his Christianity into the prescribed and traditional forms rather than into any kind of Nonconformism. For the rest, his Toryism was hardly a strictly defined political creed, still less a straitjacket. In an age when most people who had any influence (including most of his own friends) were Whigs, it suited Johnson to describe himself as a Tory. It was a badge of independence, a signal to those about him that he could not be expected to see things their way.

Was Johnson, or was he not, a 'democrat'? We cannot begin to answer that question until we have grasped that full-scale popular democracy, in the modern sense, was in the eighteenth century hardly even envisaged as an ideal. The right to vote was to be hedged about with property qualifications for a long time yet; as for universal adult suffrage, irrespective of creed or sex, that did not come until after the First World War. Even the most fervent democrat of Johnson's day would seem authoritarian to many people in ours. The notion of government by consent of the governed was, to be sure, carried much further in England than in most other countries. But it was scarcely into its stride yet.

Johnson, for his part, believed in government by elected representatives while never overestimating what that particular system would produce in terms of contentment. In an election the majority wins; and if there is a sizeable minority a good many citizens have to put up with living under a system they did not choose. When the American settlers raised their cry of 'No taxation without representation', Johnson pointed out that if this principle held good for taxation it applied equally to every kind of law; and, if the settlers were going to disobey the law merely because they were too far away to send representatives to Parliament, what should be the attitude of those whose party had been defeated at the polls, or for that matter of the majority who did not get a chance to vote at all?

Johnson believed in order and stability, which produced benefits he could see and understand, rather than heady oratory about Liberty, which might well lead to mob rule. He was at the opposite pole from an anarchist; he believed that government was there to govern. On the other hand, there is no need to represent him as a vicious reactionary on the pattern of Sir Wolstan Dixie. Far from it. Having accepted a framework of authority, Johnson was firm that the authority should not go beyond stated bounds. A really wicked and cruel tyranny, he believed, would always be overthrown by the indignation of the people. During the same conversation in which he made the remark about not giving half a guinea to live under one form of government rather than another, he went on to elaborate:

When I say that all governments are alike, I consider that in no govern-ment power can be abused long. Mankind will not bear it. If a sovereign oppresses his people to a great degree, they will rise and cut off his head.

There is a remedy in human nature against tyranny, that will keep us safe under any form of government.

Although Johnson was no friend to the only major revolution that occurred in his day, the American War of Independence, he was, as this statement indicates, fully convinced of man's right to rise in arms against an intolerable yoke. His generous indignation was aroused by any authority which, however legitimate its basis in legality, abused its power at the expense of the people who were helpless in its grasp. His blood boiled when he thought of the slave trade. He once silenced an Oxford dinner-party by holding up his glass and saying, 'Here's to the next insurrection of the Negroes in the West Indies!'

This humanitarianism was at the root of his distrust of colonial expansion. Writing to a friend – an American friend, incidentally, Dr Samuel Johnson of Connecticut – he mentions the news of a voyage of arctic exploration, and adds, 'I do not much wish well to discoveries, for I am always afraid they will end in conquest and robbery.' The red man was dispossessed, the black man enslaved, nearer home the Hebridean crofter was starved into emigration, for no morally justifiable reason but merely because the minorities to which they belonged had no economic or military power. This detestation of expansionist colonial adventuring, which he saw simply as armed robbery, was a consistent position of Johnson's through the years. As long ago as the 1740s he had given it memorable expression in the *Life of Savage*. Savage, it appears, wrote a poem called 'On Public Spirit, with regard to Public Works'. I have not read this poem and have no intention of reading it, but from Johnson's account one gathers that in its ramble over a wide political and social territory it arrives at the subject of colonial expansion; and Savage, says Johnson magnificently,

> has not forgotten, amidst the pleasing sentiments which this prospect of retirement suggested to him, to censure those crimes which have been generally committed by the discoverers of new regions, and to expose the enormous wickedness of making war upon barbarous nations because they cannot resist, and of invading countries because they are fruitful; of extending navigation only to propagate vice, and of visiting distant lands only to lay them waste. He has asserted the natural equality of mankind, and endeavoured to suppress that pride which inclines men to imagine that right is the consequence of power.

Just as Johnson hated the 'conquest and robbery' inherent in colonialism, so he hated the repressive injustice of the eighteenth-century penal system. Though all should be equal before the law, the poor and ignorant man, then as now, always saw a harsher face of the law than the comfortable and educated; this, too, Johnson condemned.

Johnson's defence of 'subordination', of the hierarchical principle in society, is another facet that needs to be seen from an eighteenth-century rather than a modern angle. It sorts perfectly well with his temperamental egalitarianism. Rather than a straight plutocracy, a society in which all men are theoretically equal but in fact the man with the most money has the best of everything, Johnson favoured a society which preserved feudal ranks and distinctions, on the excellent ground that it cuts out squabbling and envy. As he remarked to Boswell (21 July 1763), 'there would be a perpetual struggle for precedence, were there no fixed invariable rules for the distinction of rank, which creates no jealousy, as it is allowed to be accidental'. Having accepted this as a principle, Johnson moved at ease over a remarkably wide social range. While allowing due importance to rank, he was entirely free of class consciousness in the modern sense.

Perhaps we are beginning now to form a picture of Johnson's political and social attitudes. Supporting authority but hating cruelty, preferring a measured harmony to an undignified scramble, he was unfailingly rationalistic and pragmatic. He kept his eye on the qualities which actually produced happiness in day-to-day life and not on transcendent theories. His ideal was a self-contained England, feeding itself by means of a thriving agriculture and improving the quality of life by manufacture and invention. He approved of the surge of mechanical progress that went on around him, and had a remarkable grasp of it in detail – so much so that Sir Richard Arkwright, the engineer, declared that Johnson was the only person who, at first sight, understood both the principle and the operation of one of his most complicated machines. On the other hand, his enthusiasm for new processes and improvements does not make him a premature cheerleader of the Industrial Revolution. The real change, the move from an agricultural to an industrial economy, did not come until Johnson had been dead for twenty years; his opinion of it, therefore, we can only conjecture. But it seems safe to guess that he would have disapproved of the injustice and suffering it brought in its wake. And, with his firm notions of social justice, he would hardly have tolerated the way industrialism poured huge fortunes into a few pockets while degrading the bulk of the working populace.

If I had to fix upon one word that would convey the heart of Johnson's attitude towards man in society, I would choose 'compassion'. He wanted an ordered, hierarchical society because he loathed the thought of the kind of scramble in which the weak inevitably go down. That, with rule and restraint weakened, society *would* be a cut-throat business was an assumption he made on the basis of his observation of human nature, including his own. Man was not, to Johnson, inherently gentle and unselfish. On the contrary. He was a creature full of anarchic and ravening instincts, which had to be controlled by the exercise of discipline both from within the individual and from without. When he was in the Hebrides he had a conversation with Lady M'Leod of Dunvegan, in which he maintained that unselfishness and regard for others, non-existent in a young child, are implanted by upbringing:

Lady M'Leod asked, if no man was naturally good? JOHNSON: No, madam, no more than a wolf. BOSWELL: Nor no woman, Sir? JOHNSON: No, Sir. Lady M'Leod started at this, saying, in a low voice, 'This is worse than Swift.'

Johnson, in fact, found it something of a matter for surprise that ordered societies should have come into being at all. His work with Chambers on the Vinerian Lectures was a valuable experience because it threw him back on basic definitions and issues of principle. In one of the passages he supplied to Chambers, Johnson gives – in one sombre, densely written sentence – his reasons for thinking that orderly, co-operative society is something of a miracle:

> When we consider in abstracted speculation the unequal distribution of the pleasures of life, when we observe that pride, the most general of all human passions, is gratified in one order of men only because it is ungratified in another and that the great pleasure of many possessions arises from the reflection that the possessor enjoys what multitudes desire, when it is apparent that many want the necessaries of nature, and many more the comforts and conveniences of life, that the idle live at ease by the fatigues of the diligent and the luxurious are pampered with delicacies untasted by those who supply them, when to him that glitters with jewels and slumbers in a palace multitudes may say what was said to Pompey, *Nostrâ miseriâ tu es magnus*, when the greater number must always want what the smaller are enjoying and squandering, enjoying often without merit and squandering without use, it seems impossible to conceive that the peace of society can long subsist; it were natural to expect that no man would be left long in possession of superfluous enjoyments while such numbers are destitute of real necessaries, but that the wardrobe of Lucullus should be rifled by the naked and the dainties of Apicius dispersed among the hungry, that almost every man should attempt to regulate that distribution which he thinks injurious to himself and supply his wants from the common stock.

But if peaceful and orderly social organization was a miracle it was a miracle that by some means or other must be kept up. Not only so that the rich could enjoy their wealth, not only so that the learned could assemble libraries, and the subtle could tease out their speculations; but also, and perhaps most of all, so that the poor and the average could have their chance at life, that Frank Barber could be redeemed from slavery and sent to school in England, that Catherine Chambers and Lucy Porter could drink tea in the parlour at Lichfield, that old Levet could mix ointments for coachmen's lumbago, that the anonymous people in the streets could have their share of the sunlight; for, as he remarked with his usual economy, 'a decent provision for the poor is the true test of civilization'.

These were Johnson's basic positions. He was to apply them, in vigorous controversial fashion, to specific issues and events in the four political pamphlets he wrote during the 1770s.

The decision to write these pamphlets was perhaps the most purely surprising of Johnson's life. For at least ten years he had been on a pedestal as the great lexicographer and moralist, the lawgiver on letters and on experience, above every conceivable battle. Now, suddenly, he descended into the arena and began laying about him. Many people were scandalized. This was not at all their notion of how Johnson should behave. Worse, his four utterances were all in support of Government policies. Had he gone back on his resolution not to earn his pension by party propaganda? Had someone got at him?

To this last question we may answer shortly, No. There is not a scrap of evidence that Johnson was under any pressure to write for his pension. He knew, of course, that the governments formed by the Duke of Grafton and by Lord North contained many people who would be glad if he did so; but knowing that someone will be glad if you do something is not 'pressure'. Johnson never condescended to explain his motive for going back, after a silence of years, into political controversy. Quite probably a large part of the motivation was sheer enjoyment, the love of a free-for-all. Controversy, after all, is quite enjoyable, to write as well as to read. Johnson was a master of polemic writing and his gift for it had begun to rust. Certainly, if the pamphlets of the 1770s had never been written, we should lack some of his most vigorous and exhilarating prose.

The first of the four is a case in point. *The False Alarm*, published at the beginning of 1770, is a defence of the House of Commons over the affair of Jack Wilkes. Wilkes, it will be remembered, was rejected by the House of Commons as an unsuitable member, on both political and moral grounds, although he had received more votes than his rival, Colonel Luttrell. Luttrell was declared Member for Middlesex, whereupon there was a tidal wave of popular indignation that finally put Wilkes into his seat. Johnson argues that the action of the House of Commons was constitutional, that Parliament has the right to make up its own mind and ought not to be influenced by shouting from the street. The pamphlet is interesting as marking the extreme point of Johnson's anti-populist feeling. His attitude is much the same as Shakespeare's; while allowing the inalienable human right to rise against a tyrant, he has no belief in the political wisdom of the populace. The business of government should be left to the more educated and thoughtful, which in practice means the better off. Anyone who is tempted to exaggerate the liberality and modernity of Johnson's political views will soon call off the attempt on reading *The False Alarm*. In our modern 'participatory democracy' he simply did not believe. The notion of popular intervention in government policy meant nothing to him but stark mob rule. It recalled the preaching tinkers and cobblers, the ragged philosophers of the seventeenth century, the rabble of fanatics who had done so much harm to the fabric of English life. A little later, in the *Lives of the Poets*, he was to write some very mordant satiric paragraphs about these people; but no more satiric than his description of how, in his own day, signatures were collected for a petition to the King. A crowd is gathered, speeches are made, everyone is worked up into a state of excitement and then the petition is read out, approved, and signed by those present who are literate enough to write and sober enough to hold a pen:

Every man goes home and tells his neighbour of the glories of the day;
how he was consulted and what he advised; how he was invited into the

great room, where his lordship called him by his name; how he ate turtle and venison, and drank unanimity to the three brothers.

The poor loiterer, whose shop had confined him, or whose wife had locked him up, hears the tale of luxury with envy, and at last inquires what was their petition. Of the petition nothing is remembered by the narrator, but that it spoke much of fears and apprehensions, and something very alarming, and that he is sure it is against the government; the other is convinced that it must be right, and wishes he had been there, for he loves wine and venison, and is resolved as long as he lives to be against the government.

The petition is then handed from town to town, and from house to house, and wherever it comes the inhabitants flock together, that they may see that which must be sent to the king. Names are easily collected. One man signs because he hates the papists; another because he has vowed destruction to the turnpikes; one because it will vex the parson; another because he owes his landlord nothing; one because he is rich; another because he is poor; one to show that he is not afraid, and another to show that he can write.

Of such rousing knockabout stuff is *The False Alarm* made up. It is worth reading not only for its exuberant prose (and very *plain* prose, for when Johnson is writing for a popular audience he is no longer 'Lexiphanes') but as a reminder that his deep humanitarianism did not spill over into democratic populism.

For some readers of our day, this by itself will be enough to condemn Johnson's political views as reactionary and paternalistic. So be it. He shared these attitudes with virtually everyone in his time; the difference in Johnson's case being that his attitude towards the unrepresented and unproppertied commonalty was not only compassionate but respectful. He liked and admired the very people he would bar from government. When he contemplated the ordinary Englishman of his day, he found a spirit, an energy, a courage, that impressed him. Characteristically, he set about assigning reasons for this. In his essay on 'The Bravery of the English Common Soldiers', he remarked that the decay of feudalism, whatever its disadvantages, had at least resulted in an upsurge of independence:

> The equality of English privileges, the impartiality of our laws, the freedom of our tenures and the prosperity of our trade dispose us very little to reverence of superiors. It is not to any great esteem of the officers that the English soldier is indebted for his spirit in the hour of battle; for perhaps it does not often happen that he thinks much better of his leader than of himself. The French count, who has lately published the *Art of War*, remarks how much soldiers are animated, when they see all their dangers shared by those who were born to be their masters, and whom they consider as beings of a different rank. The Englishman despises such motives of courage: he was born without a master; and looks not on any man, how-

ever dignified by lace or titles, as deriving from nature any claims to his respect, or inheriting any qualities superior to his own.

The year after *The False Alarm*, Johnson was in print again with *Thoughts on the Late Transactions respecting Falkland's Islands*. This isolated speck of territory had been disputed over by Spain and England; finally, with pragmatic good sense, England had agreed to regard the islands as under Spanish sovereignty while in practice they were settled and managed by the English. Johnson approved of this commonsense solution of a theoretical difficulty; he suspected that the only people who seriously opposed it would be those who for motives of their own would be glad to see the two countries go to war. In Johnson's time and for a hundred years afterwards, England was never free of a strong lobby who wanted military and naval action as a means of guaranteeing trade routes and opening up markets. Johnson, sickened at the thought of war and what it does to its victims, detested the warmongering profiteer and attacked him in some pages of invective that put *Thoughts on Falkland's Islands* in a direct line with the anti-war literature of the 1920s:

It is wonderful with what coolness and indifference the greater part of mankind see war commenced. Those that hear of it at a distance or read of it in books, but have never presented its evils to their minds, consider it as little more than a splendid game, a proclamation, an army, a battle and a triumph. Some indeed must perish in the most successful field, but they die upon the bed of honour, *resign their lives amidst the joys of conquest, and filled with England's glory, smile in death.*

The life of a modern soldier is ill represented by heroic fiction. War has means of destruction more formidable than the cannon and the sword. Of the thousands and ten thousands that perished in our late contests with France and Spain, a very small part ever felt the stroke of an enemy; the rest languished in tents and ships, amidst damps and putrefaction; pale, torpid, spiritless and helpless; gasping and groaning unpitied, among men made obdurate by long continuance of hopeless misery; and were at last whelmed in pits, or heaved into the ocean, without notice and without remembrance. By incommodious encampments and unwholesome stations, where courage is useless, and enterprise impracticable, fleets are silently dispeopled, and armies sluggishly melted away.

In 1774 came a third pamphlet, *The Patriot*, a straight piece of opposition-bashing which need not detain us. And finally, in 1775, the year in which he published his superb *Journey to the Western Islands of Scotland*, Johnson made his most notorious *pronunciamiento* in support of George III's government, his anti-American pamphlet, *Taxation No Tyranny*.

Here again we come to one of those Johnsonian indiscretions which have become part of the caricature of Sam John Bull. The one fact about Johnson's political opinions that 'everybody knows' is that he was against American independence. Looking back from the later twentieth century we can see readily enough what a hopeless position this was. But then we see a very different America from the one Johnson saw. We see an America transformed by wave after wave of total change; by the opening of the West, by the Civil War, by industrialism, by the waves of immigration from central and eastern Europe which tipped the ethnic balance and left America no longer an Anglo-Saxon country. And we have seen the climb of America to colossal, world-dominating wealth and power. To imagine that such a country might remain tied to the apron strings of England would be hilariously absurd. But Johnson looked not at the future but at the present. What he saw was a large empty country in which a tiny handful of planters were growing rich by lashing the backs of slaves. 'Why is it', he demanded, 'that we hear the loudest yelps for liberty from the drivers of Negroes?' His attitude towards the American settlers should be seen in terms of Algeria in the 1950s, when French public opinion began to feel that it was no longer morally justifiable for the *colons* to go on sweating wealth out of the natives in a country for which they felt no patriotism.

To Johnson, the American settlers were Englishmen living abroad who refused to pay taxes to the home government. This, in itself, he considered an unbearable effrontery:

> They allow to the supreme power nothing more than the liberty of notify-ing to them its demands or its necessities. Of this notification they profess to think for themselves, how far it shall influence their counsels, and of the necessities alleged, how far they shall endeavour to relieve them. They assume the exclusive power of settling not only the mode but the quantity of this payment. They are ready to co-operate with all the other dominions of the king; but they will co-operate by no means which they do not like, and at no greater charge than they are willing to bear.

While refusing to pay taxes, the colonists nevertheless continued to accept the protection of British naval power. It has always seemed to me that Johnson had a real point here. No country in history has gone through its teething period with so little interference from outside as the United States. During the century and a half in which the country grew up, the possibility of foreign invasion was simply not a problem. And the reason, or one of the reasons, must surely be the thoroughness with which the British Navy policed the North Atlantic. A pretty handsome service to be had without paying a penny!

Such, in outline, were Samuel Johnson's ideas about how 'the great republic of human nature' could best govern itself: ideas well worth pondering today, even though changing times, changing problems, have rendered their direct application seldom possible. But his fundamental attitude towards social organization is one we can still learn from: a respect for lawful authority, tempered with compassion and informed by a never-sleeping rationality. Johnson thinks and writes within two concentric circles; he is an Englishman, and England is within Europe; the source of his ideas, the scope of his preoccupa-tions, is European; neither America nor the 'third world' figures much in his thinking, except as places with which European rapacity ought not to meddle.

And he is, of course, firmly of his historical epoch, which stretches from the Renaissance (what he himself called 'the recovery of learning') to the French Revolution, which was just about to boil over when he died.

These considerations will protect any twentieth-century person from trying to apply Johnson's solutions directly to problems of our own time, in any literal-minded way. But to ignore them, to allow them to fade from memory as 'obsolete' or 'irrelevant', would be an even worse error. Johnson is one of the finest representatives of a civilization which believed in reason and justice. It was patriotic and martial, while managing with a tiny army and navy and never even envisaging 'total war'. It was reforming and innovating, while maintaining an organic rather than a cataclysmic rate of change. Today we are told on all sides that we have broken through into a new phase of history in which the values of previous cultures will be thrown aside. Theorists have even found a name for this new epoch; they call it 'post-civilization'. If they are right, it becomes even more essential to pack a bag before taking our seat in the time machine. If we are to leave civilization behind, we should first get a clear idea of what it is we are leaving. And in this process the writings of Johnson will be invaluable: for voyagers in the intellectual spaceship a survival kit.

CHAPTER 23

The Padlock

Our last chapter was out in the sunshine. It gave some account of the outward workings of Johnson's mind during these years, the thoughts and opinions that were there for all to see: strong, confident, secure in the depth of his garnered experience, fortified by the vast resources of his reading, hooped in by that all-retentive memory. This was the Johnson the world was permitted to know, the lawgiver, the man whom Smollett facetiously yet with respect dubbed 'the Great Cham of Literature'. Alone, it was another matter. In the silence of his own mind, Johnson suffered agonies which brought him to the verge of disintegration and many times threatened to break his spirit.

We may take up the melancholy thread of this part of our story by recalling that when the Thrales took Johnson into their home in 1766 he was at the bottom of a well of depression and anxiety. Under their watchful care he made a partial recovery; there were times when his love of life was exuberant and raised the spirits of all who came into contact with him. But the recovery was never complete, the pit never more than a few steps away. Our admiration for what Johnson managed to achieve, which would surely be wholehearted if he had been the most fortunate man alive, deepens to veneration when we take into account the burden of misery he had to carry through life.

The causes of Johnson's unhappiness were twofold. There was the tension caused by his urgent and unsatisfied sexual needs. And there was the guilt and self-accusation that led him to fear that he was a sinful man, one whom the vengeful Creator threatened, once the grave closed on him, to torment for all eternity. There is no point in trying to assign any order of priority as between these two causes of disorder. Together they form a tangle which we can turn over and over in our hands without finding a beginning or an end.

Johnson's unslaked sexuality made him liable to fantasies which he could not expel from his mind, and which he regarded as sinful. If he could have accepted as a neutral fact that he was a highly potent man who for one reason and another had no outlet for his natural desires, and that in consequence he could not lay these thoughts and images to rest in his mind, he might have found the situation possible to cope with. But the starting-point of his moral thinking was that the mind is responsible for what goes on within it, and that a man will be held to account for his thoughts and imaginings as well as for his actions. Consequently, when he found himself plagued by sexual fantasies, he shrank back into self-accusation, shame and terror. Piteously, in his prayers, he besought his Creator, that God whose dreadful vengeance he dreaded with every fibre of his being, to take away from him the burden of wayward thoughts and 'tumultuous imaginations':

> Grant me thy Holy Spirit, that after all my lapses I may now continue steadfast in obedience, that after long habits of negligence and sin I may at last work out my salvation with diligence and constancy, purify my thoughts from pollutions, and fix my affections on things eternal.

His prayers were not answered. Images of lust, and of more difficult things to contain than lust, continued to prey on his mind, and these in turn sent him grovelling anew for mercy before his inexorable God. There is no doubt that Johnson's 'vile melancholy' arose very largely from guilt in the Freudian sense of that word. Freud, it will be remembered, made a sharp distinction between 'remorse' – our perfectly natural and salutary impulse of self-blame when we have done something we know to be wrong – and 'guilt'. The latter is an undirected emotion; it arises from an offence which we cannot bring to consciousness – most classically, as Freud saw it, the wish to injure or disobey the father, either the actual biological father or the father imago, the Creator. Since Johnson throughout most of his life feared rather than loved God – or his notion of God – it is probable that this wish lurked in the rebellious crannies of his being. But the prime cause of his despairing self-accusation, his sense of alienation from God, was undoubtedly his proneness to sexual fantasy.

Why – we come back to the question – did Johnson not seek lawful satisfaction for his overwhelming needs? St Paul had laid it down, with the full approval of the Church, that it was better to marry than burn; why did Johnson burn? No one can say. He was certainly attractive to women; not to all of them, but then he needed only one; and his income was sufficient for a comfortable marriage. Yet, after that brief flurry shortly after Tetty's death, it does not appear that he ever seriously looked for a wife. Why did celibacy seem preferable, attended as it was with such miseries?

No one knows. We can only speculate. One clue, a faint glimmer of uncertain light in the labyrinth, may lie in what we know of the nature of Johnson's sexual fantasies. These, apparently, were of a masochistic tendency. In 1773, while staying at Streatham, he wrote Hester Thrale a letter in French, begging her to keep him in stricter subjection, to devise a regime for him which would regulate his entire time, and, if she thought fit, lock him up except at such times as she herself turned the key and let him out.

Years later, when Hester died, there was a sale of her effects at Manchester, and one of the items catalogued was 'Johnson's padlock, committed to my care in the year 1768'. By itself, this would have a straightforward explanation. If Johnson was really afraid of losing his reason, his chief concern would be to avoid bringing his condition to the notice of the authorities. In view of the way mad people were treated in the eighteenth century, the best course was to lie low until the fit passed and he could again appear in public and behave normally. In such circumstances, to entreat Hester to attend personally to the matter of locking him away, even to give a padlock into her personal keeping, was no extravagant decision. But it does not quite square with the tone of that letter of 1773 – an extraordinary performance, especially considering that it was written to someone living under the same roof. To be sure, Hester's mother was also there and was dying, thus claiming nearly all her daughter's attention, so that she had to neglect Johnson. Perhaps the thought that she might be too busy to read his note straight away, might leave it lying about where the servants could find it, prompted Johnson to put his importunities into French. Or perhaps he simply could not endure to use English, the vehicle for his stateliest work, to drag to light material so painful. Certainly he found it painful. He speaks of her 'inconstance' which has made her neglectful,

> qu'elle a oubliée tant de promesses, et qu'elle m'a condamné a tant de solicitations réiterées que la resouvenance me fait horreur.

If the memory of his 'repeated solicitations' made him horrified, the one thing he dreaded more was that her ministrations should be at an end.

> Je souhaite, ma patronne, que votre autorité me soit toujours sensible, et que vous me tiennez dans l'esclavage que vous savez si bien rendre heureuse.

What was this bondage, this 'slavery', which Hester knew so well how to render happy? Her answer, matter of fact and in English, gives the clue:

> You were saying but on Sunday that of all the unhappy you was the happiest, in consequence of my attention to your complaint; and today I have been reproached by you for neglect, and by myself for exciting that generous confidence which prompts you to repose all care on me, and tempts you to neglect yourself, and brood in secret upon an idea hateful in itself, but which your kind partiality to me has unhappily rendered pleasing. If it be possible shake off these uneasy weights, heavier to the mind by far than fetters to the body. Let not your fancy dwell thus upon confinement and severity.

Hester, of course, is writing before the days of the clinical study of mental aberrations. The very word 'masochism' was uncoined until Leopold von Sacher-Masoch had published his series of novels *Grausame Frauen* long after both she and Johnson were in their graves. What she knew and saw both clear-sightedly and charitably was that Johnson was tormented by fantasies that could not possibly be healthy. She counselled him, in the same letter, to get out more and see people:

> Dissipation is to you a glorious medicine, and I believe Mr Boswell will be at last your best physician, for the rest you really are well enough now if you will keep so; and not suffer the noblest of human minds to be tortured with fantastic notions that will rob it of all its quiet.

By 'dissipation' she means what Johnson meant by the word; in his Dictionary he defines it as '1. The act of dispersion; 2. The state of being dispersed; 3. Scattered attention.' She does not want him to plunge into drinking and wenching, but to scatter his attention, to break the horrible concentration on his darker feelings. Her last sentence is 'do not quarrel with your governess for not using the rod enough'. We, who look back at the episode across a hundred years of chatter about perversions and psycho-analysis, across a surreal landscape of the 'Romantic agony', of *le vice anglais*, the exploits of Swinburne and the vogue of the Marquis de Sade, naturally prick up our ears at those last words, sounding as they do like the phraseology of those postcards one sees in side-street shop windows. Such associations are irrelevant. If one thing can be taken as absolutely certain, it is that Hester did *not* engage in any degrading sexual activity with Johnson, or for that matter with anyone else. She behaved admirably; she recognized that he had these fantasies, that at times they boiled over into desires of which he was ashamed but which he felt impelled to confess to her. He felt so impelled because the burden was too much to bear in utter solitude; and also, obviously, because to confess his strange cravings to the woman who had become the object of them was in itself a kind of relief.

There is – to say it again – an element of conjecture in all this. But certainly the things Johnson confided to Hester were bizarre enough for her to describe them as 'a secret dearer than life itself'. She never explicitly wrote down the things he told her, though she was a great keeper of diaries; it seemed to her, and in this she was surely right and a good friend, that if she died suddenly there would be too much danger that prying eyes would read of Johnson's intimate problems.

Something, then, it was, that needed to be guarded so closely between them. And the suggestion that Johnson's trouble was of a masochistic nature is the one that squares best with such fragments of evidence as we have. Not being Boswell, Johnson did not cover sheet after sheet with copious detail of his sufferings. Here one finds a laconic diary entry, there a few words of supplication in a prayer. Two years before the enigmatic letter in French, he had written in his diary the bald note in Latin, 'De pedicis et manicis insana cogitatio', an insane thought of fetters and handcuffs. These were the fantasies that boiled over in the early days of his relationship with Hester, and which she had to try to cope with in addition to all her other problems. Staunchly and well she stood up to the ordeal.

In the *Anecdotes* of Johnson which she published in the year after his death – a bright and lively but at the same time touching little book – Hester several times hinted darkly at the intolerable strain caused by Johnson's preoccupation with his mental and emotional sufferings; caused, that is, both to himself and to 'those he trusted', i.e., first and foremost herself:

> He had studied medicine diligently in all its branches; but had given particular attention to the diseases of the imagination, which he watched in himself with a solicitude destructive of his own peace, and intolerable to those he trusted.

This is true enough. Johnson had given deep and anxious study to the topic of mental disorder. But only of the kind that bore directly on his own case. Of the wide variety of forms that madness takes, he had concentrated on one only: the possession of the mind by fantasies which gradually usurp the place of reality and render the sufferer incapable of the ordinary adjustments and skills of living. Already, in the remarkable portrait of a monomaniac in *Rasselas* (Chapters 14–18), Johnson showed himself preoccupied with the mind that is invaded, and ultimately subdued, by 'some particular train of ideas'. The words are Imlac's, and his diagnosis continues 'all other intellectual gratifications are rejected, the mind, in weariness of leisure, recurs constantly to the favourite conception, and feasts on the luscious falsehood whenever she is offended with the bitterness of truth. By degrees the reign of fancy is confirmed; she grows first imperious, and in time despotic. Then fictions begin to operate as realities, false opinions fasten upon the mind, and life passes in dreams of rapture or of anguish.'

'Fictions begin to operate as realities' – the words are cool and diagnostic, revealing nothing of the fear, the anguished personal involvement, that underlies them. In much the same way, Johnson could discourse calmly on mental disorder, as if he had never felt the terror of its approach. One day in 1777, when he and Boswell were staying with John Taylor at Ashbourne, they had a serious conversation about madness and melancholy. Boswell records (20 September):

> Johnson said, 'A madman loves to be with people whom he fears; not as a dog fears the lash; but of whom he stands in awe.' I was struck with the justice of this observation.

Boswell of course (as the fuller rendering in his Private Papers makes clear) related this *aperçu* directly to himself, with his sweaty emotional need to be with someone he could look up to. He never dreamt that Johnson had also himself in mind. Yet, as one sees clearly in his relations with women, Johnson felt a deep need to look upward, to place the adored woman on a level higher than his own, paying her a homage which lowered him as it raised her. Up to a point this is normal; it becomes pathological only when the entire sexual situation becomes unmanageable – as in his case, ultimately, it did:

> He added, 'Madmen are all sensual in the lower stages of the distemper. They are eager for gratifications to soothe their minds and divert their attention from the misery which they suffer: but when they grow very ill, pleasure is too weak for them, and they seek for pain.'

Once again the innocent Boswell had no idea that Johnson was speaking out of a deep and tragic experience. This, it seems, was the cross he had to bear through life. And when, in his early fifties, the suffering grew uncontrollably intense, he had just one thing to bring him aid and comfort – the ability to confide in Hester Thrale. By laying himself open to her – and thus, as they both well knew, giving her the power to inflict mortal hurt on him by betraying his confidence as Dr Swinfen had betrayed it long ago – he acted out, blamelessly, part of his fantasy of total surrender, a Samson shearing himself for Delilah.

Mention of Swinfen, for that matter, recalls Swinfen's daughter, Elizabeth

Desmoulins, the girl who lay in his arms on those feverish nights in Hampstead so many years ago. She told Boswell that her love and reverence for Johnson were such that she could not have refused him anything for which he really pressed her. The restraint, then, came from him. Who knows at what cost it was achieved, this reining in of an impulse as strong as life itself? Was it, perhaps, made possible only by a deliberate raising of the warm, breathing girl into an unattainable statue, Pygmalion's act in reverse? By allowing himself to think of Elizabeth Desmoulins only in terms of a creature on a higher plane, immune to the desires which burned in him, did he succeed at last in sinking into sleep? Perhaps. And, if so, the dangerous seeds may have been sown there and then; so that, increasingly, a woman who attracted him must appear as a woman higher than himself, before whom he must bow and to whose wishes he craved to submit.

Johnson was a contemporary of the fiendish Marquis de Sade. Today, in the hungover state of Western culture through which we are condemned to live, there are people who profess, and may actually feel, a veneration for Sade. They praise him as a courageous crusader for the liberation of the instincts, martyred by a repressive society; his revolting book, *Les 120 Journées de Sodome*, is passed from hand to hand as the Bible of a new religion of total, irresponsible gratification. In these circles, Johnson would gain enormously in reputation if we could establish that he had prevailed on Hester Thrale to tie him to the bedpost and lash him. Unfortunately it is impossible to provide him with such a one-way ticket to liberated esteem. Such evidence has never been forthcoming, nor will it be. The difference between Johnson and Sade is precisely that Johnson refused to abandon himself to his fantasies and substitute them for reality. That he understood his own condition is shown by the remark that madmen seek for pain when pleasure becomes 'too weak for them'. Sade might have put it in exactly those terms. The difference was that the pull of Johnson's will was the other way. Not towards the mud but away from it.

At all events, these conjectures bring us within sight of a hypothesis as to Johnson's failure to remarry. The masochist finds sexual happiness only in the idea of total subjection to the loved person, a subjection which commonly goes so far as to involve humiliation and ill treatment. The damming up of his normal sexuality had caused this tendency, already latent in Johnson, to become marked. That is the supposition, though it can never be 'proved'. But if it is to any extent correct, then we can see why an ordinarily satisfying marriage was likely to be difficult for him. And we can also see why he preferred to stay close to Hester. Marriage to another woman would inevitably have meant removing himself from her immediate presence; and if she had become, partly or wholly, the node of his masochistic desires, his need for her would be too intense for him to face the thought of such a distancing.

To think of Johnson at such moments of crisis is inevitably to think of King Lear stumbling about the heath in the storm, heedless of the rain and wind that beat on him because the storm in his mind is the greater turmoil of the two:

> When the mind's free
> The body's delicate; this tempest in my mind

> Doth from my senses take all feeling else
> Save what beats there.

That the timbers of his mind held together, that he did not lose his intellectual powers, that he always managed somehow to bring his emotions under control, pick himself up and go on, is matter for rejoicing; it is cheering and hopeful on the widest scale; it enlarges one's idea of the power of human resistance.

CHAPTER 24

Old Acquaintance

'The man who is tired of London is tired of life.' Short, quotable, pithy, this is one of Johnson's most familiar sayings: and it is the authentic utterance of Johnson the clubman, the night-prowler, the friend of poets and wits. But, round about midsummer of every year, he began to find the close-packed streets irksome, and even the cool green spaces of Streatham too confining. He began to long for the open road.

There were many reasons for this. For one thing Johnson had a genuine fondness for the countryside. He did not wish to spend his life amid rural nature, but he missed it if a whole summer went by, as so many summers had perforce gone by in the years before the pension, without an immersion in its sights and sounds. In his seventies he could write, to Henry Thrale, 'I hope . . . to see standing corn in some part of the earth this summer, but I shall hardly smell hay, or suck clover flowers.' These are the words of one who feels the beauty and solace of the countryside on his pulses.

Then, Johnson loved motion. Just to be moving, to feel the jolt and rumble of wheels under him, was to him a pleasure. As he remarked to Boswell, 'If I had no duties, and no reference to futurity, I would spend my life in driving briskly in a post-chaise with a pretty woman. But', he added characteristically, 'she should be one who could understand me, and would add something to the conversation.' As a young student he had murmured to himself how he planned to 'see what is done in other places of learning . . . go and visit the universities abroad'. Such dreams were quickly extinguished by poverty. But once the pension came to rescue him from this state Johnson began at once to feel his wings. His first action, as we saw, was to take a six-week holiday in the West Country with Reynolds. Thereafter, hardly a summer was without its 'ramble'. He would go to visit Langton in Lincolnshire; or he would look up his Oxford friends; or, and most often, he would return to the scenes of his boyhood.

In 1767, Johnson spent nearly six months in Lichfield; in 1768, at least two months staying with Chambers in Oxford; in 1769, he made a short visit to Lichfield and a longer one to Oxford; in 1770, he was in Lichfield and at John Taylor's house at Ashbourne; in 1771, he was at Lichfield for about ten days and then at Ashbourne for a month; and so on, year after year.

As well as the pleasure of travelling, there was the happiness of old associations and old friendships. Lichfield, it is clear, meant a great deal to him (*salve, magna parens*); when he had first gone back after an interval of twenty-four years, it had seemed to him little and provincial, as he confided to Baretti; but once he got back into its rhythm he found, if not 'the full tide of human existence', at least no stagnant backwater. He had good friends there, and in a quiet way he was proud of the place. The place, also in a quiet way, was proud of him. Some five years after the award of his pension, the forty-year lease which Michael Johnson had taken on the house in Breadmarket Street ran out, and at a meeting of the bailiffs and citizens it was decided that Samuel Johnson should be granted a ninety-nine-year lease of the property at the old rent of five shillings – a financial concession which was intended, and received, as a compliment.

Not that Johnson used the house much. Lucy Porter, a pernickety old maid, would not be a hostess to his liking, and by mutual consent he commonly put up at the Three Crowns, an inn a couple of doors down. At nearby Ashbourne, by contrast, he stayed in regal comfort in the large and well-appointed house of his old friend John Taylor.

Taylor was an extraordinary man, though less extraordinary in his own age than in ours. He was a prime specimen of the shrewd, this-worldly eighteenth-century clergyman, John Bull in clerical bands. Unlike Cornelius Ford he was solidly respectable, and by all accounts solidly boring. The substantial income he derived from a plurality of livings he cannily invested in cattle farming; if Taylor could be said to have a passion, that passion had four legs and two horns. His one adventure into matrimony had ended disastrously, and for the rest of his life he was married to his prize-winning herd. 'Our talk', said Johnson sadly, after one visit, 'was of bullocks.' Johnson's letters from Ashbourne reflect, with a resigned humour, the state of mind produced by never-ending talk of livestock. For example, in July 1771: 'There has been a man here today to take a farm. After some talk he went to see the bull, and said that he had seen a bigger. Do you think he is likely to get the farm?' And again, in October 1772, 'Our bulls and cows are all well; but we yet hate the man that had seen a bigger bull.'

Bored as he was, however, it never occurred to him to drop Taylor. They had been friends since boyhood, Taylor had hurried across the road from Christ Church to Pembroke to bring Johnson his garbled account of Bateman's lectures, and such memories forge unbreakable links. So, at least, Johnson thought. During the years when he was confined in London, he was eager that Taylor, on his visits to town, should visit him and keep their friendship in repair. 'When you come to town', he wrote in 1756, 'let us contrive to see each other more frequently, at least once a week. We have both lived long enough to bury many friends, and have therefore learned to set a value on those who are left. Neither of us can now find many whom he has known so long as we have known each other. Do not let us lose our intimacy at a time when we ought rather to think of increasing it.' If a closer link was needed, Taylor had prayed with Johnson over Tetty's body, and helped to steady him through that crisis of grief. In Taylor, it is possible that Johnson found the brother he had missed in Nathaniel.

Certainly Taylor interpreted their relationship as one of great familiarity. He was never in the least overawed by Johnson, partly because of his natural sturdy insensitivity and partly through the immemorial privilege of one who had 'known him when'. Johnson wrote a number of sermons for Taylor to preach, a service which the bullock-loving pastor must have found very convenient; but there is a reliable tradition that Taylor actually refused to deliver the sermon which Johnson composed for Tetty's funeral service, on the ground that it was too flattering to the character of the deceased. To stand up to Johnson was never easy, but to thwart him in a matter like this, where his deepest emotions were invested, seems almost unthinkable. Taylor, however, calmly got away with it. In the same spirit he stonewalled, from the position of a satisfied Whig, against Johnson's political invectives. One evening in September 1777, when Boswell happened to be of the party at Ashbourne, Johnson and Taylor had a shouting match on the subject of 'the inclinations of the people of England at this time towards the Royal Family of Stuart'. Johnson loudly asserted that if the English people were to be fairly polled, the present king would be 'sent away tonight, and his adherents hanged tomorrow'. This, says Boswell, roused Taylor 'to a pitch of bellowing'. The two large, powerful men roared at each other until the windows rattled in their frames; it must have been an awesome spectacle. On cooler reflection, both must have realized that the issue over which they had allowed themselves to quarrel so vehemently was, by that date, very much a dead letter. Perhaps they knew it all the time. A real political issue as between Whig and Tory policies of that moment, something that might affect the course of events, would have gone too near the bone; but to rant and rave about the Stuarts, in the presence of a wide-eyed note-taking Scotsman, might have seemed to both men a good entertainment. They will best judge who best understand the English sense of humour.

That visit in 1777 was a good one. Boswell arrived on 14 September, when Johnson was beginning to long for some conversation. Taylor kept agricultural hours, early to bed and early to rise, and Johnson found it a relief to sit up late with Boswell. They had some of their most interesting discussions, including that on melancholy and madness quoted in the previous chapter; and Boswell saw from the inside the country society to which Johnson had given his heart in the far-off days at Appleby, with the Fitzherberts, the Meynells and the Astons. On the evening after Boswell's arrival, he notes that 'We had with us at dinner several of Dr Taylor's neighbours, good civil gentlemen, who seemed to understand Dr Johnson very well'. He is hardly able to keep the surprise out of his voice; country squires, country lawyers and parsons, who know nothing of Westminster and St James's, were surely behaving out of character by 'understanding Dr Johnson very well'.

But Boswell was a good guest, willing to be pleased, and Johnson enjoyed taking him about. They borrowed Taylor's chaise and took a trip to Derby, pausing *en route* to see Lord Scarsdale's famous house at Keddlestone. At Derby they were shown round a china factory, and Boswell 'admired the ingenuity and delicate art with which a man fashioned clay into a cup, a saucer, or a teapot, while a boy turned round a wheel to give the mass rotundity'. Josiah Wedgwood, whom Johnson never actually met, was very close to them at that moment. But Johnson, with his usual eye on the practicalities of trade and supply and the circulation of money, remarked that the china produced here was too expensive; 'he could have vessels of silver, of the same size, as cheap as what were made here of porcelain'.

Later in the day they went to see a silk mill. Johnson's interest in manufacture and inventions was always to the fore in his visits to the Midlands. Just as when he was in London he relished the intellectual pleasures of the capital, the sensation of being where ideas were revolved and political decisions made, so in the Midlands he allowed his practical side to come uppermost, and this seems to have given his conversation a special quality. When Boswell remarked that one of his ancestors 'never went from home without being attended by thirty men on horseback', Johnson immediately asked, 'Pray how did your ancestor support his thirty men and thirty horses, when he was at a distance from home, in an age when there was hardly any money in circulation?' At such times his attention to practical detail was hawklike. When Taylor, always vain of his animals, remarked of a favourite bulldog that he was 'perfectly well shaped', Johnson studied the creature for a few minutes and said, 'No, Sir, he is *not* well shaped; for there is not the quick transition from the thickness of the forepart, to the *tenuity* – the thin part – behind, which a bulldog ought to have.' Taylor took no offence. The three men were easy together, their conversation relaxed and with something of the earthiness of the farmyard. When Johnson happened to mention that in the course of his editorial work on the English poets – of which more later – he had given George Steevens the job of 'castrating' (his own word) the poems of the Earl of Rochester, Taylor remarked that if Rochester had castrated himself the offending passages in his poems would never have been written. This, one of the few remarks of Taylor's that are on record, doubtless illustrates well enough the incurably veterinary cast of his mind.

So, year after year, Johnson participated in the life of Staffordshire and Derbyshire. He was quite clear about his own habitual preference for a town existence – it was, indeed, on that very pleasant visit in 1773 that he made his remark about a man who was tired of London being tired of life – but he undoubtedly invested much thought and much sentiment in first repairing, and then maintaining, his links with the scenes of his boyhood.

This is borne out, if it needed any bearing out, by his reaction to the death of Catherine Chambers, his mother's old companion, who had been with the family for more than forty years. His diary entry for 18 October 1767 gives us the details:

18 Oct 1767, Sunday. Yesterday, 17 Oct at about ten in the morning I took my leave for ever of my dear old friend, Catherine Chambers, who came to live with my mother about 1724, and has been but little parted from us since. She buried my father, my brother, and my mother. She is now fifty-eight years old.

I desired all to withdraw, then told her that we were to part for ever, that as Christians we should part with prayer, and that I would, if she was willing, say a short prayer beside her. She expressed great desire to hear me, and held up her poor hands, as she lay in bed, with great fervour, while I prayed, kneeling by her, nearly in the following words.

Almighty and most merciful Father, whose loving kindness is over all thy works, behold, visit, and relieve this thy servant who is grieved with sickness. Grant that the sense of her weakness may add strength to her faith, and seriousness to her repentance. And grant that by the help of thy Holy Spirit, after the pains and labours of this short life, we may all obtain everlasting happiness through Jesus Christ, our Lord, for whose sake hear our prayers. Amen.

Our Father.

I then kissed her. She told me that to part was the greatest pain that she had ever felt, and that she hoped we should meet again in a better place. I expressed with swelled eyes and great emotion of tenderness the same hopes. We kissed and parted, I humbly hope, to meet again, and to part no more.

In a man of such tender-heartedness, faithfulness to old friends and old associations was to be expected. Johnson never let go of a friend. He might have said of himself what he wrote of Alexander Pope. 'It does not appear that he lost a single friend by coldness or by injury; those who loved him once, continued their kindness.' He surprised Boswell, during a visit to Lichfield, by entertaining to dinner at their inn a man named Harry Jackson, with whom he had been at school. Jackson was a loser; his cutlery business had failed, and he now pinned his slender hopes on 'some scheme of dressing leather in a better manner than common', to which Johnson listened carefully in the hope of improving it. Boswell's snobbish reaction to Jackson extended to informing posterity that he was 'a low man, dull and untaught', in 'a coarse grey coat, black waistcoat, greasy leather breeches, and a yellow uncurled wig'; his muddy complexion marked him as a beer-soaker, and indeed, as Boswell noted, 'he drank only ale'. Yet Harry Jackson had a place in Johnson's affections, and when he heard of the man's death he wrote sadly, to Boswell, 'It was a loss, and a loss not to be repaired, as he was one of the companions of my childhood.'

It was all the more natural that Johnson clung to his friendship with Edmund Hector, whose roots went just as far back and from which he had derived such solid benefits. Hector, nephew of the man-midwife who delivered him, school-fellow, companion of his melancholy young days in Birmingham; Hector, who had engineered the translation of Father Lobo, acted as intermediary between Johnson and Warren, and generally done everything possible to aid in Johnson's slow and difficult rise from obscurity, was always dear to him. So was his sister Anne, whose sixteen-year-old beauty had stirred Johnson's youthful emotions. Anne had married a clergyman named Careless, and years later Johnson introduced her to Boswell and remarked that if he had married her 'it might have been as happy' for him. If his early attempts to find a schoolmastering job in the neighbourhood of Lichfield had been successful, if he had married Anne Hector and had Edmund as his brother-in-law, if . . . if . . . one can easily plot the diagram of an alternative life that might have been Johnson's, a life which never wandered far beyond the gentle tree-lined valley of Lichfield. To Hector he wrote in very much the same strain as to Taylor, urging him to remember that old friendships were irreplaceable:

> That you and dear Mrs Careless should have care or curiosity about my health gives me that pleasure which every man feels from finding himself not forgotten. In age we feel again that love of our native place and our early friends, which in the bustle or amusements of middle life were overborn and suspended. You and I should now naturally cling to one another; we have outlived most of those who could pretend to rival us in each other's kindness. In our walk through life we have dropped our companions and are now to pick up such as chance may offer us, or to travel on alone.

Between 1772 and 1784 Johnson visited Hector, in Birmingham, at least six times. It does not appear that Hector ever made the trip in the other direction; but then he was a busy surgeon and not a pensioned philosopher. They continued to be the best of friends; what they talked about is not on record, though with Johnson's interest in medicine he probably enjoyed the opportunity to glean knowledge from a professional. And of course they would talk of old times, those days Hector had kept Johnson company as they strolled about the footpaths and listened to his monologues. The death of a friend was always a pain to Johnson, but Hector was one friend who spared him this pain; he outlived Johnson and survived to give important information to Boswell.

Oxford, Lichfield, Ashbourne, Birmingham – these were the staging-posts of Johnson's well nigh annual summer journey. He loved all of them for their own contributions to his life. If Oxford had a place in his affections that no other town, not even London, could really rival, he also felt a deep attachment to Lichfield. He had met with kindness there, and encouragement; and, though Michael Johnson had been a morose and withdrawn figure, his son remembered him affectionately in a little poem he wrote in Latin, about learning to swim in one of the tree-shaded pools near their home. The English, roughly, is this:

> *At Stowe Mill, Lichfield, Where the Streams Flow Together*
> Clear as glass the stream still wanders through
> green fields.
>   Here, as a boy, I bathed
> my tender limbs, unskilled, frustrated, while
> with gentle voice my father from the bank
> taught me to swim.
>   The branches made
> a hiding-place: the bending trees concealed
> the water in a daytime darkness.

Now
hard axes have destroyed those ancient shades:
the pool lies naked, even to distant eyes.
But the water, never tiring, still runs on
in the same channel: once hidden, now exposed,
still flowing.
Nisus, you too, what time
brings from outside, or eats away within
ignoring, do those things you have to do.

Memory had other promptings. As he walked the streets and squares of long ago, memories of his father crowded in, and his never-sleeping conscience began to accuse him. Surely he could have shown more love and obedience, done more to help that sorely tried man through the closing stages of his life? One memory in particular filled him with remorse – his point-blank refusal to go and take care of the stall in Uttoxeter. One day when he was on a visit to Lichfield – the date is unknown, but it was in his late middle age – he got up and, without telling anyone where he was going, made his way to Uttoxeter. It was raining; he uncovered his head and stood for what he recalled as 'a considerable time' in the market-place, oblivious of the staring citizens and the pelting weather: an outward and visible sign of his deep wish to be at peace with the spirit of his father.

Apart from such occasional stabs of conscience, the anxieties that were once associated with Lichfield gradually faded in later years from Johnson's mind. His mother was no longer there as a perpetual focus of self-blame and unhappiness; no one had any money worries – Lucy Porter was left a very large sum of money by her mother's brother, the one who had so begged Tetty to leave off seeing young Johnson and had promised her an annuity if she would send him packing. On his visits there, staying at the Three Crowns, he was relaxed and approachable. He enjoyed showing Boswell the place; he even allowed his disciple to get in a few little digs. Remembering the Dictionary entry for 'Oats', Boswell particularly enjoyed the fact that they were given Staffordshire oat-cakes for breakfast. 'It was pleasant to me to find', says Boswell, pointedly, 'that "Oats", the *food of horses*, were so much used as the *food of the people* in Dr Johnson's own town.' Whether this was *esprit d'escalier* or whether Boswell ventured his little joke at the breakfast table is not on record. He did, however, take the opportunity to remark – again slyly, in view of Johnson's enthusiasm for trade – that there did not seem to be much industry in Lichfield. But this time Johnson was ready, with the magisterial fending-off remark about the 'city of philosophers' already quoted on an earlier page: 'we work with our heads, and we make the boobies of Birmingham work for us with their hands'.

It was fortunate for Johnson that he had Boswell's company on some of these home visits. He enjoyed it; Boswell did him good. He chattered, and drew attention to things, and asked questions, and generally kept Johnson's mind stirred up so that it did not settle into its lees of melancholy. And then, the little man was so good-humoured; so pleased with himself and so amiable to those he met. Johnson had begun to think of Boswell as a good travelling companion from the very first year of their acquaintance; on the three-day trip to see him off at Harwich, he had shown something of the high spirits with which he often responded to a journey, and particularly a journey with Boswell. In that very year they had hit on the idea that Boswell should one day take Johnson to Scotland, and not only to Scotland but to the Hebrides. It seemed an unlikely idea but they kept hold of it during the years. And in 1773 the plan suddenly took on reality.

There were a number of reasons for this. Johnson was, by this time, installed at Streatham; he was, in fact, deep in that state of emotional dependence on Hester which led him to write her that letter in French with its scarcely veiled supplication. Hester's mother was dying; her husband had suffered catastrophic losses in business only a year earlier; she wanted Johnson off her hands, and urged him to travel with Boswell as a means of much-needed 'dissipation'.

Johnson saw the wisdom of the suggestion, but hesitated about leaving the security of Streatham. His health was bad. Earlier in the summer he had come down with a fever, and after it passed off he was far from well. His eye, the only one he could see with, was badly inflamed; for weeks he was for all practical purposes a blind man. Slowly the condition cleared. He was ready for an adventure, for a change of scene that would ease his torturing melancholy. The Hebridean journey seemed possible after all.

There was, besides, another small but distinct cause of satisfaction. Boswell had finally nerved himself to confess that he meant one day to write Johnson's life. He would use the ample time they were to spend together to put questions to Johnson and sort out the details of his early years. At this prospect Johnson was, at any rate, not displeased. He knew the strength of Boswell's attachment to him and that any biography from such a hand would be at least carefully compiled and free from malice. In this spirit he had greeted Boswell's advance warning that he intended to dig for biographical facts with a genial, 'You shall have them all for twopence.'

In this spirit, Johnson headed north, eager for Boswell's company, interested in the prospect of Scotland, confident of being able to deal with anything that might await him. In the next three months, he was to give abundant proof of how strongly the love of life still pulsed in his veins. He was to have need of all his resilience; a real adventure, a genuine testing-time, awaited him.

CHAPTER 25

A Hundred Days in a
Strange Land

The two travellers made a fine study in contrast: the huge, unwieldy Johnson, wearing boots and a very wide brown coat with enormous pockets, and carrying a large English oak stick in his hand; and beside him the perky, diminutive Boswell, thirty-two years old to his sixty-four. But the inner contrast was yet greater than the outer. Though they were very good friends (they returned from the trip liking each other even more than when they set out, which is saying a good deal for their powers of mutual tolerance and forbearance) and though they were inseparable, going side by side every step of the way, they had in fact very different expectations and very different objects in view.

In Boswell, several impulses were at work. Much as he liked to cut a figure in England, he knew that his real life lay in Scotland, and to appear in Scottish society as the acknowledged friend and confidant of Johnson would automatically make him something of a celebrity. Again, there was the bliss of having Johnson, for so long a period, entirely to himself. Normally, it was necessary to go to London to see him, and this Boswell could not always manage to do when he wished to. Family ties and his legal practice kept him at home for long periods. And when he was in London, eager to give attention to the man he called 'my great Mentor', there was competition from a host of other eager attenders; from the Club; from Mrs Thrale; and from his own riotous desires, which led him to go out drinking and whoring with men like Jack Wilkes when he might have been sitting with Johnson. Now, he had Johnson alone: and in Scotland. It would be an opportunity to introduce this arch-Englishman to the society in which he, Boswell, had been reared and educated. Naturally he wished Johnson to be interested and impressed by that society. In his published account of their journey, it is very noticeable that whenever the travellers meet anyone who is polite, cultivated, polished, learned about antiquities, has a good library, etc., etc., he always wrings every drop of juice out of the situation.

All this was sufficient motive for his persistent efforts to get Johnson to Scotland, even if the Highlands and Islands had not existed. But Boswell was too alert and intelligent not to know that his country, like many European countries in the eighteenth century, contained within its borders a fascinating mixture of

past and present. 'Mixture' is perhaps the wrong word. The elements had
scarcely begun to mix. They lay side by side. Within a few days' horseback
journey from the cultivated, outward-looking city of Edinburgh, inhabited by
some of the most sophisticated intelligences then in the world, a man could find
himself amid a tribal society, where chieftains led their private war-bands into
savage battles in the rock-strewn passes, and where such practices as raiding for
cattle and blood-feuding were regarded as, at most, technical illegalities of
which no man of spirit would be ashamed. After the involvement of the Highlanders in the forlorn adventure of 1745, and in particular after the disastrous day
of Culloden, the central government in Westminster had embarked on a policy
calculated to iron out the tribal and feudal nature of Highland society. First
there had been the harsh repression which was the immediate backlash of
Culloden; then a series of legal measures, notably the Disarming Act of 1746,
which made it a crime for a man to carry arms or wear a kilt. But the central
government was a long way away, and had many other things to attend to, and
the nature of Highland life was in any case largely determined by geographical
conditions. Boswell knew that once they left Edinburgh they would be among
scenes of which he himself had only the vaguest foreknowledge.

He was to greet these scenes with his usual raptures. A true child of the age of
Rousseau, Boswell made a cult of strong sensations and heightened emotional
states. He plunged into these states one at a time and appears not to have been
troubled by any thoughts of discrepancy. When undertaking a seduction, he
was as full of ardour as Casanova. When contemplating the sacred ruins of a
monastery, he was as rapt in piety as Bede. When he was disputing some
question at the Club, he saw himself as a philosopher like Hume. At other times
he was the young aristocrat, son of a Lord, proud of his ancient lineage and determined to be every inch a pillar of society. In politics he was a romantic reactionary, much given to rhapsodizing over the ancient glories of Scotland and the
noble loyalty of the Scots to 'the unfortunate house of Stuart'; which did not in
the least hinder him from frequently declaring, in a rather tradesmanly tone of
complacent optimism, that the House of Hanover was settling in very nicely and
would make a far more rational and efficient monarchy, as well for the Highlands and Islands as for everywhere else, since 'the plant of loyalty is there in full
vigour, and the Brunswick graft now flourishes like a native shoot'.

This was Boswell; attentive to many things at once; quicksilver, constantly in
motion; coping with Johnson and coping with Scotland; proud of his blood, yet
always ready to curry favour with persons of higher rank; resourceful; insecure;
endearingly human. Johnson's purposes were larger and steadier. What he was
looking for in the wilds of Scotland was what he was looking for everywhere:
the truth about human life. He was perhaps the last considerable traveller to
have this single-minded preoccupation with mankind. Less than twenty years
later, the entire European sensibility had turned itself towards the wilderness as a
source of inspiration. Mountains, lakes and forests, whether or not peopled with
picturesque and unspoiled inhabitants, became the prayer book of a new
theology. But Johnson remains firmly on the eighteenth-century, pre-Romantic

side of this gulf. He defends travelling in barren mountain country, but he does so on utilitarian grounds:

> Regions mountainous and wild, thinly inhabited, and little cultivated, make a great part of the earth, and he that has never seen them must live unacquainted with much of the face of nature, and with one of the great scenes of human existence.

As we noted earlier, Johnson adopted a mixed attitude towards the social and economic developments of his day. On the one hand he welcomed the improvement in trade and agriculture and the proliferation of new techniques, which relieved the stagnation of small country-towns and made a wider life possible. He appreciated that the faster flow of money gave more people a chance to raise themselves from poverty, and led to a social mobility without which such men as himself and his friends of the Club would not have been able to figure so prominently in society. All this he accepted. Yet he distrusted the gallop towards a pure plutocracy. He was for 'subordination', which to him meant the deliberate keeping alive of certain feudal attitudes and observances. His attitude to these things was emotional and aesthetic; he could have anticipated Yeats's question,

> How but in custom and in ceremony
> Are innocence and beauty born?

All these things we have already remarked. But it is worth recapitulating them because we might otherwise be in danger of overlooking a central motive – perhaps *the* central motive – for Johnson's travels in the Highlands and Islands. All his life he had longed for some means of comparing the present system with that of earlier days. Did money, social flexibility, ease of communication, really produce happiness, or was the old, fixed, earth-rooted pyramid better? What was life *really* like in historical times? He was a passionate student of history; but the professional historians, prosing on about battles and treaties and alliances, had never satisfied him. As he was later to remark to Boswell (29 April 1778), 'All that is really *known* of the ancient state of Britain is contained in a few pages . . . I would wish to have one branch well done, and that is the history of manners, of common life.' And there, all the time, within his own nation-state, governed (nominally) by the same king and parliament that governed him, was a feudal society that had lived on into his own day; a society which rarely handled money, where the laird received his rent in goods and services and had jurisdiction over his people. To travel only a few hundred miles north would have been to see this society, to mingle with it, and to gain a more vivid impression of what mediaeval feudalism must have been like than could have been gathered from all the historians who ever wrote.

But the Vanity of Human Wishes was manifested here as it was everywhere else. This state of affairs lasted only until 1745. And though Johnson might well have wished to travel to the Hebrides before that date, might have wished it as he pored over Martin Martin's *Description of the Western Islands of Scotland* in his father's shop, he might as realistically have wished to go to the moon. Now he was free and able to make the journey; he had made it; and the feudal society, in anything like its pure state, was thirty years back in the past. With his characteristic honesty Johnson does not pretend otherwise. His own words are sufficient testimony:

> There was perhaps never any change of national manners so quick, so great, and so general, as that which has operated in the Highlands, by the last conquest, and the subsequent laws. We came thither too late to see what we expected, a people of peculiar appearance, and a system of antiquated life. The clans retain little now of their original character, their ferocity of temper is softened, their military ardour is extinguished, their dignity of independence is depressed, their contempt of government subdued, and their reverence for their chiefs abated . . . Such is the effect of the late regulations, that a longer journey than to the Highlands must be taken by him whose curiosity pants for savage virtues and barbarous grandeur.

What he found was not a feudal society. But it was something equally interesting, and equally challenging to his powers of description and analysis: a society in the agonies of change.

When the Highlanders poured out of their glens and attacked the English redcoats, hoping that by sheer force they would be able to set a Stuart once more on the throne, they were in fact undertaking the last action they would ever perform in unison, as a people. Inevitably, they were beaten back. Inevitably, they were penalized, stripped, shorn of privileges. They had shown their way of life to be inimical to that of the kingdom as a whole; and when people do that they are visited first by the soldiery, with guns, and next by the administrators, with notebooks and filing cabinets. And the reformers and planners, who do not usually take the trouble to visit them at all, draw up neat little plans for giving them what is good for them.

In such a situation, everybody knows best. Everybody, that is, except the people whose welfare is being planned for. Thomas Pennant, the celebrated traveller and writer of topographical books, visited Scotland twice and wrote two books about it in rapid succession (1771 and 1774), books which Johnson knew well. There is no doubt that Pennant spoke for a large body of English opinion when he entirely approved the actions of the English government in Scotland. Reasonable opinion might well overlook 'a few excesses' in 'a day productive of so much benefit to the united kingdoms'. And if this 'benefit' included the mangling out of recognition of the Highlander's traditional way of life he could always emigrate to North America, where there was plenty of room and where he would be a nuisance to no one, except of course the Indians, who did not have any rights either. Pennant welcomed depopulation because it would 'give us a dear-bought tranquillity'. Get rid of the Highlanders and there will be no Highland problem.

Such an attitude is shocking to us because it anticipates the ruthless totalitarianism of our own century – the extirpation of races, the mass deportations and the rest of it. To kill a way of life is a form of genocide, even if the living bodies (or most of them) survive. Johnson was well acquainted with the line of argument represented by Pennant, but he showed no signs of taking it over. On the other hand, he was too honest and perceptive to take refuge in the picturesque reactionary attitudes of a Boswell, who wanted the Highlanders simply to pretend that 1745 had not happened. This way out was too easy for Johnson to take. In one of their conversations, recorded by Boswell under 25 August, he refused to echo Boswell's simple enthusiasm for feudalism. To him the question was still an open one:

> I said, I believed mankind were happier in the ancient feudal state of sub-ordination, than they are in the modern state of independency. Johnson: 'To be sure, the *Chief* was: but we must think of the number of individuals. That *they* were less happy, seems plain; for that state from which all escape as soon as they can, and to which none return after they have left it, must be less happy; and this is the case with the state of dependence on a chief or great man.'

Boswell went on to babble happily about the contentment of the French under their excellent system of subordination, praising the 'reciprocal benevolence and attachment between the great and those in lower rank'. Some ten years later the lower ranks were to demonstrate their 'attachment' to the higher-ups by guillotining them in wagon-loads. Boswell should have been a leader-writer.

Johnson was determined, then, to see for himself what Highland society was like, and to learn all that he could. The adventure started rather late in the summer; going so far north, they would probably have preferred to set out in June, but Boswell was not free to go until the end of the summer law session. Johnson travelled up in August; his friend Chambers kept him company as far as Newcastle, and another literate companion, named Scott, from there to Edinburgh, so that the journey was not especially tedious, and he arrived in good spirits on 14 August. Boswell received him rapturously at his house in the Canongate, and his wife, Peggie, though she eyed Johnson's uncouth appearance with misgivings, welcomed him politely and turned out of her bedchamber so that he would not have to sleep in one less comfortable – a kindness he remembered with gratitude. There followed four days in which Boswell showed John-son off to the *savants* of Edinburgh, and on 18 August they took the road.

At first, as they travelled by post-chaise through a cultivated and peopled landscape, there was (except for sleeping in a different place every night) no great difference from their Edinburgh sojourn. Boswell was still intent on help-ing Johnson to form a favourable impression of the learning and politeness of Scotland by introducing him to the wise and the well born. At St Andrews, Johnson examined the ruins of the Cathedral, and exclaimed against the icono-clastic zeal of Knox. Near Montrose, they paused long enough to pay a visit to the seat of Lord Monboddo, a pioneer investigator of prehistoric man in the sceptical eighteenth-century tradition, whose anticipations of evolutionary theory had aroused Johnson's defensive hostility. The two were polite enough to one another, and even found a few subjects to agree on. At Aberdeen, Johnson was entertained by grave professors and made a freeman of the city. All these things were pleasant enough. But there are signs that Johnson was impatient, inwardly, for new experiences that should mark a total change from his accustomed life. He was hungry for wildness, solitude, the untamed. Though he might only see these things as a setting for new perspectives on human nature, they nevertheless called him. On their very first day, crossing the Firth of Forth, he caught sight of the tiny island of Inch Keith and insisted that they land and explore it. Considering how many islands and how much exploration he was to encounter before the trip was over, his insistence points to a hankering to get in among wild nature from the very beginning. He clambered up a steep grassy slope; examined carefully the remains of a sixteenth-century fort; took note of sixteen head of black cattle grazing the island; and generally let nothing escape his attention. In a happily graphic sentence of Boswell's, 'he stalked like a giant among the luxuriant thistles and nettles'. It was a foretaste of what he had come to see. Inch Keith might be small beer but there was nothing like it within ten miles of Fleet Street.

He showed the same eagerness when, on their seventh day out, they were entertained at Slains Castle and he heard of the nearby 'Buller of Buchan', an enormous upright cylinder carved from the rock by the sea. Not only did the party walk round the unprotected rim of the Buller (or 'Bouloir', boiler) but at Johnson's suggestion they took a boat and entered it by one of the narrow passages connecting it with the sea. Johnson's eager attention noticed caves and he (fruitlessly) questioned the boatmen about their depth. When they got back safely Boswell was relieved. The sight of Johnson shambling round the narrow path, with a sea on either side 'deep enough to float a man of war', made him wonder if he were not leading Johnson into danger.

Having moved up the east coast, they now turned westward, and visited Forres and Cawdor with their associations with *Macbeth*, which Johnson duly solemnized by repeating some lines from the play in his deep emphatic voice. At Cawdor they were entertained by the Minister, who put his knowledge of the country at their disposal and, spreading out a map, showed Boswell the best route to take. (It is interesting that he had got this far without mapping out their journey, the first thing a modern traveller would have done.)

This accomplished, they pushed on to Inverness, where the roads ended, the chaise was sent back, and they took to horses. Boswell had brought his Bohemian servant, Joseph Ritter, and hired horses for the three of them, while two Highlanders, John Hay and Lauchlan Vass, came along on foot, to show them the way and to lead the horses over difficult ground.

Johnson himself singled out Nairn, just short of Inverness, as the place where they first saw the Highlands. But it was after leaving Inverness, the last point from which it was possible to go by road to any city in the kingdom, that their exploration began in earnest. On that day, 30 August, Johnson had his first glimpse of Highland peasant life. Riding beside Loch Ness, they came to a little stone hut with an old woman looking out of it. They stopped and conversed with her, using their Highland men as interpreters, for she spoke only the language which both Boswell and Johnson called 'Erse', though we know it as Gaelic. The interview was a successful one. Johnson was interested in everything; where the beldame slept, what she ate and drank, her sources of sustenance, the nature of her work and habits. They gave her some snuff, to her a more or less unobtainable luxury; in return, she fetched out her whisky bottle and everyone but Johnson took a dram; and they left her with a shilling.

Their 'journey to the Western Islands' had now begun. For the next two months they climbed mountains, picked their way across bogs, crossed lochs and stretches of sea in small boats, examined Druidical circles and natural wonders, noticed animals and birds, and took shelter under every variety of roof from the comely houses of lairds to unspeakable inns. On two occasions they spent the night on shipboard; on one, in a barn. They were wind-beaten, soaked in rain and deluged with spray, fatigued, benighted, parched, broiled, fried and soused. Johnson's oak staff was lost (stolen, he declared darkly, for in a treeless country what man could resist such a piece of timber?), and a pair of spurs belonging to him was washed out of an open boat by a large wave, an occurrence which wholeheartedly flouts the laws of probability. On at least one occasion he fell sprawling from his horse; on another, the animal stumbled on the brink of a precipice, which he remembered later as 'the only moment when I felt myself in danger'.

All this Johnson thoroughly enjoyed. He had always been indifferent to physical hardship, and there was a pleasure in discovering that now, as he entered old age, he could still weather an unsheltered mode of existence. He was annoyed when Boswell, before they set out, told him he had been trying to lay in a supply of lemons, so that Johnson should not go short of his customary lemonade on their travels. Johnson flashed out that he did not wish to be taken for the kind of weak man who 'could not do without anything'. From first to last he considered it beneath his philosophic dignity to grumble about cold, or wet, or fatigue, or hard fare. Once when they got soaking wet, Boswell took off his clothes and dried them as best he could; Johnson merely stood in front of a peat fire and steamed off.

Of their actual travelling time, more was spent in the islands than on the mainland. They crossed over to Skye, then to Raasay, back to Skye, over to Coll, then Mull, Ulva, Inch Kenneth, Iona, back to Mull and finally rejoined the mainland at Oban on 22 October.

There is no need to trace their journey step by step. Enough people have done it already. A Yorkshire clergyman, James Bailey, followed Johnson's route in 1787, and kept a journal of what he found. George Birkbeck Hill retraced the route for his *Footsteps of Dr Johnson* in 1890; Moray McLaren did the same thing in 1948; since then it has become an industry, with magazine photographers and television teams grinding round the well-worn itinerary. Writing in the bicentenary year, I notice that it has become the theme of a cookery book. *Und so weiter*. Let us be content to seek the essential quality of the experience for Johnson, and its effect on his thinking and feeling.

We travel, presumably, in quest of experiences that would not come our way at home. In his Scottish travels, Johnson was blessed twice over in this respect. He experienced effort, hardship and sometimes danger in a landscape of great and unfamiliar beauty. And he encountered people who were very unlike those he normally met, while being every whit as characterful and intelligent.

Let us take these in turn. Johnson is usually said to have been entirely insensible to natural beauty. This was his own opinion and it has been echoed down through the generations. Something, however, must be allowed for Johnson's fondness for deflating cant. He lived in the epoch when landscape was becoming aesthetically fashionable and he thought there was an element of mere gush in the praise of rural vistas by people who took care not to undergo the backbreaking toil of the countryside. When they rhapsodized, he made his often-quoted anti-sensibility remarks, such as that one blade of grass was the same as another. In fact, as we have already noticed in connection with his annual summer jaunt, Johnson was as fond of the countryside as the next man. His eyesight was bad, but by using it intelligently he saw a good deal (on this very journey he corrected Boswell about the exact shape of a mountain peak) and he was, moreover, fond of physical contact with the earth. Once, when staying with Langton in Lincolnshire, he went up on the hill behind the house, and, remarking that he had not had a roll for a long time, deliberately emptied his pockets, lay down on the ground, and rolled down the grassy slope. This was no mere eccentric prank. Tactile contact with the earth was important to him, as it is to those people who are always weeding their gardens because they have an emotional need to put their hands into the soil. In the Hebrides he experienced the beauty of the terrain, and bore witness to it in the book he wrote immediately afterwards. For instance:

> I sat down on a bank, such as a writer of romance might have delighted to feign. I had indeed no trees to whisper over my head, but a clear rivulet streamed at my feet. The day was calm, the air soft, and all was rudeness, silence, and solitude. Before me, and on either side, were high hills which, by hindering the eye from ranging, forced the mind to find entertainment for itself. Whether I spent the hour well I know not; for here I first conceived the thought of this narration.

Or this, recalling how on their way to Iona they were rowed forty miles in a small boat along the coast of Mull, and night overtook them on the way:

> The evening was now approaching, and we were yet at a considerable distance from the end of our expedition. We could therefore stop no more to make remarks in the way, but set forward with some degree of eagerness. The day soon failed us, and the moon presented a very solemn and pleasing scene. The sky was clear, so that the eye commanded a wide circle: the sea was neither still nor turbulent: the wind neither silent nor loud. We were never far from one coast or another, on which, if the weather had become violent, we could have found shelter, and therefore

contemplated at ease the region through which we glided in the tranquillity of the night, and saw now a rock and now an island grow gradually conspicuous and gradually obscure.

He experienced this beauty through his skin and his bone structure, through fatigue, through exposure to wind and weather. Anyone who has only *seen* a landscape (e.g., through a car window) might as well have stayed at home and watched travel films. But to experience the hills as gradient, to be toiled up; to feel the coldness of the streams, the texture of the earth under one's feet, the roughness or smoothness of the rocks, the direction of the wind, is to possess that landscape and in this sense Johnson possessed the Hebrides.

Next, people. Johnson talked to everyone he could, ranging from redcoats of the British Army to hereditary aristocrats. When he found himself among those who spoke only Gaelic, he used the nearest bilingual person as an interpreter. He seems to have met hardly anyone he heartily disliked, and a good many for whom he felt warmth and respect.

One of the first people to impress him deeply was MacQueen, landlord of the inn at Anoch in Glenmorison. This was a simple enough place; as described by Johnson, the village consisted of 'three huts, one of which is distinguished by a chimney'. The landlord, however, turned out to be a polite, literate, well-spoken man, who had serious books in his house. When Johnson praised his command of English, he replied that there was no need to wonder at it, since he had had an early grounding in 'grammar', by which of course he meant Latin grammar.

They found Mr MacQueen so interesting, and he responded so well, that he rode beside them for part of their journey on the next day, and told them something of his life and opinions. He had been out in the '45, and felt the true feudal loyalty to the Laird of Glenmorison, but regretted that since the change to money rents the laird was slowly forcing his tenants to emigrate by raising their rents to an impossible level. Seventy men from that glen alone had left for America, and he himself planned to go the following year. When Johnson, stung to a generous indignation, said that if he had his way MacQueen should stay at home and the laird should go to America, MacQueen answered without bitterness that it was better that he should go, 'for the laird could not shift for himself in America as he could do'.

When they met MacQueen, the travellers had been out only twelve days and had barely begun to penetrate the region they had come to see. It was well that Johnson should be presented, at the beginning, with such a paradigm of the best side of the Highland character: courteous, articulate, brave, quixotically loyal. Such a man, not only well educated but practical with his hands – he had built his snug wayside inn, unassisted, up from the bare ground – would be a serious loss to his country or any country. Yet MacQueen was emigrating. There was a sickness at the heart of any society that could not use such men as he. From that point on Johnson's interest and concern were deepened.

It is tempting to linger over some of the other memorable characters whom

Johnson and Boswell came across: on Lochbuy, for instance, a big, hearty ox of an old laird who seemed like a more amiable version of Sir Wolstan Dixie, and who roared at Johnson on being introduced, 'Are you of the Johnstons of Glencro, or of Ardnamurchan?' Or Sir Allan Maclean, chief of the clan Maclean, who showed them a courtesy both sympathetic and dignified, and did not think himself too grand to lie down to sleep with them in a barn, when no other accommodation could be found on the Island of Iona. (Boswell could hardly believe it was happening to him: 'When I awaked in the morning, and looked round me, I could not help smiling at the idea of the chief of the Macleans, the great English moralist, and myself, lying thus extended in such a situation.') But, with one exception, we must leave them. They are all portrayed by Boswell, and in certain cases by Johnson also. The exception is 'Col', Donald Maclean, eldest son of the laird of Coll and therefore sometimes called Young Col. He accompanied the travellers from Talisher, on 25 September, to Inch Kenneth on 19 October, and made an ineffaceable impression on them: 'We will', said Johnson, 'erect a statue to Col.'

The tragedy of the Highlands and Islands is as well illustrated by Col as by MacQueen. A small, neat young man, very tough and hardy, he was determined to make his lands profitable without squeezing the tenants, and to this end he had been to England and worked on farms in Hertfordshire and Herefordshire, tackling every kind of job and making sure he could do it himself, for on his return he would have to teach his workmen. Johnson admired Col enormously. 'He is a noble animal. He is as complete an islander as the mind can figure. He is a farmer: a sailor: a hunter: a fisher: he will run you down a dog: if any man has a *tail*, it is Col.' The reference to tails is probably a side-kick at Lord Monboddo, who held that the human race had descended from anthropoids with this characteristic; but Johnson also meant that in Col, if anywhere, they might locate the 'noble savage' so dear to the eighteenth-century imagination, who could hold his own with the animals and yet still have the full range of the human being.

Johnson added that he regretted that Col was 'not more intellectual'. But then Johnson had very high standards. Most of us would have found Col quite intellectual enough. He was not afraid to oppose Johnson in argument, though his inbred courtesy always kept him at a distance from anything resembling contentiousness.

As things fell out, Col was of the party on the one occasion during their tour when Johnson and Boswell were in serious danger. It happened at sea, on the night of Sunday, the third of October. Planning to leave Skye and make their way, by whatever stages proved possible, to Iona, Johnson and Boswell had come to Annadale, near the Sound of Sleat, where they were guests at the house of Sir Alexander Macdonald. There was some talk of their making the crossing in Sir Alexander's open boat. Johnson, who consistently left all these decisions to others, and appears never to have given a thought to questions of safety or comfort, doubtless expressed no concern at this prospect, but it cannot have been at all attractive to Boswell; the passage was a long one – some forty nautical miles, if they were trying to get to Iona in one move – and October in the

Hebrides is a season of gales and torrential rain. Darkness, at that time of year, descends at six in the evening, and from then on the only chance of visibility, for the eighteenth-century sailor, was a good moon. The entire coast of Scotland, as hazardous water as any in the world, was at that time lit by one light only, a coal fire on top of a beacon in the Firth of Forth.

Luckily, at Sir Alexander's house the travellers met Mr Simpson, a trader in kelp and general cargo, who was preparing to set sail in a decked vessel of twelve tons, and agreed to land them on the island of Mull, off whose south-western corner Iona lies. Simpson's boat was without doubt a wallowing little tub, built to cram as much payload as possible into her diminutive hold, and would be helpless against a headwind; her probable dimensions (thirty-five feet long, twelve broad) could hardly have inspired confidence when measured against the roaring tumult of the autumnal seas.

Nevertheless, Johnson as usual was so far from nervous that he gave no thought to the risks they were running. For two days they lingered in Sir Alexander's house, waiting for a favourable wind. On the third morning, soon after ten o'clock, they were hastily summoned on board; the wind had changed. Johnson, who seemed determined to treat the voyage like an afternoon trip on the Serpentine, took his time about getting down to the quay, and it was nearly three hours later when they weighed anchor.

At first the ship danced along briskly. Johnson became seasick almost at once and went below; there was a tiny cabin in the fo'c'sle, with two bunks and a fire, and this was all he saw of the ship for the next fourteen hours. Boswell, exulting in the strength of his sea-legs, whaled into a meal of boiled mutton and boiled herring, washed down with beer and punch, which speedily caused him to join Johnson on the sick list. Rather than endure his purgatory in the stuffy cabin, he went up on deck in spite of the lashing rain.

Night fell and the moon rose. So far they had been making such good time that Hugh Macdonald, Mr Simpson's skipper, was beginning to talk about landing them on Iona that same night. But now, as they rounded the point of Ardnamurchan, the wind changed, and began blowing directly out of the Sound of Mull. Headway was impossible. As the wind rose higher, a hurried consultation was held. Over to their west, downwind, lay the islands of Muck, Eigg and Canna. Col suggested that by goose-winging before the wind they might reach shelter in one of them, or in his own island which was further to the south. The skipper disagreed. He was for tacking laboriously on into the Sound. When this had been tried for some time with no result, he announced that they would try to get in close to the Isle of Mull and cast anchor.

By this time everyone present, except the oblivious Johnson below, realized that they were in trouble. All those on deck took a hand in the management of the ship: Col, his servant, Simpson, Hugh Macdonald, two sailors (one of whom had only one eye), and Boswell. There was a good deal of shouting in Gaelic, which led Boswell to fear the worst; finally, Macdonald's plan for anchoring near Mull was vetoed on the grounds that no sufficiently safe anchorage existed, and Col said that if they would make for his island he would try to bring them in. This was dangerous, the island being low-lying and difficult to see, so that there was a risk of being driven without warning on to the rocky coast; but Eigg was more dangerous still, and Canna was too far away.

At this point Johnson, whose seasickness had passed off, called up from his bunk to know where they were bound. When told that it was still a toss-up between Mull and Coll, he cried out cheerfully, 'Coll for my money.' His unconcern irritated Boswell, who by this time was badly rattled. In an effort to compose himself he asked Col how he could make himself useful; Col, without hesitation, put a rope into his hand with instructions to hold on to it until he was told to pull. Boswell obediently took the rope and stood at the ready. Hours later he noticed that the other end was connected to a masthead, so that nothing would have been achieved by hauling on it. But by that time the stratagem had served its benevolent purpose.

Having decided to run for Coll, they swung round. For a few minutes the boat lay broadside on to the sea, which was now very high; the frightful rolling can be imagined. Boswell thought of his wife and children. The ship did not, of course, capsize, or this book would end here, but they were still far from safety. It was a run of eleven miles to Coll, and when they got there they had to navigate into the harbour at Loch Eatharna, half a mile wide and with a huge, treacherous rock, Bogha More, in the middle of its mouth, exposed to sight only at low tide but a wrecker at any time. To be sure of missing it was a matter of hand's-breadth navigation, and they were moving in darkness over a wild sea whose pattern was complicated by fast currents.

Boswell, still hanging on to his rope, tried to keep his mind off Davy Jones's locker. But more refinements of torture followed. They had set out from Skye in the company of five herring boats; four of them had made better speed and gone ahead, but one, a small wherry, was in difficulty and had dropped behind them. Her master hailed Simpson's boat and begged that if they set course for Coll they would show a light. They agreed, and one of the sailors waved a glowing peat, which in the high wind showered their vessel with sparks. Boswell shudderingly remembered that Col, an enthusiastic marksman, had brought a load of gunpowder on board. More shouting in Gaelic followed.

The one-eyed seaman now took the helm, and Col, his servant, and Mr Simpson lay down in the bows, straining their eyes through the darkness for the coastline. As the sea was rising higher all the time, speed was of the essence, and they were carrying more sail than would be normal before such a wind. There was a real danger that the sheets would be torn to ribbons, which could only result in their being driven on to the rocks. 'I now saw', says Boswell, 'what I never saw before, a prodigious sea, with immense billows coming upon a vessel, so that it seemed hardly possible to escape.'

But their luck held. Suddenly, with a cry of 'Thank God, we are safe!' Col sighted the harbour of Loch Eatharna, and soon they were inside and safely at anchor. Boswell, Col and Simpson went down to the cabin and found Johnson lying calmly in his bunk, with one of Col's hunting dogs keeping his back warm. Since, although they were in harbour, it was too rough to disembark he stayed where he was. Col and the piteously exhausted Boswell were given bunks for what remained of the night by another vessel moored close by.

Less physically adventurous, but no less an adventure of the imagination and the emotions, was the visit they paid to Iona; their object, of course, being to view the remains of the monastery of Icolmkill, the tiny missionary base from which Christianity was first brought from Ireland to the British Isles generally. They arrived in the dark, having delayed themselves by the exploration of a deep cave, and spent the night, with the dignified Sir Allan, sleeping rough in a barn. In the morning, Johnson inspected the venerable ruins with great diligence, and made measurements; Boswell, who knew he could trust Johnson with this part of their survey, and that in any case the ruins had been thoroughly measured before, chose rather to loaf and invite his soul.

That visit was the last major experience. A few days later, on 22 October, they reached the mainland at Oban. Both confessed to a certain lightening of spirit on the occasion. To be in an island, amid rough seas and with unpredictable weather, is a kind of imprisonment, and they rejoiced at the freedom of movement, the availability of comforts, and the general sense of rejoining the mainstream of existence. This feeling intensified as they drew nearer to the centres of civilization; when they reached their inn at Glasgow, Johnson sat toasting his legs at a coal fire, the first he had seen for weeks, and said half to himself and half to Boswell, 'Here am I, an Englishman, sitting by a coal fire!' – as if he were resuming his familiar identity like a favourite coat that had been hanging in a wardrobe.

But to acknowledge their relief at getting home is not to miss the profound effect of the journey amid scenes always beautiful, always strange, often tragic. On the threshold of old age though he was, his mind formed by a lifetime's experience, Johnson took a strong impression, a richer and deeper colouring of his thoughts, from the Hebridean experience. As he took his place in the Newcastle coach and turned his face away from Scotland, his mind was heavy with impressions, facts, ideas, comparisons. But over it all, we must surely feel, there hung a cloud of sadness. He was far too sensitive not to realize that the Highlands and Islands, which had given him so many unique experiences and valued memories, lay in a melancholy shade. The whole region was at the beginning of a steep decline. Ahead lay three successive waves of misfortune: first, depopulation and abject poverty; second, the stockbrokers joining the express trains from Euston and King's Cross to spend a few weeks blazing away at deer and grouse and employing their betters as 'ghillies'; and finally the unspeakable havoc and degradation of the tourist industry, the caravans and hotdog stands which have sprung up where Johnson and Boswell rode and talked.

At Ostaig, in Skye, the travellers were entertained at a large farmhouse known as Coirechatachan. One evening, after supper, the company fell as usual to dancing. This time the dance they chose was one they called, simply, 'America'. Each couple, after performing the usual steps and threading among the other couples doing the same, began to whirl round in a circle; and the dance continued until every couple in the room was spinning, as if drawn by some irresistible force into the collective movement. The dance, of course, expressed their feelings about emigration, and what it was doing to the life of their community. One family decided to go, then another, then another, till the whole country was whirling in the same contagious frenzy.

All 'primitive' peoples – those who live in communities, close to their means of sustenance – express their states of mind by means of dancing. It is the physical uttering of a corporate mood, something that can be joined in by all generations, and it never survives the coming of the tourist. Johnson and Boswell were watching, as no one for a hundred years now has watched, a real Highland dance. What were Johnson's feelings, as they danced 'America'? Did his mind go back nearly fifty years, to the lonely figure of Nathaniel Johnson, and did he recall that Nathaniel, in his last dazed wanderings, had drifted to a West Country port with the vague intention of 'going to Virginia'? It hardly matters; whether or not the thought rose to his conscious mind, it must have been in his bones, the knowledge that the problems of these people were universal, that his own brother had 'danced America'.

CHAPTER 26

'The Thoughts of One Who Has Seen but Little'

Back home, Johnson immediately picked up the thread of his relationship with the Thrales, and in particular with his 'honoured Mistress'. Not that he had ever really dropped them during his three-month absence. Whenever circumstances permitted, he had sat down and written to Hester, recounting the adventure step by step. From Banff he had described their progress through St Andrews and Aberdeen; from Inverness, the Buller of Buchan; then came nine days of hard travelling, in which he had no opportunity to write, but once arrived on Skye and installed in the house of Sir Alexander Macdonald he wrote the first of a notable series of letters which shared with her the excitement of breaking new ground. 'Little did I once think of seeing this region of obscurity, and little did you once expect a salutation from this verge of European life. I have now the pleasure of going where nobody goes, and of seeing what nobody sees.' By writing Hester these journal letters, he was admitting her to an important area of his experience, and the choice was a natural one. He depended on her, confided in her, needed her, more than anyone else.

Boswell, who was just now basking in the sunshine of Johnson's approval and who was in any case not yet the jealous enemy to Hester Thrale he later became, nevertheless had to adapt, during their journey, to the knowledge that she held a more inward place in Johnson's heart than he did. Seeing Johnson dashing off page after page of one of his journal letters, he 'wondered to see him write so much, so easily' to his confidante. And he must have been aware that the Thrales were constantly in Johnson's thoughts, and Hester above all. Once, when Boswell declared jestingly that after their return he would write an Epistle to Johnson on his return, 'in the style of Mrs Gulliver to Captain Lemuel Gulliver', Johnson laughed and asked in whose name it should be written. 'Mrs Thrale's,' said Boswell unguardedly. Johnson's wrath fell on him at once. 'Sir, if you have any sense of decency or delicacy, you won't do that.' Nor would Johnson allow Hester to be toasted in whisky, when at Inverary they drank a glass to 'see what it is that makes a Scotchman happy'. He held her name in too high esteem to introduce it in the undignified context of a dram, and said they must rather drink to 'some insular lady'.

Johnson's letters to Hester Thrale naturally overlap with the book he now set himself to write. But they are much more personal. Here we find those moments of weakness and weariness which he concealed from Boswell. Proud as he was of standing up to the rigours of climate and fatigue, he confided only to her that he found the going hard:

> My eye is, I am afraid, not fully recovered, my ears are not mended, my nerves [i.e. muscles] seem to grow weaker, and I have been otherwise not as well as I sometimes am . . . this climate perhaps is not within my degrees of healthy latitude.

Again:

> I have not good health, I do not find that travelling much helps me. My nights are flatulent, though not in the utmost degree, and I have a weakness in my knees, which makes me very unable to walk.

At one point, an even more sombre note is struck. Johnson's sixty-fourth birthday has come: he would gladly have forgotten the fact, but

> Boswell, with some of his troublesome kindness, has informed this family, and reminded me that the eighteenth of September is my birthday. The return of my birthday, if I remember it, fills me with thoughts which it seems to be the general care of humanity to escape. I can now look back upon threescore and four years, in which little has been done, and little has been enjoyed, a life diversified by misery, spent part in the sluggishness of penury, and part under the violence of pain, in gloomy discontent, or importunate distress. But perhaps I am better than I should have been, if I had been less afflicted. With this I will try to be content.
>
> In proportion as there is less pleasure in retrospective considerations the mind is more disposed to wander forward into futurity, but at sixty-four what promises, however liberal of imaginary good, can futurity venture to make. Yet something will be always promised, and some promises will always be credited. I am hoping, and I am praying that I may live better in the time to come, whether long or short, than I have yet lived, and in the solace of that hope endeavour to repose.

It was to Hester with her womanly sympathy, rather than to Boswell with his 'troublesome kindness', that Johnson opened his heart. Not that the letters are gloomy. He has his brief moment of sadness, and then the bubble of the narrative floats up again. He delights in telling her of the hospitality he has met: she, who gave so unstinting a hospitality to him, should be the first to share in his happiness at finding a welcome in other houses so far away from Streatham. 'The hospitality of this remote region,' he writes, 'is like that of the golden age. We have found ourselves treated at every house as if we came to confer a favour.' If he has now and then a more disappointing experience, he shares that too. One host, and one only, was something less than hospitable – Sir Alexander Macdonald of Skye. This gentleman came to meet them when they first landed on the island, and entertained them not at his main residence but at a small house he owned near the shore. It sounds like a courteous gesture, but both Johnson and Boswell suspected – with reason – that his motive was parsimony. 'If he aspired to meanness', Johnson's letter to Hester comments dryly, 'his retrograde ambition was completely gratified.'

Thus closely they kept in touch during Johnson's travels. But, towards the end, he hankered for sight and sound of her. He knew, from the irregular letters he received, that her life was very much beset with problems. Henry Thrale's business affairs had suffered a severe setback in 1772, leaving him worried and depressed. Things were still not straightened out when a sudden scandal over-whelmed his personal life. Stories of his past amorous escapades were splashed over the newspapers and were accompanied by gleeful insinuations about his present conduct. Hester, who had suffered a miscarriage in the autumn of 1772 and was now pregnant again, was distressed by all this, yet gamely struggled to be of any help she could in sorting out matters at the brewery, for which reason she forced herself, several days in every week, to abandon the quiet comfort of Streatham and come in to Southwark. As if this were not enough, her daughter Lucy fell ill during Johnson's absence, and her mother, old Mrs Salusbury, was dying of breast cancer and suffering constant pain. There was yet more, for her troubles 'came not single spies', and she was called on to bear a severe dis-appointment. Her uncle, Sir Thomas Salusbury, had died; Hester had been brought up to expect that his estate in Hertfordshire, scene of so much of her girlhood, would come to her. But when the will was read he proved to have left it to his second wife. Writing this news to Johnson, she declared candidly, 'If I should say I was neither angry nor sorry for all this it would be very monstrous, for I am as angry and as sorry as I can be.' From Edinburgh, on 12 November, Johnson wrote her a wise and calming letter, giving sound practical advice on how to live with the disappointment, since it could not be remedied. Six days later he wrote in more general terms about her problems and difficulties, begging her to take care of herself, for she was much needed by many people:

Do not suffer yourself to be dejected. Resolution and diligence will supply all that is wanting, and all that is lost. But if your health should be impaired, I know not where to find a substitute. I shall have no Mistress, Mr Thrale will have no wife, and the little flock will have no mother.

In the same letter he tells her that they will soon be together. 'This is the last letter that I shall write, while you are reading it I shall be coming home.' 'I long to be at home.' 'Home' meant not his own house but Streatham. It was at Streatham that he sat down to write the book that would convey the lessons of his Scottish experience.

It was, for once, a book Johnson was genuinely eager to write – so much so that he quite forgot to procrastinate. There were two reasons for this. First, he knew that it would be expected of him. The thought of Johnson in the Hebrides had stirred the curiosity of many people, both among the wider reading public and in the circle of those who knew him personally. Speculation and rumour had been rife from the beginning; when Johnson and Boswell were forced by bad weather to spend such a long time in Skye, away from the mainland and out of communication, reports of their death by drowning had been printed in the newspapers. Though these rumours had not been confirmed, everyone knew that something adventurous had happened to them, and the full story was eagerly awaited. We may take as typical the remark of Topham Beauclerk in a letter to a friend: 'Johnson has been confined for some weeks in the Isle of Skye; we hear that he was obliged to swim over to the mainland taking hold of a cow's tail. Be that as it may, Lady Di has promised to make a drawing of it.' If this drawing was ever shown to Johnson, the fact is not on record.

Besides the curiosity of the public, there was Johnson's own conviction that he had important truths to communicate. He held it, as a matter of general principle, any man's duty to share with others such illumination as he had found in travelling. So firmly was he convinced of this duty that he became very exasperated with anyone who, having wandered to distant lands, came home with his mental basket empty. Once, at the Thrales', he was irritated by the silence of a man who had visited Prague. 'Surely', he said afterwards, 'the man who has seen Prague might tell us something new and something strange, and not sit silent for want of matter to set his lips in motion!' Another time, in conversation with Boswell, he remarked that it would be very interesting to see the Great Wall of China. Boswell remarked that he might almost be tempted to make the journey, if he had not responsibilities towards his children. Johnson took him up on this. 'Sir, by doing so, you would do what would be of importance in raising your children to eminence. There would be a lustre reflected upon them from your spirit and curiosity. They would be at all times regarded as the children of a man who had gone to view the wall of China.' Boswell must have grinned at this, because Johnson added firmly, 'I am serious, Sir.'

In working up his book, Johnson relied mainly on the letters to Hester Thrale, though he mentions keeping a record of his impressions; this has not survived, and probably amounted to nothing more than a few notes. Boswell was the diarist. In this, both showed their temperamental bias. Boswell, though he was so outgoing, was a compulsive journalizer; Johnson, though he kept a *journal intime*, needed the sense of a receptive listener. Boswell could sit in a room by himself and pour on to the paper his thoughts, ideas and ecstasies; Johnson, similarly left alone, would become too melancholy and withdrawn to write much. Just as, in boyhood, he had talked out his thoughts to Edmund Hector as they strolled about the green spaces of Lichfield, so now, writing down his impressions of the Hebrides, he needed to feel that he was writing *to* someone. The debt to Hester Thrale is thus twofold. Not only did she provide the sympathetic and receptive ear into which he poured out the story of his travels while it was still unfolding; she made the comfortable and secure anchorage in which the experiences could be 'recollected in tranquillity'.

There was also, of course, a debt to Boswell. The trip would never have been undertaken without Boswell's enthusiasm, and without his cheerfulness and energy it could hardly have been carried out so successfully. Boswell had earned a recompense, and Johnson gave it to him in the very opening paragraph of the book – a compliment in the high Johnsonian manner:

I had desired to visit the Hebrides, or Western Islands of Scotland, so long, that I scarcely remember how the wish was originally excited; and was in the autumn of the year 1773 induced to undertake the journey, by finding in Mr Boswell a companion, whose acuteness would help my inquiry, and whose gaiety of conversation and civility of manners are sufficient to counteract the inconveniences of travel, in countries less hospitable than we have passed.

This pleased Boswell as much as anything in his entire life. He had already welcomed the news that Johnson intended to write an account of their travels, because it would rivet in the world's attention the fact that he, Boswell, was Johnson's close friend; and apart from anything else this would be a help when he got round to writing the life of Johnson, as by now he firmly intended to do. But this accolade was more than he had dreamt of. Familiar as it was, he could not resist quoting it word for word when his own book *The Journal of a Tour to the Hebrides with Samuel Johnson, LL.D.*, in due course appeared.

Boswell's book did not come out until the year after Johnson's death and therefore has, strictly speaking, no place in our story. But it is worth pausing over for a moment or two. An enchanting book in itself, it is the record of a sunny period in both their lives. Not only that, it is the first specimen of Boswell's unique powers, and daringly original method, as a biographer. Coming out six years ahead of the great *Life*, it was a *ballon d'essai*, testing public reaction and also staking Boswell's claim to a major share in the task of recording Johnson's likeness for posterity – very necessary, this, for nimbler rivals got in ahead of him so thick and fast that his vast book was in fact the seventh in line.

Both these works of Boswell's, the *Journal* and the *Life*, provoked a storm of hostile criticism. It was felt in many quarters that by drawing Johnson warts and all, by recording his fits of peevishness, eccentricities, physical and mental peculiarities generally, Boswell had detracted from his hero's dignity. He was sensitive to this criticism, but considered it unjustified – in which he was, surely, quite right. Johnson is not lowered in anyone's esteem by the intimate portrait given by Boswell or, for that matter, by Mrs Thrale in her *Anecdotes* of 1786. On the contrary, what most of us notice is how well Johnson stands up to such detailed scrutiny. Thanks mainly to Boswell, we know Johnson's life as intimately as if we lived in the same house with him – and how little, after all, we know to his discredit! A few fits of ill-temper, a few unnecessary roughnesses which he usually regretted within the hour, that well-known lack of enthusiasm for clean linen – how small a total of defects (one can hardly call them faults) to set against his goodness and courage and positiveness! So we feel when we read Boswell. But many of Boswell's contemporaries were scandalized at the figure cut by the grave Rambler in some of his pages. It was not only the occasional revelation of peevishness or impatience that offended them, such as the account of Johnson's fit of temper when Boswell rode ahead as they approached Glenelg and left him behind ('He called me back with a tremendous shout, and was really in a passion with me for leaving him'); even worse, to many eyes, was the sheer triviality of some of the detail. Boswell disdained nothing; every remark made by Johnson could be taken as shedding some light on his character and opinions. Looking back from where we stand now, accustomed as we are to the constant purveying of trivialities about anyone who gets into the news, it is hard to imagine what a departure from established practice was Boswell's all-inclusive gleaning:

> At dinner, Dr Johnson ate several platefuls of Scotch broth, with barley and peas in it, and seemed very fond of the dish. I said, 'You never ate it before.' Johnson: 'No, Sir; but I don't care how soon I eat it again.'

Many readers snorted that this kind of thing debased the dignity of biography, and Boswell was fain to defend his method by frequent explosions of self-justification. But he had one trump card. Johnson had read the journal on which his book was faithfully based, had read it day by day as it was composed, and had approved it. He raised no objection to the minuteness of some of the fragments that Boswell stuck together to form his caddis-shell; far from it, he declared that he found the journal very enjoyable reading and that it got better as it went on. Boswell was deeply gratified and encouraged, as he was by Johnson's benign willingness to answer questions about his early life.

Boswell's book is very, very good. Apart from everything else it is the ideal preface to Johnson's more compressed and weighty account. Such episodes as the meeting with Flora Macdonald, for instance, are far more fully documented by Boswell. This lady, who in the disguise of a pageboy had played a crucial part in the escape of Prince Charles Edward after the defeat of Culloden, drew from Johnson's pen a tribute so stately that it was actually cut in stone, years afterwards, on a cross erected over her grave. 'Flora Macdonald', Johnson wrote, 'a name that will be mentioned in history, and if courage and fidelity be virtues, mentioned with honour.' But it is Boswell who tells the wild and romantic story of flight and pursuit, of small boats and dark caves, of the faithfulness of brave men to the defeated leader they called king.

We turn to Boswell, of course, not only for romantic colouring, not only for incisively etched detail, but for comedy. He must be one of the funniest writers extant. Sometimes he makes quite a good joke by intention, but more often he is hilarious without knowing it, or without completely knowing it – he has an idea there is something funny going on, but cannot put his finger on it. His psychology was, as we have noted earlier, very peculiar, and nowhere more so than in his relationship with Johnson. There was, very genuinely, love and admiration; there was the emotional dependence on a father figure; there was also, now and then, a streak of gleeful malice. It would not be true to say that he enjoyed steering Johnson into embarrassing situations in order to watch his reaction; but to say anything else would involve so many qualifications, so much shredding out of fine distinctions, that we might almost as well say so and let it go at that. His account of the visit to Auchinleck is a good case in point. He had long wanted to see Johnson at the venerable seat of the Boswell family; he had long wanted to bring his adopted father into contact with his real father. So much was genuine, and unambiguous. On the other hand, he knew that the two could be counted on to quarrel. The stiff-necked old judge was as decided a Whig and Presbyterian as Johnson was Tory and Anglican. Sure enough, the name of Cromwell happening to arise when Lord Auchinleck was showing Johnson his collection of medals, the conversation took a political turn which soon led to a free-for-all. 'I was very much distressed', says Boswell, pretending to be all of a flutter, 'by being present at such an altercation between two men, both of whom I reverenced.' With another part of his mind, of course, he was delighted at having put them both through the hoop so successfully.

Such is Boswell's account. But our main business is with Johnson's. We may approach the magnificent *Journey to the Western Islands of Scotland* by remarking that it is as centrally Johnsonian as Boswell's Journal is centrally Boswellian. It is a book that the admirer of Johnson will linger over and return to again and again. Johnson wrote it in a happy time, when everything was running in his favour. He was interested and involved, he had secure and comfortable surroundings, and he had the stimulus of knowing that the book he was writing could only come from him and from nobody else.

Everything that happens to a writer sooner or later bears fruit in a book. The cliché becomes interesting when we reflect that there is much virtue in that 'sooner' and 'later', and likewise that the tree of literature bears more than one kind of fruit. Johnson's writing was always very directly related to his experience. His earlier work, up to and including *Rasselas*, reflects his personal struggle: the succession of disappointments, the sense that the scales were impossibly weighted against him, and the compensating force and steadiness of his purpose. Starting with many handicaps, he had gradually grown into the knowledge that the strength had been given him to push ahead step by step, and by early middle life he had proved his ability to survive. This knowledge permeates *The Rambler* essays, while the colossal price he had to pay for survival is there in the melancholy of the Preface to the Dictionary and of his poetry. The later writing – everything, more or less, from *Rasselas* onward – reflects Johnson's knowledge that his immediate problems of survival are solved, that he can afford to devote the rest of his life to helping others to comb out the tangle of their conflicting impulses. There is a more relaxed, discursive, outward looking atmosphere, whether he is reminiscing, or offering general comments on life, or even laying about him as he is in the political pamphlets of the 1770s. The *Journey* is full in the mainstream of this later period of Johnson's writings. Here, and in everything that follows, there is a deep glow, as of amber, even in passages that are sombre or elegiac. Coming to it after Boswell's book, the first thing we notice is that the knockabout element is completely banished. The tone of Johnson's account is grave, dignified, compassionate. Where Boswell set himself to produce a realistic, step-by-step account of their adventures, Johnson is content that some elements of the actual experience should get lost in the reconstruction. He is concerned not to tell the story of a *divertissement* but to

paint the portrait of a society and a way of life. A good example would be their
contrasting treatment of the encounter with the old woman in her hut beside
Loch Ness. This happened on the first day of their 'equitation', when they had
the sense of breaking into wild country and strange ways for the first time, and
both make something of a set piece of it. Here is Boswell:

> When we had advanced a good way by the side of Loch Ness, I perceived
> a little hut, with an old looking woman at the door of it. I thought here
> might be a scene that would amuse Dr Johnson; so I mentioned it to him.
> 'Let's go in', said he. We dismounted, and we and our guides entered the hut.
> It was a wretched little hovel of earth only, I think, and for a window had
> only a small hole, which was stopped with a piece of turf, that was taken
> out occasionally to let in light. In the middle of the room or space which
> we entered, was a fire of peat, the smoke going out at a hole in the roof.
> She had a pot on it, with goat's flesh, boiling. There was at one end under
> the same roof, but divided by a kind of partition made of wattles, a pen or
> fold in which we saw a good many kids.
>
> Dr Johnson was curious to know where she slept. I asked one of the
> guides, who questioned her in Erse. She answered with a tone of emotion,
> saying (as he told us) she was afraid we wanted to go to bed to her. This
> coquetry, or whatever it may be called, of so wretched a being, was truly
> ludicrous. Dr Johnson and I afterwards were merry upon it. I said, it was
> he who alarmed the poor woman's virtue. 'No, Sir (said he), she'll say,
> "There came a wicked young fellow, a wild dog, who I believe would
> have ravished me, had there not been with him a grave old gentleman, who
> repressed him: but when he gets out of the sight of his tutor, I'll warrant
> you he'll spare no woman he meets, young or old".' 'No, Sir (I replied),
> she'll say, "There was a terrible ruffian who would have forced me, had it
> not been for a civil decent young man who, I take it, was an angel sent from
> heaven to protect me".'

This is brilliant reporting; it gives us the whiff of the experience as it really
happened, and it conveys that the pair were in holiday mood. Johnson makes
no such attempt. His account is short, sober, objective in its account of the facts,
but very personal in that it shows how deeply his sympathies and his moral
attitudes were engaged:

> Near the way, by the waterside, we espied a cottage. This was the first
> Highland hut that I had seen; and as our business was with life and manners,
> we were willing to visit it. To enter a habitation without leave seems to be
> not considered here as rudeness or intrusion. The old laws of hospitality
> still give this licence to a stranger.
>
> A hut is constructed with loose stones, ranged for the most part with
> some tendency to circularity. It must be placed where the wind cannot
> act upon it with violence, because it has no cement; and where the water

will run easily away, because it has no floor but the naked ground. The wall, which is commonly about six feet high, declines from the perpendicular a little inward. Such rafters as can be procured are then raised for a roof, and covered with heath, which makes a strong and warm thatch, kept from flying off by ropes of twisted heath, of which the ends, reaching from the centre of the thatch to the top of the wall, are held firm by the weight of a large stone. No light is admitted, but at the entrance, and through a hole in the thatch, which gives vent to the smoke. This hole is not directly over the fire, lest the rain should extinguish it; and the smoke therefore, naturally fills the place before it escapes. Such is the general structure of the houses in which one of the nations of this opulent and powerful island has been hitherto content to live. Huts, however, are not more uniform than palaces; and this which we were inspecting was very far from one of the meanest, for it was divided into several apartments; and its inhabitants possessed such property as a pastoral poet might exalt into riches.

I have not quoted either account in full – both go on for about as long again – but the contrasting tone is sufficiently indicated. Boswell gives a brilliant, impressionistic sketch, capturing one particular conversation on one particular August morning. Johnson has no such passion for the particular. His business is with the accurate recording and rendering of information that will help people to come to decisions. He begins with exact, minute description of what a hut is like and how it is built. He is writing for people who will not have a chance to see one for themselves. That done, he presses, as always, towards judgement and generalization. It is a scandal that subjects of the British Crown should live like the humblest savages. And such conditions are tolerated because we make the comfortable refusal to see things as they are. The dig at pastoral poetry is meaningful in the context. Johnson objected to this convention because it peopled a pretty and unreal landscape with Dresden figures, nymphs and swains who had no drudging work to do and never dreaded cold and starvation. Doubtless, from a literary point of view, there was something bull-headed in his objection to pastoral, a tradition that has given European literature many masterpieces. But he always placed life before literature, and it was his opinion that eighteenth-century pastoral poetry did precious little good and much harm, encouraging townees to take a sentimental view of the lives of the peasantry. Why, a pastoral poet might even see the lot of this old woman in her smoke-filled hut as something to write pretty poems about rather than something that should be altered.

Not that Johnson preaches. When he makes his own attitude clear, he always does so in a very few words. Brevity and concentration, indeed, are the hallmarks of this book. Short enough to be read within an evening, it leaves a lasting impression because of the weight and density of thinking and feeling behind each paragraph. In flavour it is not unlike *Rasselas*, but whereas *Rasselas* used the framework of a fictional journey to present a series of conversations, Johnson now uses the much more solid framework of a real journey and intersperses it not with conversations but with reflections like those in *The Rambler*. The wanderings of *Rasselas* and his party are a mere *donnée*; they move about, it matters not where, because Johnson wants to confront them with a diversity of human lifestyles and situations. But in reporting on his own journey he was making a definite contribution to the workings of his society. The kind of people who read his books – educated, largely urban, almost all with some kind of power and influence even if it went no further than their own parish – had, after all, considerable political power over the Highland and Hebridean people he was describing. To make the one world more intelligible to the other, to bring a very blurred portrait into clearer focus, was to perform an important service. This was not one of those travel books that serve mainly as material for daydreams, but an investigation of a corner of the kingdom Johnson himself belonged to. Hence the gravity of the book. Not that it is 'heavy', in the bad sense; the prose is lighter and swifter than anything Johnson has written before; but it has, in the good sense, *gravitas*, seriousness.

Like *Rasselas*, the *Journey* tells of a quest for illumination. But this time the objective is more limited than the prince's search for the possibility of happiness. It is a definite, concrete objective – the truth about one society in a given time and place – and yet it proves curiously elusive. The questions that arise are of considerable complexity; the easy answers seem more and more glib and dishonest as the travellers come more closely to grips with real situations. So that the *Journey* comes, like *Rasselas*, to a 'conclusion in which nothing is concluded'. Only that the people of this country are in a tragic and painful situation, and should be spared the fresh agonies that will arise from muddled decisions by centralist politicians and reformers. When he and Boswell had finished their stay on the Island of Skye, they went down to Ostaig, so as to be near the coast when a favourable wind should arise to take them on the next stage. This, apart from a couple of days at Armadale just before they sailed, was their last place of sojourn in Skye, the largest and most important of the Hebridean islands. Accordingly, when Johnson gets to the section which he heads 'Ostig in Skye', he pauses and takes a long, analytical look at the life of the island. This is the longest piece of essay material in the book, and illustrates Johnson's method so well that it is worth pausing over for a moment.

First, he gives us just the physical description, from the ground up: the air temperature, the soil, how much is arable and how much rock or marsh, what crops will grow. Next in logical sequence come the methods of agriculture. Then the animals, first domestic, then wild. Johnson has noticed everything. The cattle and horses are smaller than in England; the sheep and goats are of the usual size. Some of the cattle have horns, others do not; he has looked into the matter carefully:

We are not very sure that the bull is ever without horns, though we have been told that such bulls there are. What is produced by putting a horned and unhorned male and female together, no man has ever tried that thought the result worthy of observation.

And so on, through stags, roebuck, weasels, rats and mice. Then we come to the human beings. Still working from the natural to the man-made, Johnson begins by describing their physical characteristics; he is still dealing with the animal life of Skye, and the human inhabitants are, for the moment, grouped with the other mammals. They are 'commonly of the middle stature'; their women 'have as much beauty here as in other places'; the expectation of life is about the same as among townspeople. Golden-age fictions about the incredibly long lives of people who live close to Nature are fictions and nothing more, for 'a cottager grows old over his oaten cakes, like a citizen at a turtle feast'.

That concludes the physical side of the description of Skye. Johnson has already written half a dozen pages and he is just getting warmed up. More complex questions lie ahead, not to be dealt with by observation alone. Opinion and prejudice will henceforth lie in wait for us. So, after a short description of the social pyramid of Skye – the laird; the tacksman; the tenant – he utters a warning:

> To the southern inhabitants of Scotland, the state of the mountains and the islands is equally unknown with that of Borneo or Sumatra: of both they have only heard a little, and guess the rest. They are strangers to the language, and the manners, to the advantages and wants of the people, whose life they would model, and whose evils they would remedy.

To begin with, these Lowland blunderers have too hastily assumed that the tacksman should be thrown out as a useless middleman. The tacksman rented a large area from the laird, and sublet part of it to small tenants:

> He paid rent and reverence to the laird, and received them from the tenants. This tenure still subsists, with its original operation, but not with the primitive stability. Since the islanders, no longer content to live, have learned the desire of growing rich, an ancient dependant is in danger of giving way to a higher bidder, at the expense of domestic dignity and hereditary power. The stranger, whose money buys him preference, considers himself as paying for all that he has, and is indifferent about the laird's honour or safety. The commodiousness of money is indeed great; but there are some advantages which money cannot buy, and which therefore no wise man will by the love of money be tempted to forgo.

This is the kind of thing that the reformers, English and Lowland Scots alike, are constantly in danger of overlooking. Quick arithmetic will show that the tacksman consumes revenue that would otherwise go to the laird or to the tenants. But arithmetic does not have all the answers. The tacksman is usually a collateral relative of the laird's; he is regarded as a social superior by the tenant, being better off and better educated. A laird with wide domains cannot maintain personal contact with all his tenants, but they can all live within easy reach of a tacksman, who will give them instruction and advice and help them with their problems:

> The only gentlemen in the Islands are the lairds, the tacksmen, and the

ministers, who frequently improve their livings by becoming farmers. If
the tacksmen be banished, who will be left to impart knowledge, or impress civility? The laird must always be at a distance from the greater part
of his lands; and if he resides at all upon them, must drag his days in solitude,
having no longer either a friend or a companion; he will therefore depart
to some more comfortable residence, and leave the tenants to the wisdom
and mercy of a factor.

After a few brief remarks about domestic servants, Johnson has finished his
description of the social system of Skye. But, though he has uttered his solemn
warning against too eager meddling, he is not to be tempted into Boswellian
raptures about the happiness of the old order:

> The inhabitants were for a long time perhaps not unhappy; but their
> content was a muddy mixture of pride and ignorance, an indifference for
> pleasures which they did not know, a blind veneration for their chiefs,
> and a strong conviction of their own importance.

Nevertheless, happy, or unhappy, that state is now changed, and Johnson next
turns his attention to these changes. The people have been disarmed; the lairds
no longer have the power of jurisdiction; and rents are now paid in money
rather than in kind. All these measures produce both good and bad effects.
Johnson weighs these effects. He is at the height of his powers, reasoning like
a great lawyer while expressing the deep compassion that flows from his
involvement with common life. And, as always, he seeks to cut through the
tangle of what is accidental and incidental, and state the problem in its basic,
philosophical terms. The lairds, when they gave up their privileges, were compensated with money, becoming proprietors instead of patriarchs, and this inevitably turned their thoughts away from hereditary power and towards
transmissible wealth. Johnson accordingly clarifies this question by making
some very useful distinctions between wealth and power:

> Those who have long enjoyed dignity and power ought not to lose it
> without some equivalent. There was paid to the chiefs by the public, in
> exchange for their privileges, perhaps a sum greater than most of them had
> ever possessed, which excited a thirst for riches, of which it showed them
> the use. When the power of birth and station ceases, no hope remains but
> from the prevalence of money. Power and wealth supply the place of each
> other. Power confers the ability of gratifying our desire without the con-
> sent of others. Wealth enables us to obtain the consent of others to our
> gratification. Power, simply considered, whatever it confers on one, must
> take from another. Wealth enables its owner to give to others, by taking
> only from himself. Power pleases the violent and proud: wealth delights
> the placid and the timorous. Youth therefore flies at power, and age grovels
> after riches.

Do the lairds, as many are now saying, wring too much out of their tenants in
increased rents? Johnson is careful here; he knows that any increase in rent is
unwelcome and easily put down to rapacity. But one thing is certain: the

people are discontented. They are emigrating to America, and once they get there they send back good reports to induce others to follow them and mitigate their loneliness. Conversely, the proprietors exaggerate the miseries of emigration to keep their people at home. Between the two, the inhabitants of the Hebrides are bewildered. Once again Johnson tries to move the problem nearer to solution by stating it clearly:

Let it be inquired whether the first intention of those who are fluttering on the wing, and collecting a flock that they may take their flight, be to attain good, or to avoid evil. If they are dissatisfied with that part of the globe which their birth has allotted them, and resolve not to live without the pleasures of happier climates; if they long for bright suns, and calm skies, and flowery fields and fragrant gardens, I know not by what eloquence they can be persuaded, or by what offers they can be hired to stay.

But if they are driven from their native country by positive evils, and disgusted by ill treatment, real or imaginary, it were fit to remove their grievances, and quiet their resentment; since, if they have been hitherto undutiful subjects, they will not much mend their principles by American conversation.

Naturally, Johnson could not resist that flick at the American settlers. Every Hebridean who crossed the Atlantic not only made a gap at home, he added one more to the ranks of the illegal secessionists. But Johnson was activated by deeper motives than his dislike of American independence. He saw that a grave mistake was being made in the Highlands and Islands, and he wanted to raise his voice against it. He does so in phrases that are among the finest in eighteenth-century prose; forensic yet thoughtful, ironic yet gravely compassionate:

To hinder insurrection, by driving away the people, and to govern peaceably, by having no subjects, is an expedient that argues no great profundity of politics. To soften the obdurate, to convince the mistaken, to mollify the resentful, are worthy of a statesman; but it affords a legislator little self-applause to consider, that where there was formerly an insurrection, there is now a wilderness.

This is the high peak of Johnson's essay. It goes on to discuss the question of the migration of peoples, from a lofty historical and philosophical standpoint; thence, it modulates into a discussion of the conditions of life of the average Hebridean; thence to education, and thence to religion. Mention of religious belief leads to beliefs in general, and now Johnson pauses long enough to deliberate thoroughly on the question of extrasensory perception or 'second sight'. His marshalling of the evidence is a demonstration of fine reasoning, but his very scrupulousness will not allow him to come down on either side. 'I never could advance my curiosity to conviction, and came away at last only willing to believe.'

Stories of the second sight lead naturally to stories in general. Johnson had assiduously listened to everyone who could talk to him about past times; but in the nature of things he could expect very little in the way of accurate historical information. He and Boswell asked many questions:

> But we soon found what memorials were to be expected from an illiterate people, whose whole time is a series of distress; where every morning is labouring with expedients for the evening; and where all mental pains or pleasure arose from the dread of winter, the expectation of spring, the caprices of their chiefs and the motions of the neighbouring clans; where there was neither shame from ignorance, nor pride in knowledge; neither curiosity to inquire, nor vanity to communicate.

This leads him to reflect on the transmission of historical fact generally. His preference is strongly for the book as against the oral tradition. A book may pass out of fashion and lie neglected for generations; but once it is taken down and dusted, it is all ready to say over again what it said years ago. Whereas oral tradition, once broken, cannot be put together. A modern anthropologist would probably say that Johnson was being too sceptical here. Oral tradition in many parts of the world has shown itself capable of a range and retentiveness well equal to what the written word could have achieved within the same circumstances. Johnson cannot be blamed for not knowing this. He had not, as we have, the advantage of being able to read such books as Albert B. Lord's *The Singer of Tales*. As a result, he was disposed to rely on written evidence to the almost total exclusion of oral tradition – especially as he had had comically frustrating experience of trying to elicit information by questions. The Anglo-Saxon always finds to his cost that the Celt does not much believe in hard and fast statements, whether descriptive or narrative. He varies his account according to his attitude to the listener, or to his own mood, which in turn depends on the weather, his emotional life, and how well he is digesting his last meal. To the Celt this is normal human practice; to the Anglo-Saxon, it is evasiveness. So that the very children in the nursery are taught to distrust the Celt, and to lisp such rhymes as:

> Taffy was a Welshman
> Taffy was a thief
> Taffy came to my house
> And stole a piece of beef.

Johnson loved and respected the Hebrideans, but he had no opinion whatever of their reliability in imparting information. And if they could not convey the straight facts about something that happened two miles off on the previous day what was the value of their traditions, 'bardic' or otherwise?

Inevitably, this leads Johnson to the vexed question of 'Ossian'. The story of his involvement in this bizarre controversy is soon told, but a book at least as long as the present one would be needed to take up all the implications. In all the rich history of literature, and ideas, and attitudes, and what for want of a better word we must call 'culture', there is no tale stranger, and more productive of insights and illuminations into the ways of a bygone world, than this of Macpherson and his 'Ossian'.

Briefly, what happened was this. At the age of twenty-three in 1759, Macpherson was eating his ambitious young heart out as a tutor in a Scottish gentleman's family, when he happened to meet the Reverend John Home, the celebrated playwright whose *Douglas* had kindled many a Scottish heart. Home had heard of the ancient poetic tradition of the Highlands, and questioned Macpherson, who had some Gaelic. Macpherson, seeing a chance to attract some attention and get out of his rut, went up to his room and produced a rhapsodic monody called 'The Death of Oscar', which he showed to Home as a translation of ancient Gaelic epic poetry from manuscripts in his possession. The plan worked. Home carried off the fabrication to Edinburgh, and succeeded in interesting Hugh Blair, the *doyen* of that city's literary scholars and critics, in its merits. Where Blair led, others followed. Macpherson eagerly scribbled more of these pseudo-translations and in 1760 appeared a slender volume entitled *Fragments of Ancient Poetry, Collected in the Highlands of Scotland, and Translated from the Gaelic or Erse Language*. It had a preface by Blair, drawing attention to the excellence of this newly discovered treasure of Scots literature, and remarking particularly that the rugged bards of ancient times, working entirely from inspiration and without ever having heard of Aristotle and Horace, had given a striking demonstration of the validity of classical theories of literature; and testifying to his belief that many more remains of ancient genius were waiting to be discovered.

If that were all, the story might be one of those curiosities of literary history, to be chuckled over for a moment and then forgotten. What brings it into the centre of the stage is the incredible force and depth of the response to Macpherson's gallimaufry.

As we noted in the case of William Collins, the middle and late eighteenth century experienced a number of earth tremors which were early indications of the colossal upheaval of the human spirit that we call 'Romanticism'. Unless we adopt the view that progress is always right (a view nowadays held by no one except city developers), we cannot blame those who felt these tremors without responding to them; but not to feel them at all would argue some defect in alertness and sensibility. Johnson undoubtedly felt them, and his response was to look to the foundations of his house. After about mid-point, all his work as a literary critic was a rearguard action. He valued the tight little civilization of Renaissance neo-classicism, he respected the hard-won achievements of reason and judgement, and he saw the new wave of larger and vaguer feeling as a threat. It was, however, his fate to live into an epoch which increasingly responded to these seismic shocks, increasingly reached out towards the new order. From (roughly) 1760 onwards, all over Europe there is a hunger and thirst, which intensify year by year until they are first appeased and finally satiated by Romantic poetry, Romantic painting, Romantic music, Romantic fiction. To locate the sources of this appetite, to assign causes, to plot the graph of its growth in this country and that, has been the life's work of many a learned man. All that concerns us at the moment is that the appetite existed, and grew by what it fed on. Macpherson may have thought of himself as throwing out a book that would get him into the limelight, much as a modern young careerist will try to say something outrageous enough to get him interviewed on television. But in fact he was doing something far deeper, and with roots that were both poetic and tragic. He was co-operating with the *Zeitgeist*. The impulse that led him to fadge up the 'Ossianic poems' was at one with the impulse that had begun to sweep the Western world, and would continue its resistless course for another hundred years.

Johnson, of course, was immune to this epidemic of pre-Romantic sensibility. Country bred, he had accepted the urban Augustan culture; a man of the Renaissance (had not the very reading of his childhood been in Petrarch, the 'restorer of poetry'?), he had inherited critical principles which denied to mediaeval literature any but the most peripheral place. So that anyone hostile to Johnson could always say that he disbelieved Macpherson's claims more or less by accident; not liking 'Ossian', he had no temptation to believe in its authenticity and would not have believed even if Macpherson had had good arguments. In fact, this would be to misjudge Johnson. He did not share in the mediaevalizing enthusiasm of his friends Warton and Percy, but he respected the solid work they did. Moreover, as we have seen, he was deeply sensitive to the sublimity of mediaeval buildings and the fervent piety of mediaeval religion. He was well read in scholastic theology, the highest intellectual achievement of the Middle Ages. And he responded finely to the Highlands themselves, the landscape and the people. He was no mere John Bull snorting his contempt of everything that was strange and antique and Scotch. On the contrary he contented himself with repeating patiently that if Macpherson was translating from ancient manuscripts, he should produce these manuscripts and let people see them. Having reached the point in his narrative at which the matter presented itself for discussion, he introduced it first ironically, then with devastating bluntness:

> I believe there cannot be recovered, in the whole Erse language, five hundred lines of which there is any evidence to prove them a hundred years old. Yet I hear that the father of Ossian boasts of two chests more of ancient poetry, which he suppresses, because they are too good for the English.

Having thus flicked Macpherson on the raw, he moved in to demolish him:

> I suppose my opinion of the poems of Ossian is already discovered. I believe they never existed in any other form than that which we have seen. The editor, or author, never could show the original; nor can it be shown by any other; to revenge reasonable incredulity, by refusing evidence, is a degree of insolence, with which the world is not yet acquainted; and stubborn audacity is the last refuge of guilt.

As a final clincher, Johnson recalls a conversation with a typical believer in Ossian's genuineness:

I asked a very learned minister in Skye, who had used all arts to make me believe the genuineness of the book, whether at last he believed it himself? but he would not answer. He wished me to be deceived, for the honour of his country; but would not directly and formally deceive me. Yet has this man's testimony been publicly produced, as of one that held *Fingal* to be the work of Ossian.

Macpherson, we may reasonably suppose, chewed his fingernails on hearing that Johnson was writing a book about the Highlands and Islands; he could guess all too well what judgement would be delivered in the Ossian case. At least Johnson did not torture him by making him wait long. Working quickly, he had most of the book written by the summer of 1774; the printer was slow, but in November Johnson had finished reading proofs, and the book appeared either at the very end of that year or the beginning of 1775 – some thirteen months after Johnson's homecoming. Copies were sped northwards – Boswell received his on 18 January – and Macpherson found his worst fears confirmed. He had, in fact, already made an effort to ward off the blow he saw descending. A story, no doubt concocted by himself, was assiduously spread in Edinburgh and elsewhere, to the effect that – as Boswell informed Johnson –

Before your book came out he sent to you, to let you know that he understood you meant to deny the authenticity of Ossian's poems; that the originals were in his possession; that you might have inspection of them, and might take the evidence of people skilled in the Erse language; and that he hoped, after this fair offer, you would not be so uncandid as to assert that he had refused reasonable proof.

Johnson wrote back in dismissive vein.

My dear Boswell
I am surprised that, knowing as you do the disposition of your countrymen to tell lies in favour of one another, you can be at all affected by any reports that circulate among them. . . .

He went on to mention that Macpherson had tried to 'intimidate' him. What exactly Macpherson had said in his letter we shall never know, since Johnson did not keep a copy, but it obviously included the threat of violence, and he was a big, strong man, twenty-five years younger than Johnson. Johnson's reply is characteristic:

Mr James Macpherson – I received your foolish and impudent note. Whatever insult is offered me I will do my best to repel, and what I cannot do for myself the law will do for me. I will not desist from detecting what I think a cheat, from any fear of the menaces of a ruffian.

You want me to retract. What shall I retract? I thought your book an imposture from the beginning, I think it upon yet surer reasons an imposture still. For this opinion I give the public my reasons, which I here dare you to refute.

But however I may despise you, I reverence truth, and if you can prove the genuineness of the work I will confess it. Your rage I defy, your abilities since your Homer are not so formidable, and what I have heard of your morals disposes me to pay regard not to what you shall say, but to what you can prove.

You may print this if you will.

20 Jan 1775

SAM: JOHNSON

He also provided himself with an oaken stick, with which to defend himself if Macpherson should suddenly burst in on him; till the matter blew over, he kept it close to the chair in which he usually sat, so that he could start up with it at a second's notice. But perhaps 'stick' is too poor a word to describe this noble weapon. The sight of it was one that John Hawkins never forgot. He described it, in his *Life*, as 'an oak-plant of a tremendous size; a plant, I say, and not a shoot or branch, for it had a root, which being trimmed to the size of a large orange, became the head of it. Its height was upwards of six feet, and from about an inch in diameter at the lower end, increased to near three.'

There we must leave Macpherson, whose pate never in fact felt the impact of this shillelagh. His subsequent story is even funnier, reaching a culmination in a pitch of farce beyond the imagination of a Feydeau or a Ben Travers. But we cannot follow him. It is time to return to Johnson, whom we left writing the magnificent essay which he heads simply, 'Ostig in Skye'. That essay concludes with a characteristically laconic mention of their wild night afloat between Skye and Coll. Boswell naturally and justifiably made this episode one of his principal set pieces. But Johnson is not writing an adventure story. His thumbnail version of the affair is as follows:

Having waited some days at Armidel, we were flattered at last with a wind that promised to convey us to Mull. We went on board a boat that was taking in kelp, and left the Isle of Skye behind us. We were doomed to experience, like others, the danger of trusting to the wind, which blew against us in a short time, with such violence that we, being no seasoned sailors, were willing to call it a tempest. I was seasick and lay down. Mr Boswell kept the deck. The master knew not well whither to go; and our difficulties might perhaps have filled a very pathetic page, had not Mr Maclean of Coll, who, with every other qualification which insular life requires, is a very active and skilful mariner, piloted us safe into his own harbour.

This reticence is not mere bluffness. It has its roots in Johnson's attitude to experience generally. If he and Boswell had been exposed to danger and nearly drowned, they had asked for it. The Hebrideans had not invited them to go there in the first place. To travel or not to travel is a voluntary decision; they might have been sitting in a London tavern instead of tossing on the autumnal seas. Whereas, to the people of those islands, the dangers and hardships were an inseparable part of daily existence. Johnson's concern is entirely with them, never at all with himself. He was always ready to sympathize with poverty, and in the Hebrides he had renewed his acquaintance with it. Never far above the level of bare survival, the Hebrideans had suffered severely during the phenomenally harsh winter of 1771, when snow had covered their scanty pasturage. As Johnson did not fail to note, they were scarcely beginning to recover what they had lost. In his travels among them he saw poverty that must have reminded him of the destitution and wretchedness that he met with in his nightly walks in the London streets. The warmly compassionate tone of his book sufficiently indicates how the sight affected him.

The generosity and fulness of Johnson's response to the Highlands and Islands is shown equally in the accounts of happiness and gaiety. At Dunvegan Castle, as we know from Boswell, Johnson was so comfortable and at ease that he 'could hardly be moved from it'. When on Saturday Boswell suggested that they should leave on Monday, Johnson was firm. 'No, Sir. I will not go before Wednesday. I will have some more of this good.' He was finding at Dunvegan what he had found at Gilbert Walmesley's house in the Close at Lichfield, and with Tom Warton at Trinity, and more recently with the Thrales – good talk and a good table. But the surrounding wildness and barrenness gave the experience, this time, a new dimension. Always a huge enjoyer, Johnson delighted in the contrast between the rugged wastes outside and the elegance, neatness and plenty inside. It was an important brush stroke in his picture of Hebridean life, proving that the place was not inhabited solely by 'rough rug-headed kerns' but also by cultivated ladies and gentlemen. When he reaches this point in the story, he pays his host and hostess a noble compliment; and a few pages further on he reverts to the theme, this time finding a very evocative way of bringing the contrast before the reader's imagination. It reminds one, he says, of the old fairy tales in which the characters have only to wander for a mile or two into the forest to meet with wizards, ogres or enchantresses. Such stories arise naturally among small, hemmed-in communities living in heavily wooded country. To think oneself into such a community is to realize that the element of pure fantasy inevitably seems greater to us than it did to them. And Johnson's way of paying a compliment to his island hosts is to remark that such fictions seem very credible when one suddenly finds cultivation, hospitality, all the blessings of civilization, after trudging across a darkening moor or swaying on a cold sea:

> The fictions of the Gothic romances were not so remote from credibility as they are now thought. In the full prevalence of the feudal institution, when violence desolated the world, and every baron lived in a fortress, forests and castles were regularly succeeded by each other, and the adventurer might very suddenly pass from the gloom of woods, or the ruggedness of moors, to seats of plenty, gaiety, and magnificence. Whatever is imaged in the wildest tale, if giants, dragons, and enchantment be excepted, would

be felt by him, who, wandering in the mountains without a guide, or upon the sea without a pilot, should be carried amidst his terror and uncertainty, to the hospitality and elegance of Raasay or Dunvegan.

Yes, 'hospitality and elegance' thrive in the Highlands and Islands. But how much longer can they hold out against the steady downward drift, the depopulation and decay? Inevitably, Johnson has to face this fact. The people are emigrating, and emigration is one of the recurrent themes of the book, handled with consummate skill. Johnson knows that to harp on emigration and bring it before the reader too frequently will be to forfeit sympathy. Accordingly, he handles it like a musician. It is a *leitmotif*, never heard twice in exactly the same way. He brings in the subject now casually, now formally, first from one angle and then from another. He also bides his time before introducing it at all. We happen to know, from Boswell's account, that emigration 'was at this time a common topic of discourse' and that Johnson was involved in discussion of it before ever they left Edinburgh, and again with Lord Monboddo on their third day out. But Johnson's book says nothing of the matter until it can be heard from the lips of a man who himself intends to leave. He waits till the travellers fall in with MacQueen, the landlord of the inn who impressed them so much at Anoch. Having focused MacQueen very steadily for the reader's attention, Johnson says firmly, disregarding all the chatter about emigration that went before,

> From him we first heard of the general dissatisfaction, which is now driving the Highlanders into the other hemisphere; and when I asked him whether they would stay at home, if they were well treated, he answered with indignation, that no man willingly left his native country.

Here at least was one Scotsman who did not regard the high road leading to England as the finest sight he could hope to see! But then that joke, like all Johnson's anti-Scots quips, was receding further and further. Henceforth, when he criticized the Scots, it would be for defects they actually had, not for misfortunes that were forced on them.

MacQueen's 'indignant' reply about leaving one's native country is one that reverberates in the book. Johnson believes in nationhood, in patriotism including local patriotism, in love and respect for the *genius loci*. To uproot and go to a new and empty country might well, if the gamble is successful, result in material comfort. But a man is not an animal, to seek his habitat for physical reasons alone. Of course many people in the eighteenth century, like many people today, took the opposite view. Then as now, it was commonly argued that attachment to a place is merely a hampering illusion that we should 'outgrow'. Johnson's answer to such people is on record in the sombre and beautiful prose poem to which he is moved by visiting Iona:

> We were now treading that illustrious island, which was once the luminary of the Caledonian regions, whence savage clans and roving barbarians

derived the benefits of knowledge, and the blessings of religion. To abstract the mind from all local emotion would be impossible, if it were endeavoured, and would be foolish, if it were possible. Whatever withdraws us from the power of our senses; whatever makes the past, the distant, or the future predominate over the present, advances us in the dignity of thinking beings. Far from me and from my friends be such frigid philosophy as may conduct us indifferent and unmoved over any ground which has been dignified by wisdom, bravery, or virtue. That man is little to be envied whose patriotism would not gain force upon the plain of Marathon, or whose piety would not grow warmer among the ruins of Iona.

That passage is one of the showpieces of Johnson's work, often quoted out of context like any other purple patch. But when we put it back into its place it takes on an added dimension. If it is natural to the human heart to respond to the associations of Iona or Thermopylae, it is also natural for the Hebridean to shed bitter tears at being exiled from his native island. Comfort, even wealth, he may find; but he will leave behind so much of his identity, so much memory and tradition, that the exchange will be a poor one. As Johnson puts it with his inimitable terse finality,

It may be thought that they are happier by the change; but they are not happy as a nation, for they are a nation no longer.

Johnson's *Journey* is a complex book. He is handling many themes at once; the subject bristles with difficult – perhaps insoluble – questions, and he is concerned to hold them up to the light rather than to lay down dogmatic answers. To write such a book calls for great skill; and Johnson, the veteran journalist, has that skill. Here, as in *Rasselas*, he avoids underlining. Those points he most wishes to emphasize are introduced quietly, without insistence. They are made conspicuous by strategic placing within the narrative.

Perhaps the finest of all his demonstrations of skill occurs at the very end of the book. After getting back to Edinburgh, Johnson tells us, he went one day to see the remarkable school for deaf and dumb children run by Thomas Braidwood, who achieved excellent results mainly by the use of lip-reading. Always passionately interested in anything that can alleviate misery, always true to his principle that while suffering and misfortune are inseparable from the human condition, we have a plain duty to remedy any evil that *can* be remedied, Johnson gives a moving description of the bright eyes and smiling faces of the pupils as they await the arrival of the master who will help them to resist their tragic disadvantage; how one of the girls rapidly and correctly worked out a sum that he wrote on her slate, 'quivering her fingers in a manner which I thought very pretty, but of which I did not know whether it was art or play'. He then adds, suddenly, the short paragraph:

It was pleasing to see one of the most desperate of human calamities capable of so much help: whatever enlarges hope will exalt courage; after having seen the deaf taught arithmetic, who would be afraid to cultivate the Hebrides?

The point is typically Johnsonian. The inhabitants of the Hebrides are under great disadvantages; their climate is infertile, their soil poor, they are thinly scattered and uninstructed; they have been disarmed by law, yet in the poor state of their communications they could not summon help from the central government if they were invaded from outside, and have therefore been left powerless to defend themselves. All this is bad enough; but it is still not so bad as the plight of the deaf mute; and we who have 'seen the deaf taught arithmetic' surely owe it to the Hebrideans to make an equal effort at understanding and help towards them.

And there the book ends. All that remained was for Johnson to write the final paragraph of modest disclaimer. Every man who has travelled owes a duty to tell what he has seen; he, Johnson, is fulfilling that obligation, but he is under no illusions of being able to contribute much. Since he knows so little of the lives of crofters and fishermen, a great deal of what he has seen has struck him as new and unexpected; perhaps unnecessarily so. 'Novelty and ignorance must always be reciprocal, and I cannot but be conscious that my thoughts on national matters are the thoughts of one who has seen but little.'

Objectively, this is true. Many men of that time, including Boswell, had travelled over far more of the earth's surface than Johnson was ever able to do. What makes the *Journey* notable among travel books, what makes it worthy to stand beside such masterpieces as *Eothen* or *Black Lamb and Grey Falcon*, is the essentially Johnsonian quality of experience fully comprehended and thought out. Johnson did not have more experiences than other people, but he paid attention to his experience in a way that is very rare: at that intensity, perhaps unique to him. Even with his poor eyesight he missed nothing; and what he took in his mind revolved, examined, compared and – with its matchless retrieval system – held always ready for immediate application, so that, in a sense, every new experience that came his way happened to him simultaneously with all previous experiences. Set any five pages of the *Journey* against five pages of any other travel book and this density of thought and feeling will become apparent. But indeed it is apparent already, to anyone who reads with ordinary sensitivity.

Johnson worked quickly at the *Journey*; and he adopted what to most writers would seem the hair-raising method of sending it to the printer in chunks as he wrote it. This, which not only makes revision of detail impossible but also forbids any rethinking of the general shape of the book, would appear to guarantee a duodenal ulcer, but Johnson's experience had qualified him for it and he went sturdily on. He was determined not to admit delays which would interpose a muffling interval of time between the experience and the writing. As soon as he got home he wrote to Boswell asking him to 'quicken Dr Webster' – a statistically minded gentleman who had promised him facts and figures – but not for Dr Webster nor anyone else would he rein back his pen. In the New

Year of 1774 he wrote tersely to Boswell, 'You must make haste and gather me all you can, and do it quickly, or I will do without it.'

So the book was written and the sheets printed off. The printer was slow, and the work halted in the summer while Johnson went on a trip to North Wales, but the book was still completed and printed just over a year after his return. Only twice did he find it necessary to stop the press and go back to make a correction: once because he regretted something he had written and wished to substitute wiser and more temperate words, and once in response to a sad piece of news.

The second thoughts were these: describing a visit to the Cathedral at Elgin, he has again, as in the case of Aberdeen and St Andrews, to record that the building is ruined and disused; not, in this instance, by 'the tumultuous violence of Knox' but 'by deliberate robbery and frigid indifference'. This leads him to reflect on the sad case of many noble ecclesiastical buildings which, in that age before restoration was seriously undertaken, were often in a pitiful condition. Turning his gaze momentarily from Scotland to England, he writes,

> Let us not however make too much haste to despise our neighbours. There is now, as I have heard, a body of men, not less decent or virtuous than the Scottish council, longing to melt the lead of an English cathedral. What they shall melt, it were just that they should swallow.

This referred to a decision taken by the Dean and Chapter of Lichfield Cathedral. *Salve, magna parens!* Johnson detested these men for their decision to plunder the sacred building for the sake of the diocesan coffers. But, reflecting in a cooler hour, he decided that his ferocious recommendation that these venerable men should 'swallow' the molten lead was going a bit far. On 30 November he wrote to Strahan the printer,

> In one of the pages there is a severe censure of the clergy of an English Cathedral which I am afraid is just, but I have since recollected that from me it may be thought improper for the Dean did me a kindness about forty years ago. He is now very old, and I am not young. Reproach can do him no good, and in myself I know not whether it is zeal or wantonness.

The letter goes on to ask Strahan's advice as to how to cancel the passage; Johnson agrees to pay the cost, and to 'write something to fill up the vacuum'. Both he did; hence the gentler and unparticularized passage in the book as it stands. The 'very old' Dean whom Johnson wished to avoid wounding was a man called Addenbroke; what kindness he had done the young Johnson I do not know, but it was typical of Johnson to remember it and let it turn away his wrath.

The other correction was purely elegiac. While working on the later stages of the book Johnson's attention was caught by a report in the newspapers of a tragedy at sea. A boat crossing from Ulva to Inch Kenneth had been wrecked with much loss of life, and among those reported lost was their friend and companion 'Young Col'. Johnson at once wrote to Boswell expressing the hope that there was no more truth in the story than in the similar account of their own drowning. But the letter crossed with one from Boswell confirming the sad news. Col was lost in that dark water which had so nearly claimed Johnson and Johnson's biographer. His quick, bright energy, his intelligence and good-will were lost to the islands; his grand schemes of improvement no more than a memory. Sadly, Johnson called in the relevant sheet and wrote in a correction. Describing how Col had conducted them to Sir Allan Maclean and then taken leave of them, he wrote,

> Here we had the last embrace of this amiable man, who, while these pages were preparing to attest his virtues, perished in the passage between Ulva and Inch Kenneth.

It is not the most elaborate of Johnson's epitaphs, but it is one of the most touching.

CHAPTER 27

Countries of the Mind

The Hebridean experience had whetted Johnson's appetite for travel. He saw it, hopefully, as the gateway to a whole new period of his life, in which he would at last get about the world and explore for himself its varieties of men and manners. In 1777 the Thrales did particularly well financially, receiving at one point a lump sum of £14,000: Johnson wrote to Hester that he had been day-dreaming about what he would do if such a windfall came to him:

> If I had money enough, what would I do? Perhaps, if you and master did not hold me, I might go to Cairo, and down the Red Sea to Bengal, and take a ramble in India. Would this be better than building and planting? It would surely give more variety to the eye, and more amplitude to the mind. Half fourteen thousand would send me out to see other forms of existence, and bring me back to describe them.

And in the same year he remarked in a letter to John Taylor,

> Is not mine a kind of life turned upside side? Fixed to a spot when I was young, and roving the world when others are contriving to sit still, I am wholly unsettled. I am a kind of ship with a wide sail, and without an anchor.

The year after the journey through Scotland, he travelled with the Thrales to Hester's ancestral country of north Wales. Their chief motive was to visit Bodvel Hall, the small country house three miles north of Pwllheli, where she was born, and Bach-y-Graig, in the Vale of Clwyd, which had been her father's birthplace and which she considered as the ancestral seat of the Salusburys. They travelled up through Derbyshire ('He that has seen Dovedale has no need to visit the Highlands', Johnson noted in his diary) and proceeded by way of Chester, St Asaph, Denbigh, Bangor, then in a boat down the Menai Straits to Caernarvon. Here they visited the Castle, and Johnson's curiosity was such that he even dragged his bulk to the top of the Eagle Tower. 'I did not think there had been such buildings', he wrote. 'It surpassed my ideas.'

As usual, Johnson was alert and interested in his surroundings. He sat through a Welsh sermon and wrote in his diary that 'The sound of the Welsh in a continued discourse is not unpleasant'. He read a book by a scholar named Humphrey Llwyd, proving that the 'Mona' mentioned by classical writers like Tacitus and Pliny the Elder was not the Isle of Man, as some thought, but Anglesey, which the party visited. He did his best to decipher Welsh inscriptions on tombstones. In short, he lived up to his own precept that the traveller should not merely goggle at a new landscape but bring with him an informed mind and an enquiring eye. All in all, however, his reaction to Wales was a disappointment to Hester. Her heart beat faster among the peaks and valleys where she had been reared; but Thrale was his usual cold self, and Johnson inclined more to his side than to Hester's. The trip was, in any case, cut short by the demands of Thrale's political career. Hearing the news of the dissolution of Parliament, they hurried home so that he could fight his seat in the General Election, and on 30 September arrived in Southwark to begin canvassing; Johnson drafted Thrale's first advertisement.

Undeterred, they embarked the next year on a more ambitious journey – an eight-week visit to France. This time they took the entire clutch of Thrale children (only Queeney had been with them in Wales), and also Giuseppe Baretti, who was at this time in the Thrales' employ as tutor.

On 17 September the party sailed from Dover to Calais in calm, beautiful weather, in spite of which the Thrale offspring were vehemently seasick. They stayed on French soil till 10 November. In terms of mileage the tour was not ambitious; the main objective was to see Paris and its environs, going by way of Calais and Rouen, returning by Compiègne and St Quentin to Calais.

For both Johnson and Hester this was the first experience of a visit to continental Europe. Both were excited, though her excitement bubbled more obviously than his, and both kept careful records of the trip. Johnson's diary was in three volumes, of which only one survived; Boswell prints it entire. In contrast to the style of Mrs Thrale's journal – fluent, copious and exclamatory – Johnson's is an *aide-memoire*, a repository for facts and impressions from which, later, his memory would be able to summon up a complete impression of those precious weeks in another country. Many of the jottings are meaningless to any eye but Johnson's own; still, Boswell was right to print it without omission. It makes an impressive testimony to that curiosity about life and its processes, that hunger for knowledge and understanding in whatever area, that are so characteristically Johnsonian. The rules governing the lives of Benedictine monks; the fact that the King's dogs were almost all English; the tastelessness of lentils 'in themselves'; the fountains at Chantilly, 'eminently beautiful' although 'the water seems to be too near the house': his one shortsighted eye was constantly reporting to his active brain. Nothing was disdained. Where he happened to get a glimpse of the countryside, he was interested; on the way to Fontainebleau he found 'the appearance of the country pleasant. No hills, few streams, only one hedge. I remember no chapels nor crosses on the roads, pavement still, and rows of trees.'

The surface of life, the small details, were important. But he also observed and enquired with a deep sense of purpose. Johnson, as we have often had occasion to notice, was a European. France and England were both provinces of that large centralized civilization, European christendom, whose natural focus was 'the shores of the Mediterranean'. When introduced to French divines and *savants*, Johnson always addressed them in Latin, a policy often mistaken for mere idiosyncrasy or a quaint linguistic vanity, the wish not to be at a disadvantage when addressing French speakers in French. In fact, Johnson's use of Latin was deliberately in line with his entire intellectual attitude. He still believed in the international, Latin-based culture of Europe, and with reason: the eighteenth century saw the sunset of this culture, but it was still a brilliant radiance. Even fifty years later, it would have been eccentric to walk about Paris holding conversations in Latin, but in pre-Revolutionary France it was a means of pointing to a deeply held belief in the comity of European scholars. It is no accident that the people who smile indulgently at Johnson's quaint habit of speaking Latin to Frenchmen are the same who regard him as a John Bull to whom cosmopolitan culture meant nothing.

Johnson was in France as no idle tourist but as a representative of one major literary and intellectual nation looking attentively at the equipment of another. For this reason he seized every opportunity of being let loose in a library. His travelling companions, who failed to grasp the nature of his investigations, were often impatient as he looked into book after book. Baretti, who ought to have known better, wrote querulously that

> During our journey to and from Paris he visited five or six libraries, which is the most idle thing a traveller can do, as they are but to be seen cursorily.

Hester Thrale, for her part, dreaded the sight of a library because it always meant a tedious wait for Johnson. When a Capuchin friar courteously showed them over his establishment, she noted that 'the library was locked, and I was not sorry, for Mr Johnson would never have come out of it'.

For all his intellectual curiosity, Johnson during this French visit met no 'advanced' thinker, no one who could be called a representative of the Enlightenment. He made the acquaintance of Fréron, enemy of Voltaire and opponent of the Enlightenment; he was shown round the Jardin des Plantes by Daubenton, scientist and friend of the more celebrated Buffon. At Rouen he met Jean-Louis Roffet, a canon of the cathedral and graduate of the Sorbonne, who seems to have been a typical eighteenth-century liberal churchman. In Paris he met Mme Du Boccage, a devoutly Christian lady and an Anglophile; she had translated Milton, and was the author of an epic poem, *La Colombiade*, sub-titled *La Foi Portée au Nouveau Monde*.

With such blameless and civilized people did the party converse, doubtless to the benefit of either side. Nevertheless, Johnson's visit to France did not take rank among the important experiences of his life. He said afterwards that the chief benefit he had derived from it was that he appreciated England the more. In fact, there is an obvious explanation of the fact that neither the Welsh nor the French journey came anywhere near the adventure of 1773. Travelling with the rich, while it undeniably has its points, never permits much involvement with the everyday life of the country. Johnson never entered an ordinary Welsh home, let alone an ordinary French home, in the way that in Scotland he entered the cottages of crofters and the cabins of trading vessels and the bedrooms of low-raftered inns. Undoubtedly an opportunity was missed. One would have given a good deal to know his reactions, in each country, to the people, his observation of their life, his judgement of their hopes and fears. But, insulated in comfort, surrounded by a thicket of servants, he saw these things as in a tapestry.

Still, though travelling with the Thrales did not stimulate Johnson to the same richness of response as travelling in a less grand manner, it suited him well enough and he was eager for more of it. In particular, he was excited by the prospect of a visit to Italy, which they had planned for 1776. This would be his chance, at last, to see 'the shores of the Mediterranean'. He looked forward eagerly, and was disappointed when the journey was called off because of the sad death of the Thrales' nine-year-old son, Harry. This death, which deprived the Thrales of a male heir, was a severe emotional blow to them, and Johnson shared in their suffering. He happened to be in Lichfield, with Boswell, when he received the news in a letter as they sat at breakfast; as Johnson read it, he exclaimed, 'One of the most dreadful things that has happened in my time' – a turn of phrase that naturally led the waiting Boswell to conclude that the news concerned 'something like an assassination of the King – like a gunpowder plot carried into execution – or like another fire of London'; he was relieved to hear that the news was only something of a private nature, but Johnson would not be comforted. 'I would have gone to the extremity of the earth', he said solemnly, 'to have preserved this boy.'

Hastening back to London, to console the parents in whatever way he could, Johnson still hoped that the Italian journey might take place; he thought it would distract the Thrales from their grief. But they abandoned it and Johnson never saw those classic shores.

There remained, however, plenty to engage his attention and interest. These were good years. His social, dining-out, lionized life reached a new and strange peak when Boswell managed to engineer a meeting between him and the notorious Wilkes. Boswell's own account of this triumph, in the *Life*, is so brilliant that we must not steal his thunder by any attempt to tell the story in different words; but Johnson got on surprisingly well with Wilkes and demonstrated once again his ability to find some common ground with almost any man who walked the earth.

The charitable, compassionate side of Johnson's nature was also in evidence during these years; notably in his efforts to obtain a pardon for a clergyman named William Dodd, who was condemned to death for forgery. Dodd had been tutor to the fifth Earl of Chesterfield, successor to the recipient of Johnson's famous letter. He was a popular preacher and something of a celebrity; and, finding his expensive life style difficult to maintain, raised the wind by forging a bond for £4200 in the name of his noble ex-pupil. He hoped to be able to pay back the money by the time the imposture was noticed; and also, as Boswell hints broadly, may have counted on His Lordship's unwillingness, if it came to the pinch, to allow a former tutor and a man of the cloth to be hanged in public. When Dodd was arrested, however, Chesterfield received the news of his condemnation with aristocratic *sang-froid*. From his cell in Newgate Dodd besought Johnson's aid; not directly, though they had once met, but through the mediation of the Countess of Harrington. The Countess wrote a letter to Johnson, explaining the situation and appealing to him to use the persuasive power of his pen to sue for a Royal Pardon. Johnson received the latter, walked up and down the room for a while in agitation, and then said, 'I will do what I can.'

He was, as usual, as good as his word. That Dodd obtained no mercy was not due to any remissness on Johnson's part. He wrote a letter for Dodd to send to the King, perhaps the most moving and dignified appeal to mercy ever penned:

> Sir
>
> May it not offend your Majesty, that the most miserable of men applies himself to your clemency, as his last hope and his last refuge; that your mercy is most earnestly and humbly implored by a clergyman, whom your law and judges have condemned to the horror and ignominy of a public execution.
>
> I confess the crime, and own the enormity of its consequences, and the danger of its example. Nor have I the confidence to petition for impunity; but humbly hope that public security may be established, without the spectacle of a clergyman dragged through the streets, to a death of infamy, amidst the derision of the profligate and profane; and that justice may be satisfied with irrevocable exile, perpetual disgrace, and hopeless penury.
>
> My life, Sir, has not been useless to mankind. I have benefited many. But my offences against God are numberless, and I have had little time for repentance. Preserve me, Sir, by your prerogative of mercy, from the necessity of appearing unprepared at that tribunal, before which kings and subjects must stand at last together. Permit me to hide my guilt in some obscure corner of a foreign country, where, if I can ever attain confidence to hope that my prayers will be heard, they shall be poured with all the fervour of gratitude for the life and happiness of your Majesty.
>
> I am, Sir, Your Majesty's &c.

In a covering note he 'most seriously enjoined' Dodd not to tell anyone that he, Johnson, had written the letter. He also wrote for Dodd a sermon to be preached within the prison, 'The Convict's Address to his Unhappy Brethren'; he wrote 'Observations' to be printed in the newspapers coincidentally with the presenting of a petition on Dodd's behalf which twenty thousand people signed; and he wrote a letter to the Honourable Charles Jenkinson, presumably the appropriate person within the government, in which he repeated the point about respect for the Church: '[Dodd] is, so far as I can recollect, the first clergyman of our church who has suffered public execution for immorality; and I know not whether it would not be more for the interest of religion to bury such an offender in the obscurity of perpetual exile, than to expose him in a cart, and on the gallows, to all who for any reason are enemies to the clergy.'

It was in vain; the general principle of discouraging forgery in a rising commercial country, and the particular crime of having tampered with a Lord's money-bags, sent Dodd to the gallows, and in public at that. Johnson, when the appeal had failed, sent the unhappy man a letter calculated to do for him all that a letter could do:

Dear Sir

That which is appointed to all men is now coming upon you. Outward circumstances, the eyes and the thoughts of men, are below the notice of an immortal being about to stand the trial for eternity, before the Supreme Judge of heaven and earth. Be comforted: your crime, morally or religiously considered, has no very deep dye of turpitude. It corrupted no man's principles; it attacked no man's life. It involves only a temporary and reparable injury. Of this, and of all other sins, you are earnestly to repent; and may God, who knoweth our frailty, and desireth not our death, accept your repentance, for the sake of his Son Jesus Christ, our Lord.

In requital of those well intended offices which you are pleased so emphatically to acknowledge, let me beg that you make in your devotions one petition for my eternal welfare. I am, dear Sir,

Your most affectionate servant

SAM: JOHNSON

Dodd sent a message of overflowing gratitude – 'Accept, thou *great* and *good* heart, my earnest and fervent thanks and prayers for all thy benevolent and kind efforts in my behalf' – and in this spirit betook himself to eternity.

Johnson's endeavours on behalf of poor Dodd engaged his charitable heart. But in that same year of 1777 he was to be about another work, one which would bring into play his memory, his judgement, his learning. The whole episode, one of the most purely satisfying in all his long life, begins with a terse diary entry for 29 March 1777: 'I treated with booksellers on a bargain, but the time was not long.' (It was Easter Eve and Johnson's conscience would not allow him to spend much time on business when he should be preparing himself for the solemn festival.)

The 'booksellers' turned out to be a three-man deputation, representing virtually every important member of the trade then in London. (One of them was that same Tom Davies who had introduced Johnson and Boswell.) Their request was that Johnson should contribute a series of prefaces, biographical and critical, to a collection of the English poets. Johnson accepted promptly, naming the modest fee of two hundred guineas (the publishers made five thousand out of it, over the next quarter century), and wrote lightheartedly to Boswell, 'I am engaged to write little lives, and little prefaces, to a little edition of the English poets.'

In fact, there was nothing 'little' about the enterprise which he approached in this carefree spirit. It was a product of professional *expertise*, sharpened by Anglo-Scottish trade jealousy. An Edinburgh publisher had brought out a *Collection of the English Poets*; the London booksellers were alarmed at this poaching, especially since the edition was to be sold at a London outlet; they were relieved to find, when the volumes appeared, that they were carelessly printed and in a type too small to be read with comfort. They determined to bury the Scotch effort with a collection whose superiority would be clear to all. One committee supervised the text; a second the illustrations, engaging only well-known engravers; a third, the physical production – paper, printing and binding. Johnson was brought in as the final stamp of authority. If he wrote a Preface to the works of each poet, the edition would contain not only classic poetry but great criticism.

The booksellers' decision can only be applauded. From then until now, every reader of English literature has owed these men a debt. Johnson, as usual, was living up to the *bon mot* of Thomas Tyers, 'he only speaks when he is spoken to'. For more than fifty years he had been reading English poetry with a lover's eye and a practitioner's ear. What he had read he had thought deeply about. At the same time, unobtrusively and without effort, he had added year by year to his fund of information and anecdote. Just as, when he sat down to write his essay on Shakespeare, he had been very close to having the entire text of the plays by heart, so now he sat down to write his Lives with a memory stored with facts and associations. He did very little research – tended, indeed, to resent the suggestion that he needed to do much. Boswell, in a typical display of what Johnson once called his 'troublesome kindness', went behind Johnson's back to Lord Marchmont, who had been an intimate friend of Pope's, and made an appointment for Johnson to consult His Lordship. Johnson was furious. 'I shall not be in town tomorrow. I don't care to know about Pope.' Hester Thrale, who was present, put in soothingly, 'I suppose, Sir, he thought that as you are to write Pope's life, you'd wish to know about him.' 'Why, *wish*', Johnson repeated scornfully. 'If it rained knowledge I would hold out my hand. But I would not trouble myself to go for it.' He did, in fact, get round to consulting Marchmont; and he also wrote to his old acquaintance at Cambridge Richard Farmer, asking him to 'procure from College or University registers, all the dates, or other information, which they can supply, relating to Ambrose Philips, Broome, and Gray, who were all of Cambridge'. Farmer neglected to answer his letter. But perhaps we are not much the losers. The *Lives of the Poets* is a work of memory, judgement and love, not a work of research.

One reason why Johnson needed so little research was that he was dealing with such recent material. When these booksellers spoke of 'the English poets' they did not mean Chaucer, Spenser, Donne or Marlowe. These poets Johnson in fact knew well, but to write biographies of them would have been another matter. After their own time, very little was known about any of them before the intensive research of the nineteenth and twentieth centuries. But the poets in this collection were those whom the reader of Johnson's day thought of as 'modern'. Most of them had done their work within his own century, or, at the earliest, in the latter half of the century before. Many of them he had known personally. And if he had never actually met them his experience of their work was immediate and involved. For these were the poets of Johnson's own culture. Their writings had first established, and then constituted, the Augustan tradition to which his own work belonged. Taken collectively, as one vast cohesive work – which is the only way to take them – the *Lives of the Poets* add up to the greatest masterpiece of English eighteenth-century criticism; they offer a view of the Augustan literary culture which can never be supplanted, nor on its own terms even challenged, because it is a view from the inside, from a man who is himself one of the mainstays of the tradition he is describing.

This perspective of Johnson's gives to his judgements the sparkle of immediate interest; we are in the presence of a man who is talking about his own world, and by implication about his own work. It does more. It gives to the *Lives of the Poets* a compelling narrative structure. Starting in the seventeenth century, Johnson is naturally concerned with the question of whether the poet did, or did not, point towards the poetic practice of the eighteenth. For those who, like Waller, Denham, Roscommon and, to some extent Cowley, write like Augustans born before their time, he has appropriate praise; they 'refined our numbers', 'improved our taste', etc. This is legitimate; as C. S. Lewis remarked once, 'Inside the Chess Club, the man who is just beginning to take an interest in chess is naturally described as "coming on".' Waller and Denham were coming on; much greater poets like Milton or Butler, or Rochester, or the 'Metaphysicals' whom he discussed in a long and interesting digression, were not coming on. Their work offends against eighteenth-century canons of taste and since Johnson is using these canons he judges them severely. Even Milton, whom Johnson recognizes as a giant, is found wanting almost everywhere outside the sacred confines of *Paradise Lost*. Johnson's judgements on *Lycidas* or *Samson Agonistes* are of course not 'correct'; there are no 'correct' judgements in criticism, since criticism deals with imponderables and every opinion is valid from the point of view from which it is uttered – provided always that it represents that point of view honestly and sensitively.

When Johnson moves on to Dryden and Pope, he is at his finest. Dryden, the man who first brought Augustan poetry to maturity, and Pope, who refined it into its ultimate dazzling accomplishment, are the twin stars of Johnson's firmament. On both, he is magnificent. To both, he pays the compliment of elaboration and length; the Life of Pope, particularly, is a small book in itself. And in all his criticism there is nothing more perceptive than the sustained comparison he draws between them. It didn't, of course, stop a later and more hasty generation from inflating the dummy of 'Popendryden', and making one monstrous poet out of the two, but if they had read it carefully it would have stopped them:

> Of genius, that power which constitutes a poet; that quality without which judgement is cold and knowledge is inert; that energy which collects, combines, amplifies and animates; the superiority must, with some hesitation, be allowed to Dryden. It is not to be inferred that of this poetical vigour Pope had only a little, because Dryden had more; for every other writer since Milton must give place to Pope; and even of Dryden it must be said, that if he has brighter paragraphs, he has not better poems. Dryden's

performances were always hasty, either excited by some external occasion, or extorted by domestic necessity; he composed without consideration, and published without correction. What his mind could supply at call, or gather in one excursion, was all that he sought, and all that he gave. The dilatory caution of Pope enabled him to condense his sentiments, to multiply his images, and to accumulate all that study might produce, or chance might supply. If the flights of Dryden therefore are higher, Pope continues longer on the wing. If of Dryden's fire the blaze is brighter, of Pope's the heat is more regular and constant. Dryden often surpasses expectation, and Pope never falls below it. Dryden is read with frequent astonishment, and Pope with perpetual delight.

Once this meridian is passed, a more wary note enters the collection. Johnson's account of later eighteenth-century poetry is slightly incomplete because he leaves out not only himself (no poet still living was included) but also, owing to a difficulty about copyright, the recently dead Goldsmith. Since Johnson and Goldsmith are undeniably the two most important poets of the middle and later years of the century to remain faithful to the poetic canons of Dryden and Pope, their omission leaves the field wide open to that cluster of poets who are usually thought of as 'pre-Romantic' – poets in whom the reflective, the sentimental and the rhapsodic begin to predominate over the witty and tough minded Augustan qualities. Johnson approaches these poets with something less than enthusiasm. They were the fashionable 'movement' of his later lifetime and, just as in his Shakespearean criticism he is hostile to the lingering traces of an earlier and harsher neo-classicism inherited from Dennis, Rymer and Voltaire, so now, in the last twenty years of the century, he is hostile to those forces that are undermining the building so carefully set up and so long defended. 'Ripeness is all.' He is a man of the high Augustan moment, distrusting the doctrinaire narrowness that preceded it and the loosening and slackening that followed it. He is cool about the poetry of Collins, and (except for the *Elegy*, which is an Augustan poem) definitely hostile to that of Gray. He dislikes blank verse, which seems to him to lack the essential stiffening that poetry needs ('If blank verse be not tumid and gorgeous, it is crippled prose'); he distrusts the vogue for the mediaeval, fostered by Warton and Percy, and he is annoyed by the fashion for imitating Milton's minor poems – which is one reason why, in the Life of Milton, he criticizes those poems so severely.

The *Lives of the Poets* was intended as no placid, academic survey of fixed reputations. It expressed a point of view, and one that Johnson understood well enough to be no longer dominant in literary circles. He told Boswell that he expected to be attacked over it; and many readers were, in fact, highly incensed. The poet William Cowper spoke for many of his generation when he exclaimed, in a letter written after reading the Life of Milton, 'I could thrash his old jacket till I made his pension jingle in his pocket.'

In the *Lives of the Poets* Johnson managed to convey the full range of his attitudes to literature and to life; and this in spite of the fact that he placidly accepted the limitations of the scheme put before him by the publishers. Like the veteran professional he was, he was content to do it their way, raising no objection to the proposed list, although it contained some poets who entirely failed to interest him. When Boswell asked him if he would write about a poet who seemed to him a dunce, he replied shortly, 'Yes, Sir, and *say* he was a dunce.' Characteristically, the only alteration he proposed to the list was to increase his task by adding a few extra names – Thomson, Blackmore, Pomfret, Yalden and the pious Dr Watts. These were improving poets, and Johnson wanted them included for the same reason that had made him refuse to quote, in the Dictionary, from any writer of bad moral tendency. Apart from these additions, he rested content with the assignment as handed to him. That he managed to make a masterpiece of it was due to his willingness to take up the full slack of every topic that presented itself. Both in the biographical and the critical parts of the work, he never allows himself to be confined within the purely literary. Political and moral issues inevitably arise from the reading of literature, and in every case Johnson is ready for them. If all his other works were lost, we could still gather his essential ideas and attitudes from the *Lives of the Poets*.

To take one example: if Johnson had not written the Lives of Cowley, Waller, Milton and Butler, all of whom participated in the Civil War and lived through the Commonwealth, we should not know except from stray remarks what Johnson thought of the events of that troubled century. That he was a Royalist, and therefore out of sympathy with revolution and regicide, goes without saying. But his settled verdict on the Puritan interregnum, the solid grounds for his dislike of it, are given full expression only in this work of his old age. The Life of Milton, of course, gives the fullest treatment; Milton's poetry is the supreme literary expression of the Puritan spirit, and Johnson could not have given his opinion on the poems without doing the same for their subject matter. But a few succinct paragraphs in the Life of Butler make an adequate summary of his political judgement on the 1650s:

> It is scarcely possible, in the regularity and composure of the present time, to image the tumult of absurdity, and clamour of contradiction, which perplexed doctrine, disordered practice, and disturbed both public and private quiet, in that age, when subordination was broken, and awe was hissed away; when any unsettled innovator who could hatch a half-formed notion produced it to the public; when every man might become a preacher, and almost every preacher could collect a congregation.
>
> The wisdom of the nation is very reasonably supposed to reside in the parliament. What can be concluded of the lower classes of the people, when in one of the parliaments summoned by Cromwell it was seriously proposed, that all the records in the Tower should be burnt, that all memory of things past should be effaced, and that the whole system of life should commence anew?
>
> We have never been witnesses of animosities excited by the use of minced pies and plum porridge; nor seen with what abhorrence those

who could eat them at all other times of the year would shrink from them in December. An old Puritan, who was alive in my childhood, being at one of the feasts of the church invited by a neighbour to partake his cheer, told him that, if he would treat him at an alehouse with beer, brewed for all times and seasons, he should accept his kindness, but would have none of his superstitious meats or drinks.

One of the puritanical tenets was the illegality of all games of chance; and he that reads Gataker upon *Lots*, may see how much learning and reason one of the first scholars of his age thought necessary, to prove that it was no crime to throw a die, or play at cards, or to hide a shilling for the reckoning.

The terse, weighty sentences convey the strength of Johnson's recoil from the anarchistic chaos from which his century had managed to struggle free. How close it still was, an ever-present morass waiting for the slipping foot, is emphasized by the reminiscence of 'an old Puritan, who was alive in my childhood'. And the story of the proposed destruction of records can stand as proof that Johnson's objection to the Puritan regime was basically that it was totalitarian. Indeed, to pinpoint such a detail – that some hothead had got up in Parliament and made an unsuccessful attempt to have all historical records thrown on a bonfire – shows the penetration of Johnson's political vision. The modern forms of totalitarian government were not dreamt of in his day, yet already he understood one feature of the totalitarian mind – its hatred of the past. As the Jacobins, and later the Italian Fascists, threw away the calendar and started with Year One, as present-day Communist regimes rewrite their historical textbooks every few years and make it a crime to consult previous versions, so a member of one of Cromwell's parliaments wanted 'the whole system of life' to 'commence anew', and Johnson sees where such notions lead.

If Johnson had used the *Lives of the Poets* as a repository of critical judgements, and a means of expressing his political and historical opinions, he would already be giving abundantly. But he did more. He made the collection a vehicle for personal reminiscence. In one sense, the work is Johnson's autobiography: not a direct autobiography on a thread of personal narrative but the story of an epoch he had lived through, peopled with characters he had known, marked by events he remembered.

It is this personal involvement that gives the *Lives of the Poets* such matchless body and flavour. It is the story of Johnson's lifetime; beginning, indeed, before his birth, but getting into its stride at just about the time when his own memories link up with those of the people who were grown up when he was a child. The Life of Pope is the centrepiece of the collection, and Johnson had been thirty-five years old when Pope had died; Pope had commented on Johnson's early poems, and his favourable judgement had helped at a time when help was desperately needed. But even in the case of Pope's great predecessor, Dryden, who had died nine years before Johnson's birth, there was still a sense of direct contact. Johnson did not remember the days of Dryden, but he had grown up among people who did. Speaking of Dryden's poem *Absalom and Achitophel*, which caught the public fancy with its topical strokes of satire, Johnson recalls, 'the sale was so large that my father, an old bookseller, told me he had not known it equalled but by Sacheverell's trial'. That Michael Johnson made a profit on Dryden's poem, was helped by it to establish the household in which Sam grew up, brings Dryden very close.

But this closeness of involvement is, we soon see, everywhere in the texture of the work. Johnson is summarizing a lifetime of literary experience, and at every turn he comes upon some once familiar ghost. Scraps of information gathered from bookish customers at the Lichfield shop mingle with memories of tavern discussions long ago; faces rise up; voices sound in his ears; with love and reverence he remembers the dead. 'Such was the fate of Collins, with whom I once delighted to converse, and whom I yet remember with tenderness.'

In the Life of Fenton, he remembers Parson Ford:

> Fenton was one day in the company of Broome his associate, and Ford a clergyman, at that time too well known, whose abilities, instead of furnishing convivial merriment to the voluptuous and dissolute, might have enabled him to excel among the virtuous and the wise.

Indeed, Ford must have been often in his mind; he had known Pope, and at Cambridge had shared a room with Broome, one of the poets who worked with Pope on the translation of Homer. And to think of Ford was, inevitably, to think of Gilbert Walmesley, the man to whom in the days of his youth he had owed an even greater debt of love and gratitude. This debt Johnson now paid. In the Life of an obscure poet named Edmund Smith, Walmesley's name happened to crop up, and Johnson paused in the narrative to write that warm, glowing tribute that has become one of the most famous passages in all his work.

> Of Gilbert Walmsley, thus presented to my mind, let me indulge myself in the remembrance. I knew him very early; he was one of the first friends that literature procured me, and I hope that at least my gratitude made me worthy of his notice.
>
> He was of an advanced age, and I was only not a boy; yet he never received my notions with contempt. He was a Whig, with all the virulence and malevolence of his party; yet difference of opinion did not keep us apart. I honoured him, and he endured me.
>
> He had mingled with the gay world, without exemption from its vices or its follies, but had never neglected the cultivation of his mind; his belief of Revelation was unshaken; his learning preserved his principles; he grew first regular, and then pious.
>
> His studies had been so various, that I am not able to name a man of equal knowledge. His acquaintance with books was great; and what he did not immediately know, he could at least tell where to find. Such was his amplitude of learning, and such his copiousness of communication, that it may be

doubted whether a day now passes in which I have not some advantage from his friendship.

Once the affectionate, grateful mood was on him, Johnson allowed it to carry him forward; without pausing, he adds tributes to Robert James of the *Medicinal Dictionary* and to David Garrick:

At this man's table I enjoyed many cheerful and instructive hours, with companions such as are not often found; with one who has lengthened, and one who has gladdened life; with Dr James, whose skill in physic will be long remembered; and with David Garrick, whom I hoped to have gratified with this character of our common friend: but what are the hopes of man! I am disappointed by that stroke of death, which has eclipsed the gaiety of nations, and impoverished the public stock of harmless pleasure.

Even tenderer memories are enshrined in the *Lives*. In 1756 he had contributed an essay on Pope's epitaphs to a magazine called *The Universal Visitor*; he reprinted it now, as a pendant to the Life; it contains a reference to Molly Aston – for Molly had sometimes spoken to him of her literary preferences, during that briefly happy time when he lingered in the country while Tetty waited in London, and he told Hester Thrale that she was the 'lady of great beauty and excellence' who had objected to the fourth line of Pope's epitaph on Mrs Corbet.

Not only his memories of other people, what they had said and done and what interested them, but the image of his own younger self rose often before him. That period as a political firebrand, when he had paced the streets with Savage, 'declaiming against Walpole'! How generously indignant he had been, when the government of the day suppressed Brooke's play *Gustavus Vasa*: how he had thrashed them, or hoped he was thrashing them, in his *Compleat Vindication of the Licensers of the Stage*! Now, in the Life of Thomson, he quietly buried the issue:

About this time the Act was passed for licensing plays, of which the first operation was the prohibition of *Gustavus Vasa*, a tragedy of Mr Brooke, whom the public recompensed by a very liberal subscription; the next was the refusal of *Edward and Eleonora*, offered by Thomson. It is hard to discover why either play should have been obstructed.

The *Lives of the Poets* is Johnson's gentlest, most companionable work. It is magisterial, of course; his notion of criticism was magisterial; and he was writing out of so much knowledge and so much experience that it would have been absurd for him to offer his opinions deferentially. But he welcomes the reader, genially, to share his thoughts on all the vast range of subjects that come up. The work is a treasury of Johnson's ideas; it abounds in memorable lines and striking judgements. To read it is to feel something of the fascination of his company. I see that in one paragraph I have written 'companionable' and 'company'. Let the repetition stand. It is as good a way as another to indicate the essential quality of the work. I have been reading the *Lives of the Poets* for thirty years, and can testify that in all that time I have never known the day or the hour when I failed to find interest, instruction, amusement, somewhere in their pages. Armed with the two modest volumes into which modern publishing has obligingly packaged them (there are two cheap editions and they are both in two volumes), the longest railway journey, the dreariest wet evening in a country hotel, have no terrors. Here is the fine flower of Johnson's critical thinking; a showcase of his opinions about everything under the sun, and a wealth of personal reminiscences and striking vignettes. His vast range of anecdote supplies incident after incident that stay in the memory. Otway choking to death on a piece of bread! John Philips as a schoolboy having his hair combed 'hour after hour'! Dryden signing a contract to produce 10,000 lines of verse for £300! Gay, invited to read his poems to the Princess of Wales, approaching her with such a low bow that he stumbles and knocks over a Japanese screen, to the accompaniment of screams from the Princess and her ladies! Swift washing himself 'with oriental scrupulosity' to try to clear his 'muddy complexion'! Lyttelton with his 'slender uncompacted frame' and 'meagre face'!

This ease and richness of writing comes partly from the fact that it is a work of such marvellous ripeness. Johnson's mind is so stored that all that he has to do is take up his pen and write, on any subject, and we are made free of its wealth. But something is also traceable to the circumstances of his life at this time. The *Lives* reflect the ease of Streatham, the delightful company when he wanted to talk, the peace and quiet when he did not; behind the calm, measured sentences, we feel the warmth of the sun on the walls of the summerhouse where Johnson so often sat, writing or correcting proofs – the latter with Hester's unstinting help. Everything that could be done to make writing pleasant, to take the strain and drudgery out of it, was being done, and the relaxed tone of the *Lives* is the result. They are vigilant in judgement, but easy-going in tone and procedure. Johnson had no thoughts of producing a masterpiece. He was quite content to leave a few loose ends, to allow the work to be something of a ragbag. He was placidly willing, if it saved him trouble, to print chunks of material written by other people, or by himself a long time ago. The *Life of Young* was written by Sir Herbert Croft, a man who had once entertained the idea of producing a revised and augmented edition of Johnson's Dictionary; while, on the principle of letting nothing go to waste, Johnson even inserted the *Life of Savage*, written nearly forty years previously. It was hopelessly out of resonance with the other Lives, and the consistently high valuation of Savage's poetry gives the curious impression that Johnson thought him a more interesting writer than Swift or Addison. But in its own way it undoubtedly enriches the collection.

Johnson was four years at work on the *Lives*. The first four volumes, containing twenty-two lives, came out in 1779; the remaining six, with thirty lives, in 1781. During these years Hester Thrale had been a constant friend and helper. Remarking that the Life of Congreve was 'one of the best of the little lives', Johnson wrote to her, 'but then I had your conversation'. (That particular Life, in fact, was written in Southwark – for Johnson also had his own room at the Thrales' house next to the brewery.) She enjoyed helping him, and he was grateful and affectionate. These four years, when he worked so well and she made his life so pleasant, were the crown of their friendship.

It was well that they were; and it was even more fortunate that Johnson finished his work when he did. Unbeknown to him, the golden afternoon was over; the shadows were beginning to slant across the lawn. In 1779, while Johnson was on a visit to the Midlands, Henry Thrale had an apoplectic stroke; not only did he for some days lose the power of speech, his very reason hung by a thread. He was not a healthy man; he took his pleasures too seriously, and pursued them too wholeheartedly. Three years before his stroke he had been troubled with a swollen testicle; his doctors, in a fine demonstration of the eighteenth-century bedside manner, assured him that it was either cancer or venereal disease. In December of that year Hester wrote in her diary, 'Mr Thrale's complaint *was* venereal at last – what need of so many lies about it? I'm sure I care not, so he recovers to hold us all together.'

The time was now approaching when Thrale would no longer be there to 'hold them all together'. In spite of the warning of his stroke, he refused to moderate his gluttony or to heed Johnson's advice that he should try 'alternate diet', by which he seems to have meant abstaining from meat every other day. Ill as he was, Thrale dragged himself to the table; mountains of rich food vanished down his maw; in 1780 he had another stroke, but recovered and still refused to treat himself as a sick man. In September of that year there was a General Election, and against all advice Thrale stood again as Member for Southwark. As soon as the voters saw him totter on to the platform, his prospects evaporated. He was so obviously a dying man that it would have been out of the question to vote for him, and he was outdistanced by all his rivals.

For Hester these were bad days. She began, for the first time, to shun Johnson's company, to turn him off with excuses when he wanted to come to them in Bath or Brighton. With her husband ill and querulous, she dreaded the extra obligation of making Johnson comfortable: for he, too, was growing more infirm. In this sour, cold time only one good thing happened to her. She encountered again at Brighton a man she had met briefly at the house of Dr Burney in 1778: Gabriel Piozzi, the Italian musician who had settled in London and become something of a celebrity, giving recitals and teaching the art of singing to the fashionable world. Piozzi was in Brighton to recover his voice after some indisposition; the two became friends. Piozzi made a great impression: 'his taste is so exquisite, his manner so fine, we have never done adoring him,' she wrote flippantly to a friend; and, more soberly, in her diary: 'his hand on the forte piano is so soft, so sweet, so delicate, every tone goes to one's heart I think; and fills the mind with emotions one would not be without, though inconvenient enough sometimes'. She asked him to undertake Queeney's musical education; he assented, and the lessons began soon after the Thrales returned from Brighton to Streatham.

This new and warm friendship was pleasant, if the emotional flutterings it caused were sometimes 'inconvenient'; but for Hester at this time nothing else went right. Henry Thrale continued doggedly to dig his grave with his teeth. On the night of 3 April 1781 he was in high spirits; they were giving an elaborate party – a reception for 'the Indian Ambassadors', no less – on the following evening, and he was out in his carriage, issuing invitations. Coming home, he wolfed down an enormous dinner, with strong beer 'in such quantities!' as Hester noted, that 'the very servants were frighted'. That meal finished him. He went into apoplectic fit after fit. Johnson was sent for, and sat beside Thrale's bed while life remained; when it departed, he looked his last, sadly, on 'the face that for fifteen years had never been turned upon me but with respect and benignity'.

So, in the early morning of 4 April 1781, there ended not only the life of Henry Thrale but the good years of Samuel Johnson. Recording Thrale's funeral in his diary, Johnson wrote: '. . . with him were buried many of my hopes and pleasures'. The remark was no supernatural prophecy, just realistic commonsense. With the head of the household gone, things were bound to change. How swiftly, and how drastically, Johnson did not yet foresee.

CHAPTER 28

Alone Again

James Boswell, for one, had no doubt as to what Hester Thrale ought to do, now that she was a widow. She should marry Samuel Johnson. Boswell's entirely sincere love and respect for Johnson did not prevent him from extracting as much giggling fun as possible from the idea of Johnson as married lover, with a bride thirty years his junior. Eight days after Henry Thrale's death – one day, indeed, after his funeral – Boswell wrote a set of verses which he called 'Epithalamium', celebrating the forthcoming nuptials of the pair. To say that this poem exceeded the bounds of good taste would be an understatement; where ordinary bad taste leaves off, Boswell began. His effort opens,

> My dearest darling view your slave
> Behold him as your very scrub
> Whether to write as author grave
> Or govern well the brewing tub.
>
> While to felicity thus raised
> My bosom glows with amorous fire
> Porter no longer shall be praised
> 'Tis I myself am Thrale's entire.
>
> Five daughters by your former spouse
> Shall match the nobles of the land
> The fruit of our more fervent vows
> A pillar of the state shall stand.

And so on through eight more scurrilous verses. The joke about Thrale's entire is quite good in its low-minded way; the word 'entire', as a noun, has two meanings: it means a stallion as distinct from a gelding, and also a certain kind of beer. This kind of word-play no doubt convulsed the merry gatherings at which Boswell, incredible as it may seem, rendered his Epithalamium in the spring of 1781.

For Hester herself, things were nothing like so agreeably clear-cut. She was flustered by all the demands of her situation, beset by anxieties, haunted by emotions to which she dared not, even in the silence of her own mind, give full expression. The management of Henry Thrale's estate filled her hands with business; there were four executors, of whom Johnson was one, whose approval must be sought for every important step. The brewery, of course, had to be sold, and here at least Johnson could be of wholehearted assistance. To bustle about with a quill pen and ink horn dangling from his lapel – to discuss terms and calculate costs, to be involved in the stir of affairs, amused and interested him. He had always sturdily refused to acknowledge the mystique of buying and selling; one glance at the average business man was enough to assure him that business could not call for much intellectual subtlety; as he succinctly put it, 'Trade could not be managed by those who manage it, if it were difficult.' Now, he enjoyed meeting these people on equal terms and he did so with a grand, swaggering air. 'We are not here to sell a parcel of vats and boilers', he declared, 'but the possibility of growing rich beyond the dreams of avarice.'

His fun did not last long. At the end of May 1781 the brewery was sold to John Perkins, Sylvanus Bevan, and David and Robert Barclay. One sigh of relief, at least, Hester could now breathe; she wrote to a friend that she was glad to lose the golden millstone from round her neck: 'I long to salute you in my restored character as a gentlewoman.' But she was a gentlewoman with many problems and difficulties. Money, which her husband had for so long provided by magic, was suddenly a rebellious, unpredictable genie, ready at any moment to go back into the bottle. Streatham seemed to her enormously expensive; especially as she had failed in a lawsuit against some of her Welsh relatives, and this had involved her in the payment of a large debt, outstanding for nearly thirty years.

Underlying the practical worries were deeper personal problems. Her marriage, whatever its advantages, had been loveless; now, at forty-one, she was suddenly free to recast her life, and a happy mutual love seemed suddenly to be a possibility. Most of her friends, she knew, would take the line that as a widow with adolescent daughters to look after, she should bury her sexual emotions, regard that part of her life as over. The trouble was that it was not over; it had simply never begun. And there, on the fringe of her life, was the attractive figure of Gabriel Piozzi. Did she love him? If so, she did not yet dare to admit the fact to herself. She shrank from the upheaval that such knowledge would cause, both in herself and in others. What should she do? Tormented, harassed, she decided to gain a breathing space. She would let Streatham Park for three years and spend that time in Italy with her three oldest daughters, Queeney, Sophy and Susan. It would benefit the girls to travel and learn languages; and Queeney's musical studies need not suffer any interruption, for Mr Piozzi would guide the party. In this way she brought him into her plans while keeping him, for the moment, at a manageable distance.

On the other hand, what of Johnson? She knew, and so did everyone, how much he had longed to see Italy. If she left him behind her, how critical his friends would be, how they would castigate her selfishness! But – she had to face the fact – she simply did not want to take him. He was old; he was a nuisance; his rasping cough got on her nerves; it was not even certain that he would survive the hardships of the journey or the change of surroundings. Finally, she plucked up courage. It was her own life and she was going to live it. They would go to Italy, and they would not take Johnson. On 22 August 1782 she nerved herself to tell him of her plans. She expected anger, disappointment, protestations, pleas. But Johnson did not oblige. Deeply saddened as he must have been, he forced himself to take the news with stoical calm. Woman-like, Hester resented this too. 'I fancied Mr Johnson could not have existed without me forsooth', she wrote in her diary, 'as we have now lived together above eighteen years, and I have so fondled and waited on him in sickness and in health – not a bit on't! He feels nothing in parting with me, nothing in the least; but thinks it a prudent scheme, and goes to his book as usual.'

Obviously, Johnson's calm reaction was achieved at the cost of an enormous effort, calling on all his reserves of courage and generosity. He was to lose Hester – even if he were still alive when she returned in three years' time, she would have grown away from him – and he was to lose Streatham. For years he had loved both her and the place, and the two loves had knotted themselves into one. Now the axe was at the root. Inexorably, preparations went forward; the day of severance came nearer. The lawyers drew up the agreement; Streatham was to be let for three years to Lord Shelburne. By early October there was nothing left but to go. On the sixth of the month, Johnson dined there for the last time, read in the library for the last time, and, as usual at any solemn moment of his life, composed a prayer:

Almighty God, Father of all mercy, help me by thy Grace that I may with humble and sincere thankfulness remember the comforts and conveniences which I have enjoyed at this place and that I may resign them with holy submission, equally trusting in thy protection when thou givest and when thou takest away. Have mercy upon me, O Lord, have mercy upon me.

To thy fatherly protection, O Lord, I commend this family. Bless, guide and defend them. That they may so pass through this world as finally to enjoy in thy presence everlasting happiness, for Jesus Christ's sake. Amen.

The parting with Streatham must have seemed to Johnson like a kind of death. And indeed it severed one of the main strands that held him to life. Everywhere he looked, warmth and companionship and colour were fading. Only the previous January he had suffered a loss that nothing could repair. Swarthy, taciturn, reliable old Levet had gone to bed in his room at Bolt Court one night, and had got up no more. His death, according to Johnson's diary, took place at about seven o'clock in the morning and was 'instantaneous'. Johnson's pain can be imagined; he always hated losing a friend, and an old friend most of all, and Levet was a friend of classic vintage; they had been together in the early days of poverty, before the Dictionary, before *The Rambler*, before the death of Tetty. '*Commendavi*,' Johnson wrote sadly. 'May God have mercy on him. May he have mercy on me.'

Levet died in the depths of winter. After an uneasy summer came the sad autumn, the wrenching departure from Streatham. Thereafter events moved quickly. Freed from the twin burdens of Southwark and Streatham, Hester was able to look at her own emotions in a clearer light. She continued to see Piozzi, and the feeling between them rapidly grew in intensity until, some time that autumn, they avowed their mutual love. Hester went down to Brighton with the girls; her mind was whirling with the alternatives that opened before her, and she had no energy to spare for Johnson, who joined them briefly in a visit that no one enjoyed. He was querulous and badly behaved; she was preoccupied with the turmoil inside her. At Brighton she took the opportunity to unburden her heart to Fanny Burney, who stayed with them there, and also to Queeney. She declared that she loved Piozzi and had thoughts of marrying him. Both were horrified. Fanny pleaded with her to change her mind; Queeney vowed that she would never give her consent to such a step. Miserable, frustrated, angry with one another, they returned at the end of the month to London, where Hester had taken a house in Argyll Street for the winter.

Johnson, too, was in London this winter, at his own house in Bolt Court. He had a room in the Argyll Street house just as he had done at Streatham; a semblance of the old intimacy was preserved; but it was the shell of a relationship without the living substance. Hester was deep in the conflict with her daughters, who refused utterly to countenance their mother's remarriage. Just why the gentle and courteous musician should have been regarded as so scandalously unfit a mate for the brewer's widow is difficult, from a twentieth-century point of view, to see; but he was a foreigner, a Catholic, and had no solid position in society – for of course an artist is not solid like a lawyer or a moneylender. Then, too, the world is always cynical about the marriages of heiresses. When the news broke, Piozzi was represented as an unscrupulous adventurer who had smiled and bowed his way into a fortune; it was even confidently said that he was much younger than Hester (he was six months older, in fact), and she was jeered at as the amorous widow who marries her cicisbeo.

Almost half a century earlier, when Elizabeth Porter had announced to her family that she meant to marry Sam Johnson, exactly the same situation had arisen. Tetty had chosen to remarry for love rather than to retain the approval of her family. But the choice is a difficult one for any woman. In that winter of 1782–3 everyone was tense and unhappy. The girls were adamant, Hester in agony, Johnson puzzled and with a sense of neglect. He spent some time in Argyll Street, but mostly he moped in the house in Bolt Court. It was a melancholy place. Mrs Desmoulins had gone away, sickened finally at her incessant quarrels with Anna Williams; and Miss Williams herself was dying. Frank Barber did his best to look after both her and the ailing Johnson; but Frank was never very efficient. The house was disorganized, comfortless and probably dirty. And Levet's place at the breakfast-table was empty.

Hester, for her part, had no energy to spare for Johnson's sufferings. She was being forced to her knees by the obdurate resistance of her daughters, led by Queeney. They would not accept Piozzi as their step-father; they expected her to give her life to looking after *their* needs, running a home for *them*. Finally, worn out, she capitulated. On 6 April 1783 she bade an agonizing farewell to her lover. From that moment, her health began to crumble. The notion of living for a while in Italy was abandoned at the same time as the idea of marriage to Piozzi. Seeking a change of scene and a relief from pressures, she took refuge in Bath; immediately two of the younger children, whom she had left behind, fell ill, and one died. Sunk in her miseries, she neglected Johnson more or less completely. And now, left alone as he was, an even more appalling blow fell on him. Let him take up the story himself as he wrote it in a letter to Hester. No other voice would fall on the ear with such pathetic force:

Dear Madam

I am sitting down in no cheerful solitude to write a narrative which would once have affected you with tenderness and sorrow, but which you will perhaps pass over now with the careless glance of frigid indifference. For this diminution of regard, however, I know not whether I ought to blame you, who may have reasons which I cannot know, and I do not blame myself who have for a great part of human life done you what good I could, and have never done you evil.

I had been disordered in the usual way, and had been relieved by the usual methods, by opium and cathartics, but had rather lessened my dose of opium.

On Monday the sixteenth, I sat for my picture, and walked a considerable way with little inconvenience. In the afternoon and evening, I felt myself light and easy, and began to plan schemes of life. Thus I went to bed, and in a short time waked and sat up as had been long my custom, when I felt a confusion and indistinctness in my head which lasted, I suppose about half a minute; I was alarmed and prayed God, that however he might afflict my body he would spare my understanding. This prayer, that I might try the integrity of my faculties I made in Latin verse. The lines were not very good, but I knew them not to be very good, I made them easily, and concluded myself to be unimpaired in my faculties.

Soon after I perceived that I had suffered a paralytic stroke and that my speech was taken from me. I had no pain, and so little dejection in this dreadful state that I wondered at my own apathy, and considered that perhaps death itself when it should come, would excite less horror than seems now to attend it.

In order to rouse the vocal organs, I took two drams. Wine has been celebrated for the production of eloquence; I put myself into violent motion, and, I think, repeated it. But all was vain; I then went to bed, and, strange as it may seem, I think, slept. When I saw light, it was time to contrive what I should do. Though God stopped my speech he left me my hand, I enjoyed a mercy which was not granted to my dear friend, Laurence, who now perhaps overlooks me as I am writing and rejoices that I have what he wanted. My first note was necessarily to my servant, who came in talking, and could not immediately comprehend why he should read what I put into his hands.

I then wrote a card to Mr Allen that I might have a discreet friend at hand to act as occasion should require. In penning this note I had some difficulty: my hand, I knew not how nor why, made wrong letters. I then wrote to Dr Taylor to come to me, and bring Dr Heberden, and I sent to Dr Brocklesby, who is my neighbour. My physicians are very friendly and very disinterested, and give me great hopes, but you may imagine my situation. I have so far recovered my vocal powers, as to repeat the Lord's Prayer with no very imperfect articulation. My memory, I hope, yet remains as it was. But such an attack produces solicitude for the safety of every faculty.

How this will be received by you I know not, I hope you will sympathize with me, but perhaps

> My Mistress gracious, mild and good
> Cries, Is he dumb? 'tis time he should.

But can this be possible? I hope it cannot. I hope that what, when I could speak, I spoke of you, and to you, will be in a sober and serious hour remembered by you, and surely it cannot be remembered but with some degree of kindness. I have loved you with virtuous affection, I have honoured you with sincere esteem. Let not all our endearment be forgotten, but let me have in this great distress your pity and your prayers. You see I yet turn to you with my complaints as a settled and unalienable friend; do not, do not drive me from you, for I have not deserved either neglect or hatred.

To the girls, who do not write often, for Susy has written only once, and Miss Thrale owes me a letter, I earnestly recommend as their guardian and friend, that they remember their Creator in the days of their youth.

I suppose you may wish to know how my disease is treated by the physicians. They put a blister upon my back, and two from my ear to my throat, one on a side. The blister on the back has done little, and those on the throat have not risen. I bullied, and bounced (it sticks to our last sand) and compelled the apothecary to make his salve according to the Edinburgh dispensatory, that it might adhere better, I have two on now of my own prescription. They likewise give me salt of hartshorn, which I take with no great confidence, but am satisfied that what can be done is done for me.

O God, give me comfort and confidence in thee, forgive my sins, and if it be thy good pleasure, relieve my diseases for Jesus Christ's sake, Amen.

I am almost ashamed of this querulous letter, but now it is written, let it go.

I am, Madam, Your most humble servant
Bolt Court, Fleet Street, 19 June 1783.

SAM: JOHNSON

This paralytic stroke was a clear warning. Johnson could not hope to live long; any friend who still wanted to enjoy his company, and to contribute to what happiness he might still enjoy, would have to do so without much delay. Yet Hester, who had been so much for him for so long, continued even now to stand aloof. Her own problems of mind and body had completely overwhelmed her. Johnson struggled to his feet; that summer he was even capable of travelling into the country as usual; yet she did not suggest that he should accompany her and the girls. The gap was supplied by Johnson's devoted friend Bennet Langton, who happened to be in Rochester and had Johnson to stay there for a couple of weeks. Characteristically, still hungry for life and new experiences, Johnson went on, feeble as he was, to stay in the neighbourhood of Salisbury with a young man he had recently met, by name William Bowles. He enjoyed his stay with Bowles, who did everything possible to make him comfortable; but when Bowles suggested that they should pass a day or two at Weymouth, where he had heard that Hester Thrale was staying, Johnson showed no willingness to go. He had, quite evidently, made up his mind to avoid Hester until she came to him.

Back in London he found Bolt Court gloomier than ever. Anna Williams had died during his absence. Johnson wrote to Langton that 'her death, following that of Levet, has made my house a solitude. She left her little substance to a charity school. She is, I hope, where there is neither darkness, nor want, nor sorrow.' In this solitude, Johnson battled on, still treating life as a privilege and a challenge, still determined not to sit down tamely and wait for death. He fought gallantly against an assemblage of diseases; and to enjoy the pleasure of company and conversation he formed, in December 1783, a new Club, which met at a tavern still flourishing today, the Essex Head in Essex Street. This new association was nothing like so exclusive and distinguished as the original Club, which he still continued to attend; but it had its share of wise and witty men; Murphy was a member and so was Dr Brocklesby, Johnson's good and humane physician; so were Boswell, William Windham the statesman, and George Steevens the literary scholar.

Johnson had need of all Brocklesby's skill. That winter his health sank to the point where death was staring him in the face. He suffered from what he called 'a spasmodic asthma', and also from dropsy. In addition he was tormented by gout, and by a painful complaint which he called a 'sarcocele', which seems to have involved an enormously swollen testicle which had to be treated surgically. From mid-December to late April, a hundred and twenty-nine days by his own reckoning, he was unable to leave the house. When, amazingly, he recovered, his first excursion was to St Clement Dane's Church to give thanks for his deliverance. Dr Brocklesby was confident that warmer weather would benefit him; and it seems to have been Boswell who came up with the idea that instead of waiting for the English weather to turn warm Johnson should go to Italy. He had always wanted to go there, and now it might be the means of postponing his death for a year or two. Boswell, to his eternal credit, took the business on himself. To go to Italy Johnson would need funds. Boswell consulted Reynolds; next he wrote a letter to the Lord Chancellor, who replied that he would take the necessary steps to get Johnson a grant. 'It would be a reflection on us all', His Lordship wrote, 'if such a man should perish for want of the means to take care of his health.' Elated, Boswell hurried round to see Johnson, and steered the conversation round to the topic of a winter in Italy. Johnson confirmed that he would like to go. 'You would have no objections, I presume,' Boswell pursued, 'but the money it would require.' 'Why, no, Sir.' Boswell then poured out the story – how his friends had gone behind his back and arranged it all. Johnson heard him out; then 'This', he said, 'is taking prodigious pains about a man'. 'Oh, Sir,' Boswell burst out, 'your friends would do everything for you'. Johnson's eyes filled with tears; for a moment he could not speak: then, 'God bless you all,' he said. Boswell, in his turn, shed tears. 'God bless you all', Johnson repeated, 'for Jesus Christ's sake.' Unable to speak further, he left the room, In a few minutes he returned, having mastered his feelings, and the two made an appointment to dine with Reynolds on the following day. But that was the last time Boswell was under Johnson's roof.

They met again on the following evening. Boswell and Reynolds were happy to talk of Italy, and the enjoyment that Johnson would find in going there at last. But Johnson was gently realistic. 'Nay,' he said, 'I must not expect much of that; when a man goes to Italy merely to feel how he breathes the air, he can enjoy very little.' But he talked well, and was not melancholy. To the end, he gave Boswell good advice. To the suggestion that the possessor of fine taste was at a disadvantage, since he was harder to please than other people and must therefore be pleased less often, Johnson replied with a touch of his old positiveness. 'Nay, Sir, that is a paltry notion. Endeavour to be as perfect as you can in every respect.'

Afterwards, they took Reynolds's coach and drove to the entrance of Bolt Court. Johnson invited Boswell to come into the house; but, for once in his life, Boswell refused. He was to go to Scotland three days later, and stay there for many months; the thought that this was to be their last meeting lay heavily on his mind. He could not face the sadness of a last conversation with Johnson on their own. They said what they had to say in the coach, and Johnson got down on to the pavement. 'Fare you well', he called, and at once, without looking back, walked off with what Boswell described as 'a kind of pathetic briskness'. The first time they had parted, when Boswell as a young law student had set off for Antwerp by sea, Johnson had remained on the shore, 'rolling his majestic frame' and watching the ship grow smaller in the distance. Now, any such lingering would have been too painful, and he moved off with what speed his unwieldy old limbs would lend him.

That was on 30 June. The date was a fateful one for Johnson. Not only did he part for ever from Boswell, but Hester Thrale despatched to him on that day a letter which extinguished all hope of solace and happiness in her company.

It was, in fact, a formal letter which she sent out in four copies, one to each of the men who were executors of Thrale's estate and guardians of his daughters. It informed them that she had decided to marry Gabriel Piozzi; that she was alone at Bath, waiting for him to join her; that Queeney, Susan and Sophy were at Brighton with a suitable chaperone. At last, her sufferings had melted the hearts of her 'pelican daughters', at least to the extent that they no longer actively opposed the marriage. She might have Piozzi if she wished, though she must not expect them to have any truck with him. At once, her health began to mend;

she wrote to Piozzi, who had returned to Italy, and after a period of hesitation – for he was a cautious man, and had had quite enough of these ups and downs – he was on his way to England. To Johnson's copy of the letter she added a covering note, asking his forgiveness for having told him nothing of the matter. 'Indeed, my dear Sir, it was concealed only to spare us both needless pain; I could not have borne to reject that counsel it would have killed me to take.'

Johnson's immediate reaction was a bellow of pain and rage loud enough to be heard on Sirius and Betelgeuse:

> Madam
> If I interpret your letter right, you are ignominiously married, if it is yet undone, let us once talk together. If you have abandoned your children and your religion, God forgive your wickedness; if you have forfeited your fame, and your country, may your folly do no further mischief.
>
> If the last act is yet to do, I, who have loved you, esteemed you, reverenced you and served you, I, who long thought you the first of human kind, entreat that before your fate is irrevocable, I may once more see you.
> I was, I once was,
>
> Madam, most truly yours   SAM: JOHNSON
> 2 July 1784
> I will come down if you permit it.

With spirit, she came back at him in a letter written two days after his. 'The birth of my second husband is not meaner than that of my first, his sentiments are not meaner, his profession is not meaner . . . till you have changed your opinion of Mr Piozzi, let us converse no more. God bless you!'

Within a week of his first letter Johnson wrote again. This second message breathes all the nobility and generosity of the man. Gone is the note of rancour, gone the underlying panic. He accepts the situation, and he gives her his blessing and his gratitude.

> I wish that God may grant you every blessing, that you may be happy in this world for its short continuance, and eternally happy in a better state, and whatever I can contribute to your happiness, I am very ready to repay for that kindness which soothed twenty years of a life radically wretched.

So it happened that, on the same day, Johnson lost the two friends of a younger generation who had done most to bring warmth and animation to the last twenty years of his life. With Boswell, of course, he continued to correspond; but on his relationship with Hester a silence came down. He never spoke of her; he received no more letters from her, and destroyed those he already had. In this, even more than in the expressed anguish of his last two letters, we see the depth of his pain. He, who never let go the memory of a friendship, found that this was one he could not endure to look back on.

It remained for Johnson, now, to gather about him what courage he could summon, and what friends he could muster, for the short and painful span that still lay ahead.

PART VI

An Honourable Peace

CHAPTER 29

'I Shall Not Trouble You Long'

When a man lives into his mid-seventies, it is inevitable that he should keep company mostly with the dead. So it was with Johnson. As he sat by his fire, it was ghosts who commonly sat with him. The death of David Garrick, in 1779, had saddened him greatly. For all his jealousy of the man, he had never allowed anyone else to run him down. If the talk turned against Garrick in his absence, Johnson always defended him. There was, indeed, a deep affection between them. Garrick touched Johnson's life at so many points – pupil at Edial, companion of the early London days, *accoucheur* of *Irene*, in latter years member of the Club. His death, Johnson wrote to his widow, had 'eclipsed the gaiety of nations', and certainly it had done much to darken his own gaiety. Death crowded upon death; there would be no more epigrams from Topham Beauclerk; he would never laugh again at Goldsmith's extravagant Irish humour and comical embarrassments; Levet and Anna Williams had been snatched away so recently that he still could not reconcile himself to their absence. Brooding on mortality, he felt the impulse to poetry stir within him after a long silence; he wrote a poem on the death of Levet, and sent it – another link with the past – to *The Gentleman's Magazine*, for which he had worked so prodigiously forty years ago. Cave was long since dead, but the magazine he had founded was still flourishing, and Johnson's elegy on Levet appeared in its pages in August 1783.

> Condemned to hope's delusive mine,
>   As on we toil from day to day,
> By sudden blasts, or slow decline,
>   Our social comforts drop away.
>
> Well tried through many a varying year,
>   See Levet to the grave descend;
> Officious, innocent, sincere,
>   Of every friendless name the friend.
>
> Yet still he fills affection's eye,
>   Obscurely wise, and coarsely kind;

Nor, lettered arrogance, deny
  Thy praise to merit unrefined.

When fainting nature called for aid,
  And hovering death prepared the blow,
His vigorous remedy displayed
  The power of art without the show.

In misery's darkest caverns known,
  His useful care was ever nigh,
Where hopeless anguish poured his groan,
  And lonely want retired to die.

No summons mocked by chill delay,
  No petty gain disdained by pride,
The modest wants of every day
  The toil of every day supplied.

His virtues walked their narrow round,
  Nor made a pause, nor left a void;
And sure the Eternal Master found
  The single talent well employed.

The busy day, the peaceful night,
  Unfelt, uncounted, glided by;
His frame was firm, his powers were bright,
  Though now his eightieth year was nigh.

Then with no throbbing fiery pain,
  No cold gradations of decay,
Death broke at once the vital chain,
  And freed his soul the nearest way.

The poem is eloquent testimony that, whatever might be happening to Johnson's body, his mind was as powerful and creative as ever. Considered purely as a poem, the elegy has been frequently discussed and praised. From a biographer's point of view, two features particularly catch the attention. One is the praise of Levet as 'officious'. Human nature was in the process of changing this word into a term of dispraise; in Johnson's own Dictionary it is defined both as 'kind; doing good offices' and 'importunately forward'; the second sense was to drive out the first, but obviously Johnson meant to describe Levet as one who succoured his fellow-men by constant watchfulness and attention. He sought out sick people and brought them relief, usually at small advantage to himself; his 'useful care was ever nigh' even in 'misery's darkest caverns' – a phrase which recalls Johnson's passionate sympathy with the poor, his consistently held opinion that the treatment meted out to them was the real test of any civilization. The other point concerns Levet's 'single talent'. Among the deeply rooted fears that preyed on Johnson's mind when his thoughts turned to his religion, one of the most persistent was that he would not be able to render sufficient account of the gifts he had been born with. Prodigiously as he had worked, great as had been his charity and succour, he dreaded that the all-judging God would deem his efforts insufficient. Hence the poignancy of his salute to Levet, who, born with one meagre gift, had used it to the full during eighty years. It is a deeply personal poem, though as usual Johnson succeeds in universalizing his particular situation.

If Levet still 'filled affection's eye', so did other dead friends, and Johnson gathered about him such associations with them as he could. Frank Barber, for instance, was a living link with his beloved Richard Bathurst, that staunch friend and 'good hater'. Bathurst had died many years earlier on military service overseas; 'Havana is taken', wrote Johnson in a letter to Beauclerk at the time, 'a conquest too dearly obtained; for Bathurst died before it.' Frank Barber, owned as a slave in his native Jamaica by Bathurst's father and subsequently freed in England, had been taken into Johnson's household partly because of the association with Bathurst and partly as a gesture of opposition to the slave trade, which Johnson had the satisfaction of seeing declared illegal in 1772. Though commonly described as Johnson's servant, he was brought up more like a son. Johnson instructed him, bailed him out of various scrapes, and paid for his education at a boarding school in Yorkshire where he spent (according to John Hawkins) a full five years. Now Frank was well into middle age; he had several children by his English wife, and now that there was plenty of room in the house Johnson allowed him to bring in his family; presumably they had, all these years, been living somewhere round the corner. So the household con-sisted of Frank, Betsy and their children; Elizabeth Desmoulins was also on the scene, having returned after the death of her adversary Anna Williams, though whether she actually lived under Johnson's roof is not clear. He must have valued her, as a link with the past, though her own health was too shattered to enable her to do anything much towards his comfort.

Such was the state of Johnson's life as the summer of 1784 slowly unveiled itself. So much was changed, so many sources of happiness were gone, that he clung even more tightly to what remained. There was the new Club; there were his hopes for an improvement in health; and there was, as there had been every summer, the instinct to take the road. The peace and beauty of the countryside, and the comfort of familiar faces, seemed more attractive than ever after the shocks he had sustained. On 8 July he wrote to Lucy Porter: 'I am coming down to Ashbourne, and, as you may believe, shall visit you on my way. I shall bring a poor, broken, unwieldy body, but I shall not trouble you long, for Dr Taylor will in a few days send for me.'

So he packed, and set out. But before leaving there was one more letter to write. To Thomas Bagshaw, the Rector of Bromley, he sent on 10 July a request for permission to put a tombstone over Tetty, who had been buried there in 1752. Explaining that he had put the practical side of the matter into the hands of one John Ryland, he assured the clergyman that he would visit Bromley to see the finished work, 'if I have strength remaining'. Then, with an easier mind, he began his journey along the familiar road.

He got to Lichfield on the fourteenth, enjoyed a kind welcome, and after six days moved on to Taylor's house. A slight disappointment awaited him; Taylor had given way to the foolish passion for 'improving' his house, which so often clings to old people who should be living out their days in quiet; workmen clambered among heaps of brick and rubble; Johnson wrote to Boswell,

> On the twentieth I came hither, and found a house half built, of very uncomfortable appearance; but my own room has not been altered. That a man worn with diseases, in his seventy-second or third year, should condemn part of his remaining life to pass among ruins and rubbish, and that no inconsiderable part, seems to me very strange.

Amid this disorder, Johnson was bored and lonely:

> I have no company; the Doctor is busy in his fields, and goes to bed at nine, and his whole system is so different from mine, that we seem formed for different elements; I have, therefore, all my amusement to seek within myself.

He was in no very fit state, heart-sore and in physical affliction as he was, to find entertainment within himself; but as usual he struggled on. He wrote regular letters to Dr Brocklesby, detailing every change in his health and every measure he took to improve it ('My breath is very short and the water encroaches and retires. I yesterday took eighty drops of the vinegar of squills in one dose'). To his friend Hoole, a member of the new Club at the Essex Head, he wrote looking forward to the sociable evenings they would enjoy next winter. 'I hope we shall meet often, and sit long.' To his friend Sastres, the teacher of Italian, he wrote in September, 'I have hope of standing the English winter, and reading Petrarch at Bolt Court.' But every now and then his real forebodings show through a crack in his habitual determined optimism. To his old friend Burney he writes, simply,

> I struggle hard for life. I take physic, and take air. My friend's chariot is always ready. We have run this morning twenty-four miles, and could run forty-eight more. But who can run the race with death?

He continued to see little of his host, and when they did meet they usually discussed their ailments, for Taylor's health was also declining – though he had no difficulty in living long enough to read Johnson's burial service and subsequently to give information to Boswell. But it was no cheerful household, and after two months Johnson decamped to Lichfield, where he might find more company. There, he was pleased to find Lucy Porter and her neighbour, Jane Gastrell, who had both seemed very ill when he left for Ashbourne, much recovered. 'It is a great pleasure to a sick man', he wrote in a letter to Ryland, 'to discover that sickness is not always mortal; and to an old man, to see age yet living to greater age.' So stubborn was his hold on life.

It was now autumn, and Johnson knew that there was to be, for him, no escape from the English winter. Auspiciously as it had begun, the scheme for sending him to Italy had fallen through. Precisely who turned it down, and for what reason, is not clear; but Thurlow, the Lord Chancellor, was moved by the *débâcle* to a private act of generosity; he conveyed to Johnson, through Reynolds, the offer of a loan of 'five or six hundred pounds' against a mortgage of Johnson's pension; the part about the mortgage, His Lordship explained to Reynolds, was simply a gesture to avoid making Johnson feel that he was accepting charity. Johnson, of course, saw through the benevolent ruse. He wrote gratefully to Thurlow; but told him that he would not be going to Italy. The time for such measures had gone by. 'If I grew much better, I should not be willing, if much worse, I should not be able, to migrate.'

In short, the old bear was at bay. Johnson had made up his mind to face death. To skulk in Italy, away from his friends, was to risk dying among strangers; or – perhaps even worse, for an old man who drew so much of his life from well-tried friendships – living among them. He was ready for London. Richard Brocklesby had written suggesting that, as Johnson was comfortably installed in Lichfield, he might consider staying there, away from the noise and bustle and smoke of the metropolis. Johnson replied firmly:

I am not afraid either of a journey to London or a residence in it. I came down with little fatigue, and I am now not weaker. In the smoky atmosphere I was delivered from the dropsy, which I consider as the original and radical disease. The town is my element, there are my friends, there are my books to which I have not yet bidden farewell, and there are my amusements. Sir Joshua told me long ago that my vocation was to public life, and I hope still to keep my station, till God shall bid me *Go in peace.*

By 'public life' Johnson means the life of a townsman, mingling in the world, meeting and exchanging ideas with people of every kind. Rural retirement, though he found it pleasant and even essential from time to time, was not his 'element' – and, like most of us, he wanted to meet death in the strength and security of his own element.

So towards London he turned his face. But there was no hurry. First, he must pass through Birmingham, to pay his respects to Edmund Hector; then a last visit to Oxford, where he stayed with Adams. Both men found him responsive and affectionate. 'He was very desirous with me', wrote Hector to Boswell, 'to recollect some of our most early transactions, and transmit them to him, for I perceived nothing gave him greater pleasure than calling to mind those days of our innocence.' Adams, too, communicated to Boswell his impressions of Johnson's visit. 'We had much serious talk together, for which I ought to be the better as long as I live.' Once more, Johnson walked the streets and squares which recalled his youthful dreams and ambitions.

Back in London, he sent a short, affectionate note to the Burney family:

Mr Johnson, who came home last night, sends his respects to dear Dr Burney, and all the dear Burneys little and great.

Perhaps Johnson was hoping for a tranquil period in which he might renew old friendships. But it was not to be. His illnesses gave him no respite. Very shortly after his return to London, both dropsy, his 'original and radical disease', and the asthma attacked him with redoubled vigour. His doctors clustered about him; in addition to the faithful Brocklesby, who at the time when there was talk of financing a trip to Italy had offered Johnson a hundred pounds a year for life, there were three others, Heberden, Warren, and Butter, besides a surgeon, Cruickshank. But there was little they could do for him. The colossal strength that had held him upright amid the onslaught of so many diseases was now fading with every painful breath he took.

While some of it remained, there were a few tasks yet to do. He had seen to the business of Tetty's tombstone, down in Bromley; he had settled the details, in letters to Ryland, before leaving Lichfield. Now, his mind went back to his parents and to 'little Natty'. He had, in old age, sometimes thought of Nathaniel, that shadowy figure who seems to have been banished from his thoughts for over half a century; in 1780 he had written to a woman he knew in Frome, Somerset, asking if Nathaniel's name had ever come to her ears. There would be no point in making enquiries about a man who had put down no roots in the neighbourhood; but she might have chanced to learn something.

What can be known of him must start up by accident. He was not a native of your town or country, but an adventurer who came from a distant part in quest of a livelihood, and did not stay a year. He came in '36, and went away in '37. He was likely enough to attract notice while he stayed, as a lively noisy man, that loved company. His memory might probably continue for some time in some favourite alehouse.

A man might have a worse epitaph. But now Johnson determined that his parents and brother should be worthily commemorated in his and their *magna parens*. To Richard Greene, apothecary of Lichfield, he sent an elaborate Latin inscription with a request that it should be 'engraved in the large size, and laid in the middle aisle in St Michael's church'. As in the case of Tetty, he seems to have been particularly anxious that such traces of their physical presence as remained should be protected from disappearing altogether:

The first care must be to find the exact place of interment, that the stone may protect the bodies. Then let the stone be deep, massy, and hard, and do not let the difference of ten pounds or more defeat our purposes.

Perhaps this obsessional care to hold on to mortal remains, to prevent the bodies of those who had been close to him from mingling peacefully with the anonymous dust, reflects Johnson's own horror of dissolution. Certainly, in his brave fight for life there was a negative element as well as a positive; if he loved life, he also feared death. His letters, in the last year or two of his life, are full of frank avowals of this fear. 'Death, my dear, is very dreadful,' he had written to Lucy Porter in the dark days of the previous winter; 'let us think nothing worth our care but how to prepare for it; what we know amiss in ourselves let us make haste to amend, and put our trust in the mercy of God and the intercession of our Saviour.' His fear, as this passage indicates, was not of the process of death but of the judgement after death. In his late years, talking once with Adams at Oxford, Johnson had admitted his fear that he might be one of the damned. Adams, sweetly reasonable as became a don and a clergyman, started to take the line that God might not intend the damned to be utterly outside His mercy; what, he asked in the tone of one conducting a seminar, did Johnson precisely mean by 'damned'? 'Sent to hell, Sir,' Johnson roared out, 'and punished everlastingly!' Compared with this fear, physical suffering was nothing. When the surgeon lanced his swollen legs to let out the water, Johnson guided the man's hand to cut deeper; afterwards, left to himself, he took a pair of scissors and inflicted such wounds as to lead Hawkins, quite mistakenly, to toy with the notion that he intended suicide. 'I will be conquered,' he exclaimed to a friend, 'I will not capitulate.'

Those who loved him came to pay their last respects. One of them was Fanny Burney, the gifted daughter of his old friend Charles, of whom he had made such a favourite in the happy Streatham days, full of praise for her gifts as a sharp-eyed satirical novelist, doting on her with avuncular affection. On one visit he even managed to joke with her about death. Recalling that Tetty in her last illness had tried the experiment of sleeping out of town, in the hope of resting better in the purer air, he said he had a mind to follow her example, and went on to recall how Tetty had found fault with the shabby lodging that had been found for her. The staircase was in bad condition, with the plaster knocked off the wall in great lumps. 'Oh', said the landlord when it was pointed out to him, 'that's nothing but by the knocks against it of the coffins of the poor souls that have died in the lodgings!' He and she laughed over the macabre little joke, but she noted his 'apparent secret anguish'. In the same conversation – they must have been very close together, their talk running without reserve – she ventured to bring up the name of Hester Thrale. Did Johnson ever hear from her? 'No,' he cried. 'Nor write to her. I drive her quite from my mind. If I meet with one of her letters, I burn it instantly.'

Hester Thrale's letters were not the only papers that Johnson burnt, during these last days. In the last week of his life he incinerated a large mass of letters and private papers, after (and, perhaps, in consequence of) an incident which was a further cause of bad blood between Boswell and John Hawkins. According to the account by Hawkins in his *Life*, what happened was this. On Sunday, 5 December, Johnson took the sacrament in company with a large number of his friends – how many, Hawkins does not say, but enough to fill a room. The office was performed by a young clergyman friend of his, by name Strahan, to whom he had already entrusted the publication of his *Prayers and Meditations*, which Strahan duly carried out in the following year. While he was preparing

for the solemnity, Johnson suddenly missed a piece of paper containing confi-
dential instructions to his executors. A search was set in motion, and Hawkins,
as one of the searchers, found himself handling 'a parchment-covered book',
which he found to contain 'meditations and reflections, in Johnson's own handwriting'. Hawkins – still following his own version – had been warned against a
certain unscrupulous character, an agent of the book trade, who was determined
to pilfer any item of this kind, and had been known to force his way into the
house and up the stairs after being told that Johnson was not to be visited. So, to
save the book from falling into such hands, he put it into his pocket.

Sharp eyes, however, had seen him, and as soon as the service was over
Johnson was told, by 'a friend', that Hawkins had pocketed the book. Immediately, in great agitation, Johnson demanded it back. Hawkins handed it over
and gave his explanation; this calmed Johnson, but he still said, 'You should
not have laid hands on it', adding that on missing it he would 'probably have
run mad'.

The 'friend' who nailed Hawkins was probably Boswell, who, in an indignant
footnote to his *Life*, comes close to saying that Hawkins was lying about his
motive for taking the book, and also hints darkly that Johnson would never
have burnt his private papers – 'those precious records which must ever be
regretted' – so hastily and with so little discrimination, if Hawkins had not
given him a scare.

Be all this as it may, the fact is that Johnson burnt a mass of papers in the
last week of his life, and all that we know for certain is that some of them were
letters from his mother; his friend Sastres remembered him weeping copiously
as the sheets on which his mother had written, his last physical link with her,
blackened finally into ashes; and how he took up a fragment here and there, to
see if a word were still legible – though whether this was out of sentimental regret
or to make sure that prying eyes could decipher no part of her message, does
not appear.

The secretive and unpleasant Hawkins doubtless merited Boswell's disapproval. One substantial good turn, however, he did for Johnson at this time:
he nagged him into making a will. Johnson, like so many people, had always put
off this duty, probably sharing the widespread feeling that to make a will is to
signify a willingness to have done with life. Now, obviously dying as he was, he
would probably have procrastinated till it was too late. But Hawkins insisted,
and the real beneficiary was Frank Barber. Johnson had always intended to
leave Frank a competence; he had very little opinion of the man's powers of
survival, and thought a small regular income the best way of keeping him and
his family out of the gutter. How much, he asked Dr Brocklesby, would be
a proper annuity for a man to leave to a favourite servant? Brocklesby, with a
physician's wide experience of wills and settlements, replied that it all depended
on the circumstances of the testator, but 'in the case of a nobleman, fifty pounds
a year was deemed an adequate reward for many years' faithful service'.
'Then shall I be *nobilissimus*,' Johnson replied, 'for I mean to leave Frank seventy
pounds a year, and I desire you to tell him so.'

Frank was accordingly named Johnson's principal legatee. But Johnson's protecting care did not stop there. He had always loved and shielded Frank; he would never risk wounding his feelings in any way, for instance by sending him out to buy fish for their cat, Hodge; Johnson always went himself, so that Frank would not feel lowered by having to attend on an animal. Now, he gave serious thought to Frank's future, in this world and the next. Calling him often to his bedside, he explained to him passages in the Scriptures, and prayed with him. He gave him solemn advice: after his death Frank should leave London and go to Lichfield, where there were fewer risks that he would be swindled out of his money or be tempted to squander it. Frank agreed but Johnson still worried about him. He was weak-willed and scatterbrained; someone must look after him. Among the friends who came to sit by him was the brilliant William Windham, already entering on his resplendent career as a statesman, though he had not yet risen to high office. Windham had been a pupil of Robert Chambers at Oxford, and soon afterwards had got to know Burke, who had great respect for his political judgement, and Johnson. Windham would make a good protector for Frank. So, on his next visit – but let Windham's diary tell the story:

> He told me that he had a request to make to me, namely, that I would allow his servant Frank to look up to me as his friend, adviser and protector in all difficulties which his own weakness and imprudence, or the force or fraud of others, might bring him into.
>
> ... Having obtained my assent to this, he proposed that Frank should be called in, and desiring me to take him by the hand in token of the promise, repeated before him the recommendation he had just made of him, and the promise I had given to attend to it.

So the end came nearer. Tenderly, solemnly, his old friends watched him go towards death. Burke, in particular, was very deeply affected. When Johnson rallied his strength to pay him a generous compliment, Burke said in a voice breaking with emotion, 'My dear Sir, you have always been too good to me.' After visiting Johnson in company with Charles Burney, he turned to Burney on the pavement outside, and said fervently, 'His work is almost done – and well has he done it!'

For Johnson, the voices of his friends grew fainter as he drew near to that Presence he had always dreaded. Sometimes his fear was strong upon him. Once, when Brocklesby was attending him, he burst out in the words of Macbeth:

> Canst thou not minister to a mind diseased,
> Pluck from the memory a rooted sorrow,
> Raze out the written troubles of the brain,
> And with some sweet oblivious antidote
> Cleanse the full bosom of that perilous stuff
> Which weighs upon the heart?

To which the good doctor, a literate man, replied in the next words of the play,

> Therein the patient
> Must minister to himself.

Johnson assented to this. 'Well applied,' he murmured. 'That's more than poetically true.'

Johnson trusted Brocklesby. On a date Boswell does not specify – but it must have been near the end – he asked Brocklesby to tell him, without mincing words, whether or not he had a chance of recovery. Brocklesby hesitated; asked if Johnson was prepared to face the truth, whatever it might be; receiving his assurance, told him that only a miracle would save his life. 'Then', said Johnson, 'I will take no more physic, not even my opiates; for I have prayed that I may render up my soul to God unclouded.' Whatever were the terrors of death, he wanted to face them with a clear mind.

His reward was great. In those last days, from whatever source it came, he was granted mercy. On 28 November, when he had just over two weeks to live, Hawkins visited him and found him asleep, with a number of friends watching by his bed. Waking and seeing them, Johnson began to speak, solemnly, of his own spiritual condition. 'You see the state in which I am', he began; 'conflicting with bodily pain and mental distraction; while you are in health and strength, labour to do good, and avoid evil, if ever you hope to escape the distress that now oppresses me.' Having delivered himself of this warning to his friends, his mood lightened; he went on, 'I had, very early in my life, the seeds of goodness in me: I had a love of virtue, and a reverence for religion; and these, I trust, have brought forth in me fruits meet for repentance; and, if I have repented as I ought, I am forgiven.'

He went on to speak of moods that visited him, in which he felt a loathing of sin, and especially of that sin that was within himself; this loathing, he said, was not merely the result of fear, for it did not lessen when his fear happened to lift. 'At these times', he told his friends, 'I have had such rays of hope shot into my soul, as have almost persuaded me that I am in a state of reconciliation with God.'

Whether we choose to call it reconciliation with God, or reconciliation with himself, the fact is there: calm descended at last. On 5 December, with a mind peaceful and composed, he wrote his last prayer:

> Almighty and most merciful Father, I am now, as to human eyes it seems, about to commemorate for the last time, the death of thy son Jesus Christ, our Saviour and Redeemer. Grant, O Lord, that my whole hope and confidence may be in his merits and in thy mercy: forgive and accept my late conversion, enforce and accept my imperfect repentance; make this commemoration [of] him available to the confirmation of my faith, the establishment of my hope, and the enlargement of my charity, and make the death of thy son Jesus effectual to my redemption. Have mercy upon me and pardon the multitude of my offences. Bless my friends, have mercy

upon all men. Support me by the Grace of thy Holy Spirit in the days of weakness, and at the hour of death, and receive me, at my death, to everlasting happiness, for the sake of Jesus Christ.

The pious George Strahan, when he printed this prayer, left out the words 'forgive and accept my late conversion'; he was afraid, perhaps, that the uninstructed reader would think of Johnson as a man who had passed a large part of his life in doubt or disbelief. He might as well have let the sentence stand, for Johnson in his Dictionary had defined 'conversion' as 'Change from reprobation to grace, from a bad to a holy life'. That, blessedly, was how he saw his situation; he had changed from reprobation to grace. And surely this prayer, by itself, would indicate that he was right. It is so humble, so wise, so beautiful. 'Bless my friends, have mercy upon all men.' Characteristically, he made it one of his last thoughts to commend 'his friends', and 'all men', to the mercy of that God in whom he so fervently believed.

The shepherd in Virgil grew at last acquainted with Love, and found him a native of the rocks.

On 13 December Johnson had a new visitor; 'a Miss Morris, daughter to a particular friend of his'. Thus Boswell. No one actually knows who she was, this girl; scholars write learned footnotes trying to establish which 'particular friend' of Johnson's her father might have been. But she would see Johnson; she told Frank that she must see him; she wanted to ask for his blessing. Frank went into Johnson's bedroom; the girl, too anxious to wait outside in case he came out with a refusal, followed at his heels and stood there while Frank explained what she wanted. Johnson's almost helpless body turned over in the bed; he looked at her and spoke. 'God bless you, my dear.' They were his last words.

At about seven o'clock that evening, Frank and Elizabeth Desmoulins were sitting in Johnson's room when his breathing ceased, quietly and with no disturbance. It was some minutes before they realized that he had died.

CHAPTER 30

Afterwards

Frank Barber took Johnson's advice, retiring to Lichfield with Betsy and the children. Even this wise move was insufficient to protect him against his own improvidence; he managed, somehow, to get his hands on the lump sum which had been invested to produce his annuity, and squander it. In dire poverty he moved to the village of Burntwood, three miles from Lichfield, and kept a little school, the education provided at Johnson's expense proving his last and best resource. He died in Stafford Infirmary in January 1801. Betsy came back to Lichfield and continued to teach a school, ending her days exactly like the widow Oliver. Their eldest son, Samuel, wandered to the north of the county and ended up in the Potteries. First, he worked for a surgeon named Gregory Hickman, grandson of that Gregory Hickman to whom Johnson's first known letter is addressed; then he was apprenticed to the famous potter Enoch Wood. His children in turn were absorbed into the labour force of the pottery industry, so that today, if you see a man or woman in the streets of Stoke-on-Trent with a slightly mulatto cast of countenance, you are possibly looking at one of the descendants of Frank Barber.

James Boswell, after years of toil and discouragement, brought out his *Life of Johnson* in 1791, and had the satisfaction of seeing it sweep aside his rivals', notably Hawkins and Hester Thrale. He died at the age of fifty-five in 1797, worn out by his literary, legal, familial, convivial and sexual endeavours.

Hester Thrale, as it turned out, was exactly half-way through her life when she parted from Johnson. After a happy sojourn on the Continent immediately after her marriage, she returned home with Piozzi and soon built a beautiful house overlooking the Vale of Clwyd, to which, with a fond wish to unite the two languages of her heart, she gave the name 'Brynbella'. They lived a placid life there until she finally nursed her husband through his last painful illness; then she gave up the house and lived mainly in Bath. On her eightieth birthday she gave a large party, and led the dancing with her adopted son, Sir John Salusbury. Two years later she died as the result of an accident while travelling.

Charlotte Lennox died in poverty in Dean's Yard, Westminster, in 1804, her powers extinct and her reputation forgotten. She was buried at the expense of George Rose, a last faithful admirer of her talent.

Johnson sleeps in Westminster Abbey, and David Garrick, who was beside him when he first took the road from Lichfield to London, is beside him still.

A Note on Sources

There is no research in this book. Every fact it contains was previously known to scholars and to any reader who kept abreast of scholarship. The basic narrative is taken from two works published at Oxford by the Clarendon Press: Dr L. F. Powell's monumental revision of George Birkbeck Hill's already monumental edition of Boswell's *Life*, the 'Hill–Powell Boswell' (1934–64), and R. W. Chapman's edition of *The Letters of Samuel Johnson, with Mrs Thrale's genuine letters to him* (1952). The facts of Johnson's working life are mostly to be found in *A Bibliography of Samuel Johnson* by W. P. Courtney and David Nichol Smith (Oxford, 1915; reissued with facsimiles, 1925). Contemporary lives other than Boswell's are collected in, and here cited from, Birkbeck Hill's *Johnsonian Miscellanies* (Oxford, 1897). The basic research on Johnson's ancestry and early life, as well as on such interesting ancillary matters as the life story of Frank Barber, was done by Aleyn Lyell Reade in his ten volumes of *Johnsonian Gleanings* (privately printed, 1909–46). It was Reade, for instance, who discovered that Johnson and Chesterfield were relatives.

In quoting from Johnson's writings I have modernized spelling and punctuation. Most of the background information about them is taken from the ongoing Yale edition of his *Works*, and particularly from Volume I (*Diaries, Prayers and Annals*, edited by E. L. McAdam, Jr, with Donald and Mary Hyde), Volumes VII and VIII (*Johnson on Shakespeare*, edited by Arthur Sherbo) and Volume IX (*A Journey to the Western Islands of Scotland*, edited by Mary Lascelles). For Johnson's poems, the edition consulted was that of D. Nichol Smith and E. L. McAdam (Oxford, 1941), with additional information from the edition by J. D. Fleeman (Penguin Books, 1971).

As far as possible I have avoided reading modern studies of Johnson, preferring to take my impressions directly from eighteenth-century sources, however packaged and illuminated by modern scholarship; but everyone who knows his way about Johnsoniana will recognize my debt to certain modern studies in fields where my ignorance was too great to allow of my consulting original sources: notably Donald J. Greene's *The Politics of Samuel Johnson* (Yale, 1960) and Mary Hyde's *The Impossible Friendship: Boswell and Mrs Thrale* (Harvard, 1972).

Index